GEORGE MARSHALL

GEORGE
MARSHALL

A BIOGRAPHY

DEBI AND IRWIN UNGER

WITH STANLEY HIRSHSON

HARPER

www.harpercollins.com

HarperCollins books may be purchased for educational, business, or sales promotional use. For information, please e-mail the Special Markets Department at SPsales@harpercollins.com.

FIRST EDITION

Designed by William Ruoto

Library of Congress Cataloging-in-Publication Data has been applied for.

ISBN: 978-0-06-057719-3

14 15 16 17 18   OV/RRD   10 9 8 7 6 5 4 3 2 1

To Elian with love

CONTENTS

CHAPTER 1

CHILDISH THINGS

George Catlett Marshall was born on the last day of 1880 between two worlds. His birthplace was Uniontown, Pennsylvania, a grimy industrial town fast becoming the coke capital of America. George's father was a "coke baron," a man who converted bituminous coal into a high-carbon ash used in blast furnaces for reducing ore to metallic iron. For a time George Senior rode the growth wave that transformed America into the world's manufacturing powerhouse. Yet in George's boyhood Uniontown was still geographically and culturally close to the rural countryside. His earliest memory was climbing up a ladder in the family barn, where the Marshalls kept a horse and a cow, to get a haymow, a piece of farm equipment. George indulged fully in the boyhood pleasures of nineteenth-century rural life. He never enjoyed cities and in later years would regret what industry had done to his hometown.

There was an even more significant divide in George's youth and childhood. His parents represented a tradition at odds with the texture of life in southwestern Pennsylvania. Though both

his father's family, the Marshalls, and his mother's, the Brad-
fords, had long resided in Kentucky, they traced their ancestry to
Virginia. That pattern was not uncommon; hordes of old-stock
Americans could claim Virginia origins, for the Old Dominion
had scattered thousands of its sons and daughters across the nation's landscape to merge and blend with streams of people from
other commonwealths and other countries. Yet many of these
Virginians, wherever they lived, held themselves special for their
ancestry and their ancestral values.

The proud claim was based in part on a myth of royalist forebears fleeing Oliver Cromwell's Puritan England. These high-
toned Cavaliers had fought for King Charles I and fled Britain for
America in the 1640s, when Cromwell's low-born Roundheads tri-
umphed and beheaded their monarch. In fact few English royalists
actually sought refuge in the infant colony named for the Virgin
Queen, Elizabeth I; far more Puritan Roundheads settled in frigid
New England. Yet the legend of Virginia's Cavalier heritage, reinforced by the century-long struggle between North and South over
slavery and states' rights, would prove potent as a formative cultural
influence among its children, whether at home or abroad.

One result was inflated collective pride, as expressed by the lineage society the Order of the First Families of Virginia (FFV), a
state version of the Daughters of the American Revolution (DAR)
or the Sons of the American Revolution (SAR). The full myth
went beyond the Cavalier-Roundhead distinction, however. More
legitimately, it also drew on the critical role of Virginia in the
events leading to the Revolution, and on the fame of its revolutionary sons—Washington, Jefferson, Madison—in the creation
of the early republic. For George's family the esteemed forebear
was John Marshall, the fourth chief justice of the U.S. Supreme
Court, who established judicial supremacy as the cornerstone of
American constitutional practice.

Though at best a distant, "collateral" relation, the famous jurist loomed large in Marshall's family lore. George Catlett Senior revered John Marshall and treasured his connection to the chief justice. However, as a boy his younger son never had much use for the puffed-up family pride that infused his father. In fact he believed that "continual harping on the name of John Marshall was a kind of poor business."[1] George at one point offended his father when, thumbing through a history of the Marshall family, he fastened on the pirate Blackbeard, husband of one of the ancestral Marshall women, as the only interesting character in the work, and boasted to his classmates about his raffish forebear.

But if indifferent to his own pedigree, George was susceptible to the Virginia myth as a force for molding character and personality. In reality, from the outset, the settlers of colonial Virginia and their descendants enjoyed a mixed reputation, one that included proclivities for hard drinking, boisterous sports, reckless gambling, and heedless extravagance. But at its best the ideal of "Virginian" shaped a code of values and behavior that appended pride with honor, grace, and integrity that George somehow absorbed on the road to adulthood. Among those who seriously practiced what they preached, it included a love of place and country, an exalted standard of personal honor and public rectitude, an avoidance of overt self-serving, and a respect for women, children, and the weak. Alas, in George's case, it also discounted humor. Many people had words of high praise for Marshall over the years, but few ever called him funny. Years later, when he presided over his country's military operations in the greatest war in history, a colleague in the War Department recalled his manner of giving orders. "He was a demanding man," an aide, Col. Frank McCarthy, later told an interviewer. "There was nothing except, 'Take this' and 'Do this' and so on, and 'Yes sir.' . . . Never with humor, never with warmth, but with correctness and politeness."[2] Few of the published pictures of Marshall show him with a smile on his face.

For George as a boy the Virginian myth was steeped in the special mystique of George Washington. Close to his Uniontown home was Fort Necessity, where in 1754 the French had defeated the young lieutenant colonel of the Virginia militia sent to oust them during what became a dress rehearsal for the French and Indian War. When George Junior was seven his father took him on a memorable tour of the fort, then in ruins. In 1957, in his first interviews with his biographer Forrest Pogue, Marshall seemed almost obsessed with Washington and his early military exploits. It is not surprising that as he evolved into an adult George would borrow the attributes of his childhood hero and make them his own.

Interestingly, Washington's own self-creation had foreshadowed George's. According to his recent biographer Ron Chernow, the Father of His Country "tended his image with extreme care." He "trained himself to play the gentleman in polite drawing rooms. . . . People sensed something a bit studied about his behavior."[3] Chernow says that Washington's model was the British aristocracy as he perceived it before the Revolution, but Marshall in his turn learned much of what manhood meant, or should mean, from Washington directly. One telling instance of imitation was Marshall's devotion to horseback riding. The first president was famous for his superb horsemanship, and it appears likely that Marshall's almost compulsive attachment to riding was inspired by his great predecessor.

Marshall's exposure to noble Virginians and their attributes intensified at Virginia Military Institute, where George would receive his military training as a young man. At VMI in Marshall's day the Civil War victories of Confederate general Thomas "Stonewall" Jackson in the Valley Campaign, at Antietam, and at Fredericksburg remained heroic legends. His classmates at the institute, moreover, were predominantly Southerners, many from the wealthier classes who cherished and emulated the Virginia type. Reinforcement came from that still-more-famous Virginia general, Robert E. Lee, the commander of the Army of Northern Virginia and general in chief of the Confederate army. After the South's surrender at Appomattox in 1865 Lee had settled in Lexington, adjacent to VMI, to serve as president of Washington College. He was a potent presence, both literally and figuratively, in Marshall's early manhood.

And then, to further strengthen the Virginia affinity, there was Marshall's first wife and her family. Lily Coles was descended from a long line of Virginia gentry. Her mother, Elizabeth Childs Pendleton Coles, a member of the FFV whose forebears included a signer of the Declaration of Independence, harped on her ancestry. As Marshall later recalled, she was "a very ardent Virginian" who thought that the name Uniontown "sounded rather common and was rather ashamed of where I came from."[4] Marshall claimed that his mother-in-law's pretensions amused him, but they could not have failed to reinforce his sense of how important the Virginia connection was in the eyes of many people.* These influences left their deep mark on the later man in the form of a cast of mind, a mode of behavior, a way of relating to others. It showed in his taciturnity, social reticence, and even in his notably erect posture and stiff physical bearing. However they may

---

*Whatever his actual roots, Marshall was often assumed to be a Virginian. Late in his life an interviewer asked him if he regarded himself as a Virginian. His answer was equivocal, almost evasive: "My family are Kentucky," he replied. "I myself was the only member of the family born up north. . . . I married two Virginians, very ardent Virginians, and I went to school in a very ardent, historical Virginia section school, and I have many friends that are Virginians. I might say also that I pay taxes in Virginia and I know all about that." (Marshall Interviews, April 11, 1957, Tape 7, p. 250)

have questioned his military judgment or his intellectual prowess, virtually no one who knew him doubted Marshall's elevated character. Gen. Alan Brooke, chief of the Imperial General Staff, who for more than four years during World War II was Marshall's British counterpart and frequent opponent, invariably scorned the American general's strategic grasp. But never his character. In a radio broadcast in 1958 Lord Alanbrooke—as he was by then known—though still no fan of Marshall's generalship, described the American as "amongst the biggest gentlemen . . . that I've ever met. [He had] a sense of extraordinary integrity. One could trust him with anything. . . . He treated his inferiors almost the same as his peers."[5] Nor was Brooke alone in his admiration. One of Marshall's staff during World War II, Gen. Frederick Osborn, whose rich and influential New Jersey family had known a half dozen presidents and other distinguished men, later claimed that none of them compared to Marshall in strength of character. "I never had any . . . impression from any of them as I always had of General Marshall. I had always the sense that I was in the presence of a man who was altogether my superior . . . in his tremendous control over himself, and in his tremendous determination. When he came to the conclusion that something should be done, he said it with such firmness and with such lucidity that you just agreed with him. You knew he was right."[6]

However acquired—whether inherent or contrived—Marshall's austere persona was undoubtedly useful. It reassured many of those with whom he had important transactions—his British allies, newspaper reporters, members of Congress, the president of the United States, the American public—and often resolved their doubts on thorny and controversial issues. It also protected Marshall from his enemies. During his years of power and prominence Marshall would make mistakes, some serious; his performance as a decision maker, as we shall see, was not always stellar. But seldom did his critics penetrate the shield of his reputation. Almost invariably he survived without serious damage. To the end the carpers would be dismissed as bigots and extremists by the conventional thinkers, as many were; in the eyes of most informed midrange Americans he would remain a great man.

A qualifier is in order here: The full array of these personal qualities remained buried in the struggling junior officer, as indeed they could not fail to be, not becoming fully manifest until Marshall attained high rank.

But George belonged to two worlds. In contrast to this tradition and these values was the reality of his early life. He was born in a Pennsylvania town of some five thousand, fifty miles southwest of smoky industrial Pittsburgh. Uniontown was located on the old National Road built by the federal government in the early nineteenth century before the railroads, to provide connections between the Atlantic coast and the nation's trans-Appalachian interior. The road was a monument to enterprise, and this is where his ancestor-proud father had come in the early 1870s to make his fortune. Besides its importance as a transportation hub the town abutted the famous Connellsville coalfield, the site of some of the best "coking coal" in the world. Here Henry Clay Frick constructed his banks of earth-covered "beehive" ovens to create the coke that fed the new Bessemer converters making cheap steel. At about the time of Marshall's birth Frick became an executive in the thriving steel business run by the Scottish immigrant Andrew Carnegie, eventually becoming one of the richest industrialists of his day.

George's father never attained the eminence of Frick. But for a time he was an affluent coke baron, with wide-ranging commercial and real estate interests. Following the collapse of a Virginia land development venture in 1890, his fortunes waned and the family struggled to stay solvent, but George Senior never ceased to be a man of business, a part of the great industrial surge of America's Gilded Age.

On the other hand, in Marshall's youth Uniontown retained most of its rural roots, and the general never lost his attachment to country life. In his account of his childhood taped for Forrest Pogue, he described with affection the bucolic pleasures of turn-of-the-century western Pennsylvania. George remembered how much he enjoyed working on the prosperous farm of his friend Andy's grandfather, and how he was not above getting down to earthy agricultural basics. He helped, he recalled, to "distribute the manure on the parts of the land [that] needed refreshment." George retained his affection for farming and the natural land-scape. He deeply regretted the destruction wrought on the land by industrialization. When he saw the farm again in the mid-1950s, he noted "it had been ruined by the coal veins being taken out from under it."[7] He also recalled the arrival of the railroad in Uniontown as a blight on the town—the source of periodic floods, soot-filled air, and grimy black surfaces.

And yet, pointing again to his two worlds, as a schoolboy he was inspired as much by profit and enterprise as by the Arca-dian activities of the remaining unspoiled Pennsylvania coun-tryside. An observer of his boyhood activities might have sworn that he was destined for success in the world of business. At one point he and his buddy Andy established a hand-poled ferry that crossed a small stream, for which they charged a toll. The boys printed up tickets for their ferry on a toy typewriter and sold them to the local girls. One day in midstream the girls decided that they would not pay their pennies. In retaliation "Captain" Marshall pulled the boat's cork plug, sinking it in the shallow water while the passengers screamed in dismay.

George and his friend also raised tomatoes on the site of an old barn where the soil, enriched by years of animal waste, produced giant fruit. The local grocer snapped these up eagerly for pennies until the boys, advised by George Senior, insisted on getting more money for their labor. At this point the grocer refused to buy any more.

Whether agrarian or commercial, life in Uniontown in the last decades of the nineteenth century was insular. His environment made George acutely conscious of the local past. Within a few miles of town, besides the remains of Fort Necessity, was the grave of British general James Braddock, who had died leading a failed military expedition to annul Washington's earlier defeat by the French. The battles and campaigns of the Civil War, moreover, were still part of living memory in the Uniontown area when George was growing up. But his intellectual environment included little about the great contemporary world outside his corner of Pennsylvania. By his own admission, George's early education was seriously deficient. He attended private elementary schools run by local gentlewomen, but apparently he learned little there beyond the most basic skills, and when his father entered him in the local public school the admitting officer was dismayed at the boy's inability to answer simple factual questions. There is no evidence that George the boy knew much about Europe, Asia, or Africa, places that would loom large on his later military and diplomatic world stage. Nor did his reading expand his horizons by much. It can be argued that few Americans of that day, adults included, knew much more. Still, George's background was not equal to that of a contemporary boy in large port cities like New York, Boston, New Orleans, or San Francisco, who might have absorbed through his pores, as it were, considerable knowledge of the wider world.

There is little evidence that George's formal higher education expanded his horizons very much either. What it did do was reinforce the aloof, Olympian "Virginia" persona he would inhabit in his adult life.

As he reached his midteens George, like other middle-class boys, faced the prospect of training for a profession. Unfortunately he had limited options. With his deficient school record he was not suited to the "learned professions." Temperamentally he was not fit for a life behind a desk or a counter. (He would always despise the work environment his career would actually impose on him.) What about the army? As a lad from a semirural environment, active in fishing, hunting, and camping, the life of a soldier must have seemed congenial. There was also the inspiration of Washington, Jackson, and Lee. But there remains a puzzle. The military life was not widely esteemed in 1890s America. Disrespected, the army was small and poorly funded. In that decade it was a shadow of the proud and powerful Grand Army of the Republic that had paraded down the capital's Pennsylvania Avenue at the great victory review in May 1865. In 1897, the year of George's admission to VMI, the U.S. Army budget was $35.3 million out of a total federal budget of $366 million. The army consisted of fewer than thirty thousand men scattered across the Western frontier primarily to keep the restless Indian tribes on their reservations. The rank and file was largely composed of the castoffs of society, men who could not compete in civilian life. As the *New York Sun* noted in March 1888, "The regular army is composed of bummers, loafers, and foreign paupers." The lives of these soldiers were hard. A new enlisted man received only thirteen dollars a month (though he was also fed, clothed, and sheltered). With discipline harsh and workloads heavy, personnel turnover was high, often 25 to 40 percent a year in some units. Officers' circumstances were not much better. A second lieutenant's pay was fourteen hundred dollars a year, from which he had to buy his own uniforms and many other personal items to make his life comfortable on post. Worst of all, promotion was snail-like. Many officers were in their forties before reaching the rank of captain.

George's father was fully aware of the drawbacks of the military as a career. His older son, Stuart, had already attended VMI, but he had majored in chemistry and after graduation found work as an industrial chemist, an acceptable vocation. But however skeptical, George Senior sought to get his younger son a place at West Point, where he could receive a free education at the United States government's expense. But a placement at the U.S. military academy required a recommendation by the aspirant's local member of Congress. George Senior, a lifelong Democrat, had little influence with the district's Republican representative, and George Junior was not admitted to the prestigious academy. VMI was the next best thing. Stuart, however, did not want his cutup, ill-educated kid brother to go to his alma mater. He would disgrace the family name, he told their mother. George overheard Stuart's remarks and was enraged. It "made more an impression on me than all the instructors, parental pressures or anything else, and I decided right then I was going to 'wipe his face' as we say or 'wipe his eye' and I ended up at the VMI." This eruption of sibling rivalry, George later claimed, not only propelled him into VMI; it fueled his drive to excel for the rest of his career.[8] It was just as well that George failed to get into West Point. He probably would have flunked out academically: George had not yet learned how to study.

In the end it proved easy to get George into the freshman class at VMI despite his unimpressive school record. The institute required no entrance exam. The only hurdle to admission was Superintendent Scott Shipp, a former Confederate general who respected the distinguished Marshall ancestry as much as George's father did and simply admitted the young Pennsylvanian on sight.

Founded in 1839 in Lexington, Virginia, at the site of a former state arsenal, VMI had graduated its first class of sixteen cadets in 1842. Thereafter, during the antebellum years, it played a minor role in the Old South's system of higher education. Not until the Civil War would its graduates make their mark on Southern life. There was one exception. During the 1850s the professor of "Natural and Experimental Philosophy" was Thomas Jonathan Jackson, a West Pointer and a veteran of the Mexican War, who later, as a Confederate general, would acquire the nickname "Stonewall." A notoriously poor teacher while there, Professor Jackson's memory would be revered at the institute in later years.

VMI indelibly etched one side of George's life and personality. The institute's collective culture and atmosphere were decidedly Southern through the nineteenth century. Besides the Jackson connection, during the Civil War, VMI cadets fought in fourteen battlefield engagements wearing Confederate gray. Fifteen of its graduates rose to the rank of general in the Confederate army. In May 1864 VMI cadets fought as a unit in the Battle of New Market. Ranging in age from fifteen to twenty-four, the cadets suffered ten killed and forty-two wounded, but they captured a Union artillery emplacement and helped turn the tide of battle. After Appomattox the memory of the "Baby Corps" and the South's "Lost Cause" in general permeated the school's atmosphere. The Confederate association was fortified, as we saw, by the veneration of Robert E. Lee, general in chief of the Confederate army. After the general's death his presence was felt through Lee Chapel at the college, which housed his remains.

Lee was more than a respected former soldier. Son of a Revolutionary War general and former governor of Virginia, like Washington he embodied all those qualities—integrity, honor, dignity, breeding, generosity—associated with the Virginia elite. Marshall later acknowledged that he had been "greatly influenced

by the traditions concerning General Lee and General Jackson."
He had gone "to frequent services in the Washington and Lee
chapel" and had often reflected on the traditions that these men
represented.[9] In Marshall's day VMI was unself-conscious about
announcing its mission to fashion Southern gentlemen. Superintendent Shipp, who had actually led the brave VMI cadets at
New Market, caught the spirit of the institute in his 1901 report.
School life, he wrote, should emphasize "habits of obedience, self-
denial, and self-restraint." It should encourage "respect for lawful
authority and to that self-respect which the consciousness of duty
well done carries with it."[10]

As a Yankee, George stood out. He was one of fourteen North-
erners in a freshman class of eighty-two. Taunted for his Pennsylvania accent, he modified it to conform to his peers' way of
speaking. He also revised other ingrained habits. The four years
at VMI suppressed the bumptious Tom Sawyer in George and
helped mold him into a gentleman imbued with dignity and the
spirit of noblesse oblige.

VMI's coursework was not demanding, yet even so Marshall
absorbed only a modest amount of what was offered. He considered a complete waste the time he spent there learning French
and German, two languages that he could have used profitably
in later years. He also regretted that his instructors had never
taught him how to express himself well either orally or in writing. "What I learned most at the V.M.I.," he later said, "was self-
control, discipline, so it was ground in."[11] His academic failings
did not affect his standing among the leading voices in the cadet
corps, however, for what he lacked in intellectual achievement
he made up in strength of character, however acquired.

Besides indoctrination, VMI's character-molding ends were
abetted by a system that subjected its freshman class—the
"Rats"—to a brutal hazing regime. The institute forbade inflict-

ing bodily harm on the novices, but promoted the "Rat Line," which it admitted was "among the toughest and most grueling initiation programs in the country."[12] Under it freshmen were expected to walk a prescribed straight line—the Rat Line— when moving in barracks from place to place, all the while with shoulders held stiffly back and heads up in an exaggerated sort of mobile "at attention." Rats were subject to verbal abuse from upperclassmen who could also impose on them humiliating and arduous physical penalties—exhausting push-ups and the like— for supposed infractions of rules or slippage of proper demeanor. One former Rat recalled the cruel rituals of his first week at VMI with revulsion. He and a group of fellow freshmen were subjected to a "Sweat Party"; the freshmen were crammed into a shower stall wearing their fatigues and raincoats and ordered to run in place and perform push-ups until they were drenched in perspiration. Then the upperclassmen turned on scalding water, ostensibly to wash the sweat off the exhausted freshmen. On one occasion at the end of this ordeal, an upperclassman taunted the novices: "Well, rats, what do you think of Friday nights at your new school?"[13]

The Sweat Party account describes a Rat Line experience almost half a century after Marshall's years at VMI. No authorized explanation of the purpose of the freshman hazing system survives from Marshall's time at VMI. But it was widely believed that by the mid-twentieth century the system had been moderated, not intensified. In any case, in 1897 freshman George felt its sting literally. One of the most appalling aspects of the Rat Line routine was its capriciousness. Upperclassmen were indeed forbidden to inflict bodily harm, but almost anything could pass muster if perpetrated out of sight of the faculty and administrators. Tall, skinny George, with his Pittsburgh twang, was a natural target for the sadists, and at one point he was ordered by some upperclassmen, as a test of physical stamina, to squat over a naked bayonet fixed point up in the ground. George had just arrived at the institute weakened by a bout of typhoid fever and soon slipped from his position, barely missing a serious wound to his buttocks if not to more vital parts of his anatomy. He might have reported the upperclassmen for their extreme punishment, but to their great relief he chose not to. In the end, then, the event elicited the respect of the cadet body for Marshall as a coolheaded, gutsy young man.

In addition to the Rat Line, VMI stood out from other schools for its strict honor system. At the institute doors were left unlocked. Exams were unproctored. Students attested in writing to the authenticity of all submitted papers and reports, and that was enough. Cadets were not only expected to abide by the rules; they were expected to report strictly all violations of the rules. Failure to do so was itself a violation, and like other infractions of the code resulted in immediate dismissal from the institute.

And then, as a further character builder, there was the overall austerity of cadet life. Wake-up call was in the very early morning, a requirement that George despised. Food was atrocious. The main dish at mess, Marshall recalled, was "growlie," a concoction of "most anything . . . that was around . . . handy to dump into it." There was little time off: just "part of a day here and part of a day there." Moreover, "there were . . . no arrangements practically to amuse the cadets . . . . It was pretty much a case of looking after yourself and the old cadets chasing you."[14] Marshall would remember this recreation deficiency and as chief of staff would seek to alleviate it in the World War II citizen army.

It is not entirely clear how George managed in his senior year to become first captain, the place of highest honor in the VMI cadet corps. The process required recommendations from the four cadet senior captains, and from the institute's tactical instructors, as well as the school adjutant and school quartermaster. How did George secure these accolades? Perhaps his stoicism and reticence on the occasion of the bayonet mishap contributed to the favorable response of the top cadets, But clearly he had also captured the attention of the faculty and administrators by his diligence, which had already won him the rank of first sergeant. He had worked very hard at this secondary post to win the favor of his peers and his superiors. "As first sergeant. I fell the company in, called the roll, kept tabs on it, and marched the detail to guard mount every morning," he later recalled.[15] These were routine duties of the first sergeant, but George performed them so well— with commanding posture and a bullhorn voice—that it deeply impressed the cadets.

As first captain George's performance was equally notable. The cadets inevitably tested his mettle, and he proved equal to the job. He accepted their challenges, sternly responding without losing their goodwill and respect. It was at this point in his career, apparently, that he adopted the cool, aloof persona that later set him apart from many other army officers."What I learned at the V.M.I.," he later declared, "was self-control, discipline, so it was ground in, and the problem of managing men which fell to the cadet noncommissioned officer and cadet officer."[16]

While still a cadet, Marshall managed to find a wife. His choice fell on Elizabeth Carter Coles, called "Lily," a red-haired, fair-skinned beauty six years his senior. As we noted, Lily came from an old Virginia family that was inordinately proud of its connections with the Old Dominion's glorious past. A cultivated young woman with a heart condition, she lived with her widowed mother in Lexington, in a house near the institute's outer gate. George knew of Lily through his brother, Stuart, who had courted her for a time while he attended VMI, but it was when he stopped outside her house one evening in his senior year to listen to her play the piano—pieces his mother had played—that she truly captured his heart. Lily found the lanky cadet to her liking as well. Though still a student, with uncertain prospects, he was intelligent, well mannered, and devoted. Besides, she was already twenty-seven, in those days perilously close to spinsterhood, and with a heart condition at that, and could not hold out for a "brilliant" match to a rich, settled man. Though she would probably be fated, as an army wife, to spend years in remote, primitive Western "forts" and "camps" the match was still appealing. She and the first captain were soon seeing much of each other. The courting process required George to violate VMI rules. He often left the institute barracks and grounds after hours to see her, though if caught, he might have been expelled from school.

In the normal course of events Lily and George might have chosen to marry when he graduated. But even after the VMI commencement ceremonies George's future remained uncertain. Unlike graduates of West Point, those from VMI were not automatically commissioned as army officers. In fact, though a military school, VMI did not send many of its graduates into military service. In 1890 only ten VMI graduates were officers in the regular army. Of the 122 young men who started the class of 1901, only six became professional soldiers. VMI graduate Marshall was, then, faced with the prospect of winning a commission and beginning a military career against serious odds.

Fortunately 1901 was an auspicious year for a young man to begin the long upward climb in the U.S. Army. Though long ignored, the army's deficiencies had been exposed by the Spanish-American War. The United States had won that "Splendid Little War" against a feeble, decayed European empire, but the army's performance had been disappointing, marked by inefficiency, poor training, corruption, and incompetence. Too small to fight a European nation possessing superior arms and tactics, it had relied on volunteers, including most famously Theodore Roosevelt's Rough Riders. The logistic conduct of the war was worse than the actual fighting. The War Department chose the small city of Tampa, Florida, as the assembly point for the invasion of Cuba. The town lacked proper rail and port facilities. Freight cars carrying troops, munitions, and military supplies were soon backed up on sidings as far north as Columbia, South Carolina. Meanwhile, officers fought one another for ship space to assure their units were not left behind and arrived late in Cuba, at the scene of fighting. The provision of food, clothing, tents, weapons, and medical supplies was mishandled. Men wore woolen uniforms in the tropical heat; ate tasteless, stringy canned beef; and fought with outdated Springfield rifles. They died in droves of yellow fever, malaria, dysentery, and other diseases.

Had precedent been followed. peace would have encouraged Americans to return to their miserly, neglectful prewar military policies. But Marshall was lucky. Despite the incompetence, victory after scarcely 150 fighting days brought the United States a small overseas empire including Puerto Rico in the Caribbean and the Philippines, the large, diverse archipelago off the East Asian coast. Most Americans saw their acquisition of colonies as a liberation of the "little brown brothers" from European oppression. They were rudely awakened when in East Asia local Filipino nationalists rose up against the American successors to the defeated Spaniards. The force authorized in the wake of the "Philippine Insurrection" more than doubled the size of the former peacetime army. Obviously the expansion created the need for new officers, greatly improving Marshall's immediate chances for a commission.

And there was more. After the scandalous wartime failures came a cascade of military reforms that would deeply affect Marshall's future career. Pushed by the new secretary of war, the New

York lawyer Elihu Root, successor to the bungling Russell Alger, the changes ended the confusing division of military authority between the secretary of war and his bureau subordinates and the commanding general of the army by creating the post of chief of staff. The new chief would serve as top military adviser to the president and, under the secretary, would in effect reign as the uniformed head of the army. Under him, in turn, would be a new general staff to prepare plans for future military contingencies. To upgrade old-fashioned officer training, Root also created a number of schools for various broad divisions of the army such as the infantry, field artillery, cavalry, engineers, and medical corps. Serving to round out the new reeducation institutions would be the Army War College.

Yet another of Root's changes, reform of the National Guard, would impinge on Marshall's career. The antique state militia system, composed of part-time local volunteers, which had served—and often misserved—the nation since colonial times when dangers threatened, was inadequate. It was underfunded, its officers were often untrained political appointees, and its rank and file was composed of men interested largely in camaraderie and boozy good cheer. It was better known as a strikebreaking device than a military organization. Under Root's reforms the inept guard would be subject to new standards; Guard units would now be instructed by regular army officers; guard officers would have to pass federal examinations; guardsmen would participate with regulars on military training maneuvers.

These postwar changes undoubtedly offered new opportunities for aspiring officers, but how was the fledgling VMI graduate, without West Point credentials or family military connections, to qualify for the required second lieutenants' exam? Happily a combination of George Senior's string pulling, the new graduate's own enterprise, and sheer good luck got George on the applicants' exam list. In late September he came to New York for three days of tests. These were pitched at so low a level that a diligent high school student could have passed. But George could not be sure of his success, and he returned to his summer appointment as an instructor at Danville Military Institute, a Virginia secondary school, seriously worried about the results.

On October 8 the examining board issued its report. Marshall had passed with a score of 84 and was judged "well qualified for the position of a commissioned officer in the United States Army."[17] In fact Marshall had done so well that he would be eligible for service in the artillery, a competitive branch considered more desirable than the infantry.

Marshall resigned from his job at Danville and returned to Uniontown to await orders. Just after the New Year he received them. To his surprise they were for service in the infantry. Apparently no vacancies existed in the artillery for second lieutenants, and Marshall would be assigned to the Thirtieth Infantry Regiment, stationed in the Philippines. Though his posting was a disappointment, Marshall submitted his signed oath of office on February 3.

A week later Lily and George were married in a simple ceremony at the Coleses' home in Lexington, with the bride's brother standing in for Lily's deceased father. The next morning the married couple took the train to Washington for what they assumed would be a one-day honeymoon before George would have to report to Fort Myer. He would then depart immediately for early transport to the Philippines. Happily, when George appeared at the War Department, a compassionate officer noted his recent marriage and took pity on the newlywed. He could delay his departure for five extra days, he was told.

Army rules did not allow the wives of junior officers to accompany their husbands to their posts. But even if they had, Lily's uncertain health would have precluded it. All of six days, then, would be the extent of George and Lily's "wedded bliss" for two years. Meanwhile, the new bride returned to her mother's house in Lexington while George entrained west to the Presidio in San Francisco. In mid-April he took ship aboard the *Kilpatrick* sailing for Manila and the new American colony across the Pacific. He was about to begin his life as an officer in the U.S. Army.

CHAPTER 2

LEARNING AND YEARNING

The next seventeen years in Marshall's life were a time of learning how to be a hands-on soldier and how to climb the steep professional military ladder. Both processes began with his initial assignment, the Philippines. In the newly won colony he would learn the skills of military command and begin the slow advance toward the rank of general, the ultimate goal of any career army officer. Then, too, as a lowly second lieutenant, he would be compelled to forgo life with Lily, his new bride.

When Marshall arrived in May 1902, the Philippines, except for Manila, the archipelago's capital, was a primitive place by Western standards. The scattered seven thousand islands off the East Asian coast had been a Spanish colony since the late sixteenth century, and Spain had left its imprint on the predominantly Malaysian people in the form of the Spanish language, the Catholic Church, and the Gregorian calendar. But the Spanish rulers had bestowed only a thin layer of schools, roads, and hospitals, located particularly in the lowlands of Luzon and a few other large northern islands.

Filipinos, led by Emilio Aguinaldo, had joined the Americans in the brief struggle to oust the Spanish rulers in 1898. Though the uprising was a by-product of the Spanish-American dispute over Cuba thousands of miles away, the McKinley administration had resolved to retain the islands as a dependency. Aguinaldo and his followers had different goals. In early 1899 fighting broke out between Filipino rebels determined to achieve independence and the Americans, now seen as colonial occupiers. The Philippine Insurrection proved to be a major war. Before it ended in 1901, following Aguinaldo's capture, it would take the lives of more than 4,200 American soldiers and 34,000 Filipino guerrillas. The war, like most "asymmetrical" guerrilla conflicts, had fostered appalling atrocities on both sides.

When Marshall arrived in the Philippines most of the northern islands had been pacified and the American army in the islands cut back from its peak of 120,000 to 34,000 men. After a few days in Manila he took up his assignment with the Thirtieth Infantry on Mindoro, a four-thousand-square-mile, thumb-shaped island of mountains and rain forest southwest of Luzon, with scattered towns along the coast. The island was now peaceful except for some bandits and leftover *insurrectos* in remote areas. It was not a prime assignment, but, as he later noted, "there isn't anything much lower than a second lieutenant and I was about the most junior second lieutenant in the Army at the time."[1] His local posting was Calapan, the island's capital, an overgrown village of 5,600 where he was, in the temporary absence of a superior officer, placed in charge of a small American garrison consisting of fifty bored and unruly men. "They were about the wildest crowd I've ever seen before or since," he later reported.[2] However unlikely, Lieutenant Marshall managed to create an entertainment program that converted sulky troops into enthusiastic performers. He also helped fight off a devastating cholera epidemic that had descended on the islands shortly before he arrived. Instituting rigorous hand-washing, water-boiling, and mess-kit-scouring practices in the camp, he was able to avoid the scourge. None of the American soldiers died of cholera, though it did not spare hundreds of Mindoro's Filipino population.

In September, Capt. Henry Eames finally appeared to take over the post from Lieutenant Marshall, and soon after, the whole company was transferred to Manila, the Philippine capital. There, outside the cosmopolitan city of a quarter of a million, Marshall could finally relax. Garrison duties and chores occupied only the morning hours, and to fill his day he took up riding, borrowing his mounts from the U.S. Cavalry. For the rest of his life riding would be his chief exercise and recreation.

In late November 1903, after a brief, distasteful stint with Company G guarding hard-bitten, dangerous military prisoners on Malahi Island, Marshall and the Thirtieth Infantry boarded the military transport *Sherman* and embarked for California. There the young lieutenant set out for his next posting, Fort Reno on the Canadian River in what was then still Oklahoma Territory. Though now back in America, the new assignment kept George and Lily apart for still another few months. Apparently the lieutenant was not given leave time to visit his wife in Virginia, and meanwhile the frail Lily remained at home.

Fort Reno was adjacent to several Indian reservations and, in many ways, was as isolated as Calapan from mainstream contemporary America. It was a haven of the "Old Army" that, in the generation following the Civil War, had served primarily as a frontier police force to keep the Indians in check. With little to do after the end of the Indian wars in the 1890s, it devoted its energies primarily to spit-and-polish routine—clothing, kit, and barracks inspections; parading and close-order drill; punctilious saluting; and guard duty. The military force molded by this regimen was well suited to parades but not fit to fight a serious foreign enemy. Though the reform mood had been unleashed by Secretary Root and others, and Marshall would joyfully embrace its spirit, it had not yet reached this arid outpost in the still-wild West.

Though Marshall was now back in the United States, the reunion with Lily was further delayed by his assignment in the spring of that year to map a vast area of southwestern Texas, a rugged, empty region of desert, mountains, and dry riverbeds. It was, he later remarked, among the most rigorous duties he had ever performed in the army. The food was bad and water scarce. At one point he and his small platoon of soldiers and civilians went eighteen hours without a drop to drink. And his body would show it: He lost more than thirty pounds from his lanky frame from dehydration and sparse food supplies.

But he was rewarded at the end. The chief engineer officer of the Southwestern Division considered Marshall's map "the best one received and the only complete one" of the several assigned to other officers that summer.[3] To show their appreciation his superiors granted him four months' leave that Marshall spent back east visiting Uniontown and spending time with Lily and her Coles relatives in Albermarle County, Virginia. We do not know whether he enjoyed the stay with Lily's relatives, but he found the reunion with his own family somber. His parents no longer lived in the house on Main Street where he had grown up; it had been torn down. His father, stouter and slower, had begun to decline; his sister, Marie, soon to be married, was about to move away. And Uniontown itself seemed alien. Even Trip, the friendly dog of his close pal Andy, had forgotten him. But at least he had been reunited with Lily, and it was probably at this time that she finally joined him when he returned to Fort Reno.

Despite the consolation of Lily's presence, at this juncture in his army career Marshall felt suffocated and frustrated. After almost five years he was still a second lieutenant and relegated, besides, to a military backwater. He was soon seeking some way out of his uncomfortable position. In a March 1906 letter to VMI's Superintendent Shipp, he asked to be considered for a "detail" appointment from the army as professor of military science and tactics at the institute. The effort to escape failed. Unfortunately, Shipp wrote back, the institute preferred an older man and an officer of higher rank. It must have appeared to Marshall that he was truly stuck in place. But abruptly a brighter prospect appeared, one that would open up a new avenue of advancement and set on track the rest of Marshall's military career.

The break was selection for the two-year course at the Infantry and Cavalry School at Fort Leavenworth, Kansas. The school had been created by Secretary Root as part of his reform agenda and was imbued, though as yet imperfectly, with the new concept of a mobile and agile fighting army. Its teachings and approaches, considered "Germanic," were resisted by older officers, but Marshall knew that it was the portal to higher rank in the new peacetime army. He had applied for admission two successive years and come out first on the Fort Reno qualifying tests, only to lose out to senior officers with more influence. These men had returned to Reno at the end of their course skeptical of the new philosophy and were discouraging others at the post from applying. Their negativism helped Marshall. The third year he was the only Fort Reno applicant, and received the appointment for one year at the school with a second to follow if he excelled at the prestigious general staff course.

Leavenworth was a shock to the overage second lieutenant. Many of his classmates, especially those from the cavalry, had been coached for a year in the material of the courses and were well prepared for the race for advanced standing. Marshall was

not. Overhearing some of his fellow students discussing the probable winners of a second year without mentioning his name reminded Marshall of his brother's dismissive attitude years before
when he was considering whether to attend VMI. He responded
as he had to Stuart's put-down. He would show them! "I taught
myself to study very, very hard," he later recalled. "If it was a simple statement, I memorized the statement. . . . It was the hardest
work I ever did in my life."[4]

The rigors of that first year at Leavenworth took a toll on his
personal life. Though better than at Fort Reno, living accommodations were not ideal. Marshall lived with Lily and her mother in
cramped married officers' quarters. The three had dinner together
each evening after his classes, before Marshall hit the books to
prepare for the challenging day ahead. Bedtime was late and, apparently, sleep intermittent. We do not know the dynamics of the
relationships among the three and should be wary of the live-in
mother-in-law cliché, but the presence of Mrs. Coles cannot have
made life easier for the beleaguered student of war.

Despite the new army spirit and the influence of a military
reformer, Gen. J. Franklin Bell, former fort commandant and
later army chief of staff, the pedagogy at Leavenworth was still
primitive, predominantly rote memorization. With exceptions: A
number of instructors, particularly Maj. John Morrison, used different methods. Though considered too unorthodox by the old-
guard staff still hanging on at the school, Morrison was popular
with the students. "He spoke a language that was new to us and
appealed very much to our common sense," Marshall later noted.[5]
Morrison's forte was "tactics" as opposed to "technique," and the
replacement of memorization by problem-oriented pedagogy using maps, most of them foreign in the absence of American versions. "He spoke a tactical language I have never heard from any
other officer," Marshall later wrote. On the other hand, Marshall

added, he was "a miserable judge of men" and "understood nothing of the necessity of compromise."[6]

At the end of the rigorous year Marshall came out first in the class, one of the twenty-four first-year students to be asked to stay on and attend the Army Staff College the next year. Equally valuable, he had earned the favor of General Bell, who learned of the lieutenant's success when he attended the class graduation. Bell's good offices won Marshall a prestigious detail for the summer as an instructor with the Pennsylvania National Guard. There, though his stay at the Mt. Gretna Guard encampment in July 1907 was brief, he made his mark as a successful instructor and motivator of the civilian soldiers and was invited back for the next year's encampment. Marshall would continue to serve National Guard units periodically, learning from them many of the problems—if not necessarily the solutions—of turning clerks, workingmen, farmers, and bookkeepers into effective soldiers.

The second year at Leavenworth was easier than the first. The long-awaited promotion undoubtedly helped. In December, after hard study, he had taken five days of stiff exams for promotion, and in March received his silver bar as first lieutenant. His personal response reveals the depth of his ambition and his frustration. The promotion, he later said, "was the most thrilling moment of my life."[7] An added bonus was a salary raise: He would now be paid $183 a month.

The year 1907–8 at Fort Leavenworth was less competitive than the one before. Marshall took courses in military history, on the duties of the general staff, and on the organization of foreign armies. He sailed through easily. His impressive record, added to the good report of his summer National Guard service, earned him an invitation to stay on at Leavenworth as an instructor, only one of five students so honored. Though Marshall had "aced" Leavenworth, he never fully approved of its methods of instruction or its curriculum. As late as February 1939, when serving as deputy chief of staff under Gen. Malin Craig, he sought to thaw the school's "frozen . . . routine procedure" and especially its unfriendly response to airpower.[8]

The next two years as an instructor were among the more personally satisfying times in Marshall's life. He enjoyed teaching and was good at it. There were also exhilarating hunting trips in the saddle with his fellow officers. Marshall bought dogs and deployed them to hunt game birds in the countryside surrounding the post. Pleading his wife's fragile health, he could also avoid the frequent dances at the officers' club. For Lily, her husband's freedom from academic pressure ensured the more placid domestic life she cherished. During part of his extended leave from Fort Reno in 1905 he had spent time with Lily's kin in verdant Albemarle County, Virginia, south of Charlottesville. The couple had clearly enjoyed their visit, and in the summer of 1909 they returned to Albemarle County, where they lived, surrounded by Coles relatives and longtime neighbors and friends, in a white 1870s clapboard house owned by Lily's aunt, Sally Coles. It was a timeless atmosphere that might have existed a hundred years before. The older relatives dwelled much on Virginia's noble past. "Miss Sally" remembered hearing the rumble of the final Civil War battle at Appomattox Courthouse on Palm Sunday morning, April 9, 1865, as the family went to church. As Forrest Pogue writes, "The young lieutenant fell in love with this little world, its graciousness and hospitality, the charming serenity of the countryside, the horseback rides down tree-lined country lanes, the canoe trips on the James."[9] Though at first a little suspicious of this Pennsylvania-born officer, the Albemarle circle soon embraced Marshall as one of their own. That summer made a deep impression on Marshall. Ever after he found the charms of the rural Virginia countryside irresistible, and many years later he would chose a similar environment for his retirement home. The experience inevitably also fortified his adopted persona as a Virginian.

With his four-year stint at Leavenworth as a student and an instructor finally over, in the late summer of 1910 Marshall, joined by Lily, took a cut-rate vacation of five months in Europe, visiting England, France, Italy, and Austria. The assignments that followed in quick succession on his return, though mostly brief and frustrating for an officer seeking a more expansive career, nonetheless brought useful experience. Having done so well as an instructor for Pennsylvania National Guard troops, Marshall received regular assignments with other state guard units, including those of Massachusetts and New York. With the guard he learned the valuable lesson of how to maneuver large masses of troops—large at least for that day of a pygmy army. He also landed brief assignments on Governors Island, New York, and posts near Minneapolis and Galveston. In 1913, after seven years of detached domestic postings, he applied for foreign service. His list of preferences included Hawaii, Alaska, and China as the top three. He made a special plea to avoid the Philippines for a second time on the grounds of Lily's health. But on July 5, 1913, he boarded the transport *Logan*, assigned to the Thirteenth Infantry in Manila. Reassured that a posting in the modern capital city would not be medically detrimental to her health, this time Lily came along.

They would not be disappointed. "Living conditions," Marshall later noted, "were very much better [than during his first Philippine posting] because you had good houses and very good servants. And you had a very good general commissary to bring things out [from the United States] so that you got good things to eat and sufficient fresh things to eat."[10] During this Philippine interval Marshall's most valuable professional experience was the maneuvers of 1914, when he was introduced to the difficult prob-

lems of amphibious landings. Though they were primitive compared with the dilemmas he dealt with at Anzio and Normandy
thirty years later, he considered the lesson useful. "[I]t gave me
some familiarity with what you had to do," he later recalled.[11]

Once more working above his rank, and still driven by his
fierce will to succeed, Marshall felt obliged to deal diligently and
thoroughly with every detail of his Philippine assignment. Despite
Lily's comforting presence, he soon buckled under the strain. In
both 1912 and 1913 he experienced bouts of what was then diag-
nosed as "acute dilation of the heart" and was hospitalized for ten
days in Manila and forced, the second time, to take four months
of combined sick and regular leave to restore his health. He and
Lily took the opportunity on this occasion to visit Japan, Manchuria, and Korea. The experience taught Marshall a lesson: He was
working himself to death. Writing to Gen. Bruce Magruder years
later, he noted that he had been too intensely focused on "detail
work." But besides the damage to his health, he had acquired "the
reputation of being merely a pick and shovel man." When he finally
"woke up" at age thirty-three, he wrote, he determined to "relax as
completely as I could manage in a pleasurable fashion."[12]

The stresses of the second Philippine posting probably reflected
frustration as much as overwork. In October 1915, still a first
lieutenant, he wrote to the VMI superintendent, Gen. Edward
Nichols, Shipp's successor, of his professional discontents and for
advice about leaving the service: "The absolute stagnation in promotion in the infantry has caused me to make tentative plans
for resigning as soon as business conditions improve somewhat."
Marshall was not encouraged by the growing public awareness of
America's military unpreparedness since the outbreak of war in
Europe the previous year. "Even in the event of an increase as a
result of legislation next winter," he observed, "the prospects for
advancement in the army are so restricted by law and by the ac-

cumulation of large numbers of men of nearly the same age all in a single grade that I do not feel it right to waste all my best years in the vain struggle against insurmountable obstacles."[13]

By the time the Marshalls returned to the United States in the summer of 1916, the great European powers had been at war for almost two years, with two powerful alliances, the Central powers, linking Imperial Germany and Austria-Hungary, and the Allies, a coalition of France, Russia, and Great Britain, striking ferociously at one another on land and sea, and in the air. Eventually, Italy, Japan, Turkey, and other nations would be pulled into the war's vortex. Since several of these powers had colonies scattered over all the populated continents, the conflict quickly became a genuine world war. Despite Marshall's earlier pessimism, however, World War I broke the logjam on professional military advancement.

The events in Europe also transformed the combat mission of the American army. Though elsewhere in the war's many theaters the ground fighting had taken on the shape of a war of movement, in the most important theater, the Western Front, where France and Britain clashed with Imperial Germany, it had degraded into static trench warfare. There, running north and south from the English Channel to the Swiss border, inside the former boundaries of France and Belgium, both sides had literally dug in, creating a line of trenches where their troops could be relatively safe from artillery and other deadly attack. But the trenches did not prevent unbearable casualties. Periodically the British-French Allies and the Germans would launch massive frontal assaults against the other in hopes of breaking through their static defenses, sweeping into open country, and ending the excruciating stalemate. Preceded typically by hellish artillery bombardments directed at the enemy's trenches, troops armed with rifles and bayonets would go "over the top," against the barbed-wire defenses and the deadly machine-gun fire of their opponents. At the Marne, Verdun, the Somme, Passchendaele, and other battlefields, casualties were fearsome. At Verdun in the first half of 1916 French losses reached 163,000 dead and missing. German casualties in the same extended engagement included 100,000 dead and missing. The first day of the Battle of the Somme in mid-1916 inflicted 58,000 dead and missing on the attacking British forces. In these battles, through at least mid-1918, little was achieved by either side. A few trenches captured, a protruding salient in the line reduced, some prisoners taken were all the attackers had to show for the bloodbath they had inflicted and experienced.

As Americans looked on during the early months of the Great War they felt uneasy and unprepared. President Woodrow Wilson had asked his fellow citizens to be "neutral in fact as well as in name during these days that are to try men's souls." But gradually the United States, the most powerful of the remaining neutral nations, was drawn into the struggle through its financial stake in Allied victory and the public's growing anger at German submarine attacks on unarmed American vessels and transatlantic passenger liners. During the months preceding the American declaration of war, a "preparedness movement," sparkplugged by former president Theodore Roosevelt, captured the imagination of an elite, primarily on both coasts. It soon became stylish for the more patriotic young college men to volunteer for summer training camps sponsored by the army to learn to be officers. In June 1916 a preparedness-minded Congress passed the National Defense Act, authorizing an army of 175,000 men, increasing the National Guard to 450,000 men (and allowing its members to be drafted into federal service in time of war), creating a Reserve Officers Training Corps (ROTC) to turn qualified civilians into army officers, and giving the president enhanced powers over war matériel production.

Marshall was an early beneficiary of this martial surge. He had expected to be sent to join Gen. John J. Pershing in northern Mexico, where American troops were hunting down the Mexican rebel Pancho Villa, who had attacked American towns along the border. Instead he was dispatched to the Presidio in San Francisco, where his patron, General Bell, assigned him to a new officer-training camp located at coastal Monterey. Before beginning duty in California, Marshall finally got his captain's bars, after fourteen long years in the army. Soon after, he settled in a tent on the spacious grounds of the Del Monte Hotel, prepared to instruct the twelve hundred gentlemen "hot bloods of San Francisco" with their "Rolls-Royces and other fine cars" on the routines of army life and how to command and maneuver soldiers.[14]

The assignment was anything but arduous. There were champagne lunches in the field with wives and sweethearts, down from San Francisco and its wealthy suburbs. After training hours the men took their ease at the adjacent luxury hotel. Marshall tried, with indifferent success, to instill in them some discipline with close-order drill. Though he was probably considered a bit of a martinet by the men in his charge, several became his lifelong friends. After the Monterey encampment closed, Marshall helped open another officer-training camp, near Salt Lake City. Then, in late January, after concluding that the war would end before the United States could bring its military weight to bear, the Imperial German government resumed unrestricted submarine warfare against neutral shipping. On April 6, 1917, the United States declared war on Germany.

The war changed everything for Marshall. General Bell was reassigned to Governors Island, where he was placed in command of the army's Eastern Department. Captain Marshall came along as an aide and was put in charge of two officer-training camps near Plattsburgh in far-northern New York. He acquitted himself well as usual, cutting red tape, for example, to assure that his men had warm blankets for cold weather.

However challenging the training mission, Marshall craved active duty in France. General Pershing, now the designated commander of the AEF, the American Expeditionary Force, had sailed to Paris in June. Soon after, the U.S. Sixteenth Infantry Regiment paraded through the streets of Paris, lined with cheering crowds. This early show of strength was misleading, however. In May, Congress had passed the Selective Service Act, the first military draft measure since the Civil War. Eventually it would register almost twenty-four million men and provide more than a million and a half "doughboys" for the AEF. But for months after the United States joined the Allies, the available manpower of the American army was pitiful, no more than 190,000 officers and men. Meanwhile, British and French missions in Washington were pleading for American bodies to replace the Tommies and *poilus* killed in action or worn out and demoralized by two and a half years of trench warfare.

Having narrowly missed out on accompanying Pershing to France, Marshall lingered impatiently in New York. He soon contacted Superintendent Nichols, who apparently brought his virtues to the attention of Maj. Gen. William Sibert, the newly chosen head of the First Division, assigned to early combat duty overseas. Sibert got Bell to release Marshall so he could serve as the division's operations officer in France. With only thirty-six hours' notice of his departure, Marshall sent Lily off to Charlotte, North Carolina, to visit her brother and then to return to Lexington to sit out the war. In New York he collected his own gear and settled his personal affairs.

Marshall joined the First Division as it assembled on the New Jersey Meadowlands near Hoboken to prepare for departure for the fighting front. He found it a ragbag of a unit. One of the standard "square divisions," composed of four regiments, it was made up of Southwesterners, mountaineers from Kentucky and Tennessee, and hundreds of recent immigrants, many with little command of English. The First's noncoms were mostly old regular army veterans with no experience of the trench warfare they were about to encounter. Its officers were even more callow, largely recent civilians with, at best, six months of military training. As for the privates, they were as green as could be. "They had no knowledge of how to drill," Marshall later recalled, "no knowledge of how to handle their rifles."[15] When they arrived in France their slipshod appearance and careless demeanor would dismay the French. As for their equipment, it was in no better order. Marshall would later remark that most of them "had never heard of the weapons of which they were supposed to be equipped."[16] Probably no one, least of all Captain Marshall, had any illusions about the fighting quality of this human miscellany, but it was important to get combat troops to France as soon as possible to buck up sagging Allied morale and prove American determination to seriously engage the common enemy.

On June 14 the USS *Tenadores*, with Marshall and a large contingent of the First Division aboard, slid slowly down the Hudson and bore east for France. On the way over, Marshall would share a stateroom with Maj. Lesley McNair, who during the next great war would become his close associate in the task of molding American civilians into soldiers. During the jittery crossing the officers and noncoms tried to learn something about trench warfare but discovered that practically nothing useful was available in print. The appalling state of the nation's military preparedness was vividly illustrated when the naval gun crew attempted target practice with the transport's six-inch guns. The firing was wild. "The only thing they succeeded in hitting," Marshall later wrote, "was the horizon and the foreground."[17]

The transports and escorts arrived in Saint-Nazaire twelve days after leaving New York to be greeted coolly by the French, by now skeptical of would-be foreign saviors and depressed by the recent horrific casualties at the Somme. After several weeks camping out near Saint-Nazaire, the division set up headquarters at Gondrecourt in Lorraine, not far from the village where Joan of Arc had been born. There, though the troops were short of equipment and transportation, Marshall drew on his extensive experience with National Guard summer volunteers and devoted his energies to turning civilians into soldiers. It was a taxing though essential task. The French had little faith in American military prowess. They wanted the Americans to push training in trench warfare early and to incorporate American units into their own command structure, where the inexperienced troops could learn from French veterans. They also expected the novices to be led by French officers. Pershing refused to comply. American troops would fight in American units under American officers, he insisted. As for Marshall, he believed that before learning the fine points of trench fighting, the men under him needed more elementary instruction: how to march and how to acquire proper military demeanor and practice military courtesy.

Anxious to show his army's mettle, as the weeks passed Pershing grew impatient with delays in the training program. A former cavalry officer, though stern and aggressive he valued education, was warm in private, and would tolerate criticism himself. But he was not averse to dishing it out. During the late summer he drove out frequently to Gondrecourt from AEF general headquarters at Chaumont, an hour away. He often did not like what he observed. Exercises were too slow and too sloppy; proper terminology was not being used for facilities. He blamed General Sibert for the unit's failings, and on one occasion in early October, he harshly disparaged him in front of his subordinates. Loyal to his immediate chief, Marshall was offended by both Pershing's charges and his breach of courtesy. As a lowly captain he might well have repressed his resentment. Instead he confronted the general, putting his hand on his arm as he was leaving, forcing him to listen to his defense of Sibert. Marshall recited the extenuating circumstances for the unit's deficiencies and noted that some of them were the result of failings at Chaumont headquarters. Pershing listened as Marshall, "just mad all over," defended his unit and its commander. Shaking off the insubordinate captain, Pershing walked off, muttering, "Well, you must appreciate the troubles *we* have."[18]

The encounter horrified all who witnessed it. Sibert himself deplored the captain's action, though it was on his behalf. Marshall's friends told him he "was finished" and would "be fired right off." He shrugged. At the worst, he told them, he would lose his staff job and get duty with the troops, and that would be all to the good.[19] In the end, however, the incident would work to Marshall's advantage. Pershing never mentioned the event during the war. Years later he admitted to Marshall that he had been "pretty hot" at the time, but the incident had a paradoxical effect on their relationship. Unconvinced by Marshall's defense of his superior, Pershing replaced Sibert as commander of the First Division, but thereafter, when he visited the division, he often took Captain Marshall aside to question him about the state of affairs. Eventually Pershing would make Marshall his top aide and become his sponsor and patron through the AEF commander's long life.

If the Pershing episode had been an isolated event we would not question its source: Marshall had acted spontaneously to right an injustice. But a very similar confrontation with a powerful leader would take place some twenty years later, and it too would accrue to Marshall's advantage.

While the AEF and the First Division were painfully learning and improving, the Allied position on the Western Front deteriorated. In December 1917 the Russians, under their new Bolshevik leaders, Vladimir Lenin and Leon Trotsky, concluded an armistice with the Central powers at Brest-Litovsk, freeing many thousands of German troops to shift to the Western Front. Thus reinforced, and hoping for a knockout blow, in March 1918 the Germans launched a major offensive in the West that quickly inflicted 150,000 casualties on the British, bringing them once again within artillery distance of Paris. At this dangerous juncture the Allies chose a single officer, the French general Ferdinand Foch, as supreme commander of Allied forces in the West, though with limited powers over the Americans. It was under this unified command that the *Boches* would be finally defeated. Marshall would not forget in later years that command unity was a valuable military asset.

In those final months of the war the American forces, still thin on the ground, helped to check the German offensive by a successful First Division counterattack at Cantigny, a village in the Somme district. Marshall did much of the elaborate staff planning for the assault. He also got a taste of personal danger when he and two other officers made a preliminary night reconnaissance in front of the village to learn the lay of the land and found themselves at dawn crawling on their bellies in shallow trenches for hundreds of yards to escape the sharp-eyed German machine-gunners. But this bit of action was exceptional and only underscored Marshall's discontent: He craved combat assignment with troops. Such duty was the essence of soldiering, of course, and no true warrior could fail to seek it. But it also seemed vital for advancement. His old acquaintance from Leavenworth days, Douglas MacArthur, had arrived in France soon after him. But combat with the Rainbow Division had brought him seven silver stars and the rank of brigadier general at the age of thirty-eight, before the Armistice was declared. Marshall, surely, could not avoid making an invidious personal comparison.

But combat assignment in France would escape him. To Marshall's dismay and frustration, his staff work for the Cantigny attack was too well appreciated; he was too valuable as a tactical planner to be released to lead troops. Partial salvation came when, in mid-July, he was transferred to Pershing's headquarters at Chaumont, becoming chief of the Operations Division of the U.S. First Army. He would now operate on a wider stage—one, moreover, where he would be under the command of chief of operations Col. Fox Conner, and in close proximity to Pershing himself.

By now the German spring offensive had lost its momentum, and German hopes for final victory had evaporated. Drained of manpower, energy, and will, the Germans also confronted the growing size and experience of the still fresh and aggressive troops of the AEF, now pouring into France at the rate of more than 250,000 a month. Yet much fighting remained before the stubborn enemy would surrender, and a substantial part of it would be borne by the Americans. During the next four months Marshall helped plan major American offensives against the Saint-Mihiel salient, and in September, in conjunction with the French, he contributed to planning the American part in the Allied grand offensive in the Meuse-Argonne sector. Fifteen U.S. divisions joined the broad-fronted attack, later increased to twenty-two. It developed into the bloodiest single battle in American military history till then, but in the end it helped break the German will to fight.

On October 5 the German government sent a telegram to Washington through the neutral Swiss requesting the United States to "take steps for the restoration of peace," on the basis of President Wilson's generous terms as announced in his Fourteen Points of the previous January. On November 11, at 11:00 a.m., hostilities ceased on the Western Front. For America, and for Marshall, the war was over.

From Marshall's professional perspective the Great War had been a mixed experience. He had not learned all there was to know about the training and personnel problems of a large army. In the greater war to come he would make mistakes both of omission and commission. But compared to most of his peers he had acquired valuable knowledge of how to organize, manage, and sustain large bodies of troops for, and in, combat. He had also honed the useful skill of dealing with difficult allies. His expertise as a staff officer was widely recognized, moreover. Gen. George Van Horn Moseley, another Pershing staff officer, would later explain that it had been Marshall's job to "work out all the details of the operations, putting them in clear practical workable order which [could] be understood by the commanders of all the subordinate units. The order must be comprehensive, yet not involved. It must appear clear when read in poor light, in the mud and rain. It was Marshall's job and he performed it 100 per cent. The troops which maneuvered under his plans always won."[20]

On the other hand, he had not leaped ahead in rank, as had many of his colleagues who led troops in the field. He had more than once been recommended by friends for field service. In August 1918, marine general John Lejeune had requested that Marshall be made commander of the Twenty-Third Infantry Regiment in the battle shaping up, only to have the request denied: Marshall was too valuable where he was. At forty he emerged from the war still a temporary colonel, reverting to major as his permanent peacetime rank in 1919.

With the fighting over, most American troops went home, of course. But not all. Pershing and a nub of regulars, officers and men, including Marshall, remained after the Armistice to

perform occupation duties, to be ready in case final peace negotiations failed, and to help compose a final report on the AEF's
wartime achievements. In April 1919 Pershing asked Marshall to
be one of his official aides, to serve as his adviser, and to take
his place at times in routine matters. The appointment was an
honor and the connection with Pershing invaluable. "Black Jack"
Pershing was now America's greatest war hero who, after November 1918, would be feted in France, Britain, and Italy, and back
home in America when he and his staff returned the following
September. In 1919 he would be made "General of the Armies"
by a grateful Congress, and in 1921 he would become army chief
of staff. It was by no means a grim fate to be closely associated
with such a man, and in the long run it would pay valuable professional dividends for Marshall. Perhaps, in the end, it more than
compensated for the combat deficiencies that Marshall so much
lamented.

But meanwhile there was the reunion with Lily after two years
of separation. Lily was at City Hall in Manhattan, waiting for her
husband when the SS *Leviathan* docked in New York Harbor.
Along with other staff families the Marshalls were put up at the
luxurious Waldorf Hotel, a fit setting for what was clearly a joyful
reunion. Banquets and parades followed in the city and then the
last of the victory parades in Washington, with Pennsylvania Avenue lined with cheering spectators.

Marshall was now back to the concerns and vicissitudes of
the military services in a nation that had little use for soldiers
and sailors—with their high cost of maintenance—when danger
seemed remote. Now, in peacetime again, would the frustrating
professional experiences of his first military decade and a half
simply be replayed?

CHAPTER 3

BETWEEN THE WARS

As Pershing's aide, Marshall accompanied the AEF commander to Washington, where his chief would serve for the next five years, first as General of the Army and then, after July 1, 1921, as army chief of staff. In the fall of 1919, now reduced to the peacetime rank of major, he settled in with Lily at 2400 Sixteenth Street, N.W., an apartment hotel. Their fellow tenants were mostly transients—diplomats, academics, military officers, and members of Congress who retained their permanent residences in their home districts. The Marshalls took their meals most evenings in the hotel dining room, where, like other residents, they had their own special table and assigned waiter.

We get a rare glimpse into the Marshalls' years at Sixteenth Street because it was where the major met Rose Page, the eight-year-old daughter of a University of Virginia economist serving a term in Washington on the U.S. Tariff Commission. As a middle-aged woman Rose would publish a memoir of her friendship with Marshall, a friendship that would last until his death forty years later.

Rose—later Rose Page Wilson—was a lively, curious, intelligent little girl who met the thirty-eight-year-old major when she hailed him by name as they rode down the hotel elevator together. Marshall was enchanted by her. He and Lily would never have children, though they enjoyed their company, and they virtually adopted Rose. The perky little girl and Marshall took walks in Rock Creek Park, went horseback riding together, and talked endlessly, with Marshall recounting his years at VMI, his service in the Philippines, his courtship of Lily, and advising Rose on proper decorum and soothing her small discomforts after childish misadventures. Rose preferred Marshall to her own distant and inaccessible professor father. Detecting his by-now perfected persona, she remembered Marshall's dashing manner and, at the same time, his great poise and dignity. The major was a man of "incorruptible honor," the adult Rose wrote, chivalrous and meticulously courteous to women, who admired him as an amusing dinner partner.[1]

Rose provides one of the few insights we have into the Marshalls' day-to-day domestic relations. The major, she reported, was extra-attentive to his wife's needs and wishes. "He delighted in indulging [Lily] in every way he could. . . . [He] showered Lily with a hundred little attentions; he fetched and carried; he planned little surprises. He was ever solicitous about her health and comfort. He relieved her of mundane financial budgeting and any like chores and decisions; and if he teased her, he paid her innumerable little compliments. . . . In short, he gave her his unremitting consideration, smoothed the path before his queen and led her by the hand."[2] Though Rose did not record it, as we shall see, he was also at times her overseer and executive director.

The years in the nation's capital would be an especially happy period for the Marshalls. The hotel was full of congenial people, and Washington was still sufficiently Southern and gracious enough to please Lily. There were also friends nearby, some made before the war in Marshall's peacetime postings, and newer ones he had acquired in France. During these months Pershing became more than a respected superior; he became a mentor and a warm friend to both George and Lily. In a December 1920 letter to the general the Marshalls would sign off: "We both send you our love."[3]

The early years of the postwar decade were an unsettled time for the military services. True, America had won its war, but its performance as a combatant had not been outstanding. The nation had been unready for war. The United States already possessed the world's most productive economy, but its mighty industrial machine had been unable to gear up in time to produce the guns, ships, planes, and tanks required by twentieth-century warfare and it had been forced to borrow much of the doughboys' equipment from its French and British allies. Moreover, as the experience of the First Division in France illustrated, American troops were raw, unprepared for combat. Not until the last months of the fighting in France did the AEF earn the respect of their British and French compeers. Marshall himself, writing soon after the war, noted that the experience of 1917–18 "taught one great lesson": that "the unprepared nation is helpless in a great war unless it can depend upon other nations to shield it while it prepares."[4] Now, after Versailles, as the American military and their civilian masters in Congress considered the war's lessons, they knew they must avoid repeating the mistake of too little, too late.

But any program of prudent change was undermined by the American public's disappointments and disillusionments with the peacemaking process at Versailles, and its reversion to the deep-rooted American inwardness and disdain for supposedly corrupt Europe. It was in these years of the early 1920s that the term "isolationism" would be first widely used for the mood of determined detachment from Europe's problems. Concentrated in the country's Midwestern heartland, it would remain a powerful force throughout the interwar years. In the view of its proponents, Americans could take refuge behind its two great ocean moats, ignoring threats and dangers from abroad. We might need a powerful navy for this purpose, but there would be little use for a large land army.

Serious discussion of the army's future course and shape had been initiated by Secretary Newton D. Baker in the War Department soon after the Armistice. At the department's request Pershing sent Col. John McAuley Palmer, Marshall's former student and old friend from Leavenworth, to Washington to contribute his knowledge and expertise to the discussion. Palmer had long advocated a small core military to be used in emergencies, but also a National Guard capable of converting into a large citizen army to meet any needs of an overseas expeditionary force as in 1917. This view was assumed to represent Pershing's preferences as well.

In any event it clashed with the plans of Chief of Staff Peyton March, a fine administrator but an irascible man who, Marshall later said, had "a great weakness of antagonizing everybody."[5] General March disdained the guard and preferred a large peacetime army of regulars that in time of war could absorb draftees directly into its ranks. March and Pershing did not get along. Though he was theoretically Pershing's superior, in fact March held permanent rank inferior to General of the Armies Pershing, who treated him as a subordinate. The conflict of egos exacerbated their differences over the pending Army Reform Bill, jointly sponsored by March and Secretary Baker, that called for a substantial regular army of five hundred thousand. The clash worsened when Pershing endorsed a Palmer-like bill. Testifying before a joint congressional committee on military affairs in October–

November 1919, he proposed a three-hundred-thousand-man army that could mobilize and train the National Guard if needed, along with a provision for universal military training (UMT), in effect, a peacetime draft.

Marshall approved of his chief's plan. These expressed his faith in UMT for the nation and his own confidence in the utility of the guard based on his experience as a guard trainer during prewar summers. He accompanied Pershing to the congressional hearings, where, though only an observer, he learned much about congressional processes and about managing the nation's elected representatives. But Marshall personally refused to take sides in the dispute. "They had it out, and I'm not an umpire on such things," he later told an interviewer.[6] Yet he did not approve of Pershing's unrestrained and public feuding with the chief of staff. Both men, he believed, were at fault. The unpleasant publicity, perpetuated by the later published memoirs of both officers, would make a deep impression on Marshall. Ever after he would make it a point never to allow his personal judgment of generals and prominent civilians to become public knowledge. (His reticence, unfortunately, would impoverish his own recorded oral memoirs for historians and laymen alike.)

Pershing's congressional testimony reinforced the public's related moods of parsimony and isolation. The Republican Congress passed the National Defense Act of 1920 roughly on the Palmer-Pershing model. The law provided for a regular army of only 280,000, backed by a National Guard totaling 430,000 additional men, It dropped the UMT provision both Marshall and Pershing supported, but strengthened considerably the power of the general staff. The structural features of this imperfect measure remained in force through the remaining two decades of peace and formed the military framework within which Marshall had to work when he became chief of staff in 1939.

Paltry as were the authorized dimensions of the new army under the 1920 law, the actual numbers grew progressively worse as Congress became more and more stingy. In January 1921 it reduced the number of authorized troops to 175,000 and soon thereafter to 150,000. In 1922 the number declined further: 12,000 officers and 125,000 enlisted men. The decay also affected funding. During most of the 1920s the War Department's annual appropriation plateaued at about $300 million, with the ground forces increasingly forced to compete for resources with the air corps, then a division of the army. Meanwhile, the National Guard dwindled as well from its authorized strength, stabilizing at roughly 180,000.

Soon after his decisive congressional testimony Pershing, at Secretary Baker's behest, embarked on a tour of army posts and munitions factories to determine which should be retained and which closed in peacetime. Accompanied by Marshall, the general was greeted by lavish banquets and adoring audiences. By now Pershing had caught the presidential bug. His hero status as AEF leader and his acquiescence in the parsimony of the Republican congressional leadership made Pershing for a time seem a possible GOP candidate in the 1920 presidential race. Marshall disapproved of the move. "Some of his friends," he later observed, had "deluded him."[7] In the end Pershing proved to have little political savvy and his presidential boomlet quickly fizzled out. Marshall believed it had diminished Pershing's reputation, and the episode confirmed one of his basic precepts: Generals and politics should not mix.

In July 1921 Pershing superseded March as army chief of staff and moved to Fort Myer, Virginia, just across the Potomac from Washington and connected to the city's downtown by a short streetcar ride. Marshall remained his aide, and he and Lily now ended their idyll at Sixteenth Street and moved to Fort Myer's

Quarters No. 3, close to Pershing's own house. There their comfortable lives continued relatively unchanged. Lily remained socially inhibited by her heart condition; she could not tolerate the cigarette smoke that usually enveloped the parties and balls they were invited to. But she occasionally was able to fill in for her husband at gatherings he could not attend. Living nearby, in Washington, was the captain's aged mother, Laura, now a widow and largely bedridden. Marshall dutifully visited her once or even twice a day, sometimes bringing General Pershing along to please the old lady.

Marshall's years in Washington, as personal aide to Pershing, were invaluable for his future. He accompanied the general everywhere, sitting in on discussions with the president and congressional leaders. He got to know Washington's movers and shakers from both parties. Among them was Charles Dawes, director of the newly created Bureau of the Budget, former AEF chief of supply procurement during the war and a future Republican vice president of the United States. Another influential friend was the New York financier Bernard Baruch, an adviser to President Wilson and a major financial contributor to the Democratic Party. During the war Baruch had headed the War Industries Board, the federal agency that coordinated the production and shipping of vital war matériel. In later years he became an influential adviser to another Democratic president, Franklin Roosevelt.

Pershing's retirement from the army in 1924 marked another pivot point in Marshall's career. He had by now grown tired of staff positions and serving as an assistant to high-ranking officers. In August he was promoted to permanent lieutenant colonel, but further advance depended on command of troops. With the world at peace, he could not expect to lead men in combat, but he needed experience as a leader of soldiers if his career was to prosper. Even if he had wished to remain in Washington, moreover, army rules did not allow him to continue. Marshall's solution was to seek an overseas posting, and in April 1924 he was assigned to the Fifteenth Infantry in Tientsin, China, effective July 1. He would not be leading soldiers into enemy fire, but at least he would not be buried under paperwork in some obscure domestic corner.

Though a very long way from home, Tientsin was considered a cushy post, one whose amenities would allow Lily to accompany him. Lily herself looked forward to a three-year posting in China. "A lot of our friends are over there," she wrote to her aunt, "& *all* are wild about it—One of my friends now in Tien Sien . . . says she has *nine* servants, for the price of *one* in the States—Everyone over there lives in the most unbelievable luxury. Beautiful houses—wonderful food & tremendously gay and interesting."[8] An added bonus for Lily was that her mother could come and stay with them. On July 12 the Marshall party boarded the army transport *St. Mihiel* in New York and, after stops with friends in San Francisco and Honolulu, landed at Ch'in-huang-tao, China, on September 7, reaching Tientsin regimental headquarters soon after.

Tientsin was a city on the North China coast, not too distant from the Chinese capital, Peking (now Beijing). The Fifteenth Infantry post had been established in early 1921 in response to the persistent turmoil that swept across China following the 1911 revolution, which had replaced the corrupt and incompetent imperial Qing Dynasty with a republic on the Western model. Though the Chinese republican ideal assumed a unified nation, the country soon collapsed into civil war, with a multitude of ruthless, tyrannical warlords vying for pelf and power. Other Western nations had long-established "concessions" in Tientsin, Western islands in the midst of an alien culture where the institution of "extraterritoriality" (judicial self-rule by the foreign residents) prevailed. There were as many as seven of these foreign enclaves in Tientsin, but none was American. In the interests of economy the U.S. government was content to limit its presence to a small troop contingent to protect its citizens' lives and property. It was this community that Marshall—and Lily—now joined.

Marshall's job was not onerous. He was officially only regimental executive officer, though for a time, until the arrival of Col. William Naylor in November, he was in de facto charge of the approximately 850 officers and men of the Fifteenth. Having inherited the abandoned former German enclave with its fine brick barracks, the regiment had pleasant physical accommodations. The troops' mission was well defined: They were in China to guarantee the safety of American citizens and protect the railroad connecting the coast to the capital, where the American Embassy was located. The major difficulty the regiment faced was the disunity and turmoil in this "warlord period" in twentieth-century Chinese history. The armed forces mustered by these freebooters were ill equipped and ill led, but they far outnumbered the foreign troops. It required tact more than brute force to keep their clumsy clashes with one another from spilling over into the foreign enclaves and endangering foreign lives and property.

For the women, however, life in Tientsin lived up to its reputation in army circles. A ten-room house rented for fifteen dollars a month. Servants were plentiful and cheap: The typical officer employed five (not nine, like Lily's friend) at a total cost of some forty or fifty dollars per month. Since Marshall's lieutenant colonel's pay ran to about $6,800 a year, he could easily afford them. Yet there were reasons for complaint. While it was true that living costs were low compared with those in the United States, army families, warned one writer for the *Infantry Journal*, would find that they had little money to spare after raising their sights to equal their Western military peers' in China. If nothing else an officer's wife would "inevitably" accumulate "a rather impressive store of rugs, silver, linen, lingerie, embroideries, and other impedimenta, that would be utterly beyond his means if priced on Fifth Avenue."[9] Lily appreciated the amenities. "We quite adore it over here," she wrote one of Pershing's former aides, "and find life so easy. Many servants and much liquor make things so simple."[10] She seems also to have acquired the standard complement of household furniture, rugs, and assorted bric-a-brac.

While immersed in regimental desk work, keeping a careful eye on the likes of warlords Chang Tso-lin, Wu Pei-fu, and Feng Yu-hsiang, and monitoring growing antiforeign feeling among Chinese students, Marshall diverted some of his energies to recreation and self-improvement. He took his personally trained Mongolian pony on eight- to ten-mile jaunts followed by a top-speed run around the Tientsin racetrack. He organized an informal regimental cavalry troop mounted on the local ponies. Besides satisfying his equestrian passion, riding was how Marshall kept in physical—and also psychological—shape. He supplemented the riding by playing squash and tennis at the American country club.

Self-improvement also took the form of learning Chinese, a difficult language for Westerners unused to bewildering vocal tonalities atop a vocabulary without European cognates. Despite his poor performance at VMI as a student of French, Marshall made good progress in Chinese at the regimental language school. On July 18, 1925, he reported to a friend back home that "I can now carry on a casual conversation in Chinese with far less difficulty than I ever could manage in French. And I can understand even the wranglings and squabbles of the coolies and rickshaw men."[11] It is hard to believe that Marshall ever became truly fluent in Mandarin, but he apparently did learn enough to engage in useful dialogue and negotiations with Chinese officials and military leaders.

Marshall also came to understand the Chinese mind and sympathize with Chinese grievances against the West. He did not "go native," of course. He scarcely knew any Chinese men or women of his own class. Typically for his set, his social life was confined to European venues, including the Race Club (that is, riding club) and the luxurious Tientsin Country Club, with its pool, tennis courts, and pavilions. Few if any who enjoyed these facilities—as opposed to working staff and servants—were Chinese. Nevertheless he came to understand the feelings of the Chinese people, especially their deep sense of humiliation at foreigners' hands, and to grasp how difficult it would be to settle the tangled relations between China and the West. "How the Powers should deal with China is a question almost impossible to answer," he wrote to Pershing in late December 1926. "There has been so much of wrong doing on both sides, so much of shady transaction between a single power and a single party; there is so much of bitter hatred in the hearts of these people and so much of important business interests involved, that a normal solution can never be found."[12] His remarks would be prophetic.

In this letter to his former chief Marshall mentioned the intrusion of a new force into his own North China neighborhood. "At present," he wrote to Pershing, "the Cantonese troops are waging very successful warfare in central China and are threatening Shanghai. Officials in Peking have their wind up pretty badly fearing the Southern part will leap into North China any month." Though Marshall did not note it, the "Southern part" referred to was led by a young officer named Chiang Kai-shek, who had recently assumed leadership of the Kuomintang, the southern-based Nationalists, following the death of Sun Yat-sen, founder of the Republic of China. Chiang was not content to govern the country's south and was, as Marshall wrote, threatening to move against the northern warlords who ruled in Peking and the northern provinces, and unite all of China under his Nationalist rule. The American lieutenant colonel could not know it, of course, but the events he described were a foreshadowing of China's history for the next generation, a history in which he would eventually play an important role. The two and a half years in Tientsin did not make Marshall the expert on China that influential people in later years, including the president, would believe. But it did provide an important context for his crucial diplomatic mission just after World War II. He would at least understand the depth and complexity of the problems then at hand.

With his Tientsin posting about to end, Marshall once again had to consider his future and again he found himself faced with the realities of the peacetime army: small size, slow promotion, and the tyranny of seniority. "Administrative desk jobs have always been my pet abomination," he wrote to VMI superintendent William Cocke just after Christmas 1926. "But with so few regiments and so many lieutenant colonels, one has little choice."[13] Under the circumstances, he told Cocke, he had already accepted the position offered by Gen, Hanson Ely, an infantry colonel friend from AEF days, as instructor at the Army War College in Washington.

The Marshalls sailed for home in May 1927. Lily's health was not good, and their trip by car from San Francisco to the East Coast was unavoidably by slow stages. They stayed two weeks in Lexington and then moved into the unoccupied Washington apartment of Marshall's old friend General Palmer, who was away on duty in Panama.

Lily's health soon deteriorated further, and in August she entered Walter Reed Hospital for diagnostic tests. The doctors determined that her heart condition had been aggravated by a thyroid malady that required an operation. But given her coronary problems, the surgery would have to wait until her strength had been enhanced by rest and better nutrition. In the meantime the Marshalls moved from their temporary quarters to an attractive house on the War College grounds, where Lily gained weight to the point where the doctors believed a thyroidectomy safe to perform. The operation on August 21 at Walter Reed proved difficult but successful. Lily remained in the hospital for three weeks slowly regaining strength, being cheered by her husband's visits. "George is so *wonderful* and helps me so," she wrote to her aunt. "He puts heart and strength in me."[14] A week later, about to be released to return home, Lily slumped over and died while composing a letter to her mother.

Marshall was devastated. The austere, laconic officer had truly loved her. Lily had been more than his partner. Though in poor health throughout their marriage, she had been in many ways at the core of his life. She, and her family and friends, had helped to define who he was. If he had developed a male "club life," as so many military men did, he might have been better able to endure this blow, but he had not, he wrote to General Pershing; Lily had filled all his emotional space. Rose Wilson, who had attended the funeral at Arlington National Cemetery with her mother, visited Marshall several days later. He found Rose a comfort and asked her to join him for a car ride as in the old days. She later wrote that as they drove she could see that "his face was haggard and drawn with grief; his eyes lifeless, clouded by such utter sadness." His "sorrow" seemed to her "as profound and awesome as is possible for a man to bear." When she took his hand to comfort him, he murmured: "Rosie, I'm so lonely, so *lonely*."[15]

Still, grief is seldom endless, and the army was quick to help its own. Chief of Staff Charles Summerall offered Marshall several job choices, including the option of staying on at the War College. Finding Washington a stifling place after Lily's death, Marshall accepted the post of assistant commandant at the Infantry School at Fort Benning, Georgia. There he would head the Academic Department, with control over the curriculum. At Benning he would be able to try out ideas about infantry tactics he had long favored, and could exercise his strong teaching instincts. Marshall explained the appeal of the Benning assignment to Gen. Stephen Fuqua, a former classmate at Leavenworth, soon after leaving Benning. He would "always have a soft place" in his "heart for Benning," he declared. "It caught me at my most restless moment, and gave me hundreds of interests. . . . At a War College desk, I thought I would explode."[16] Marshall was pointing here to the pull of the wide-open outdoor life of the extensive Benning post, but he was also alluding to its power to cushion him from his bereavement.

Marshall's four and a half years at Benning, then, promised emotional refuge. Unfortunately it did not promote his physical health. At Benning, Marshall remained trim, but he developed a thyroid condition that triggered an irregular pulse and coronary arrhythmia that would periodically flare up. It also provided valuable experience for the middle-aged lieutenant colonel. But, most important, it made a difference to the U.S. Army, for the Marshall regime would leave a deep imprint on the Infantry School.

The core of the Marshall approach to training officers was an extension and reinforcement of the realistic tactics—as opposed to rote, "set-piece" exercises—that he had learned under Morrison at Leavenworth. He preached the need for simplicity and flexibility. Army orders, he taught, had always been too detailed and complex, slowing down movements and responses. They must be made brief and clear. Though he could not foresee that the tank and the airplane would negate the trench warfare of World War I, he worked to undercut the static "war of position" doctrine that had clamped its deadly hand on the Western Front in 1915–18, and sought to replace it with a "war of movement" creed, of "fire-and-flank" maneuver, that would prevail in the later and greater war. He also sought to compel trainees to improvise, to "think on their feet." In one instance, a student later wrote, he led a class on horseback on a seventeen-mile cross-country jaunt and at the end, "without previous warning," told them to draw a sketch map of the terrain they had covered.[17] He placed high value on originality and encouraged and rewarded the officer who thought of novel ways to achieve a tactical goal. According to Capt. J. Lawton Collins, later himself army chief of staff, Marshall helped create "the spirit at Benning" that "if anybody had any new ideas he was willing to try them instead of saying, 'Why don't you let the thing alone instead of stirring things up.'"[18]

Among many of the officers who were exposed to Marshall's principles, his success at Benning was widely acknowledged. An instructor who taught during his first year later wrote that in his "opinion Col. Marshall did more for the Infantry School than any one who ever served there. We were in a 'slump' and he pulled us out."[19] Omar Bradley, who served as a tactics instructor at Benning under Marshall, noted in 1964 that Marshall had "really established the standards of instruction as we know them today," insisting "that a maximum of our training take place on the ground, not in the classroom."[20] A later scholar has noted that under Marshall the Infantry School represented the army "school system at its best."[21]

Time and often bitter experience would show that even under the Marshall regime, the school failed to instill in its pupils the aggressive leadership qualities required of officers in the war to come. And indeed some later officers would question its timid focus on flanking tactics. But his stint at Benning would exert enormous influence on the men who led the army ground forces in World War II. All told, during Marshall's tenure, 150 future generals were students at Benning, and an additional 50 served there as instructors; many of these—including Omar Bradley, Joseph Stilwell, J. Lawton Collins, Walter Bedell Smith, and James Van Fleet—would attain high rank in World War II.

During the years at Benning, Marshall filled his leisure time with strenuous activities, especially "riding to hounds." These hunts on horseback appealed particularly to Anglophile upper-class Southerners and suggested how much of the "Virginia" identification remained in Marshall's persona. Beginning early in the fall and into early spring, twice a week several score officers and their wives rode out from Benning in pursuit of the gray or red fox. Marshall was often the inspirer of these outings and shared in the thrill of the exuberant chase. He also enjoyed quiet solo canters across the Georgia countryside.

If the Benning interlude was intended to foster emotional "closure" for the grieving widower, it did not fully work. Besides his duties Marshall sought consolation in the young. As with Rose, he doted on children and now often invited them to his house for refreshments or took a colleague's borrowed son or daughter to a theatrical or musical performance on the post. Apparently these contacts did not fully assuage the desolation he felt. Marshall's sister, Marie, made several long visits to Benning during her brother's posting and was dismayed to find that he had made his house a shrine to Lily, with photographs of her displayed in every room.

Then, in the fall of 1929, his ordeal came to an end. One evening while dining with friends Tom Hudson and his wife in Columbus, the town adjacent to Benning, he met Katherine Tupper Brown, a rich widow with three children: Molly, fifteen, Clifton, thirteen, and Allen, eleven. Katherine was forty-seven at the time, a year younger than Marshall. She was a vivacious and intriguing woman with an unconventional background. Though the daughter of a Baptist minister, after college in Virginia she trained as an actress in New York. She later joined an English repertory company, playing Shakespeare and the Restoration playwrights in the British provinces. She returned to America after two years, married a successful lawyer, Clifton Brown, and settled down in Baltimore as a wife and mother. In 1928 a disgruntled client shot and killed Brown at his law office, leaving her devastated. Fortunately her deceased husband had invested his money well, and she and her children were provided with a comfortable income to live on.

Katherine later recalled her first glimpse of Marshall. "My first impression was of a tall, slender man with sandy hair and deep-set eyes." She remembered that he had attracted her interest when he refused a cocktail at a party they both attended. These were Prohibition times, but most worldly people, including military men, drank—and, in fact, the Volstead Act had made bathtub gin and bootleggers prime conversational topics in such circles. "You are a rather unusual Army officer, aren't you?" Katherine exclaimed when he refused the drink.[22] Marshall asked her how many officers she had known. The ice was broken. Conversation at dinner flowed easily, with Marshall telling amusing stories about Southern hospitality. He drove Mrs. Brown home that evening, and by then both parties seemed to know that more was to come.

Katherine had not expected to marry again, but the meeting with Marshall undermined her resolve. During the summer of 1930 the colonel spent five weeks with Katherine and her offspring at their vacation cottage on Fire Island on Long Island's South Shore. There he got to know the children and discovered that he and they were compatible. In fact, in the years ahead, Marshall would come to consider Molly, Clifton, and Allen his own children, growing especially attached to Allen, the youngest, who accepted him most comfortably as surrogate father.

Katherine and George were married on October 15, 1930, in Baltimore's Emmanuel Episcopal Church. The affair was intended to be simple, with a few family members and a small number of invited guests. Attendance would have been modest, but the local papers reported that General Pershing was to be best man, and his presence drew crowds of onlookers who filled the chapel and spilled over on to the sidewalk. After the ceremony the newlyweds boarded a train to Atlanta and arrived at Fort Benning the following afternoon.

That evening, at a reception on the lawn of Commandant Campbell King's home, Katherine ran the gauntlet of all the Benning brass and most of George's friends and colleagues. Marshall instructed his new wife how to greet particular individuals as they passed her on the reception line. Nevertheless it was an ordeal. As she later wrote, "It was with fear and trembling that I took my place in the receiving line, praying to make good. I shall never forget that night."[23] After the first five hundred or so greeters, Katherine felt that her face had frozen into a permanent smile. Still, George believed she had done well overall, though she was, he noted, a little slow to pick up the signals he gave her regarding topics to mention to individuals as they passed by. In the days and weeks that followed Katherine learned more and more about the idiosyncrasies of army social life. She apparently met all the challenges. "At the end of our two years at Fort Benning," she later wrote, "I was a fair Army wife."[24]

Marshall's four-and-a-half-year tour of duty at Benning ended in the spring of 1932, just as the nation, and much of the Western world, approached the grim nadir of the Great Depression. In America the economic crisis would soon elevate Franklin Delano Roosevelt and the Democratic Party to power in Washington. A Wilsonian internationalist and former assistant secretary of the navy, FDR, though initially constrained by falling federal revenues, would be less frugal about military spending than had been his Republican predecessors. Eventually he would also surmount the nation's self-imposed isolationist posture toward the foreign world. The military as a whole would benefit from his policies, though the navy and air corps more than the army. Marshall himself would be a prime recipient of Roosevelt's favor. The two had met briefly when, as New York's governor-elect, Roosevelt had visited Fort Benning in 1928. Though they never became close personally, it would be FDR who would finally end Marshall's long career drought and raise him to the status his talents deserved.

Meanwhile, in Europe, the same economic crisis that brought Roosevelt to the White House also made Austrian-born Adolf Hitler chancellor of Germany. Determined to rearm his adopted nation and establish its preeminence in Europe, Hitler soon destroyed Germany's fragile post-Armistice democracy and replaced it with a brutal, totalitarian, racist regime that horrified democrats everywhere and threatened the delicate European balance of power established by the Versailles Treaty of 1919. Marshall was never attracted to the thuggish barbarity of the Nazi regime and ideology, as were a few American military men—but by making Americans feel vulnerable the Nazi menace would be a professional godsend.

For the army as a whole, however, things got materially worse before they got better. Fearing to antagonize the nation's military personnel in the face of rising social unrest in the nation's cities and farms, President Herbert Hoover had dissuaded Congress from mandating a 10 percent across-the-board pay cut for the military services. Yet, in its effort to offset mounting budget deficits, Congress authorized payless furloughs for soldiers and a wage freeze for both officers and enlisted men. In the case of junior officers this policy reduced their income to a fifth below the level of 1917; the salaries of privates plummeted almost 45 percent; those of sergeants more than 20 percent.

Marshall observed the dire effects of these cuts on his men and their dependents at his next assignment, Fort Scriven, Georgia, where he took command of a four-hundred-man battalion of the Eighth Infantry Regiment. The post was on Fort Tybee Island near Savannah, and, though small, he wrote to Pershing, it allowed him to escape the tedium of "office work and high theory."[25] As post commandant he sought to help his men and their families cope with the current hardships. He encouraged military families to plant vegetable gardens and build chicken coops and hog pens to supplement their diets. He ordered the base mess sergeants to prepare large extra servings of the lunch meal to be sold to enlisted men for ten cents to take home after duty to their hungry wives and children. In May 1933 Marshall's promotion to full colonel finally came through, and in June he left Scriven to take over command at historic Fort Moultrie in Charleston Harbor, where the bulk of the Eighth Infantry Regiment was stationed.

At both Scriven and Moultrie, Marshall distinguished himself as an organizer and administrator for the Civilian Conservation Corps. A New Deal agency created by Congress in early 1933 to provide useful work and income for unemployed young men from the cities, the CCC established military-style camps in national forests and on other public lands, where the recruits, receiving thirty dollars a month, cleared brush, built roads, trails, and bridges, stocked fish, erected ranger stations, planted trees, and performed other heavy outdoor work to preserve and enhance the country's rural infrastructure and develop its natural resources. All told, some three million jobless, undernourished, and predominantly ill-educated young men, aged eighteen to twenty-five, passed through the CCC, leaving behind an awesome number of rural "improvements." The program ended in

1939, after the economy, stimulated by growing defense outlays, began to contract the pool of unemployed young men. The CCC would prove to be the most popular of all New Deal work programs.

The army played a large role in its success. Under the law the Labor Department would recruit the personnel; the Agriculture and Interior Departments would define the work. But the army would provide the housing and camp facilities, administer discipline, and oversee the lives and work of the participants. Not all professional military men welcomed the task of supervising thousands of unemployed civilian youths, many undisciplined and ignorant of proper hygiene. In late May 1933, as the program got under way, Col. Laurence Halstead wrote to Marshall that the work assigned the army by the CCC program was "onerous and probably distasteful" to military men. But, he noted, it had also silenced much recent talk of reducing the army by a further four thousand officers.[26]

For Marshall, if not for others, the CCC project was a exhilarating and worthy challenge, however. His long and successful association with the National Guard had given him an understanding of and respect for citizen soldiers. These CCC boys were not so different from the young National Guardsmen he had met in Pennsylvania, California, and Massachusetts on summer encampments. The experience also reinforced his interest in universal military training—a peacetime draft—as a solution to the country's evil cycle of military boom and bust: unpreparedness followed by hasty mobilization, followed by complacency once again, and then another hurried, and imperfect, mobilization.

Marshall's work with the CCC was an impressive performance. In the first few months he helped establish a flock of camps in Florida and southeastern Georgia, housing 4,500 men. When transferred to Moultrie, he inherited another "forestry district" that covered all of South Carolina. During his stay at Moultrie he twice visited all fifteen CCC camps of his district, where he focused on orienting the camp commanders in the unfamiliar work of running a post composed primarily of civilians. As early as mid-July the new full colonel had concluded that "this CCC affair" was "a major mobilization and a splendid experience for the War Department and the army."[27] In a speech to a local civic club in the Charleston area, he called the project "the greatest social experiment outside Russia."[28]

In the end it probably, indirectly, also advanced Marshall's career. The CCC was a particular favorite of FDR's, meeting both the nation's urgent need to help the jobless and the president's long-term devotion to conservation and natural resource development. Though Marshall's definitive biographer, Forrest Pogue, emphasizes his subject's scrupulous avoidance of partisan politics then and later, Marshall's enthusiasm for the CCC program and his enterprise in making it a success could not have gone unnoticed in the White House. And yet, if his enthusiasm for the "Forestry work," as Marshall called it, had been noted, it was not immediately rewarded. Marshall and Katherine had enjoyed Fort Moultrie and, expecting to spend at least two years at the post, had gone to the expense and trouble of redecorating a large house. Katherine had brought in from Baltimore a load of expensive furniture to refurbish the new quarters. Now, unexpectedly, Marshall received orders to report to Chicago as senior instructor to the Illinois National Guard. True, Marshall liked working with civilians, and the guard brought civilians and the military together, but once more he would be removed from command of troops, once more deprived of a career-promoting experience. Though a full colonel as of September 1, 1933, he might be denied that all-important step to brigadier-general rank—without which all further advance was impossible.

The instigator of the transfer was Douglas MacArthur, with whom Marshall had first crossed paths at Fort Leavenworth and later in France with the AEF. Son of a Civil War hero, first in his class at West Point, reputed to be the second-most-decorated U.S. officer in World War I, a brilliant, flamboyant soldier, MacArthur had risen far more quickly through the ranks than had Marshall. In 1930, already a major general, he became army chief of staff, the youngest man to hold the job. Like most professional soldiers, MacArthur was politically conservative, a law-and-order man. But unlike many officers, certainly unlike Marshall, he was also overtly political. In 1932 he had commanded his troops to oust the needy, unemployed World War I veterans—the so-called Bonus Army—from their makeshift encampment at Anacostia, near downtown Washington, D.C., where they had squatted for two weeks, waiting for Congress to provide early payments under a proposed 1924 veterans' bonus plan. Convinced that most of the protesters were communists, MacArthur exceeded his orders. On June 28 he led the Twelfth Infantry Regiment, bayonets and gas canisters at the ready, on a sweep into the encampment. Halfway through the attack President Hoover ordered it halted, but MacArthur ignored him and completed the job of dispersing the protesters. Hundreds of veterans were injured in the attack, and several died. Though the Bonus Army incident hurt MacArthur with many moderate and liberal citizens, it heightened his popularity with conservatives. Thereafter the flamboyant general never ceased to harbor presidential ambitions or failed to attract the hopes of citizens who yearned for a charismatic, Napoleonic figure to save them from the forces of disruption and unwelcome change.

It is not clear if, in reassigning Marshall to the Illinois National Guard, MacArthur was seeking to injure him. Yet the two men, destined to cross paths many times in the future, were scarcely natural allies. Markedly different in temperament—Marshall reserved, scrupulous, unassuming; MacArthur showy, freewheeling, egotistical—they were also separated by differing allegiances. In MacArthur's eyes Marshall was part of a hostile cabal, one of the "Chaumont crowd," the circle of loyal former aides and staffers around Pershing at AEF headquarters in France. At one point he himself had described Marshall as having "no superior among infantry colonels,"[29] yet when Marshall protested the new posting he was rebuffed. The order, MacArthur noted, would stand. If it cannot be shown that MacArthur was biased in any way toward Marshall, it is hard to believe that—despite denials—the colonel for his part did not resent MacArthur's act and, given their troubled later relationship, that he was not swayed at times by that disheartening assignment of October 1933.

Marshall was well aware of the implications of the posting for his professional future, as Rose Page would later note. After the Marshalls settled into their Chicago apartment, Rose, now an observant college student, visited them several times. The visits did not go smoothly. Katherine was polite but cool, as if she resented Rose for reminding her husband of Lily and his life before her. For her part Rose admitted that her "personal feelings about Mrs. Marshall . . . were never very warm." When Rose once stayed overnight in the apartment, Marshall revealed his fears for his future. When she asked him how long it would be before he became chief of staff, he replied with a laugh, "Well Rosie, it looks now as if I never will. . . . If I don't make Brigadier General soon, I'll be so far behind in seniority I won't ever be in the running."[30]

Yet Marshall did not abandon hope. He would now have to make the best of the new assignment. Fortunately the guard appointment was not necessarily a dead end. In Chicago his sponsor was the Thirty-Third Guard Division head, Maj. Gen. Roy D. Keehn, a Democratic activist, who was currently under attack by the archconservative *Chicago Tribune* for mismanagement of the guard and failure to deploy them when needed against strikers. It was Keehn who had solicited names from MacArthur for a regular army officer to reinvigorate the division and restore its reputation. The role of the Illinois State Guard seemed particularly important in 1933. Chicago was deep in the Depression, with thousands out of work, and lurking beneath the surface the possibility of dangerous civil disorder. Nor was the city's ominous atmosphere much improved by the Century of Progress world's fair, which brought thousands of visitors to the Windy City from all over the country and from around the world.

Despite the fair the Marshalls did not find the city to their liking. They had arrived in Chicago in late October and, after much hunting, found an apartment in the Near North Side, close to the Drake Hotel. Marshall never liked cities or apartment living, and in Chicago he could not avoid either. "Those first months in Chicago, I shall never forget," Katherine later wrote. "George had a grey, drawn look which I had never seen before, and have seldom seen since."[31]

By the second year, according to Katherine, things had improved. Marshall's spirits perked up as he got to work reorganizing and retraining the Thirty-Third Division. His success soon became widely known and widely praised by the media and influential men. The Marshalls also found new friends when Gen. Frank McCoy of the Sixth Corps and his wife moved into an adjacent apartment in their building. The two couples were soon spending many evenings in each other's company; the two wives went to auctions together in quest of bargains in furniture, lamps, mirrors, and other household items.

Meanwhile, Marshall never lost sight of the career difficulties ahead: He would first have to make brigadier, itself a formidable hurdle. But besides, the promotion would have to come soon enough for him to be eligible for the army's top post. He was already fifty-four, and the prevailing rule required that the chief of staff have at least four years left to serve before he reached retirement age at sixty-four.

Marshall would always deplore the use of influence and self-praise in military career advancement. But he found he could not avoid pulling strings himself. He felt uncomfortable, he wrote to Pershing in November 1934, trying to "exert political influence in my effort to be recognized." He did not want to solicit letters of support from fellow officers since the "War Department is flooded with them." Feeling that his record spoke for itself, he asked Pershing to forward to the War Department his efficiency reports since 1915.[32] Pershing went an important step further: He telephoned FDR on Marshall's behalf. Roosevelt waited a while and then in late May 1935 sent Secretary of War George Dern a memo: "General Pershing asks very strongly that Colonel George C. Marshall (infantry) be promoted to Brigadier. Can we put him on list of next promotions?"[33] Even this endorsement did not work, however: Marshall did not make the 1935 promotion list, perhaps because MacArthur, though still outwardly friendly, did not push it. But then, in October 1935, MacArthur retired as chief of staff to take the job of military adviser to the newly formed Filipino army. His successor was Malin Craig, an old Marshall friend from both Fort Reno and AEF Chaumont headquarters days. The path to brigadier and beyond now seemed open. But even General Craig seemed unable to break through the sclerotic seniority system, and the promotion stalled, throwing Marshall into a funk: "I have possessed myself in patience," he wrote to Pershing in late December 1935, "but now I'm fast getting too old to have any future of importance in the army. . . . This sounds pessimistic," he admitted, "but an approaching birthday . . . rather emphasizes the growing weakness of my position."[34]

And then abruptly the dam broke. In April two of Marshall's friends, Gens. Charles Herron and Frank McCoy, arranged a private meeting between Marshall and Dern. The secretary had already heard of Marshall's brilliant work in Chicago and elsewhere and, after his talk with the colonel, approved the promotion. In August 1936, after a sixteen-year-wait, Marshall received notice that he had been promoted to brigadier general. He was also reassigned to command the Fifth Brigade of the Third Division at Vancouver Barracks, in Washington State.

Located on the north bank of the Columbia River, close to Portland, Oregon, the post dated from the early nineteenth century when it was headquarters of the British-owned Hudson's Bay Company. With the Oregon Treaty of 1846, the United States acquired from Britain the part of the immense Oregon country that included the fort. In 1849 the U.S. War Department established Columbia Barracks adjacent to the existing trading center. It was soon renamed Vancouver Barracks.

Arriving at the post after a cross-country drive in their new Packard, a replacement for their old Ford, the Marshalls, including stepdaughter Molly (whose brothers were in boarding school) and their Irish setter, were greeted by the barracks band and a guard of honor. "Thus began," Katherine later wrote, "two of the happiest years of our life."[35]

For both Marshalls the months at Vancouver Barracks were a delightful interlude. The Marshall home on post was a two-and-a-half-story Queen Anne house with a view of majestic, snowcapped Mount Hood. Nearby Portland offered many social amenities for the wife of the commanding general at Vancouver. Katherine was impressed with the beautiful gardens Portlanders maintained, and, as she wrote, "their clubs are excellent and their hospitality informally lavish."[36] The new post offered many attractions for the newly minted brigadier as well. He was once more commanding troops, his first professional love. He was also now in charge of thirty-five CCC camps in the Washington-Oregon area, a task he had come to relish. Living conditions in the Northwest, despite the incessant winter rains, were also congenial. He had left behind the big Midwestern city, with its abrasiveness, noise, and congestion, and could now hunt, fish, ride, and generally enjoy the great outdoors. Yet he remained close enough to a substantial urban center where he could continue to meet men of parts and influence. Marshall already knew Oregon's governor, Charles Martin, and through him soon got to know many members of the state's power elite.

During the Fort Vancouver posting he also improved his health. By 1936 the effects of the thyroid disorder first detected at Benning—rapid and irregular pulse and general irritability—were becoming severe, and he had it checked out, first in Portland and then at Letterman General Hospital at the Presidio in San Francisco. At the latter a diseased lobe of his thyroid gland was removed and, after five weeks in the hospital, he returned to duty. In some ways he was a new man. For the first time in years he began to gain weight. More significant, he seemed less jumpy and irascible. Friends noticed that not only was his general health better but also "that the old nervous intensity had been replaced by an unfamiliar calmness."[37] Nevertheless his health remained a problem if for no other reason than that it was a potential peril to professional advancement. Rumors that he was a sick man would have to be denied if he was not to be passed over for future assignments and promotions.

The Marshalls' comfortable stay in Vancouver ended in June 1938, after twenty months. He had already rejected by letter a proposal from his VMI classmate John L. Cabell that he accept the institute's superintendency since it would entail taking a pay cut of two thousand dollars a year. In another letter to Cabell in

April 1937, Marshall hinted at a more significant consideration: "the question of abandoning the possibilities of the next eight or nine years, so far as that pertains to a professional soldier." As he explained, "With the world in its present turmoil no one can prophesy what the outcome will be, and as I made my life occupation that of a soldier I hesitate to take any decision which might leave me eliminated at the critical moment."[38] In a word, the general would gamble that the burgeoning world crisis of the late 1930s would make his final goal a reality.

And well he might. Within the administration, and abroad in the country, opinion regarding the nation's future military needs was growing more positive. Overseas, militaristic, antidemocratic regimes had turned to brute force to achieve national ends. In 1933 a Depression-torn Germany had elevated to power a charismatic, fanatical hater of democracy, communism, Jews and other "inferior" beings—a man dedicated to restoring Germany's preeminence in Europe. Adolf Hitler soon abrogated the detested Versailles treaty and began the rapid rearmament of Germany. In 1935 Benito Mussolini, the Fascist dictator who had destroyed Italian democracy in the 1920s, ordered an invasion of Ethiopia, Africa's last independent nation, and despite timid League of Nations sanctions, brutally conquered and occupied it. Italy and Germany had already signed treaties of friendship in 1936. In 1939, recognizing the natural affinity between their regimes, the two dictators signed the "Pact of Steel," allying their nations' militaries and creating the Rome-Berlin Axis. Meanwhile, in Spain, another strongman, Francisco Franco, rebelling against the existing democratic republic, was turning Spain into a battleground between a Far Right supported by Fascist Italy and Nazi Germany and a broad Left pro-Republican coalition supported by the Soviet Union and, less effectively, by many Western democrats and far left and liberal intellectuals.

The story in the Far East was similar. After a period of relative nonbelligerence following World War I, Japanese leaders, driven by hunger for natural resources and markets, had launched a series of aggressive moves against the Republic of China, still weakened by political divisions and crippled by poverty and chronic underdevelopment. In 1931 Japan occupied Manchuria, a weakly held northern province of the Chinese republic, turning it into a puppet dependency called Manchukuo. China asked the League of Nations to condemn Japan. After an on-site investigation it did so but with little effect. Instead, Japan simply quit the league as a gesture of defiance. Then, beginning in July 1937, following a contrived shooting "incident" at the Marco Polo Bridge near Beijing, Japan launched a military campaign that sought to turn all of China into a Japanese satellite that could provide the manpower and resources the "have-not" island nation coveted and felt it needed to become a world power.

Japanese behavior in China probably offended more Americans in the 1930s than did the Nazi-Fascist aggression in Europe and Africa. For generations China had been viewed by Americans as an object of solicitude and a field for Christian missionary labors and benevolence. The United States had refused to join the late-nineteenth-century European scramble for special privileges in China. In 1900 Secretary of State John Hay had announced the Open Door policy, renouncing any desire for an exclusive American sphere of interest in China and asking other nations to respect China's territorial integrity. In early 1932, on the occasion of the Manchuria attack, President Hoover's secretary of state, Henry L. Stimson, announced that the United States would not recognize any act that impaired the "territorial and administrative integrity of the Republic of China." Steeped in isolationism and enfeebled itself by economic crisis, the United States did nothing more, however. For years Americans had been lectured by the Hearst press and other xenophobic opinion molders that Japan represented a "Yellow Peril" in the Pacific. Then, by the end of the decade, recognizing their shared expansionist goals, the three aggressor nations formed a military alliance, making the German-Italian pact into the Rome-Berlin-Tokyo Axis. The events of the 1930s confirmed and reinforced American fears, but for the moment few citizens could imagine taking effective action to counter the aggressors' threats.

Initially, in fact, the world turmoil drove the American public deeper into its shell. Impressed by the plausible revelations of the Senate's Nye Committee in 1934–36 that the United States had been misled into an unnecessary European war in 1917 by greedy, mendacious bankers and munitions manufacturers, many Americans concluded that the current quarrels of nations abroad were none of their business. Isolationist sentiment soon took legislative form in the passage by Congress of the Neutrality Acts, a set of measures designed to avoid the supposed mistakes that had led the country to join the Allies in the Great War. Enacted between 1935 and 1939, the laws imposed an embargo on all arms shipments to belligerents in both international and civil wars, forbade U.S. citizens from traveling on belligerent vessels, and made illegal all loans and credits to belligerents. The 1937 measure made one concession to President Roosevelt's fear of aggressors by permitting "cash and carry": Belligerents willing and able to pay cash on the barrelhead and transport the purchased goods in their own ships were permitted to buy arms and other matériel in the United States. This proviso, however, would expire after two years.

Yet no matter how xenophobic and isolationist the American public in this period was, the unfolding events in Europe and Asia could not fail to awaken widespread anxiety about the nation's safety. The president himself had no illusions that America could avoid entanglement in the emerging world crisis. In October 1937, in a brief speech in Chicago, he reminded his audience that the world political situation had "of late . . . been growing progressively worse." The "unjustified interference in the internal affairs of other nations" and "the invasion of alien territory in violation of treaties" had reached a "stage where the very foundations of civilization" were "seriously threatened." The "peace-loving nations," he continued, "must make a concerted effort in opposition to these violations of treaties and these ignorings of humane instincts which are creating a state of international anarchy and instability." He went on to insist that he would "pursue a policy of peace." But to stop the "epidemic of world lawlessness" the peace-loving nations should impose a "quarantine" on the aggressors. However, if Roosevelt hoped to rally the American people behind some version of "collective security," he was disappointed. After several initial days of applause, the speech came under severe attack. As FDR wrote to a friend soon after the speech, "As usual we have been bombarded by Hearst and others who say that an American search for peace means, of necessity, war."[39] The response confirmed to the president and his advisers—if confirmation was needed—that public opinion was deeply averse to any entanglement in foreign affairs that threatened strict American neutrality.

The stormy international climate of the mid- to late-1930s affected the military services at home in profound ways. To some isolationists, military preparation was anathema; it would only encourage overt bellicose actions. Others, however, saw modest rearmament as an alternative to intervention. No matter what happened abroad, they claimed, a rearmed United States could feel secure behind its two ocean moats. This attitude tended to favor the navy over the army, but it spilled over to the land-based service as well. Slowly, but with gathering momentum, the nation began to rearm. Military appropriations in 1934 had dropped to an abysmal $541 million. By 1936 they were up to $916 million; by 1938 to just over $1 billion, and in 1940 would reach $1.57 billion. As for personnel, between 1934 and 1940 the number of army enlisted men would grow from 138,400 to almost 270,000; the number of officers from 13,761 to 18,326.

Marshall could not help but gain by this expansion and he would work hard to encourage it. Yet his rise to the very top command still remained problematic. In May 1938 Chief of Staff Malin Craig asked the general to come to Washington as chief of the army War Plans Division, to take the place of Stanley Embick. Craig had told him that the job was a stopgap, that he would soon appoint him deputy chief of staff. Marshall's doubts were not assuaged, however. The post of deputy had only once in the past been the road to the apex. He knew that Craig himself intended to retire in a year and wanted Marshall to succeed him. Yet Marshall remained skeptical. For one thing, it made him uneasy that in the new post he would be outranked by a flock of generals to whom he would be giving orders. He also still craved "command work." As he wrote to Pershing, "I am fond of Craig personally, but I loathe a desk."[40] Deputy chief of staff was still a desk job.

In fact the position promised to be unusually challenging and problem laden in the months ahead. Marshall would be walking into a bureaucratic hornet's nest in the War Department. The new secretary was Harry Woodring, the successor to George Dern, who had died in 1936 of influenza complications, His assistant secretary was Louis A. Johnson, former head of the American Legion. The two men were natural adversaries with different temperaments, personal styles, and opinions. In the emerging debate over the way to treat the "aggressor nations," they deeply disagreed. Woodring, a Kansas isolationist, opposed any aid to nations resisting the bellicose policies of the Axis. Johnson favored universal military training to prepare the country for war and was an outspoken advocate of aid to Britain and France, the guardians of the European status quo and the natural enemies of the Axis nations. Fortunately both men supported Marshall, but inevitably, as the general moved up the command chain, he would be compelled to confront seriously discordant voices in the War Department.

Marshall arrived in Washington in early July to take up his assignment in the War Plans Division. Katherine detoured to her summer home on Fire Island, only to be caught in the ferocious hurricane of September 1938 that devastated Long Island and New England. Reading in the press that Fire Island had been "wiped out," Marshall commandeered a small plane at Bolling Field and flew to the South Shore of Long Island. Fortunately Katherine and Molly had been taken in by a neighbor whose house was a concrete structure, and they were safe. But as she later wrote, "I was blown into Washington in the autumn of 1938."[41]

The U.S. Army was at an important juncture in its evolution when Marshall returned to Washington that summer to take up his new job. Since the end of World War I military minds had pondered the meaning and future of air power. Led by the maverick colonel William ("Billy") Mitchell, one group of younger army officers believed that the advent of the airplane had transformed the art of war. Mitchell's famous demonstration in the early twenties of the vulnerability of naval vessels to aerial bombing was not, in fact, a fair test of airpower under realistic combat conditions. But it convinced the American public, already beguiled by heroic World War I aerial combat and disillusioned by the meat-grinding trench warfare of 1914–18, that the airplane deserved a high priority in any future military planning. Though never a disciple of the "victory through air power" doctrine that some military gurus purveyed, Marshall himself endorsed expanded army investment in its air arm. But he opposed the group of younger army officers—backed by a substantial portion of the general public—pushing hard for massive commitment to pilots, bombers, and pursuit planes at the expense of badly needed personnel and equipment for the anemic and technologically backward traditional ground forces.

The most consequential partisan of airpower, besides Mitchell, was the president himself. FDR was a navy man. He had served before and during the First World War as assistant secretary of the navy under Josephus Daniels. He loved the sea and was an enthusiastic sailor who spent much of his summer vacation time before and after the war navigating a small sailboat on Passamaquoddy Bay, at his vacation home on Campobello Island, between Maine and New Brunswick, Canada. But, like many of his countrymen, he had also succumbed to the airpower romance and the desire to avoid in the next war the heartbreaking infantry casualty lists of the conflict two decades before.

As promised, Marshall did not stay long at the War Plans Division. One of five general staff sections,* it was sometimes reckoned the most important since it was charged with planning for future wars against potential enemies. War Plans was the source of the array of secret "color plans," in effect blueprints for virtually every possible international conflict between the United States and a foreign power or powers. Especially prominent was "Plan Orange," the military scenario for a potential war in the Pacific against Japan. Three years later it would also be the source of the important "Victory Plan," authorized by Marshall as chief of staff, that laid out the economic and manpower requirements for winning a war against the Axis. However important a post—in which he was supported by Woodring, Johnson, and Craig, each

---

*It was informally designated G-5. The others were: G-1 (Personnel); G-2 (Intelligence); G-3 (Operations); and G-4 (Supply).

for his own reasons—Marshall left it after three months to become, as promised, deputy chief of staff.

His quick elevation coincided with rapidly escalating American fears of a major European war. In September 1938, following months of tension between the democratic Czechoslovak government and the pro-Nazi leaders of the country's Sudeten German minority, Hitler demanded that the German population be given "self-determination," that is, autonomy within the Czechoslovak republic. The British and French governments feared that these demands, following close on the German annexation of Austria, would be a first step in Hitler's eventual dismembering of Czechoslovakia and its absorption into a greater Reich. But they also were terrified that Europe might be drawn into a general war that would duplicate the horrors of 1914–18. Though France was bound by treaty to protect Czech independence, and Britain in turn was committed to backing France, neither democratic nation was prepared, militarily or psychologically, for war. In a series of September meetings with Hitler and a final conference in Munich, which included Italy but not the Czechs themselves, British prime minister Neville Chamberlain and French premier Édouard Daladier pledged not to oppose German annexation of Czechoslovakia's Sudeten region in exchange for Hitler's agreement to desist from future European aggression. Denied support by the democratic European powers, the appalled Czechs were forced to accept the crippling Munich terms. Returning to Britain after this act of dishonorable appeasement, Chamberlain famously (or infamously) waved the Munich document to cheering London crowds and was roundly applauded when he delivered his "Peace for Our Time" speech in the House of Commons. In March 1939, the Munich pact notwithstanding, German troops marched across the new Czech-German border and occupied the rump of the small democratic republic. Feeling betrayed and now fully alert to the German expansionist threat, Britain and France pledged to aid the Reich's neighbor, Poland, in the event of an attack by Germany. Since Hitler had made demands on Poland, too, the fuse was now lit for a major European war.

Despite their own aversion to war, Americans were alarmed by the cascading developments in Europe. A survey in *Fortune* magazine showed that a large majority condemned the Munich pact and almost as many believed their country could not avoid being sucked into a general European war. The events of the fall of 1938 and spring of 1939, the editors concluded, "had shattered our sense of . . . reliance upon the sentiment: 'Thank God for two wide oceans!' "[42]

For FDR, and for Marshall, a major lesson to be learned from the debacle was how French-British weakness at Munich derived from military unpreparedness. Both European nations had long neglected their military forces and were now lagging dangerously behind the Germans, particularly in airpower, the new weapon's effectiveness already so woefully demonstrated by the devastating Luftwaffe attacks on civilians in the civil war raging in Spain. Something must be done by the United States to fill the gap and done quickly, the president believed. It was vital not only to bridge the chasm in American airpower but, more immediately, to enhance the country's ability to supply planes for the British and French. On October 12 FDR told the press that he wanted another $500 million in defense funds to beef up the Army Air Corps. He also asked Secretary Johnson to prepare for an air corps of fifteen thousand planes.

Roosevelt's push for airpower conflicted with the War Department's own plans. Marshall and his colleagues were not averse to more planes. But even the Army Air Corps head, Gen. Henry ("Hap") Arnold, believed the needs of his branch of the service must be balanced against the army's overall requirements. And

what about the needs of the now rearming European democracies? How would these conflict with America's? On November
14 the president called together his military and civilian advisers,
including Craig, Arnold, and Deputy Chief of Staff Marshall,
along with Treasury Secretary Henry Morgenthau, Solicitor General Robert Jackson, WPA administrator Harry Hopkins, and a
group of assorted White House military aides. The United States
must have an air force strong enough to deter any potential aggressor against the Western Hemisphere, he told them. Some twenty
thousand planes would suffice, although Congress would probably not pay the bill for such a large increase in aircraft strength.
Listening from a back row, Marshall recognized that FDR was
at this moment thinking primarily of the needs of Britain and
France faced with Hitler's belligerence. That presented the army
with problems. Marshall had no argument with the efforts to
check the German dictator, but he feared that the president's
plans would deflect resources from America's own military needs.
Whatever he himself believed, it seemed that all the others at
the meeting agreed with the president or were unwilling to differ
openly with him. When, at the end of his presentation, the president asked his listeners for their opinion they all either praised his
views or deftly evaded criticism. Finally FDR turned to Marshall
and said, "Don't you think so, George?" Marshall bridled. He objected to the familiarity of the first-name address—even from the
president of the United States. And besides, he did not agree with
FDR's conclusions. "Mr. President," he responded, "I am sorry,
but I don't agree with that at all." As Marshall remembered the
incident, "The President gave me . . . a startled look, and when I
went out they [the other conferees] all bade me good-bye and said
that my tour in Washington was over."[43]

What could in fact have been a career stopper may have turned
out to be, like the confrontation with Pershing in 1918, a career

maker. Were both challenges unpremeditated? Were they merely impulsive acts by a man with a hair-trigger temper? Or were they in some sense calculated? Did Marshall instinctively grasp that he needed some propellant to accelerate his career? Whether Marshall deliberately used "speaking truth to power"—in the cliché of sixties political rebels—as a contrivance to get the attention of a man in whose hands rested his fate, or whether the response emerged spontaneously from his deep trait of honesty, is unclear. But the effect was positive. As Marshall later noted: "It didn't antagonize him at all."[44] More significantly, it may have been the inspiration for the president's approval of Marshall as chief of staff.

There was more to that appointment than catching the boss's attention, however. Marshall was competing against a field of at least five officers with greater seniority. At the top of the list was Maj. Gen. Hugh Drum, the former chief of staff of the First Corps in France, former army inspector general, and currently commander of the prestigious Second Corps on Governors Island in New York. Drum was an active campaigner for the post and the leading candidate in the spring of 1939. He had the support, moreover, of the president's chief political adviser, Postmaster Gen. James Farley. But Drum was a puffed-up blowhard who was too full of himself to please FDR. Besides, the president had little respect for Farley's judgment of men, whatever his skill in political maneuvering and infighting.

Marshall had behind him more impressive endorsers than Farley. He, of course, had Pershing on his side, and the former chief of staff at one point early in the selection process had written to the president for support of his protégé. William Frye, Marshall's first biographer, also mentions a Pershing visit to the White House on his behalf. "Mr. President," he is reputed to have said to FDR, "you have a man over there in the War Plans Division who has just come here—Marshall. He's Chief of Staff material. Why don't you send for him and look him over? I think he will be of great help."[45] Other significant sponsors were the feuding Woodring and Johnson, each of whom, curiously, saw Marshall as a potential ally against the other.

But above all Marshall had won the support of Harry Hopkins, the man whose opinions FDR considered more valuable than virtually anyone else's. A tall, skinny, habitually profane former social worker from Iowa, Hopkins had met FDR at the onset of the Depression, when the future president was governor of New York. Brought to Washington when FDR moved into the White House, he had administered some of the largest New Deal work programs, including the massively funded Works Progress Administration. Hopkins offended the president's opponents, who depicted him as a sinister figure, the hidden real power behind the throne. But FDR considered him indispensable and consulted him on a range of matters far beyond issues of unemployment relief. During the war soon to come he would serve as the president's eyes and ears abroad and chief intermediary with Winston Churchill, the leader of Britain's war effort against Germany.

Hopkins was an impassioned enemy of Hitler and his Axis allies, and a man who strongly supported the rearmament policies that Marshall favored. Undoubtedly he also had taken note of Marshall's good work at the CCC, one of the New Deal's signature programs. Well before generous congressional appropriations arrived, he and the deputy chief of staff conspired secretly to divert funds from the WPA for machine tools to produce ammunition for army rifles. At the very end of 1938 he and Marshall met to talk over the army's proposal for a military budget better balanced than the president's air force–heavy plan. Hopkins soon took the balanced budget proposal to the president himself and helped persuade him to scale down the proportion allotted to the air arm. Thereafter Hopkins and the deputy chief of staff met and talked frequently, in the process becoming close friends and confidants. Marshall even allowed Hopkins to call him "George," a favor he never extended to the president of the United States.

The suspense over Marshall's professional future ended in the early spring, just as the great powers were about to plunge into the greatest war in history. On April 23 FDR summoned Marshall to the White House and, in his second floor study, offered him the post of chief of staff. At the presidential desk, disordered by the paraphernalia of the president's stamp collection, the two men talked for half an hour. Marshall sketched briefly some of his ideas of how to defend the country in dangerous times. He also told FDR that he always expected to be able to be direct and honest about his views though some of them might not be pleasant to hear. Was that acceptable? Roosevelt tersely responded, "Yes." Marshall then rose. "I feel deeply honored, sir," he announced, "and I will give you the best I have."[46]

Actually Marshall was to be only acting chief of staff until Craig's resignation took effect on September 1. But as the promotion announcement was sure to create a hullabaloo, Marshall asked the White House to delay the press release until he had left Washington on a scheduled West Coast inspection tour. In fact he did not even tell Katherine, who only learned of the appointment when, as she lay in bed with an acute case of poison ivy, he came to say good-bye. "The papers will probably have it in a day or two," he remarked, "and now I must be off."[47]

The interview with the president at the White House had been a low-key affair, but with war imminent in festering Europe, the new chief of staff knew that both he and his country now faced the challenges of their lives.

CHAPTER 4

PREPARING FOR WAR

Clearly Marshall's most pressing concerns as chief of staff were the proliferating crises in Europe and Asia, yet his first assignment was a goodwill mission to Brazil. In May 1939 this could be justified by the president's fears—exaggerated, time would show—that Brazil, with its large German and Italian communities, was the potential site of an Axis "fifth column." However overblown the danger, the administration believed that the new chief of staff could do some good by a visit to Brazil.

Marshall's trip was a resounding success. For twelve days he attended receptions, made ceremonial inspections, watched parades, met government officials, and talked to high-ranking military officers with whom he discussed ways to achieve military cooperation between Brazil and the United States. By June 20 he was back in Washington prepared to take up more important work.

September 1, 1939, was a momentous day for Marshall—and for the rest of the world's people. At 3:00 a.m. he was awakened by a call informing him that the German army had invaded neighboring Poland. Later that morning he was handed his promotion to the permanent rank of major general and officially sworn in as chief of staff of the U.S. Army. Immediately after the brief ceremony he was summoned to the White House to discuss the rapidly evolving European crisis. On September 3 Britain and France would declare war on Germany. World War II, and Marshall's career as the highest-ranking officer in the American army, had almost exactly coincided.

The future promised a tidal wave of trials and emergencies for the new chief of staff. "I do not anticipate peaceful years ahead," Marshall wrote to his Chicago friends, Frank and Frances Mc-Coy, on September 2.[1] His first priority, of course, was to prepare the nation's army to meet the challenges of a global war. The task promised to be monumental. Congress and a majority of the American public were still bone-deep isolationist, and even Roosevelt was not anxious to create a political storm over the issue of military preparedness. During the September 1 meeting FDR told his advisers to pay attention to the diplomatic dilemmas that the war might create for the United States, but not to concern themselves with preparing for war "because we are not going to get into war."[2] FDR would soon ask Congress to make permanent the temporary two-year "cash-and-carry" proviso of the 1937 Neutrality Act and authorize a small increase in army and National Guard strength. Yet the president remained cautious. To avoid roiling the isolationists, he squelched Marshall's ambitious requests for much-needed new military equipment and an additional 25,000 soldiers for the existing force of 175,000 regulars. In the next weeks, during the struggle in Congress over the cash-and-carry extension, FDR carefully avoided any move to prepare the country militarily for war. However discouraging to Marshall, the president's caution helped get the Neutrality Acts revision through Congress in early November. Ironically, though the country's own armed services might be put on short rations, the United States could now be a major source of arms and supplies for the Western armies confronting Hitler.

Roosevelt continued to resist asking Congress for substantial increases for the armed forces even after his success with cash-and-carry. Marshall understood the president's dilemma. His "feeling politically [was] that the Middle West was so solidly against him," he later told an interviewer, "that if he moved suddenly into an enlarged military effort he would encounter such opposition . . . that he wouldn't be able to manage the affair."[3] And the chief of staff could do little to move him. As yet he had little influence at the Oval Office. He and Roosevelt would eventually develop a deep mutual respect. Indeed, FDR came to rely to an extraordinarily degree on the Joint Chiefs of Staff, where Marshall was first among equals.* In July 1939 he created more direct links between himself and the nation's military leaders by transferring the existing Army-Navy Joint Board to the newly established Executive Office of the President. As Mark Stoler, the historian of the Joint Chiefs, has noted, the president was also at pains to take the chiefs to all his wartime summit conferences. His esteem for Marshall individually would eventually know few bounds, and when the time came to choose the Allied commander for the cross-Channel attack on Hitler's *Festung Europa* (Fortress Europe)—the crowning Anglo-American military operation of World War II—FDR would pass over the chief of staff on the grounds that he needed him close by rather than in distant Europe.

---

*The Joint Chiefs at this point had no legal standing. It was merely an informal arrangement prompted by Marshall in 1942 to ensure interservice cooperation. Its legal status was not established until the unification of the War and Navy Departments and the creation of the Department of Defense in 1947 under the National Security Act.

And yet Marshall and his chief never established a warm personal relationship. They were very different men. The general was guarded and formal, a man who prized dignity over affability, who sought clarity over complexity. FDR was a glad-hander who bantered and joked with advisers, associates, and reporters, and who, with a party, a nation—indeed, a world—to run, encouraged diverse opinions and seldom offered clear answers to major issues. Whether by plan or by ingrained trait, the general would never allow FDR to get too close personally. He did not allow the president to call him "George"; he refused to laugh at his jokes. Fearing to fall under FDR's famous spell, he would never accept invitations to Hyde Park, the president's Hudson Valley home. In those last peacetime months Marshall did not even respect the president, beloved by so many. Not until after Pearl Harbor, he later admitted, did he grow to admire his boss.

Moreover, at this early moment in their relationship Marshall was particularly cut off from the president by the absence of his new ally, Harry Hopkins, the former social worker and supposed New Deal éminence grise who had become FDR's most trusted adviser, now temporarily sidelined by a chronic digestive disorder. Further muffling the general's voice was the ongoing struggle between the civilian heads of the War Department, Woodring and Assistant Secretary Johnson, each of whom demanded his sole fealty, a pledge he refused to give either.

And yet Marshall needed somehow to awaken the country and especially Congress to the hazards of inaction on the nation's serious military deficiencies. The war that followed the September 1 attack on Poland did not go well for Hitler's enemies. Poland fell to German blitzkrieg in a month. On September 28 the Soviet Union, having concluded a friendship pact with Hitler just before the German attack, invaded Poland from the east and divided it with its former Nazi enemy. The Soviets would now have a common border with Nazi Germany. But then, after Poland's defeat, blitzkrieg turned into *Sitzkrieg*. For six months, until early April 1940, the war in Europe became dormant, marked only by small-scale actions at sea and in the air and minor, feckless French military operations along the Franco-German border. During this so-called Phony War Hitler's enemies let down their guard. In the United States any uneasiness about the country's weak defenses subsided.

Though handicapped by the nation's complacency, Marshall persisted in pushing for upgrade and expansion of the army. At the end of December, at the annual meeting of the American Historical Association in Washington, he criticized American schools for failing to teach military history and caught public attention by estimating that the army's ability to fight stood at less than 25 percent. In a mid-February radio broadcast, drawing on the experience of 1917–18, he warned his listeners that in any war a time lag of a year or even two usually followed between orders for vital military equipment and its delivery to the fighting men. In late February, in his first testimony before Congress as chief of staff, he warned the House Appropriations Committee that if Europe "blazes in the late spring or summer, we must put our house in order before the sparks reach the Western Hemisphere."[4]

Marshall wanted Congress to fund a mountain of new equipment—tanks, the new Garand rifles, heavy artillery—sufficient for an eventual force of about a million men, though his immediate objective was to equip the regular army, now authorized for 227,000 men, and the National Guard, another 235,000. He got little of what he wanted. The committee chair, J. Buell Snyder, insisted that the federal budget be cut and the military not be exempted from the pruning. In the end the House committee slashed the armed forces budget by close to 10 percent. The Army Air Corps was to receive only 57 planes of the 166 Marshall had requested.

The Phony War ended abruptly on April 9, 1940, when the German army invaded neutral Norway and Denmark. The unprepared Danes surrendered virtually without firing a shot. With the limited help of the Royal Air Force, the Royal Navy, and British and French troops, the Norwegians bravely resisted, but in a matter of weeks the German attackers had subdued large areas of the country. In early June the remaining Allied forces were withdrawn from Norway to meet the far greater German challenge in France and the Low Countries: On May 10 the Wehrmacht smashed across their borders and swept west and south toward Paris and the English Channel. The defeat in Norway and the new crisis across the Channel toppled the Chamberlain government in Britain, and replaced the indecisive prime minister with his chief critic, the fiery, eloquent, and determined Winston Churchill, leading a coalition government. By late May the German onslaught, led by tanks and Stuka dive-bombers, had crushed the French, Dutch, and Belgian armies and forced the retreating British Expeditionary Force in France into a tight pocket at the Channel port of Dunkirk, from which thousands of troops were evacuated successfully to Britain, though forced to abandon most of their equipment. On June 10, fearing to be left out of the imminent division of spoils, Mussolini joined the war against the faltering Allies. On June 22 the French government signed a surrender agreement with the Germans at Compiègne. The following day a triumphant Hitler visited a vanquished Paris with his favorite city planner, Albert Speer, to marvel at the city's architectural wonders.

Under the June armistice terms, much of northern and western France became a German-occupied zone, leaving an autonomous rump in the south and east. In July the elderly World War I hero, Marshal Philippe Pétain, established at Vichy in the unoccupied zone a right-wing regime that repudiated French democracy and agreed to collaborate with the Germans, including doing their dirty work against France's Jews. Many, but by no means all, French citizens deplored the Vichy regime and its policies. A segment, small at first, rallied behind Gen. Charles de Gaulle who had fled to Britain where, as leader of the Free French Forces, he vowed to continue the fight against the Germans and to challenge Vichy's control of the extensive French empire in Africa, Southeast Asia, and elsewhere.

Meanwhile, the end of the Phony War drastically altered the debate in America over the European war. The lightning German victory shocked and dismayed most Americans. Suddenly Congress loosened the defense purse strings. In late May it raised the defense budget by $1.2 billion beyond the president's request. A month later it appropriated an additional $1.7 billion to expand the army to 375,000 men, also granting FDR the power to call the National Guard into active service. At this point, however, only a minority of Americans expected, or wanted, their nation to intrude directly into the events in Europe. But many now feared that Germany might win, and realized that their country must act to defend itself. During these confusing and unsettling months following the German invasion of France, Roosevelt and his closest advisers—sensitive to ambivalent public opinion—continued to eschew direct U.S. military intervention. They hoped that a middle-of-the-road policy—massive matériel aid to Hitler's surviving enemies—might be sufficient to check the Axis onslaught and decide the war's outcome. Deep-dyed isolationists disagreed, arguing that doing so would merely weaken America's own defenses. FDR was not deterred, however. Soon after the fall of France he dropped from his cabinet the two most committed isolationists—War Secretary Woodring and Navy Secretary Claude Swanson—and replaced them with Henry Stimson and Frank Knox, respectively. Both new cabinet members were strong advocates of rearmament and ardent interventionists who believed in stepped-up aid to Hitler's enemies. Both were also Republicans. The appointments, the canny commander in chief believed, would establish a needed bipartisan foundation for the aid-to-Britain policy.

For Marshall, Stimson's appointment would prove a blessing. A graduate of Yale and Harvard Law School, the seventy-three-year-old New Yorker was an impeccable representative of America's elite at its best—men of established wealth and social standing who felt morally obliged to devote their skills and knowledge to public service. Stimson had served as secretary of war in President William Howard Taft's cabinet before World War I, gone to France with the AEF as a colonel in the field artillery, and returned to public life as Hoover's secretary of state in 1929. Stimson and Marshall had met in France, and the starchy Wall Street lawyer had flagged Marshall as an exceptional young officer. Marshall and the new secretary would mesh almost flawlessly during the trying months ahead, their relationship lubricated by the general's respect for "the wisdom of the founders . . . in subordinating the military to the civilian authority."[5]

The most significant consequence of the pro-Allied shift in public opinion after France's defeat was passage on September 14, 1940, of the Selective Training and Service Act, establishing the first peacetime military draft in American history. Curiously, the measure was not initiated by the administration at all, but by a group of preparedness-oriented civilians and World War I officers, receiving only guarded and largely behind-the-scenes support from FDR, Marshall, and Secretary Stimson.

They had good reasons for their caution. The president was moved by continued sensitivity to isolationist feelings, especially in an election year when he was running for an unprecedented third term. As for Marshall, then and later he strongly supported an American military draft to prevent repeating the country's ragged mobilization performances in the past. But he had valid reservations. Could the army and the country, he asked himself, find the personnel to train, and the means to equip, the avalanche of callow young men to be mustered into uniform by a draft? Testifying before the Senate Military Affairs Committee on July 12, 1940, Marshall warned the senators that "we do not have the trained officers and men—the instructors to spare; also we do not have the necessary matériel. We lack the special training set-up at the moment, and we cannot afford to create it."[6] And like his boss, the chief of staff was also constrained by his fear of offending the isolationists. "People have forgotten today," he told an interviewer in 1957, "what a difficult time we had raising an army, how bitter was the opposition to raising it. . . . We had to move cautiously. If I had ignored public opinion, if I had ignored the reaction of Congress, we would literally have gotten nowhere."[7]

As passed, the Selective Service Act required men between the ages of twenty-one and thirty-six to register with local draft boards. These would decide their military status based on health, age, civilian skills, and other criteria. If selected, they would be sent off to training camps, with no more than nine hundred thousand training at one time, and assigned to units to complete one year of service. During that year they could not be sent outside the United States or its overseas possessions. In August, Congress had nationalized the National Guard. Add the guard to the conscripted soldiers who would emerge from the camps and, Marshall believed, he would now have the manpower he needed for a successful defense of America and the Western Hemisphere.

For Marshall, aid to Britain continued to present a dilemma, however. Helping Hitler's enemies was all very well, but the issue came down to priorities. American factories were still not capable of providing the vehicles, tanks, munitions, and planes the U.S.

Army itself badly needed to become a respectable fighting force. How could the country afford to divert much of this limited output to Britain, especially when, after Dunkirk, that country's very survival long enough to use the equipment was in serious doubt? On this issue Marshall found himself at odds with the more generous president. He also disagreed with FDR, in those pre–Pearl Harbor months, on airpower and on the navy's role in America's defense.

Unlike many senior army officers, Marshall understood the need for an effective military air arm. He did not support the "flyboys'"demand that the air force be made a separate service equal to both the army and navy. This would require an act of Congress, and neither he nor his good friend Hap Arnold believed such a move wise during the ongoing military crisis. Accordingly, during the war, the air corps remained under army command. To compensate, Marshall later insisted that Arnold be made a member of the Joint Chiefs of Staff, equal to himself and the chief of naval operations, despite the corps' nominal subordinate status.

Marshall would later defend the expanded use of airpower through airborne parachute attack, but at a time when scarce resources were being allocated for the various military services, he refused to go overboard on the offensive dimension. For many months he would fight for a "balanced" military expansion plan, one that would recognize the proper roles of land, sea, and air simultaneously, At times he clashed directly with the president— who, Marshall believed, had been taken in by all the hoopla over the effectiveness of the dive-bombers in the blitzkrieg against Poland and the Allies. The American people too had bought the thesis that airpower was now the decisive factor in any war. Marshall demurred. "The airplane is very photogenic," he later told Forrest Pogue. It was "a new weapon" that "had been very heavily advertised by the initial fighting in Europe."[8] In late September 1940, as the rearmament program began to gather steam, Marshall and Stimson were summoned to a White House meeting called by FDR to consider sending some of the new Flying Fortress (B-17) bombers to Britain. As FDR made the case for shipping Fortresses to embattled Britain, he was startled when the chief of staff informed him that the United States had only forty-nine of the new machines. Congress had, perhaps unconstitutionally, mandated that any foreign purchases of American military equipment be approved by the chief of staff, allowing Marshall legally to overrule the president in this matter. He was uncomfortable with this power, however, and, in the end approved the transfer of fifteen Fortresses to Britain for "experimental purposes." The rationale for caution in fact proved valid: Many of the transferred planes, when deployed in European combat conditions, revealed serious mechanical flaws not detected at home, and had to be modified by the air corps for actual military use.

The chief of staff also feared the president's romance with the navy. The U.S. Fleet, too, had glamour on its side in the interservice rivalry, but in addition the president was a devoted weekend sailor and a former assistant secretary of the navy. FDR's pro-navy bias was transparent. In 1956 Marshall recalled that at one point during the war he had to ask FDR to stop speaking of the navy as "we" and the army as "they."[9]

In the fall of 1940, just as rearmament moved into high gear, the nation found itself in the midst of a presidential campaign. Running for a chancy third term and still fearful of the isolationist voice—which now had an effective platform in the influential America First Committee—FDR rashly promised the voters that their "boys [were] not going to be sent into any foreign war." Yet as they watched developments across the Atlantic, Americans could not help becoming ever more uneasy. After the German triumph in France and the Low Countries, the Luftwaffe had

launched a massive campaign to destroy the RAF as the preliminary to an invasion of Britain, Germany's one remaining serious
foe. During the crucial Battle of Britain, Americans heard the
terrifying sounds of air assault against British airfields, ports, and
cities over the newly activated transatlantic radio. They listened
to the soaring rhetoric of Prime Minister Churchill telling the
British—and American—people that success in the skies over the
British Isles would decide the fate of "Christian civilization." "If
we can stand up to [Hitler]," Churchill declaimed, "all Europe
may be free and the life of the world may move forward into
broad, sunlit uplands. But if we fail, then the whole world, including the United States, including all that we have known and
cared for, will sink into the abyss of a new Dark Age."[10]

During this grim period between Dunkirk and Pearl Harbor, Britain stood essentially alone. Inspired by the eloquence
of Churchill, the British refused to consider a negotiated peace
with Nazi Germany, despite its vast superiority in numbers,
skill, wealth, and military prowess. They would fight on, trusting that their command of the seas, resolute aid from the British
Commonwealth and empire, and massive bombing, combined
with armed uprisings in occupied and oppressed Europe, would
save them. But above all they hoped—certainly Churchill
hoped—that the New World would come to the aid of the Old
to balance the unequal score.

The remaining months of 1940 brought some improvement
in British fortunes. By the fall, the intrepid RAF had won the
Battle of Britain, beating off the Luftwaffe's ferocious air assault
and forcing the Germans to abandon their plans to invade the
British Isles. Meanwhile, in the last months of 1940, British and
empire forces under Gen. Sir Archibald Wavell in Egypt struck
the Italians in North Africa and delivered a stinging defeat to
Hitler's Axis partner. Perhaps Britain would survive after all, and

become a worthy partner for any American defense against the German juggernaut.

During this period Marshall's views of America's future military direction were in flux. He was not yet totally convinced that the well-being of the United States was tied to Britain's fate. Unlike the admirals, American generals had frequently emphasized "continental," rather than transmaritime, dangers. The United States, they held, would not have to fend off an invader from abroad. Though that did not preclude military operations in Mexico or Canada, the nation would not, as in 1917–18, be required to send armies to Europe or farthest Asia. Such officers, especially prominent in G-2, were often antagonistic to Britain, indifferent to its plight, and skeptical of Churchill's aggressive leadership.

Marshall absorbed some of these views through his friend Lt. Gen. Stanley Embick, chief of the Joint Strategic Survey Committee, a planning division of the Joint Chiefs that Marshall had worked to establish. The craggy-faced Embick had worked closely with Marshall on the important spring 1940 Louisiana maneuvers and had loyally supported him in his bid to become army chief of staff. But he was no friend of Britain. Like more than a few other army planners, including his own son-in-law, Col. Albert C. Wedemeyer, he suspected the British of duplicity and selfish imperial goals and disagreed with the administration's view that Britain's survival was essential to America's own safety. Embick had favored the appeasement of Hitler at Munich in 1938 and despised Churchill for his determined opposition to the Nazi regime. He was basically an isolationist whose continentalism led him to oppose offensive operations against Japan, including defense of the Philippines, in the event of a Pacific war as proposed in Plan Orange. If carried out, he declared in late 1937, the plan would be "a potential national disaster."[11]

Embick's views did not go unchallenged. There was another faction among army planners and decision makers, most notably Col. Joseph McNarney of the Joint Army-Navy Planning Committee, and, at the top, Secretary Stimson himself, who were all-out supporters of Britain and Churchill. These men might validly have been labeled "warmongers" by the isolationists. American entry into the anti-Axis battle was inevitable, they held, and the sooner the better. Though Marshall is often treated as a resolute interventionist, in these early months of the war he was indecisive. As Mark Stoler notes, at this point he "remained respectful of both viewpoints and [was] still making up his own mind."[12]

But the navy, naturally resistant to the continentalist virus, was not. If the army chief of staff did not know what to think of the war abroad, Adm. Harold Stark did. A bland-looking, mild-mannered man, nicknamed "Betty" as a plebe at Annapolis, he had made up his mind. In late 1940 the chief of naval operations, Marshall's navy counterpart, composed a memo ("Plan Dog") as part of a statement of strategy in the event of war against the Axis powers. It was a far-seeing projection that transcended the Pacific theater of operations, certain to be the navy's particular turf during any future war. It assumed that British survival was vital to America's interests. "If Britain wins decisively against Germany we could win everywhere," Stark's memo noted. But "if she loses the problem confronting us would be very great; and, while we might not *lose everywhere*, we might, possibly, not *win* anywhere."[13] Presciently, Stark was also sure that such a strategy required sending large U.S. forces to Britain. The only way to defeat the Germans, he wrote, was "by military success on shore" and for that, "in addition to sending naval assistance, [the United States] would also need to send large air and land forces to Europe or Africa or both, and to participate strongly in this land offensive."[14]

Stark's Dog Memorandum accurately anticipated in outline
the grand strategy that the United States would follow in the war
years, and reflected a level of strategic thinking then in advance
of Marshall's and the army's. For a time, then, Plan Dog, even
as modified by Colonel McNarney and navy captain Richmond
Kelley, remained controversial in army circles. Soon after its circulation Marshall and his planners gave it their "general agreement," but they continued to warn of Britain's narrow interests
and expressed concern lest any American troops sent to Europe
end up under British command.

It would be a mistake to ascribe the shift of the military planners' thinking to a single document, however trenchant. In many
ways Plan Dog merely reflected new realities. By the time it appeared, the defeat of France had raised the specter of a German-
dominated Europe and North Atlantic. Yet it now also seemed
likely that following the defeat of the Luftwaffe in the air battles
over Britain, England and the empire would survive to fight another day and would be worthy of American military investment.
Stark's proposal must be accounted, as the historian Louis Morton has written, as "perhaps the most important single document
in the development of World War II strategy."[15]

The changing view of U.S. strategic interests led, from late January into March 1941, to a series of unprecedented secret peacetime talks in Washington with Britain on mutual defense needs.
In fourteen meetings high-ranking members of the American and
British air, sea, and army staffs discussed joint action in the event
the United States should enter the war. At these American-British
Conversations (known as ABC-1) both sides recognized the tentative nature of the discussions, with the Americans making fully
explicit that any plans adopted were contingent on America's future relations with the Axis powers.

Marshall and Stark greeted the visiting British officers in person when they first arrived in Washington but warned them of the need for strict secrecy. Congress was at the moment debating the Lend-Lease Bill to provide further matériel to Germany's adversaries, and a leak, they were informed, "might well be disastrous."[16] Neither Marshall nor Stark attended the meetings. Instead, to head the army delegation, Marshall inexplicably chose Embick. Surprisingly, given the circumstances, the "Europe-first" (essentially "Germany-first") view prevailed. The negotiators concluded that in the event the United States entered the war against the Axis powers, both nations would focus on defeating the European enemy; while, if Japan should join Germany and Italy, holding at bay the Asian one until later action. The British sought to commit the United States to the defense of Singapore, their major naval base in Southeast Asia. It was essential, they said, to protect Australia and New Zealand and preserve the empire in the Far East generally. Its safety "must be assured."[17] The American delegates adamantly refused to accept their proposal. The United States, they insisted, could never justify sending men to die to preserve the British Empire. Their anti-imperial response foreshadowed a divisive theme that would surface many times in the upcoming four-year alliance of the two English-speaking nations. Fortunately, on this occasion, Churchill intervened and told his subordinates to drop the Singapore scheme.

"Europe First" was, then, an already established American strategy before Pearl Harbor. Although it would be dauntlessly defended by Marshall against all comers in the months ahead, it did not rely solely on one man's perception. Rather, it was based ultimately on undeniable political-military realities: Germany was the strongest of the three potential American antagonists, and its defeat, though more difficult than defeat of the potential Pacific enemy, would assuredly be decisive. Besides, though seriously weakened by its failure in France, Britain remained a significant military and naval power in its own right, able to contribute major forces to any common effort. That contribution must be protected. Moreover, Britain's location close to occupied Europe made it an obvious base for any attack on Germany. The strategic decision made in Washington that winter of 1941, though perhaps predictable, was the most important the Western Allies made during the entire war. Marshall would embrace the Europe-first principle and eventually become its strongest partisan, but he was not its father.

But that spring in Europe, another top-level strategic decision would be even more fateful for the war's outcome than the conclusions reached at ABC-1. Determined to seize the lebensraum in the East that Germany had long coveted, and to eradicate what he considered the poison of international Communism, Hitler abruptly abrogated the August 1939 Nazi-Soviet Nonaggression Pact. On June 22, 1941, German tanks, planes, and infantry stormed across the eastern border of occupied Poland into Soviet-controlled territory. In a matter of weeks the Wehrmacht had carved away vast slabs of eastern Poland and western Russia, killed or captured hundreds of thousands of Soviet troops, and virtually destroyed the Soviet air force. By the late fall, as winter descended, the Baltic states, White Russia, and Ukraine, and almost all the major cities of western Russia were in Nazi hands, and Wehrmacht officers in the farthest-advanced units could see through their binoculars the spires of Moscow's Kremlin, less than twenty miles away.

American feelings about the German attack on the Soviet Union were ambiguous and volatile. Russia and its cruel dictator, Joseph Stalin, were not popular with most Americans. Besides their repugnance for, and fear of, Soviet Communism the American public could not forget the unprovoked Russian attack in 1939 on little Finland—the only nation, it was said, that had repaid its debts to the United States. Among the top Anglo-American decision makers, however, pragmatism prevailed. Churchill, a fierce anticommunist, on learning of the German attack in June, is reported by his private secretary to have observed: "If Hitler invaded hell I would make at least a favorable reference to the Devil in the House of Commons."[18] The prime minister immediately pledged to help the Russians in any way Britain could. FDR soon seconded Churchill, but the president, like many British and American military experts, had serious reservations about Russia's ability to survive the German juggernaut. During the Soviet-Finnish "Winter War," the Finns had successfully fought off their Russian attackers for many months until smothered by overwhelming numbers. Recently, moreover, Stalin had brutally purged the Soviet army of its most experienced officers. Why throw away precious military resources on such a shaky enterprise when Britain, not to speak of the United States itself, could put them to better use?

At the outset Marshall essentially agreed with the skeptics. FDR himself soon shifted ground, however. In mid-July he brought before his cabinet a list of Soviet arms needs running to $2 billion in cost. High on the list was the request for planes. Marshall bridled. *He* needed the planes, and besides the American public would object to shortchanging the air corps to help the Russians. The president insisted, and Marshall yielded in part because his friend Harry Hopkins stood behind FDR. Still, he later admitted, he "was opposed to any . . . undue generosity which might endanger our security. I thought," he continued, "that we gave too much at times."[19] In the end the Russians had little reason to criticize American aid. In November, as the German army approached the outskirts of Moscow, the Soviet Union was officially admitted to the Lend-Lease program. Many problems would plague the delivery of American and British supplies to the besieged Russians. Dealing with the ferocious losses to U-boats of Allied matériel on the sea route to Murmansk and Archangel, Russia's Arctic ports, would prove a difficult and contentious issue. And there would be others. But by the end of the war the Soviet Union had received more than $11 billion worth of trucks, food, planes, and other war matériel from the United States, a volume of aid second only to Britain's.

If Marshall did not take an early lead in the Anglo-American grand strategy, he was, or so it would be largely believed, the helmsman of American mobilization. One of his first moves as chief of staff was to replace the World War I four-infantry-regiment "square" divisions, appropriate, he felt, primarily for trench warfare, with the three-regiment "triangular divisions," better suited to a war of movement, as touted by numerous military theorists and put into practice by the German army. An important part of the mobilization process was training recruits for war, and for that purpose Marshall, who recalled all too well how unprepared the AEF had been for major operations in France, believed that large-scale army maneuvers were indispensable. The Louisiana maneuvers in 1940 had revealed the woeful inadequacy of the army's equipment. The opposing forces had to fake weapons by labeling iron pipes as "cannon," trucks as "tanks," and single-engine Piper Cubs as "bombers." By the fall of 1941 the equipment deficiencies had been drastically reduced. More significant, the lessons of German blitzkrieg, the rapid, tank-spearheaded attack used so successfully in Poland, France, and Russia, had been absorbed and acknowledged as a major challenge to the American army.

The August–September 1941 General Headquarters Maneuvers in Louisiana and Texas were in every way far more realistic than those of the previous year. Marshall expected them to prepare the American army for the dangers ahead. "I want the mistakes [made] down in Louisiana, not over Europe," he told one senator, "and the only way to do this thing is to try it out, and if it doesn't work what we need to make it work."[20] Some four hundred thousand men were engaged that summer, more than twice the number in the whole army in 1940. The exercises deployed an entire armored corps with real tanks and a thousand military aircraft. The performance of the men and their leaders was a significant improvement over that of the year before, with the skills of three or four officers standing out. One winner was the Third Army commander, Walter Krueger. Another was his chief of staff, a middle-aged, prematurely balding colonel named Dwight David Eisenhower, whom Marshall had first met in 1929 when they had both been asked to edit the ungainly manuscript of Pershing's memoirs. Finally there was the flamboyant major general George S. Patton. Marshall knew Patton well, their friendship going back to France in 1918 when Patton had been an aggressive, profane young captain in the newly formed tank corps. Marshall had only a passing acquaintance with Eisenhower, but he apparently accepted the media's celebration of the officer's skills during the maneuvers (praise that should probably have applied to Krueger). Perhaps he also recognized in the colonel a temperament similar to his own: cerebral, organized, conciliatory, and provident. Thereafter Ike would remain in his mind a "fair-haired boy" who deserved his special favor. Marshall supposedly added the names "Eisenhower" and "Patton" to his "little black book"—whether its existence is valid or dubious—a list of promising officers to be considered for promotion.*

And what of the rank and file, the common GIs, as they would be called in World War II? How had they performed? At the ma-

---

*There is some dispute over whether such a notebook ever existed. One of the skeptics is Thomas E. Ricks. See Ricks's recent book, *The Generals: American Military Command from World War II to Today* (New York: Penguin Press, 2012), pp. 24 and 470 n24.

neuvers' conclusion Marshall praised the men for their "zeal and energy" as well as their "endurance." "The spirit of the troops have been a model of excellence," he wrote Lesley McNair (now a general), one of the maneuvers' organizers. On the other hand, he admitted, they had "much more to learn," but believed that "the mistakes of the past two weeks will be corrected."[21]

Many of the foot soldiers on maneuvers slogging through the marshes and forests of Louisiana and East Texas, swatting mosquitoes and crushing ticks, were draftees getting their first taste of combat's rigors. Though Marshall had been only marginally involved in passage of the 1940 Selective Service Act, once it was on the books and in operation, the measure assured him the manpower the army needed for a major confrontation with the Axis.

The actual draft process had begun that October 16 when more than sixteen million young men registered for the military lottery. The first numbers were drawn two weeks later, and soon thousands of conscripts were streaming off to army camps for basic training. They quickly encountered the usual unfamiliar, uncomfortable aspects of military life: screaming drill sergeants, harsh discipline, exhausting drilling, route marching, KP, guard duty—and boredom. By the terms of the original bill, the draft and the draftees' term of service were to expire at the end of a year, and by the summer of 1941 many of the conscripts had resolved that no matter what was happening overseas they intended to be OHIO—"over the hill in October." In the nation at large, a formidable partnership of isolationists and parents strongly supported these sentiments.

But this attitude meant disaster to America's mobilization plans, and early in the spring, well before the October crisis struck, Stimson and Marshall decided to fight back. In July Marshall used the War Department's annual report to Congress to warn the nation that if the draft act were not amended, a large proportion of the army's divisions would be riddled by mandatory discharges and rendered ineffective. The report specifically recommended that, as a first step, the ban on sending draftees overseas be repealed. Marshall and Stimson had not reckoned with public opinion, however. The request implied the much-dreaded "foreign war," instantly igniting isolationist wrath. Administration supporters in Congress were soon angrily telephoning the White House to complain that they had not been warned of the War Department's initiative.

It may be difficult for readers today, when the United States has become a world leader, to understand the depth of resistance from Americans in mid-1941 to any act that entangled the nation in the war raging overseas. But the contemporary public fear was real and powerful. In Congress particularly, isolationism was amplified by fierce anti-Roosevelt sentiment. Many anti-interventionists detested "that man in the White House" and opposed his entire agenda, not just his foreign policy. In allaying isolationist dread, Marshall had to be careful not to trigger the strong current of FDR hatred in many of the same people.

For a brief moment following the report the chief of staff was in disgrace on Capitol Hill. "I am being called—a Benedict Arnold, a skunk, . . . a stooge, traitor, etc," he wrote to a friend.[22] Fortunately Marshall was now widely seen as a man whose views were not tainted by political ambition or partisanship. With his awesome dignity and patent sincerity, his command of ideas and facts, his lack of offensive ego, and his political neutrality, his goals could only be considered honest and disinterested. Marshall, House Speaker Sam Rayburn informed his colleagues, was the very man to overcome isolationist and anti-Roosevelt fears and resentments. "Let us remember," he said, "that we are in the presence of a man who is telling the truth."[23] Rayburn and the other interventionist Democratic leaders now turned to Marshall as the best man to save and improve the draft law.

Marshall opened his campaign to rescue the Selective Service with testimony before Congress. He pointed out to the Senate Military Affairs Committee, and later to the corresponding House panel, the inadequacies in past wars of a volunteer army; he reminded senators and representatives of Hitler's recent victories; he assured them that a strong defense was the best insurance policy against war. Marshall was careful to detach himself from FDR, depicting the president as a military conservative who did not fully understand the urgency of the army's needs.

In the Senate, action was quick. In early August, after dropping Marshall's request that draftees, with congressional approval, serve for as long as the president believed necessary, the Senate approved the renewal bill. The House was more recalcitrant. Every member faced reelection in 1942, and representatives from isolationist districts were balky. Even vulnerable Democrats were dubious. In early August the House majority leader, John McCormack, reported that forty-five Democrats were opposed to extension and another thirty-five were wavering. But pure partisanship also played a role in the deliberations. Joseph Martin, the House Republican leader, though himself in favor of the draft extension, chose to rally his party against the measure on the grounds that by opposing it the Republicans "might yet funnel the winds into our sails and blow us back again to the commanding position [we] . . . enjoyed in the 1920s."[24]

As the debate in Congress and the media heated up, morale among the new soldiers themselves continued to slip. Angry draftees and guardsmen turned on the administration, and even Marshall fell victim to their rage. A *Life* magazine article of mid-August reported one private as railing: "To hell with Roosevelt and Marshall and the Army and the Germans and the Russians and the British. I want to get out of this hole."[25] The revolt disturbed Marshall. Poor military morale, he worried, would damage the nation's ability to defend itself. Writing to his friend Bernard Baruch, Marshall blamed much of the issue on the media. "Parents became stirred up and individual soldiers were taught to feel sorry for themselves," he noted. He had been surprised "that in our democracy we were able to achieve a Selective Service system late last summer, but I guess I was hoping too much." Calling it a "delicate problem," he added that "with such a slender margin of public opinion to back us" it would be "no easy matter to build up the highly trained and seasoned fighting force that we must have available."[26]

As the final House vote on the draft extension bill approached, Marshall asked his friend Congressman James W. Wadsworth, a Republican interventionist from upstate New York who had co-sponsored the original 1940 bill, to assemble a group of skeptical Republican representatives so he could try to change their minds. Forty of these men met with Marshall in a private dining room at Washington's Army and Navy Club and listened to his arguments from seven in the evening until two in the morning. It was rough going despite the general's eloquent patriotism and masterful marshaling of facts. At one point, Marshall recalled, one of the congressmen turned to him and exclaimed: "That's all very well. You put the case very well, but I'll be damned if I'm going to go along with Mr. Roosevelt." An angry Marshall shot back: "You're going to let plain hatred of the [president's] personality dictate to you to do something that you realize is very harmful to the interests of the country?"[27] At the end of the long session he had, Marshall believed, induced twelve of the group to change their minds.

Marshall's efforts, and especially the dozen conversions, would be crucial. On August 12 the draft extension bill came up for a final House vote. Republicans and a few Democrats denounced the measure. One of the skeptics, Everett Dirksen of Illinois, later the Republican Senate minority leader, asked acerbically how long it would be before the president managed to send U.S. soldiers to serve outside the Western Hemisphere once the year limit on service was lifted. Opponents sought to bury the bill under amendments. With contingents of isolationist Mothers for America and the America First Committee watching intently from the crowded Capitol gallery, the House voted 203 to 202 in favor of the bill. Some sixty-nine Democrats had defected, but twenty-one Republicans had voted yes. On August 18 FDR signed into law the bill extending selectees' obligations to eighteen months of military service.

The nation now could count on a steady supply of military manpower, but whether the draftees' training would fit them well for war remained another matter entirely.

Saving the draft, and with it America's mobilization for war, had occupied Marshall's energies for much of the fall. Meanwhile, however, the international crisis continued to worsen, raising new challenges for the army and for the military planners who would chart its course in the months ahead.

In their arguments for the draft and its extension, partisans claimed that a strong defense would make war unnecessary. Yet many of them knew that the assertion was misleading. By late 1940 Roosevelt and his advisers had come to accept privately that the United States could not avoid becoming a belligerent. In mid-December, following a meeting with Navy Secretary Knox, Admiral Stark, and Marshall, Stimson wrote in his diary that "all four agreed that this emergency could hardly be passed over without this country being drawn into the war eventually."[28] And bit by bit, despite FDR's public protestations, the administration was clandestinely committing the nation to the struggle against the aggressors in both oceans. Well before Pearl Harbor the interventionists determined to remedy Britain's shortage of the "tools of war" through modification of the cash-and-carry principle. In September 1940 Roosevelt concluded a deal to transfer fifty mothballed U.S. World War I destroyers to the Royal Navy in exchange for ninety-nine-year leases of British military bases in the Western Hemisphere. In early 1941, following his reelection, he had proposed the Lend-Lease program to help Britain, then running out of cash, to continue the flow of American arms. In March 1941 Marshall would testify twice before Congress in support of the bill. As passed soon after, the Lend-Lease Act authorized the president to designate any country he deemed vital to American defense as a recipient of American arms on credit. Under its terms an enormous fifty billion dollars in equipment and other war aid would eventually flow to Britain and other enemies of the Axis powers.

But how would this matériel safely reach its destination? From the outset of the war German U-boats and surface raiders had taken a brutal toll on Allied shipping in the Atlantic. The fifty over-age destroyers promised to help but were clearly not enough, and by the spring of 1941 the U.S. Navy began to patrol large portions of the western Atlantic to detect U-boats to ease the strain on the Royal Navy. Confrontations with submarines were inevitable. In September a German sub attacked the USS *Greer*, an American destroyer patrolling off Iceland. Roosevelt immediately issued a "shoot-on-sight" order to the navy. At the end of October the Germans sank the U.S. destroyer *Reuben James*, convoying British merchant ships, with the loss of one hundred American sailors. In effect, by the fall of 1941, the United States was engaged in a virtual naval war against Germany in the North Atlantic.

Dangers were also boiling up in the Far East. By 1937 the Japanese advance in China, coyly named the "China Incident" by the aggressors, had turned into a full-scale drive for conquest that had brought much of the North China coast under their harsh rule. The American government, still inspired by its traditional "Open Door" policy in China, had protested the Japanese aggression but without effect. In fact, taking advantage of the German victories in Europe, the Japanese had now begun to encroach on the French and Dutch colonies left exposed by their defeated colonial rulers. In July 1940 Japanese troops moved into northern French Indochina and, defying the feeble protests of French officials, occupied several strategic cities. In September, Japan formally joined Italy and Germany as the third member of the Axis powers.

By mid-1941, to Marshall and War Department planners, urged on by the president, the time appeared ripe for an economic blueprint for a war that now seemed close at hand.

Marshall gave the task of estimating the industrial, manpower, and transport needs of a major war abroad to the War Plans Division, headed by Gen. Leonard T. Gerow. Gerow promptly dumped the assignment into the lap of Maj. Albert Wedemeyer, General Embick's son-in-law, a tall infantry officer recently assigned to the WPD. In its economic projections Wedemeyer had the help of the New Deal economist Robert Nathan of the government-run Office of Production Management (OPA).

At first glance, Wedemeyer seems an eccentric choice to plan a possible anti-Axis war. A West Point graduate, in the mid-1930s he had spent two years as an exchange student at the Kriegsakademie, the German War College in Berlin. His experience convinced him that the Nazi regime was not without its virtues, and he had even come to endorse the German yearning for expansionist Lebensraum. Not surprisingly, like his father-in-law, he was an ardent isolationist who perceived, as he later wrote, that the "administration's war preparations, and its unneutral actions [were] calculated to provoke the Axis powers to declare war on us."[29]

Yet in his work on the assigned logistical and industrial plan of action, Wedemeyer kept his prejudices in check. In the document that emerged from the deliberations there was no hint of an isolationist or pro-German bias.

The "Victory Program," as the document was labeled, has been touted as the farsighted military and economic master plan that guided American leaders in World War II. In the words of one military historian, it was "the blueprint both for the general mobilization of the United States Army for a war not yet declared and for the operational concept by which the United States would fight the war." It "predicted the future organization for an army that did not yet exist, outlined combat missions for a war not yet declared, and computed war production requirements for industries that were still committed to peacetime manufacture."[30]

And indeed, in many ways, its drafting was a formidable accomplishment. Working through the torrid Washington summer in the War Department's un-air-conditioned Munitions Building, the army planners collected advice and information from a wide array of industry leaders and government agencies, which they then marshaled skillfully. But the document had serious failings. Much of it centered on manpower needs. Wedemeyer estimated that the army, both ground and air forces, would require some 8.8 million men to win the war. This figure was remarkably close to the total size of the wartime army at its peak in March 1945, but bitter field experience would show that this figure was too low for the tasks at hand. The program was also deficient in allocating military manpower within the overall figure. Wedemeyer believed that the almost 9 million men would yield 250 combat infantry divisions. Instead, by war's end there were only 90 to fight the Axis. In fact, the number of actual available ground combat troops in 1941–45 would be fewer than in 1917–18, though the army in World War I was only half the total size as in the later war. One problem that Wedemeyer had not counted on was the need for truck drivers, mechanics, clerk-typists, military police, intelligence officers, and the rest of the "long tail" of logistical and technical troops that seem an unavoidable part of modern military forces, certainly those of the United States. Still another serious defect in the program, time would show, was its failure to provide an adequate replacement system for combat casualties, an issue to be considered later.

Besides manpower needs, the Victory Program dealt with industrial mobilization. Here, too, Wedemeyer and his colleagues overestimated. In reality, it would be America's incredible industrial cornucopia that won the war. The "arsenal of democracy" would smother the Axis under the tanks, planes, shells, guns, ships, trucks—and the wheat, cotton, corn, and beef—that poured out of its factories and farms into the arms, packs, and bellies of American, British, French, and Russian soldiers. But the army planners miscalculated even America's capacity to produce the tools of modern war. They had, for example, estimated the number of armored divisions needed by U.S. forces at sixty-one. Instead the army could field only sixteen. In the end the number of proposed armored divisions exceeded the capacity of American plants to produce the necessary tanks and other armored-force equipment.

Whatever its shortcomings, Marshall and Stark approved the plan in early September. For Marshall and the army generally, it served to legitimize their convictions about the vast economic and logistical needs ahead.* Unfortunately, as a manpower blueprint it

---

*On December 4, 1941, the isolationist *Chicago Tribune* revealed the existence of the Victory Program on its front page and condemned it as an example of the Roosevelt administration's secret, dishonest schemes to drag the country into war. Interventionists, certain the revelation would help the Axis, were appalled. Secretary Stimson called the *Tribune*'s story unpatriotic and "damaging to our defense." There was talk of federal prosecutions for the leak, but the issue became moot on December 7, when the Japanese attacked Pearl Harbor.

led Marshall astray, a misstep that would produce serious short-ages and other deficiencies later in the war.

Though he deserved much of the credit for passage of the draft renewal bill, Marshall had not been at his desk when it passed the House in mid-August. He, along with Hap Arnold of the air corps and Admirals Stark and Ernest King, then commander of the U.S. Atlantic Fleet, were with the president at Argentia Bay in Newfoundland, conferring with Prime Minister Churchill and a full panoply of British military and civilian staffers and experts.

The meeting was instigated by Churchill, who understood the depressing reality of Britain's existing position in the war after the defeat of France. Russia was now a cobelligerent against Hitler, but its survival was in serious question. America alone appeared able to provide the aid that Britain desperately needed to sur-vive and finally prevail. The prime minister's ultimate goal at the Atlantic Conference was to further enmesh Britain's "American cousins" in the anti-Axis war. As for Roosevelt, FDR had often expressed interest in meeting the dynamic British prime minister, the man who had so eloquently rallied his discouraged people after Dunkirk. But Roosevelt had no intention of being trapped into a premature commitment to war. He would meet with the British only if the issue of U.S. entry was off the table, along with any discussion of postwar economic, demographic, and territorial changes. The military staffs of both nations would have the op-portunity to discuss how to make Lend-Lease aid effective, but in no way would they make joint war plans. The chief result of the meetings should be, he believed, a joint declaration stating in very general terms the goals of the two nations following the war.

In the event, this limited agenda was pushed aside, and the two parties discussed actual military cooperation. Here Marshall and the other American military men were ill prepared for nego-tiations with the British. Their staffs were far smaller than the

British, and perhaps understandably, they did not have detailed plans for how to win the war. By contrast, the Imperial General Staff, headed by Sir John Dill, had prepared a long paper on the strategy for eventual victory. The proposal reflected British reality and history and would be the prototype of many future ones by Churchill and the Imperial General Staff through to 1944. It rejected the idea of defeating the Wehrmacht in direct head-on combat. "We do not foresee vast armies of infantry as in 1914–18," the paper read. Instead, Hitler's Western adversaries would seek a "peripheral" approach. A tight blockade and a prolonged bombing campaign would undermine German morale and war industry. Simultaneously every effort would be made to stir the peoples of Nazi-occupied Europe to rise up against their oppressors. Meanwhile, a string of military assaults from the edges of the German-occupied Continent, especially north from the Mediterranean, would weaken the Axis powers. At this point the enemy would be softened sufficiently for final defeat by "armoured divisions with the most modern equipment."[31] Besides these broad strategic proposals for the future, the British staff also urged the Americans to help the cause immediately by joining in an attack on Vichy-controlled French North Africa and by sending combat troops posthaste to the endangered Middle East.

However unsure of the future course of his country, Marshall was unimpressed and unmoved by British plans. He knew that the United States was not ready for direct intervention on the fighting fronts. But he already believed that to defeat Germany there could be no substitute for operations on the European continent, deploying masses of ground troops against the enemy. This scenario had been foreshadowed by Stark's Dog Plan proposal. But the perspective was not new to the American military ethos. According to the historian Russell Weigley, Ulysses Grant's successful strategy of "annihilation" through "head-on grappling" with the Confederates in the Civil War had deeply embedded itself in the American military mind.[32] World War I had reinforced the conviction among American generals that "fire and maneuver," as used by the Allied armies in France in 1914–18, however valuable as a *tactical* approach, did not work as an overall *strategy* in an era of mass armies. The brute-force view was widely disseminated in American military circles in the interwar years by various military historians and theorists. Plan Rainbow 5, in April 1941, had urged "the building up of the necessary forces for an eventual offensive against Germany." And for that matter, the Victory Program had also suggested that ultimately the United States would have to defeat German ground forces in direct combat. Marshall himself had no doubt that in the event of war the United States could not avoid taking on the formidable Wehrmacht. Whether it was his personal experience in the First World War, the American military culture in which he was immersed, or his own extensive study of military history and theory, he would defend the direct-confrontation strategy, battling over and over in the next four years against those who hoped to avoid the heavy costs it threatened.

Though he disagreed with the proposals of the Imperial General Staff, Marshall found the meetings at Argentia Bay valuable. He had nothing to say about the Atlantic Charter issued at the end of the meetings that laid out idealistic principles that the two democracies hoped would govern humanity in the postwar world. But he and the other American staffers had taken the measure of their putative future ally, and they were impressed. At the conference they had been outclassed, they recognized. Clearly the British were better prepared than the Americans to argue their case. On a lighter note, they also knew how to put on a better show. As Elliott Roosevelt, FDR's air corps son who accompanied his father, later wrote, in their dress uniforms the British staff

were "so resplendent as to put us Americans . . . to shame."[33]
Also—unbelievably—they were better cooks. The U.S. Navy had
served roast chicken when Churchill and the British staff ate dinner aboard the American flagship on Saturday. On Sunday the
Americans aboard HMS *Prince of Wales* were treated to choice
grouse shot in Scotland just hours before Churchill and his party
had taken ship for Newfoundland.

The Atlantic Conference would reinforce the sense, already
manifest at ABC-1, that America's prospective allies were interested not just in saving the British homeland from the enemy, but
in preserving the whole of Britain's immense empire. Marshall
and Stark also learned that their soon-to-be allies were grossly
ignorant of America's existing military unpreparedness and of the
continued power of the administration's isolationist foes. Amid
the negative impressions, one important plus for Marshall was
that he got to know and to admire Field Marshal Dill, who then
led the British Imperial General Staff. The friendship between
the two, begun at Argentia Bay, would flower and become an
indispensable element in the success of the British-American collaboration when, after Pearl Harbor, Churchill sent Dill to Washington as head of British military liaison with the Americans.

Returning to his office on August 14, Marshall confronted the
urgent problem of growing Japanese intransigence in the Pacific.
Army strategic planners in the 1930s, led by Embick, had rejected
as too costly a major far-Pacific campaign in the event of war with
Japan. America of course would fight to save Hawaii, but this
position precluded a commitment to saving the Philippines. By
mid-1941 army opinion had changed. As FDR's resolve to thwart
Japanese ambitions in China stiffened he was compelled to shift
direction. In July he created a new army command in the Philippines and appointed Douglas MacArthur, then retired as army
chief of staff, to head it. MacArthur's authority included the new

Filipino army, created to provide a local defense against rampaging Japanese forces if war should erupt in the Pacific.

Meanwhile, relations with Japan grew edgier as reports of Japanese designs on the British Malay States, French Indochina, and the Dutch East Indies filtered into Washington. In late July, Japanese forces completed their occupation of Indochina. Britain and the United States now froze all loans and credits to Japan, making it difficult for it to import from the United States vital strategic resources like oil. Stark and Marshall both voiced objections to the move, believing it likely to provoke an attack on the Dutch East Indies while the United States still remained unprepared for the consequences. Their voices did not deter the president. Along with the freeze, FDR warned the Japanese ambassador that further aggression in the Far East would goad Washington to take strong "measures toward ensuring the safety and security of the United States."[34]

Still, FDR held back. Fearing war in the wrong place at the wrong time, he responded positively to an overture for direct talks with Prime Minister Fumimaro Konoe. They never took place. Japan's bellicose army leaders were in no mood for negotiations and refused to consider any serious promise to abandon their campaign of conquest in China, a minimum requirement for a settlement with the United States. When the American government rejected Tokyo's proposals, the Japanese warlords in mid-October forced Konoe to accept as minister of war one of their militant own, the aggressive Hideki Tojo.

By now the influential war party in Japan had decided that hostilities with America were inevitable. The end of British-American credits had cut the vital Japanese oil pipeline to America. The oil embargo of the Dutch East Indies government that followed soon after, promising to pinch off the last remaining source of diesel oil and aviation fuel, threatened to cripple the Japanese army and navy as well as starve important civilian functions. Clearly Japan must find a way to neutralize the United States while it pursued its campaign of subordinating resource-rich Southeast Asia to its imperial designs. For months the naval leaders in Tokyo had been developing a plan to subvert American naval power by a surprise attack on Pearl Harbor in Hawaii, headquarters of the American Pacific Fleet. Though the United States and Britain had broken the Japanese diplomatic code and could read Tokyo's Foreign Office dispatches, the decipherment process (code-named "Magic") did not disclose the Japanese navy's plans for an attack on American targets. These were effectively hidden even from the Japanese Foreign Office and much of the civilian Japanese government. The White House and leading American officials knew that further Japanese troop and fleet movements were imminent, but these, they believed, were pointed either south at the Dutch possessions and British Singapore and Malaya, or perhaps north against Russian Siberia.

Meanwhile, in late November, last-ditch talks had begun between Secretary of State Cordell Hull and the Japanese emissaries over the two nations' overall relations. In Washington, Ambassador Kichisaburô Nomura and special envoy Saburô Karusu demanded that the United States accept Japan's policies in China, that it resume full trade relations with their country, that it aid it to acquire oil from the Dutch, and that it cease its naval expansion in the Pacific. Secretary Hull countered with demands once more that Japan exit China and end its expansion in East Asia. During these talks the American intelligence services, using Magic, informed the White House and the State Department that the negotiations were largely a smokescreen hiding Japanese plans to move aggressively in the Pacific.

Marshall, of course, was aware of Japan's imminent moves in Asia, but favored stringing out the negotiations as long as possible while the United States continued to strengthen its defenses in the Pacific area. Seconded by Admiral Stark, he urged the president to make "minor concessions which the Japanese could use in saving face."[35] Now, with the Embick policy superseded, he was particularly concerned about the Philippines, whose strategic location jeopardized any Japanese expansion southward and so seemed likely to be targeted. Lobbied by MacArthur, during the final months of peace Marshall ordered the shipment of scores of the new Flying Fortresses and B-24 heavy bombers to the Philippines. These, he hoped, along with better training of Filipino regiments and additions to the U.S. regulars already dispatched, would enable MacArthur to thwart any Japanese incursion, or to hold out until reinforcements could be sent.

By now FDR and his advisers had lost patience with what seemed at best a forlorn hope for peace through negotiation. In fact, the two Japanese envoys in Washington themselves hoped that a settlement between the two nations remained possible, and asked their superiors for more time. But Tokyo wanted results, not hopes. The "deadline absolutely could not be changed," Tokyo signaled Nomura and Kurusu; November 29 was the absolute latest by which any agreement must be signed: "After that things are automatically going to happen."[36] On the twenty-sixth Roosevelt received information that Japanese warships and troop transports were moving toward Singapore, the East Indies, and the Philippines, and Hull, seething over Japanese duplicity, delivered to the two emissaries a final American proposal that neither he nor FDR believed would do any good. Negotiations, they were certain, were for "all practical purposes at an end," and a Japanese attack somewhere was "possible at any moment."[37]

On November 27 a War Plans Division alert, bearing Marshall's signature, went out to the commanding generals in the Philippines, San Francisco, the Canal Zone, and Hawaii. Negotiations with the Japanese government, it said, appeared "to be terminated." Though "future action [was] "unpredictable, . . . hostile action [was] possible at any moment." The message went on to advise the commanders to take such precautionary measures as they deemed necessary but that these be carried out so "as not to alarm civil population or disclose intent."[38]

By this time Vice Adm. Chûichi Nagumo's Operation Z task force was already steaming under radio silence toward Hawaii. The Japanese armada consisted of six of Japan's most modern aircraft carriers and several battleships, along with a flock of cruisers, destroyers, and submarines as escorts. Aboard the carriers were more than four hundred planes—high-altitude and dive-bombers, torpedo planes, and nimble Zero fighters. On Sunday morning, December 7 Hawaii time, the armada approached Oahu and, from three hundred miles to the north, launched its planes in two waves toward the American military and naval bases. The attack caught the army and navy totally unprepared. The navy's Pacific carrier force was, fortunately, at sea, but many of the other vessels, including the core vessels of the battleship fleet, were moored at their berths. Nor was the army more alert to danger. Believing sabotage more likely than an actual enemy physical attack in the event of war, Gen. Walter Short had, for safety's sake, clustered the air corps planes at Hickam, Bellow, and Wheeler Fields wing-to-wing, making them sitting ducks for the Japanese bombers. The few American fighters that rose to engage the enemy proved to be no match for the Zeros; most were shot down. In two hellish hours the planes with the rising sun emblem on their wings sank four U.S. battleships and crippled four others; destroyed a small armada of lesser vessels; demolished 188 planes, and damaged another 155. The Japanese attack killed 2,345 American servicemen and wounded 1,274 others.

All told, the top Japanese naval planner, Adm. Isoroku Yamamoto, had achieved his ends: American power in the Pacific had suffered a shock that would prevent it for months from responding effectively against the major Japanese offensive against the British, Dutch, and American possessions in East Asia that now unfolded. But the admiral had also unleashed the concentrated might of the enraged American people against his country. On December 8 Roosevelt appeared before a joint session of Congress to ask for a declaration of war against Japan. December 7 had been a "day that will live in infamy," he famously announced. While their negotiators in Washington were holding out hope for peace, the Japanese government was preparing for attack. This "dastardly" assault would unite the American people and, in "their righteous wrath" they would "win through to absolute victory." Congress, with a single dissenting vote, voted for war against the Japanese empire. Three days later Germany and Italy, meeting their Axis obligations, declared war against the United States.

Roosevelt was essentially right about American opinion: Pearl Harbor did silence most of the administration's isolationist critics. Soon after the attack the transatlantic flyer Charles Lindbergh, the most visible member of the isolationist America First Committee, announced "now that war has come we must meet it as united Americans regardless of our attitude in the past toward the policy our government has followed." Newspapers from every part of the nation declared that the isolationist versus interventionist debate was over. The *Chicago Daily News* predicted that "thanks now to Japan, the deep division that has rent and paralyzed our country will be swiftly healed."[39] But Pearl Harbor did not end the resentment of many men and women who had fought mightily to avoid war. For diehard isolationists, resentment soon transmuted into blame: FDR and the interventionists collectively had deliberately goaded Japan to attack the United States as a devious, dishonest way to bring the United States into the war against Hitler. And Marshall, many would claim, had been a party to this conspiracy to make America a belligerent in a deadly, unnecessary war. The charges would nip at Marshall's heels, like some mad persistent terrier, for the remainder of his life, and even beyond.

Was there any substance to the charges? Many of the critics were the same Roosevelt haters who deplored the domestic New Deal, decried pro-British interventionism, and had sought to end the draft in 1941. Their motives were blatantly partisan or ideological. But however partisan, the indictment could draw on reality. The Roosevelt administration had not been candid with the American people. FDR and his close civilian advisers believed by the end of 1941 that America's entry into the war was both unavoidable and warranted to preserve international order and protect the nation against aggressors. But how should this be accomplished? They had goaded the Germans into attacking U.S. Navy convoys of British ships in the Atlantic, but that course failed to incite Hitler, who had his hands full with Russia and preferred at this point to avoid war with the United States. Would Japan do instead—as the critics claimed? By November 1941 the crisis with Japan had reached a climax. But in fact war in the Pacific was not what the administration wanted. "Europe first" remained the watchword, and war with Japan seemed to the White House likely to be a dangerous distraction. Yet a case can be made that the responses of FDR and Secretary Hull to Japanese aggression—and especially the oil embargoes—were, as Marshall believed, more belligerent than necessary or expedient, and were a possible tripwire for Japanese aggression.

Despite this view, however, the charge that the administration deliberately made Pearl Harbor into bait to lure the Japanese into an attack can be clearly dismissed. Supposedly a piece of evidence that confirms the cynical conclusion about administration motives is the White House meeting on November 25, attended by Marshall, described in Secretary Stimson's private diary. At this gathering the president, drawing on the Magic decrypts, stated that "we are likely to be attacked perhaps next Monday for the Japanese are notorious for making an attack without warning."* From this conclusion, in Stimson's words, flowed the key question: "how we should maneuver them into a position of firing the first shot without allowing too much danger to ourselves."[40]

In fact the words quoted do not implicate the administration or Marshall in a malign conspiracy. An attack by Japan, the attendees knew, was certain to come soon; war was unavoidable. But surely, in reality, there was no way the United States could avert it short of a Munich-like appeasement or a preemptive strike, which the American people would never condone. The men gathered at the White House that late November day were confronted with the same dilemma as Abraham Lincoln as he grappled with the crisis of Fort Sumter in Charleston Harbor in April 1861, and they reached the same conclusion as the Great Emancipator: Let the enemy fire the first shot.

But hadn't those same men criminally dangled the bait of Pearl Harbor to tempt the enemy strike? The answer is no. They did not know where and when the blow would land. It is true that at various times in the past American military planners had speculated about a Japanese attack on Hawaii, but no one believed in November 1941 that Pearl Harbor would be the current Japanese target. Certainly no one in the administration, least of all Roosevelt, would have knowingly jeopardized the U.S. Navy, the service he truly cherished. And if they had known they could

---

*Here the president was referring to the Japanese surprise attack on the Russian fleet in the 1905 Russo-Japanese War.

have intercepted the Japanese attackers and have had their casus belli without the need to sacrifice the Pacific Fleet.

The role of Marshall was an inevitable component of the conspiracy indictment. Marshall had tried to avoid too close an identification with the Democrats and the Roosevelt administration; the appearance of political neutrality had been one of his strong points, especially in his dealings with Congress. But his views of rearmament and military preparedness largely coincided with those of the reigning Democrats, and he could not escape the contumely heaped on them by isolationists and the Far Right. So was Marshall part of the plot? The answer here too must be no: Since there was no plot he could not have been a plotter. But beyond this, is it conceivable that Marshall would connive with FDR and his chief advisers to endanger the navy and the Army Air Corps on Oahu? The answer again is no. It is preposterous to believe that a man who had built his career, and indeed his life, on his reputation for personal integrity, and for whom the army was everything, would have lent himself to such a project.

But what about a charge of incompetence? In their eagerness to assign blame, a substantial segment of the Pearl Harbor critics was willing to forgo conspiracy for ineptitude. The administration and its military and naval agents had been obtusely complacent, needlessly exposing vital American weapons to enemy attack, they said. And the army chief of staff was not blameless in the debacle. Marshall, along with his peers, had failed in his responsibility to protect Pearl Harbor from Admiral Nagumo's Operation Z task force.

Was Marshall, in any way, culpable in the failure of the army's defense at Pearl Harbor on December 7? Had he been careless or deficient in interpreting the danger to Pearl Harbor and/or in transmitting his fears to General Short? Any answer is inevitably informed by the lessons from the terrorist attack on the World

Trade Center, sixty years later, and from successive jihadist assaults or attempted assaults on the United States and its allies: Human communications and perceptions are always imperfect, and it is easy to assign blame after the fact.

Marshall did not anticipate an attack on Pearl Harbor. In a letter to Short, he had urged the commanding general of the Hawaiian Department to keep in mind that the army's mission in the islands was to protect the naval base. But he *was* complacent: "If no serious harm is done us during the first six hours of known hostilities, thereafter the existing defenses [of Hawaii] would discourage an enemy against the hazard of an attack," he wrote to Short on February 7.[41] By late fall the situation in the Pacific had obviously deteriorated, and though it was clear that the Japanese were on the move, most observers believed that their most likely direction was south against Singapore, Malaya, the Dutch possessions, and the Philippines, not east against Hawaii. Though critics have uncovered a few warnings from intelligence officers that the Japanese might target Pearl Harbor, none of these were authoritative in light of the overwhelming idée fixe that the naval base on Oahu was too far from Japan and too well defended for the Japanese to attack it successfully. It is true that Short misinterpreted Marshall's warning of November 27 as a caveat against sabotage by local people, many of them of Japanese ancestry, and so failed to disperse his planes on the Oahu airfields. But was Marshall at fault? It has been noted that MacArthur in Manila also allowed his close-clustered bomber force to be destroyed on the ground, though he had learned of the Pearl Harbor attack nine hours earlier. But of course that does not absolve Marshall of blame. As a number of official investigations would assert, Marshall's role in the events immediately preceding Pearl Harbor was not above reproach. His response to the warnings of imminent Japanese aggression in Asia seems less than meticulous. He could not know that Task Force Z was steaming toward Hawaii, but it was clear that the Japanese moves threatened to sever relations with the United States. Yet he was not convinced that this meant certain war. Perhaps this removal from reality was encouraged by his hope that war could be delayed until the nation's military forces were better prepared.

His complacency was epitomized for later critics by his failure to cancel his usual fifty-minute horseback ride on December 7, an important feature of his established health regimen, reinforced by a recent recurrence of his irregular heartbeat. While Marshall cantered along the north bank of the Potomac that Sunday morning Col. Rufus Bratton, chief of the Far East Section of Army Intelligence, was reading the late-arriving part 14 of the long message to envoys Nomura and Karusu that U.S. intelligence had already deciphered. The bulk of the communication had made it clear that Tokyo totally rejected Hull's counterproposals. After reading the intercepts of parts 1 to 13 on December 6, the president had remarked, "This means war."[42] But part 14, clearly ending further negotiations, and a supplement ordering that the final word be delivered to Hull precisely at 1:00 p.m., startled Bratton. It amounted, he saw, to a de facto breaking off of diplomatic relations with America and, alarmed at its implications for immediate military action, he telephoned Marshall at his private quarters at Fort Myer. When an orderly informed him that the general was on his morning ride Bratton asked that Marshall be found and told to call back immediately.

When the general returned to his house at 10:00 that morning he received Bratton's message and, after showering, left for his office in the Munitions Building. There, while methodically plowing through the whole of Tokyo's fourteen-part response to Hull, he asked Bratton what he thought was the significance of the 1:00 p.m. delivery time. The colonel replied that it probably meant that the Japanese intended to launch an early-morning attack on the United States somewhere in the Pacific. Marshall now wrote out a new dispatch warning the army commanders in the Philippines, Panama, San Francisco, and Hawaii that the Japanese were "presenting at 1 p.m. Eastern Standard Time today what amounts to an ultimatum." This was clear enough, but its impact was muffled by the next sentence: "Just what significance the hour set may have we do not know, but be on the alert accordingly."[43]

To further weaken the impact of the note, its transmission was bungled. Marshall sent his handwritten orders to the Army Signals Room for forwarding to the four command posts. When Col. Edward French in the signals room finally deciphered his scrawl he found that direct army radio contact with Hawaii was down. The warning would have to be sent to General Short via Western Union, the commercial telegraph company. In Oahu, the Western Union motorcycle messenger boy, a Japanese American, was stopped several times on his way to Short's headquarters by suspicious MPs. But in any case, by now it was too late. As he approached army headquarters the messenger could hear the sound of American antiaircraft guns firing at the planes with the rising sun insignia on their wings. Marshall cannot be held responsible for these almost comical mishaps, but it is difficult to avoid the feeling that the chief of staff did indeed lack the sense of urgency that the circumstances warranted.

Marshall would survive the avalanche of criticism he would eventually have to endure, but for the rest of his life, to the circle of disgruntled erstwhile isolationists never reconciled to their repudiation by Pearl Harbor, he would remain a surrogate for the detested FDR. But meanwhile there was a war to be fought, and as December 8 dawned it was clear to the army chief of staff that America faced a hazardous and painful struggle to win it.

CHAPTER 5

RETREAT

To Churchill and his countrymen the Japanese attack was a godsend: Britain and the empire would survive. That night the prime minister went to bed and "slept the sleep of the saved and thankful." But much pain and suffering remained for the new cobelligerents. The weeks following Pearl Harbor were a time of agonizing, unrelenting retreat for the Allied forces facing Japan. On December 8 Japanese troops invaded and quickly subdued independent Thailand and British-ruled Malaya; on December 10 Japanese torpedo planes sank the Royal Navy's powerful capital ships *Prince of Wales* and *Repulse* on the South China Sea. That same day Gen. Masaharu Homma landed his army on the beaches of northern Luzon, the major island in the Philippines. The attack on Pearl Harbor had mysteriously failed to alert MacArthur to imminent danger. Just hours after news arrived in Manila by cable of the devastating blow to the American Pacific Fleet in Hawaii, the general's entire air force, parked wing-to-wing on Clark Field, was wiped out by Japanese Mitsubishi bombers and Zero fighters swooping in from Formosa.

And on and on the bad news continued. In early December, Japanese troops seized the U.S. possessions of Guam and Wake Island and occupied British Hong Kong. Meanwhile, MacArthur's force of army regulars and half-trained Philippine Scouts abandoned Manila and retreated to the narrow Bataan Peninsula and the bastion of Corregidor island in Manila Bay. There, cut off from reinforcements, they would hold out for four months, fighting bravely but hopelessly against overwhelming enemy forces.

Through early 1942 the Japanese rampage in the Pacific continued. In January the forces of Emperor Hirohito invaded the Dutch East Indies and overwhelmed its local defenders in a matter of weeks. At the end of the month British troops withdrew from the Malay Peninsula under relentless Japanese attack and retreated to Singapore, the key British naval base in the Far East. On February 15 the Singapore garrison, after a mismanaged defense, unconditionally surrendered, an act that Winston Churchill would call "the greatest disaster" in British history. Later that month the British abandoned Rangoon in Burma (now Myanmar), allowing the Japanese to cut the Burma Road, the principal route for vital supplies to the troops of China's Nationalist leader Chiang Kai-shek, Japan's chief opponent on the Asian mainland. On March 8 Japanese troops came ashore on the vast mountainous island of New Guinea, just north of Australia. An invasion of that island continent, part of the British Commonwealth, now seemed imminent.

Nor did the military landscape on the vast plains of Eastern Europe appear less dire in those early months of war for America. Despite crushing losses of men and equipment during the summer and fall of 1941, in December the Red Army had counterattacked and pushed the Wehrmacht back from the gates of Moscow. But it had not ended the German threat. The Soviet winter gains were limited, and by March the battle lines between the enemies had stabilized. With spring, however, the rested and resupplied German army promised to renew the offensive. In the eyes of the Western Allies, Russia's survival in these months remained in serious doubt, and with it the chances of eventual Anglo-American victory over Hitler.

At home Pearl Harbor ended the careers of both Adm. Husband Kimmel and Gen. Walter Short, chiefs of their respective services in Hawaii. Blamed for neglecting the official warnings of imminent Japanese attack, both men were sacrificed to the public's quest for scapegoats following the December 7 disaster. Admiral Stark also fell victim to public anger after Pearl Harbor. Accused of failing to warn Kimmel in Oahu aggressively enough of imminent danger, he was removed as chief of naval operations and replaced by Ernest King. Marshall survived the post–Pearl Harbor recriminations, but the catastrophe in the Pacific affected him profoundly. According to his biographer Forrest Pogue, Pearl Harbor was one of "the most staggering blows sustained by Marshall in the course of the war."[1]

In these early catastrophic weeks the chief of staff worried particularly about the Philippines, where he had spent much time as a junior officer and where MacArthur and many of his own army friends and colleagues were now caught in the perils of a major war, faced with death or capture. Though army planners had long doubted the ability of the United States to defend the islands from a determined Japanese attack, in the months before Pearl Harbor they had changed their minds and sent MacArthur B-17 bombers and other new military equipment, and promised more, in hopes that a strengthened Philippine bastion might deter, or at least slow, any Japanese Pacific attack. As Marshall described the then new defensive policy to a small trustworthy group of Washington correspondents on November 15, three weeks before Pearl

Harbor the United States, in great secrecy, was "building up its strength in the Philippines to a far higher level than the Japanese imagine." General MacArthur was "unloading ships at night, . . . building airfields in the carefully guarded interior, . . . allowing no one within miles of military reservations."[2]

Unfortunately the chief of staff had not realized till too late how little time remained for a credible military buildup in the islands or how grossly unprepared MacArthur was, psychologically as well as materially, for a major Japanese attack. The crippling blow to the U.S. Navy on December 7 made it obvious that the islands could not be relieved or even reinforced. But the government chose not to be candid with MacArthur. Through the months-long Philippine ordeal, both Marshall and the president misled the general. More planes and supplies were on their way, they assured him. On December 11 Marshall cabled: "We are making every effort to reach you with air replacements and reinforcements as well as other troops and supplies."[3] On the twenty-sixth, after noting the "splendid conduct" of MacArthur's "command and troops," Marshall assured him that "yesterday the President again personally directed the Navy to make every effort to support you." The general could "rest assured the War Department will do all in its power to build up at top speed the air power in the Far East to completely dominate the region."[4] Not until the very end, with final collapse imminent, did they admit that the defenders were on their own.

Yet the failure was not for want of trying. Faced with heartrending pleas from Bataan for more men and supplies, Marshall struggled to find some way to break through the Japanese cordon. The War Department shipped disassembled planes and supplies to Australia, hoping that they could then be sent by commercial freighter to MacArthur. The plan to run the blockade foundered on reality. No private ship captain would risk the job; nor would shipowners offer vessels for hire at any price. A thousand tons of supplies eventually reached the Philippine defenders by submarine, but this met only a tiny fraction of their need.

Though there was no denying the logistical realities, MacArthur and his soldiers could not help feeling abandoned by their countrymen—resentments that have to be taken into account in explaining the later tensions between MacArthur and his boss in Washington.

As a sort of recompense the army promoted MacArthur to four-star general. In January, bowing to public opinion at home and hoping to reassure the nervous Australians now awaiting attack, Roosevelt and Marshall approved a daring rescue of the general, his family, and his staff by swift navy PT boats. Safely in Australia by mid-March, MacArthur was assigned command of all Allied forces in the Southwest Pacific. He would now have a far wider role in the Pacific war than as commander in the Philippines. But driven by survivor's guilt and by a deep sense of loyalty toward the Filipino people and the soldiers left behind, he promised redemption. On his arrival Down Under, the general told reporters in Adelaide that he had been rescued for the purpose of "organizing the American offensive against Japan." A "primary object of that offensive," he noted, was the "relief of the Philippines," and, he famously asserted, "I shall return."[5] For the remainder of the war MacArthur would battle, primarily against the navy, to point the American counteroffensive against Japan due northward through the Philippines.

As he looked on helplessly at the advancing tide of Japanese conquest in the Pacific, Marshall's attention was deflected to the pressing issues of British-American cooperation and grand strategy. It has been said that coalition warfare is the most difficult kind to conduct, and so it has been many times in the past. From this long perspective, the Anglo-American alliance in World War II, the way smoothed by a shared language and a shared institutional and legal history, was a triumph. And yet there would be occasion after occasion during the three and a half years following Pearl Harbor when the interests, goals, and preferences of the two nations would clash and the differences be resolved—only imperfectly—toward the end, primarily by the clear ascendancy of American manpower and matériel. Several of the fault lines between the two nations had already become visible at the Atlantic Conference at Argentia Bay. Now, with America finally in the war, they would take on new meaning and urgency at the marathon "Arcadia" meetings in Washington between Churchill and Roosevelt and the British and American staffs in the fading, fraught days of December 1941 into mid-January 1942.

The Arcadia Conference was the brainchild of Britain's larger-than-life prime minister. Eager to seize the initiative in guiding Allied military strategy now that the United States was on board, on December 22 Churchill and his cohort of experts and top brass arrived in Washington prepared to convince the Yanks that *they*, the more experienced partner, should lead. Above all, they felt that the Allies' motto must remain, without reservation, Europe First, a goal undoubtedly jeopardized by the Japanese attack in the Pacific.

The success of the project, the prime minister believed, depended in large part on establishing cordial relations with the president, and Churchill shamelessly, then and later, cultivated FDR who, at Arcadia at least, allowed himself to be beguiled by the prime minister. As for Marshall and Churchill, according to the historian Andrew Roberts, at Arcadia the chief of staff "started to exercise a fascination over the Prime Minister." Jock Colville, Churchill's private secretary, later noted that "there were few people who could mesmerize Churchill," but "Marshall was one of those few who came close to doing so."[6]

Inevitably, the Americans had their own agenda. Before the "cousins" appeared on the scene the president gathered his chief war advisers, civilian and military, at the White House to discuss the U.S. positions in the forthcoming conference. One of the more prominent topics under consideration was America's possible role in North Africa. Even before Pearl Harbor, FDR had been intrigued by suggestions that either Dakar, directly opposite the great eastward bulge of Brazil, or French North Africa, edging the south shore of the Mediterranean, might be profitable targets for early American military action. Marshall had objected, primarily because of shortages of manpower and equipment. Now, at the pre-Arcadia meetings, with the United States finally at war, the president once more raised the Africa issue, and once more Marshall demurred. With the needs of the Pacific and recently formulated plans to relieve the British garrisons in Iceland and Northern Ireland with American troops, there simply was not enough manpower to go around, he said. And yet in a memo to the president at about this time the chief of staff also speculated that the United States could mount an attack on North Africa, but only if the Vichy authorities would "invite the United States and Great Britain jointly to occupy and defend North Africa," a highly remote likelihood.[7] Having failed to insist that the African options were strategic errors, not merely supply and diplomatic problems, Marshall apparently left FDR with the impression that once the logistical difficulties were solved, one or more of the African operations might be worthy goals. If so, the failure had consequences that Marshall would later regret.

The strategic meetings in Washington between the two national leaders were held at the White House, where the charming, garrulous, bibulous, and self-indulgent prime minister was put up in the East Wing in a bedroom close to both Harry Hopkins and the president himself. FDR and Churchill had lunch together almost every day, often joined by Hopkins, and dined at the White House in the evenings, though these meals were more social. They also met together with both military staffs. The combined staffs, in turn, convened some twelve times at the new Federal Reserve Building on Constitution Avenue. Heading the British delegation at these meetings were First Sea Lord Sir Dudley Pound, Field Marshal Sir John Dill, and Air Marshal A. T. ("Bomber") Harris. In the months to come Marshall would deal extensively especially with the first two. At Arcadia he did not meet his top equivalent on the British side, Alan Brooke, the newly designated chief of the Imperial General Staff (CIGS); he had been left behind in Britain to mind the store. The American contingent, besides Marshall, consisted of Admiral Stark, still chief of naval operations; Admiral King, then commander in chief of the U.S. Fleet; and General Arnold, head of the Army Air Corps.

Now as at Argentia, the experienced British were bursting with detailed plans for the future and, FDR's African musings aside, the Americans were not. Rather, the American planners, though still wary of their allies' apparent obsession with their own imperial needs, were open to suggestion. Churchill and his colleagues from the outset were determined to deflect the understandable, if unspoken, urge of the Americans to concentrate on the Pacific, where they had so recently been treacherously attacked and where they were already grappling with the enemy. In fact, for virtually the rest of the war British leaders would worry that their ally might abandon Europe to channel its energies and resources against Japan. And they had reason to be concerned. Though in the end Stimson, Marshall, and their colleagues would remain committed to defeating Germany first, at times over the next three and a half years, often urged by the navy, they would play the "Pacific First" card to coerce and intimidate the uneasy British at a point of disagreement. Before long they would be joined by MacArthur in Australia, who would fire barrages of demands for redistributing resources to the Pacific from Europe. And perhaps still more worrisome was the state of grassroots American public opinion. It was not easy in the months after Pearl Harbor to explain to average midcontinent citizens why their country's war effort was centered on Germany and Italy when it was Japan that had perfidiously attacked the United States. In fact polls in the weeks immediately following Pearl Harbor showed that as many as 25 percent of the American public favored an immediate end of the war with Germany through negotiation. Some 10 percent even endorsed peace with Germany on any terms.

In all, then, the British could not be certain of their ally's resolution, and Churchill's strategy proposals at the opening session of leaders and staffs at the White House on December 23 sought to reinforce the Europe First principle. Germany, the PM announced, must be the chief target of the Allies' war effort, while in the Pacific theater they must conduct only a holding action. Despite all the British doubts, however, at the Arcadia meetings there was no overt divergence on this issue; the Americans had already accepted Europe as the primary theater. But the prime minister also made it clear that the British version of Europe First differed from the American. Britain was a sea power, not a land power. With the exception of the disastrous 1914–18 experience in France, it had not sent large armies to the Continent in the past; it had historically relied on allies to do its ground fighting. And what, in the end, had that deviation from traditional practice during the Great War brought but the slaughter of an entire generation of young Britons? In the months leading up to D-Day, the Allied invasion of Normandy, British planners were haunted by images of mangled Tommies strewn on the Flanders fields, as had happened a generation before, or their massed corpses bobbing in the Channel. And the British lacked the resources for a full-throated cross-Channel invasion. A nation of forty-eight million in 1941, with a GDP one-third of America's, two years after the onset of war Britain had almost reached the limits of its manpower and matériel reserves. If there was to be a cross-Channel invasion the Americans must inevitably lead it.

Now in Washington, Churchill explained that the Allies must rely on a campaign of attrition, as hinted at in Argentia, not a direct confrontation with the enemy's military might. Germany should be subjected to a rigorous naval blockade and devastating air bombardment while the subjugated peoples of German-occupied Europe were incited to rise up against their conquerors. Meanwhile, opportunistic limited sorties, particularly if German power faltered, should be launched directly against Hitler's forces on the Continent, in part to help the beleaguered Soviet Union. Finally, perhaps in 1943, there might be a major Allied invasion of the occupied Continent itself. In later months the Allies would argue boisterously over whether the centerpiece of their grand strategy should be a mass cross-Channel assault or nibbles at the edges. In these debates the Americans might have confronted the PM with Gallipoli in 1915, when First Lord of the Admiralty Winston Churchill had sought to finesse the lethal head-on assault deployed in France with a "peripheral" strategy that had served England so well in the past. That attempt to knock Turkey out of the war had been a disaster; it had not helped to avoid the murderous trench warfare in France and Belgium or advanced the Allied cause one inch. Fortunately for Anglo-American comity at Arcadia in 1941 no one was willing to mention that embarrassing precedent. In the end Arcadia would nail down Europe First as Anglo-American policy but leave unsettled the way that strategy would be expressed. The resulting uncertainty would fuel many months of debate and raise a cloud of confusion, resentment, and outright rancor.

Yet even as they wrangled over Europe, the conferees in Washington could not ignore the disaster unfolding in the Pacific. To meet the danger the Allies agreed to establish a Pacific command to be called the ABDA after the American, British, Dutch, and Australian national jurisdictions and forces in the theater of operations. It was at this point that Marshall made his chief contribution to the conference. Starting with the ABDA, all theaters of war, he urged, should be subject to a "unity of command" principle, by which a single designated commander of whatever service, of whatever nationality, would organize and execute all operations, including those on land, sea, and air, of all the forces engaged. Marshall cited his own experience in support of his bold proposal. It represented, he declared, his "personal views and not those as a result of consulting with the Navy" or even with his "own War Plans Division." The scheme was inspired, he noted, by what he "saw in France" in the previous war, where until the Allies chose the French general Ferdinand Foch, in 1918, as supreme commander of the Allied armies, "much valuable time, blood, and treasure was needlessly sacrificed." But Marshall proposed to go even beyond that precedent. Foch had been assigned primarily a coordinating function: He did not have the authority to give orders to his British and American allies. The proposed new supreme commander would have this power in his theater. "I am convinced," Marshall noted, "that there must be one man in command of the entire theater—air, ground, and ships." "Human frailties," he acknowledged, "are such that there would be emphatic unwillingness to place portions of troops under another service." But if adopted, the plan "would be a great advance over what was accomplished during the World War."[8]

The British at first balked at the proposal. Churchill objected that the experience of the Great War was not relevant. Unlike the Western Front in World War I, where there was a continuous line of battle, in the current Far East the Allied forces were widely scattered. Besides, the final authority would be even more concentrated than in Foch's day. The British admirals were also skeptical. The Royal Navy was, as its American counterpart, not willing to surrender its autonomy in any theater of operations to an army or air corps general, even one of their own, who obviously could not fully understand the special nature of naval operations. As for CIGS, though not present in Washington to object, he, too, was uneasy with the unity-of-command principle and would largely remain so through the war.

Churchill finally yielded to strong pressure from Roosevelt and Marshall. The American chief of staff, the PM wrote to his cabinet colleagues, had come with Hopkins to his White House room and "pleaded his case with great conviction," and he had yielded.[9] Katherine would later colorfully depict the occasion, with—as she learned from her husband—Churchill in his White House room "propped up in bed with his work board resting against his knees and his ever present cigar in his mouth or swung like a baton to emphasize his points."[10] The American navy, though never fully reconciled to the scheme, also yielded. Thereafter, through the rest of the war in each theater there would be one general (or admiral)—a "supreme commander"—responsible for the Allied operations to defeat the enemy.

Though at times challenged, and in practice sometimes relaxed, the system overall would work well. Given the special hazards of coalition warfare, it was probably indispensable to final victory. Marshall considered it "basic to the whole control of the war" and one of his chief contributions to that victory.[11] And indeed it was; he deserves unstinting praise for its achievement. But it did not invariably produce successful results. During the conference itself, in the first instance of unified command, the British general Sir Archibald Wavell, initially victorious over the Italians in North Africa, was, at Marshall's suggestion, chosen as chief of operations of the ABDA theater, with his mission defined as holding the "Malay Barrier" against further Japanese advance. Unfortunately the mission quickly collapsed. It took only a few weeks for the barrier to crumble as Japan's early momentum carried its forces past the Allies' key defensive points. By the end of February the command's headquarters in Java was overrun by the Japanese. ABDA was dissolved soon after and the Pacific theater redivided so that its western portion was assigned to MacArthur, now headquartered in Australia.

Arcadia produced another important command innovation. Clearly there had to be some final link in the joint military chain of command. It had been agreed early on that there would be a top military council to represent both British and American staffs, called the Combined Chiefs of Staff (CCS). (In the event, it would convene primarily at major Allied strategic conferences.) Foreshadowing the inevitable American preeminence, the Combined Chiefs would be headquartered in Washington, where the British would be represented by a Joint Staff Mission. For most of the war this group would be headed by the genial field marshal John Dill, whom Churchill considered too lackluster and pessimistic and had fired as CIGS in London, replacing him with Brooke. Since the RAF would be represented on the Combined Chiefs, it proved necessary to elevate Hap Arnold to that body, though the U.S. Air Corps remained officially only a subordinate branch of the army. The first meeting of the CCS would convene on February 9, and it thereafter would function by and large successfully. Meeting some two hundred times during the war, it effectively coordinated the strategies of the two allies. Churchill later noted that it was at these sessions "that the most important [military] decisions were taken."[12] Though its power to override national preferences was unprecedented, even the skeptical Gen-

eral Brooke agreed in the end that the CCS was "the most efficient [organization] that had ever been evolved for coordinating
and correlating the war strategy and effort of two allies."[13]

Among the few specific Atlantic-oriented military operations
proposed at Arcadia was a British plan, code-named Gymnast,
that coincided with FDR's scheme to invade Vichy-controlled
North Africa. The plan ignored Marshall's diplomatic and logistical reservations. Churchill believed the ostensibly neutral
French forces there might welcome an American landing in Morocco. Moreover, having recently defeated Mussolini's ill-led, ill-
equipped troops in Libya, the British, he claimed, could contribute to the operation some fifty thousand troops already in place.
Between the two nations, all of North Africa might drop like a
ripe fruit into Allied hands.

The Gymnast proposal was the germ of the later British-
American invasion of French North Africa, and from the outset
many American military planners remained skeptical. For one,
the Anglophobic General Embick, still Marshall's senior strategy
adviser, was sure that UK politics—to protect the Suez Canal and
Britain's lifeline to India—were the real motives behind the plan.
As for its viability, Embick insisted, the British claim that control of the southern shore of the Mediterranean would "afford an
advantageous area from which to launch an invasion of Europe"
was a delusion.[14] Marshall kept quiet on the North Africa issue,
remaining strangely indecisive at Arcadia. At one point in the discussion of North Africa he did directly object, but obliquely and
on political rather than strategic grounds. Asked by Roosevelt
whether it would be feasible for American troops to land at Casablanca if the French chose to resist, Marshall declared that the
operation would be "extremely hazardous" and its failure would
have a "very detrimental effect on the morale of the American
people."[15]

A consummate politician, the president saw such a result as the very opposite of his intentions. Whether or not wise strategically, it made sense domestically, both politically and psychologically. The U.S. armed forces were expanding at a furious pace. They had to be used. The voters were impatient; they wanted action; the troops must be not allowed to remain idle in the Atlantic area, certainly not if Germany's defeat was to be the country's first priority. With the president pushing them, American planners refined the details of a possible "Northwest Africa Project," noting the need for far more troops than the original British estimate and the difficulty of finding sufficient shipping to move large forces from the continental United States to the French North African colonies. In the end the planning at Arcadia for a North African invasion ended without a firm conclusion, the issue to be raised in more urgent form months down the road with many of the same arguments marshaled, for and against, as at Washington during the winter of 1941–42.

The final meeting of Arcadia dealt with allocating munitions production quotas among the Allies. Marshall insisted that the new Munitions Assignment Board to be created be placed under the authority of the CCS and not divided between London and Washington. So strongly did he feel about this matter that he told FDR, Churchill, and the staffers present that if his view was not accepted he would resign as chief of staff. Marshall's impassioned plea produced a compromise: The single board would be tried for a month and then evaluated. This satisfied Marshall, and ultimately his scheme worked so well that it was retained for the remainder of the war.

Besides its primary strategy-planning mission, Arcadia provided an opportunity to formalize the emerging coalition of anti-Axis powers. Calling themselves the "United Nations," in Washington twenty-six countries at war with one or all of the

Axis nations—including the United States, Britain and its dominions, China, the European governments-in-exile, and the Soviet Union—pledged to fight and defeat "the . . . forces of conquest" in the name of "life, liberty, independence, as well as the righteous possibilities of human freedom, justice and social security . . . throughout the world," and to coordinate their military efforts to these ends. Little more initially than a convenient tab for the wartime anti-Axis coalition, the UN became the germ of the international peacekeeping body organized in 1945 at San Francisco to replace the failed League of Nations. Marshall had nothing to do with the UN's creation; at Arcadia British-American war strategy was his sole concern. He would, however, later be intricately involved in the affairs of the postwar international body.

Churchill had intended to leave Washington in a week, but his stay was extended to include a visit to Canada to address the parliament in Ottawa, and a weeklong trip to Florida to relax in the sun. After dinner with Hopkins and FDR on January 14 Churchill finally left for home by plane. He could be satisfied that much had been achieved to cement the alliance between the two English-speaking nations, but he had little reason to be happy at the way the war was going. Japan's easy victories over imperial forces in the Far East had shaken the British people's confidence. A failed operation in mid-1941 to rescue Greece from German invaders only demonstrated once again Britain's skill in evacuations. The regiments sent to Greece had weakened the forces of Gen. Claude Auchinleck, Wavell's successor in North Africa. The initial British gains against Italian marshal Rodolfo Graziani in Libya were soon being reversed by troops under Gen. Erwin Rommel, now arriving to rescue the Germans' ineffectual Italian allies. Whatever had been achieved in Washington, when Churchill returned home he would have to face angry critics in the House of Commons.

Arcadia had not laid out a road map for the war. But if the next move was not to be French North Africa, then where would the Allies strike? As the weeks passed with no effective American action against the Axis, public opinion at home, briefly united by Pearl Harbor, began to fragment. Apathy toward the war, or Pacific First sentiment, took hold, especially in the Midwestern isolationist belt. Meanwhile, Admiral King began to push for more of the nation's limited military resources to be allotted to the Pacific.

One answer to the puzzle of "what next" was provided by Dwight Eisenhower, the fifty-one-year-old officer whose talents Marshall had spotted at the 1941 General Headquarters maneuvers, had befriended, and had recently brought to Washington to head the Army's War Plans Division to replace Gen. Leonard Gerow, who Marshall believed "was growing stale from overwork."[16] In a late February 1942 paper and in a memorandum prepared some weeks later, Ike laid out a well-argued blueprint for an Anglo-American war strategy. Though he devoted some space to the Pacific theater, his focus was on the Atlantic. But Ike rejected the southern coast of the Mediterranean as the major theater of operations. In line with Marshall's thinking he concluded that the best way to defeat the Axis was an "attack through Western Europe," with England serving as the operations base.[17]

A vital piece of his reasoning was Russia's continuing plight. In early 1942 and for months thereafter, the outcome of the titanic struggle between the Soviet Union and Hitler's Reich remained in serious doubt. As expected, after pausing for the winter the German offensive had resumed with major advances into the Caucasus, which threatened the vital Russian oil supply and even promised to bring German divisions into contact with Japanese forces moving westward against Burma and India. Not until the winter of 1943, at remote Stalingrad, would the German army suffer a major defeat. Yet even after the victory at Stalingrad, in their savage struggle to survive the Russians would sustain immense losses in manpower and economic resources and at times barely hold on.

Marshall and his colleagues fully understood the vital role of Russia in the war against the German enemy. Army planners had told the president in late December that "Russia alone possesses the manpower potentially able to defeat Germany in Europe." They were preaching to the already fully converted. That March FDR wrote to Secretary Morgenthau: "Nothing would be worse than to have the Russians collapse. I would rather lose New Zealand, Australia, or anything else than have the Russians collapse."[18] The Western Allies had accepted the necessity to supply the Soviet Union with as much war matériel as they could spare, transporting the bulk of it by sea, despite remorseless U-boat attack and heavy losses, to Murmansk and other Russian Arctic ports. But to Stalin and his colleagues this effort was not enough. What Russia needed was a "second front," a powerful Allied attack in the West against Nazi-occupied Europe that would draw off many Nazi divisions from their murderous work in the East. British and American planners, then, were fully alert to Russia's critical role in the struggle with Germany and feared for their own fate if it went under. Recalling perhaps the disastrous Russian surrender to the Germans in 1917, in his March memorandum Eisenhower had keeping Russia in the war very much in mind. Russia "must not be permitted," he wrote, "to reach such a precarious position that she will accept negotiated peace, no matter how unfavorable to herself, in preference to a continuation of the fight."[19]

Eisenhower's memos solidified the thinking of army planners and strongly influenced the chief of staff himself. The historian Richard Steele claims that they "marked the end of the army's ambivalence toward the peripheral strategy and the beginnings of unified, consistent support of the immediate concentration of American forces preparatory to an assault on German-held territory."[20] Steele overstates the case, but the memos undoubtedly clarified Marshall's and the War Department's thinking.

Marshall wasted no time conveying his new resolve to the president. On March 25, along with King, Stimson, Knox, Arnold, and Hopkins, he lunched at the White House and presented Eisenhower's suggestions to FDR. His was not the only perspective proposed that day. King had just written the president a note warning against neglecting the Pacific. Playing the race card that was never entirely absent from the Pacific-Atlantic debate, he declared that the United States could not allow Japan to conquer the "white man's countries" of Australia and New Zealand "because of the repercussions among the non-white races of the world."[21] If FDR was immune to the racial argument, he was not indifferent to the navy's perspectives, and initially endorsed a Pacific First approach. But he was obviously uncertain of his direction and seized on Eisenhower's memo when Marshall brought it to his attention at the meeting. Would the chief of staff work out the details? he asked. The War Department planners quickly assembled a document for FDR's consideration.

The proposal Marshall submitted later that day, though it has been called the "Marshall Memorandum," was not his alone. It had been worked on and worked over by Eisenhower and several planning staffers in the War Department. It was more specific and more decisive than Marshall's previous versions of Europe First. The document vigorously defended an early cross-Channel second front and sketched out the scope of the operation, including the possible area of the Allied landings, their timing, and the forces to be used. It also divided the operation into several distinct phases and provided names for each. As phase one of the plan, it proposed putting ashore Allied forces on the French coast

as early as the fall of 1942. Labeled Sledgehammer, this operation would not, however, be the massive cross-Channel assault
against the Wehrmacht designed to deliver the coup de grâce to
Germany. Rather, it would be a large-scale raid that would draw
German troops and planes from the eastern front and thereby
relieve the excruciating military pressure on the Soviet Union.
The true second front, Roundup—the British-American cross-
Channel invasion in force—would come in mid-1943. Both operations would be preceded by Bolero, a massive buildup in Britain
of American combat divisions along with their equipment and
3,200 warplanes. FDR gave it his stamp of approval when Marshall and Stimson brought the detailed proposal to the White
House, authorizing the chief of staff and Hopkins to proceed
quickly to Britain to clear the proposal with the "former naval
person"—that is, the British prime minister.

The joint mission to London in early April was a bare-bones
affair. Besides Marshall and Hopkins it included as Marshall's
planning aide Albert Wedemeyer, the Victory Program author,
but few others. Marshall and the colonel traveled in civilian
clothes aboard an amphibious Boeing "flying boat," the only plane
then in commercial transatlantic service. Landing in Northern
Ireland after a freezing twenty-four-hour flight, the Americans
were whisked off to grimy, bombed-out, war-worn London to
meet Churchill and General Brooke. Marshall and Brooke, the
top commanders in their respective armies, would meet many
times subsequently, both as collaborators and opponents.

As an adversary Brooke was a formidable figure. A small, sar-
donic, dark-eyed, dark-haired Anglo-Irish Ulsterman of distinguished
military lineage (with a very British passion for birdwatching),
Brooke had fought in France in 1940 and had helped organize the
extraordinary Dunkirk evacuation that saved the British army after
the Allied rout. Another prominent British general, Bernard Mont-

gomery, would later call him "the greatest soldier—soldier, sailor, airman—produced by any country" during the war.[22] In December 1941 Churchill appointed him to replace Dill. An outwardly dour, rather supercilious man, the new CIGS was skeptical of the Americans from the start. They had, he would note, never encountered the German army and did not know how formidable a fighting machine it was. Absent from Arcadia, he had never met Marshall, and was now not overly impressed with him. Writing in his diary on April 9 he noted: "I liked what I saw of Marshall, a pleasant and easy man to get on with, rather over-filled with his own importance. But I should not put him down as a great man." Brooke and his colleagues were scornful of Sledgehammer, whose chief burden would have to be borne by British troops since few trained Americans were yet available. In his later comment on this original diary entry, Brooke would remark: "In the light of the existing situation his [Marshall's] plans for September of 1942 were just fantastic! Marshall had a long way to go at that time before realizing what we were faced with."[23] The observant Hopkins did not need to read Brooke's diary to perceive his doubts; Brooke had said enough for him to "indicate that he had a great many misgivings."[24]

Despite their reservations, the British were initially happy to embrace the American proposals. If nothing else, Bolero reinforced the American commitment to Britain and to Europe. But in London the Americans quickly learned, or rather relearned, that British priorities were different from their own. Defeating the Axis remained of course their shared primary interest, but Britain's specific agenda—understandably—did in fact include preserving its prewar empire. Protecting the Mediterranean lifeline to the Persian Gulf, India, and the Far East would at times obscure the larger goal. But more to the point, they were terrified that the cross-Channel operation as proposed by the Americans would be a disaster.

Now, at meetings at Downing Street and at Chequers, Churchill's country estate, that often lasted till early morning, Marshall and Hopkins argued with the PM and Brooke over the American proposals. The British forcefully attacked Sledgehammer, which they perceived as a more ambitious operation than Eisenhower, at least, had intended. How could it possibly succeed? Most of the troops at this stage, Brooke reminded the Americans, would have to be British, and no more than seven infantry and two armored divisions could be mustered for the operation. These forces, even if successfully landed, could not hold out against a concerted German counterattack. They would not be "strong enough to maintain a bridgehead against the scale of attack which the Germans could bring against it," and it was "unlikely that we could extricate the forces if the Germans made a really determined effort to drive us out."[25] Churchill emphatically agreed. As he would later write in his massive history of World War II, "The Allies would be penned up in Cherbourg and the tip of the Cotentin peninsula and would have to maintain themselves in this confined bomb and shell trap for nearly a year under ceaseless bombardment and assault."[26]

And Brooke and the prime minister were certainly right. Sledgehammer was a suicide mission. Given their limited resources of skill, numbers, matériel, and shipping, the Allies were not realistically prepared in mid-1942 to cross the English Channel in force and take on the Germans entrenched behind massive fortifications, especially on Cotentin or in the Pas-de-Calais area where the landings were to be effected. No better evidence for Sledgehammer's folly was the outcome of the Dieppe Raid in mid-August, when, by orders of the overimaginative Lord Louis Mountbatten, British chief of Combined Operations, a force of six thousand predominantly Canadian troops landed at Dieppe on the French Channel coast to test German defenses and collect intelligence. More than half the attackers were killed or captured, while the RAF lost 106 planes to the Luftwaffe's 48. The disaster would starkly disclose the hazards of any cross-Channel operation against *Festung Europa* so early in the process of the Bolero resource buildup and the American troop-training process.

If better disguised, British skepticism also extended to Roundup, the later main thrust, as well. That phase lacked strategic understanding, CIGS wrote in his diary. It did "not go beyond just landing on the far coast!! Whether we are to play baccarat or chemin de fer at Le Touquet, or possibly bathe at Paris Plage is not stipulated!" he wrote sarcastically. "I asked him [Marshall] this afternoon, do we go east, south or west after landing? He had not begun to think of it!!" Moreover, Brooke insisted, the proposal did not take into account logistical realities. As Brooke later observed: "With the situation prevailing at that time it was not possible to take Marshall's 'castles in the air' too seriously!" The availability of shipping was another problem. "We were desperately short of shipping and could stage no large scale operation without additional shipping." And this issue directly affected the choice of Axis targets. It "could only be obtained by opening the Mediterranean and saving a million tons of shipping through elimination of the Cape [of Good Hope] route." Brooke was not opposed, he claimed, to an eventual direct ground attack on Germany. "We might certainly start preparing for the European offensive," he added, "but such plans must not be allowed to interfere with the successive stages of operations essential to the execution of this plan."[27]

Brooke eventually came to respect and honor Marshall as a man, but after these discussions he would consistently dismiss him as a strategic mediocrity. The American chief of staff, he noted, was "a good general at raising armies and providing the necessary links between the military and political worlds. But his strategical ability does not impress me at all!!" He went on, "In fact, in many respects he is a very dangerous man whilst being a very charming one."[28] Not all the British military leaders were as critical of Marshall as Brooke. Gen. Hastings Ismay, Churchill's personal military adviser and link to the CCS, would be more generous, though he like many others emphasized the American's strength of character rather than his military acumen. As Ismay later wrote, "Marshall was a big man in every sense of the word, and utterly selfless. It was impossible to imagine his doing anything petty or mean, or shrinking from any duty, however distasteful." He agreed that he was "somewhat cold and aloof" at first. "But he had a warm heart, demonstrated, he confessed, by his pain when forced to fire a subordinate for incompetence."[29]

Still brooding over the humiliating British defeat in the Norway campaign of the previous year, Churchill privately preferred a scheme to invade northern Norway (Operation Jupiter) that even his own generals thought dimwitted. But the volatile PM still feared the Americans might turn to the Pacific as a course that made political sense to them. He also did not want to offend his new friend, the American president, who had approved the Marshall Memorandum, and at an all-night session on April 14, the PM agreed to "offensive action in 1942, perhaps, and in 1943 for certain," while still expressing fear of a linkage of the Germans advancing eastward through the Middle East and the Japanese westward though India.[30]

Despite all the warning signs of underlying dissent, Marshall unaccountably expressed satisfaction with the Anglo-American discussions at this April meeting in Britain. He and Hopkins both believed they had reached a firm agreement about Roundup. Marshall admitted he was somewhat less certain about Sledgehammer, but the Americans left England generally pleased with the overall results. In fact it is now known that the British leaders had not been candid with the Americans. However frank in his diary, Brooke had failed to convey fully in person his dismay at the American proposals. And the British deception, apparently, went beyond CIGS. As General Ismay later wrote: "Everyone seemed to agree with the American proposals in their entirety. No doubts were expressed; no discordant note struck." But, he added, "I think we should have come clean; much cleaner than we did."[31] The dissimulation was compounded by a cable from Churchill to FDR on April 12. In a review of the discussions at Chequers, he lavished praise on the American plan. "I am in entire agreement in principle with all you propose," he wrote, "and so are the Chiefs of Staff." If, he added, "as our experts believe, we can carry this whole plan through successfully, it will be one of the grand events in all the history of war."[32] And the PM not only endorsed the full-throttled cross-Channel invasion for 1943, but Sledgehammer as well. In truth, America's allies did not intend to go through with Sledgehammer and even had reservations about Roundup. For the next two years the British would continue to blow hot and cold on Roundup (later renamed Overlord), to the despair of the Americans.

And, though devious, they were right to question seriously the proposed 1942 attack. It was in fact grossly premature. Pressing for Sledgehammer in 1942 was a serious error in judgment on Marshall's part. Steele's conclusion is convincing:

> Responsibility for the fumbling American strategy-making and its near disastrous results rests mainly with the chief of Staff. He was in a position to know the facts that made SLEDGEHAMMER a false vision, yet continued to press for the operation long after the high costs and probable negative results were apparent. To the extent the President depended on Marshall for military on the first offensive, he was ill-served.[33]

Marshall, then, was clearly wrong to push Sledgehammer as a key part of the American strategy that he and Hopkins brought to Churchill and Brooke that April. His defenders have insisted that the chief of staff thought the operation justified only if German successes became "so complete as to threaten the imminent collapse of Russian resistance." It would then be "a sacrifice in the common good."[34] But how could such an acute observer of American public opinion as Marshall believe that a bloody defeat on the French beaches so early in the war could avoid being a political disaster to American leadership, civilian and military, and not have serious consequences for the entire conduct of the war? His myopia can only be explained by the profound American fears of Soviet collapse and its consequences. In hindsight, the issue is further muddied by the reality of the astonishing Russian military turnaround at Stalingrad that winter of 1942, making the second front militarily—though surely not politically—irrelevant.

On April 18, before returning to Washington, Marshall visited American troops in Northern Ireland. Just before flying back the next day he sent a top-secret message to the president: "I think our trip has been successful"[35] He was mistaken. In the end Sledgehammer was never carried out. The British, for their own cautious reasons, would rescue Marshall from an almost certain military catastrophe.

Amid the strategic trials and acute professional anxieties of early 1942, private life for the Marshalls went on apace. They lived simply at Quarters No. 1 at Fort Myer, close to the War Department, still headquartered at the old Munitions Building. Repelled by the capital's social whirl, Marshall learned how to deflect the engagements and speaking requests that came in a flood after his appointment as chief of staff. For those parties he could not avoid he invented an effective dodge: arrive early for cocktails, chat with the hostess and a few guests, and arrange to be called away by emergency messenger as soon as possible. Meanwhile, Katherine was up to her hairline performing as a good army wife, attending meetings, serving on committees, constantly on the telephone for some cause to benefit military wives and families, while at the same time keeping in touch with widely scattered members of her own family. In September, before Pearl Harbor, she slipped on a loose porch rug and broke four ribs. She recuperated too slowly to suit her husband, who fretted that she was spending too much time and effort on duties and not taking enough rest for a speedy recovery.

In his private capacity Marshall was not a traditional "family man" deeply immersed in domesticity and well connected to relatives. His job, peripatetic and crisis driven, would not have permitted it at this point in his life—or, for that matter, ever after. But more than this reality, his own parents were dead, and he was never close to his brother, Stuart, though he kept in affectionate touch with his sister, Marie, now Mrs. John J. Singer. Over the years, however, the childless Marshall did develop ties to his stepchildren, Molly, Clifton, and Allen. Katherine's children were now already in their twenties and had embarked on adult lives. In 1942 all were directly or indirectly associated with the military. Molly, a new mother, was married to Maj. James Winn, a field artillery officer. In mid-1942 the Winns were living at Fort Bragg, North Carolina, where James was commander of the Fourth Field Artillery Battalion. Clifton was in Army Officer Candidate School, and the youngest, Allen, also married and a father, was a trainee at the Armored School at Fort Knox and, after attending OCS, would be commissioned a second lieutenant in the tank corps.

Marshall followed a strict hands-off policy regarding his military stepsons and son-in-law, a practice that Allen, for one, applauded. But not Katherine. She could not help intruding where she could to advance her children's interests. Allen asked his mother to back off, but, Marshall noted in a letter of September 1942, "whether or not she will scrupulously carry out your request I do not know."[36] Marshall's self-denying policy did not preclude offering professional advice to his military children, however. In this same letter the chief of staff suggested that the tank corps would suit Allen: "I think you would find your interest greatly stimulated there and a fertile field for the future as a commissioned officer."[37] It was advice that Marshall would surely come to regret.

In 1940 Katherine bought Dodona Manor, in Leesburg, Virginia, thirty-five miles from Washington. Located in "a quaint and very old Virginia town," the estate was, Katherine proudly wrote, "as unreconstructed a place as you could find, alluringly replete with tradition and history."[38] The main residence was a two-and-a-half-story white-painted brick house with a four-column portico. The entrance survived from 1786, though the house itself dated from the early nineteenth century. It had been renovated by a previous owner, but there remained much work to do on the grounds to make the property comely and comfortable. During the general's April absence in England, Katherine hired a flock of landscapers and contractors to build a garage, construct brick walkways, and tear down unsightly old sheds and outbuildings. The work was done in time for Marshall's return from Britain. After a brief stop at his office, the chief of staff drove down with Katherine to Leesburg. Marshall examined the property as if on a military tour of inspection and declared himself pleased: "This is home, a real home after forty-one years of wandering," he announced.[39] Marshall would find that Dodona Manor eminently suited his self-image, and he would retire there as a Virginia squire after his many years of public service.

When Marshall was not busy arguing America's strategic case

to his British allies and mapping out sweeping military initiatives, he was superintending a vast bureaucracy with literally millions of clients and thousands of managers. His job required improving the efficiency and effectiveness of an agency growing exponentially and charged with turning hordes of callow American civilians into fighting men capable of facing the veterans of the Axis, supplying them with the food, transportation, moral support, and weapons needed for their tasks, and finding officers fit to lead them in battle.

The first priority for Marshall on assuming his rank as chief of staff in 1939 was to streamline a creaky, decrepit army structure in which, despite the reforms earlier in the century, Civil War agencies and practices lingered on. As Marshall noted just after the war, the general staff, created as part of Elihu Root's reforms in 1903, had "become a huge, bureaucratic, red-tape-ridden oper-ating agency" that "slowed down everything."[40] Specifically, too many officers had direct access to the chief, while heads of au-tonomous agencies and offices jealously guarded their entrenched privileges. These arrangements entangled the chief and his three deputies in endless details and petty disagreements. It took days to get "a paper through the War Department," Marshall wrote soon after Pearl Harbor. "Everybody had to concur."[41] Recogniz-ing the immensity of the task, in late November 1941 Marshall recalled Joseph McNarney, now a general based in London, to head a department reorganization committee. A frank, laconic air corps officer who had graduated from West Point in Eisenhower's class, McNarney quickly chopped out much of the underbrush that had clogged decision making in the War Department. He and his deputies abolished outright the agency of the chief of arms and cut back the powers of the chiefs of infantry, cavalry, field ar-tillery, and coast artillery. The number of individuals who would have direct access to the chief of staff was reduced from sixty to six and three new commands—Army Ground Forces, Army Air

Forces, and Army Services Forces—to serve under Gens. Lesley McNair, Hap Arnold, and Brehon Somervell, respectively—were created.

Newly installed in office, Marshall ruthlessly slashed deadwood from the existing officer corps. He remembered Pershing's troubles with incompetent officers in 1917–18 and resolved to do better. When, in an October 1939 off-the-record interview, the military columnist George Fielding Eliot asked the newly appointed chief of staff how he intended to avoid Lincoln's long, frustrating quest for a winning general during the Civil War, Marshall acknowledged that "the present officers of the line" were mostly "too old to command troops in battle under the terrific pressures of modern war." Their minds, he noted, were set in "outmoded patterns," and could not change to meet new conditions if the United States became involved in a European war. He did "not propose to send our young citizen-soldiers into action . . . under commanders whose minds are no longer adaptable to the making of split-second decisions in the fast moving war of today."[42]

Even before appointment, as deputy chief of staff, Marshall had sought to replace the seniority system for officers' promotion with one based on merit. "I wanted to be able to put your finger on the man you wanted, and he would work like the devil . . . instead of being interested in something, besides the two cars and his wife's bathrooms he wanted at the end of his career."[43] Fortunately, over the years he had kept track of men who had impressed him as bold, intelligent, loyal, and, preferably, young. Initially he drew heavily for the surging ranks of officers on men he had met and admired in France or at Fort Leavenworth. It has often been said that Marshall was an incomparable judge of military talent. Omar Bradley, one of his choices for top leadership, later wrote: "In the choice of his commanders General Marshall evinced his almost unerring judgement of men."[44] And the recent military author Thomas Ricks would more or less agree. "While sometimes mistaken," he writes, "the Marshall system generally achieved its goal of producing military effectiveness."[45]

Yet in fact the selection process did not work as well as Bradley and Ricks believed. More than occasionally Marshall was dismayed when, elevated to new wartime responsibilities, his choices failed the competence test. In the end the quality of Marshall's selections was mixed. On the one hand we note the names of fighting generals Patton, Robert Eichelberger, Courtney Hodges, J. Lawton Collins, and Lucian Truscott. Among his appointments as administrators were distinguished performers like Somervell, whom Marshall made head of the new Services of Supply, and of course Dwight Eisenhower, whom he would elevate to top leadership in both the Mediterranean and for Overlord. But he was far from infallible, and there would be more than a few duds and mediocrities on the list of those he favored.

As a salient feature of Marshall's reorganization of War Department and army personnel, he insisted that his subordinates, including combat commanders, be autonomous, self-activating agents. His formula with both generals and civilian aides was: "You know what the right thing to do is, so do it; don't bother me." The approach is perhaps best illustrated by his initial relations with Dwight Eisenhower, whom, just days after Pearl Harbor, he brought to Washington to head the Far East section of the Army's War Plans Division. In his Munitions Building office he had briefed the new brigadier on the perilous status of the American military and naval position in the Pacific and asked him to outline what he thought the strategic response should be. Directed to an empty desk in the War Plans Division, Eisenhower quickly managed to come up with a few written suggestions; when he showed them to his boss, Marshall said, "I agree with you." Then the chief of staff explained his management theory:

"Eisenhower, the Department is filled with able men who analyze their problems well but feel compelled always to bring them to me for final solution. I must have assistants who will solve their own problems and tell me later what they have done."[46]

This early example of delegated authority was not aberrant. It remained Marshall's management style through his entire public career, often disconcerted his colleagues and subordinates—and at times served him ill. Marshall justified his hands-off policy as a way to reduce bureaucratic red tape and preserve his time for high-level decisions. But it was also a way to conserve his own limited energies and uncertain health. The doctors had warned him even before the First World War to avoid overwork, and he had responded by restricting himself to a modest daily schedule that often ended at three or four o'clock in the afternoon. This habit, too, at times troubled observers, especially those who encountered it for the first time.

Changes in army personnel policy are never achieved without cost. And so it was with the early personnel housecleaning. Some officers forced into retirement with reduced benefits never forgave the chief of staff for their plight.

Marshall proposed one more major reform to improve the structure of military command at the very top. Because the air corps, an army subdivision, was represented on the Joint Chiefs of Staff, the navy was, in effect, outvoted. To even the score the president, he felt, should appoint a chairman for the Joint Chiefs from the navy. Though an admiral, this person, Marshall anticipated, would serve as a "neutral agency" to minimize interservice disputes. Marshall had a preference for the post: Adm. William D. Leahy, then U.S. Ambassador to the Vichy French government. Roosevelt was frankly puzzled by Marshall's proposal for another member of the Joint Chiefs, but agreed to go along. In the end Leahy ended up being FDR's personal representative, his "legman," much like Hopkins, rather than an autonomously functioning member of the Joint Chiefs, a development that did not please Marshall entirely.[47]

As the uniformed head of the army one of Marshall's most critical functions was converting millions of young American civilians into soldiers. The Victory Program had projected training some 8.8 million men to serve in the army, with approximately 2 million of that number in the air force. As a manpower blueprint the program had serious flaws. In any case, it said nothing about how these men were to be made into soldiers. Marshall had more than a little experience with training men to fight. His work in the thirties CCC camps had taught him how to impose discipline and order on raw civilians. His many dealings with the National Guard had provided further lessons, as had the rebellious OHIO movement of 1941. By the time he became head of the U.S. Army he had developed some strong views regarding the proper way to create a powerful military force out of the human material available in the country.

First, he felt, traditional forms of discipline must be revised. In place of the "monotonous drilling which . . . achieved obedience at the expense of initiative," and "excluded 'thought' of any kind," he favored "respect rather than fear; the effect of good example by officers; and the intelligent comprehension of all ranks of why an order has to be and why it must be carried out."[48] Easier said than done. Yet Marshall understood that morale was all-important and tried to achieve these ends. He sought to improve the safety of his men by replacing the shallow helmets of World War I doughboys with the deeper, more protective steel "pots" seen in the pictures of their World War II GI successors. When a visit to a small Southern army-base town showed him the squalid off-duty recreation facilities available for men at the nearby post, he returned to Washington and helped create the USO (United Service Organization), a joint military-civilian group that throughout the war would schedule performances for army audiences of such Hollywood and Broadway headliners as Betty Grable, Bob Hope, Glenn Miller, Marlene Dietrich, and Martha Raye.

Marshall was also determined that American soldier-civilians be enlightened on the reasons for their efforts and sacrifices. In the spring of 1941 he directed army commanders to remind recruits of their country's democratic heritage and link this heritage explicitly to their military service. Under his aegis the army produced a series of paperback textbooks in American history and international relations, made widely available to the men. Most famous of the morale-building devices was a series of seven movies, produced and directed by one of Hollywood's top directors, Frank Capra, collectively titled *Why We Fight*, explaining the origins and meaning of the war in both oceans. The films were not objective; the American cause, not surprisingly, was depicted as without blemish. Today World War II is still—rightfully—held to be the "good war." Unfortunately, in the manner of the day, racist elements, especially concerning the Japanese enemy, were a part of the war and part of the series. Whether Marshall endorsed these views or not, at the end of each film the narrator quoted the chief of staff's words: "The victory of the democracies can only be complete with the *utter defeat* of the war machines of Germany and Japan."[49]

Were these educational programs effective? Compared to the Wehrmacht soldiers' fanatical, bitter-end defense of the Nazi cause, American GIs, particularly in the European-Mediterranean theaters, would often seem uncertain of the reasons for their risks and painful sacrifices. Yet Marshall had identified a serious problem of morale and sought constructively to correct it.

On the matter of race and its problems for the army, Marshall was probably a little ahead of his time and his place. The United

States fought World War II—against the most brutal and blatant proponent of racist ideology in history—with a racially segregated military. In the army black soldiers, airmen, and sailors were assigned almost exclusively to all-black units, generally under the command of white officers. They were also largely restricted to service functions; few ever saw combat. The arrangement, of course, echoed the unequal social system that prevailed by law through the entire South and, informally, was widely observed in the North as well. It was reinforced by the large proportion of white Southern officers and noncoms who made the military their lifetime careers. Marshall of course was not Southern-born, but he was in his own mind a Virginian, and accepted many of the racial values of his adopted state, including a defense of "separate but equal." When liberals, including the president's wife, Eleanor, pushed for racial integration in the armed forces, Marshall pushed back. Responding to a memo calling for integration from the black judge William Hastie, dean of the Howard University Law School and recently appointed by FDR as a civilian aide to Stimson, Marshall noted that what Hastie proposed would be "tantamount to solving a social problem which has perplexed the American people throughout the history of the nation." The army could not "accomplish such a solution and should not be charged with the undertaking."[50] In a September 1941 letter to Assistant Secretary of War John McCloy, by pointing out that American Communists had come out for military integration, he implied its subversive nature.

Yet, while acting within the racial limitations of most contemporary white Americans, Marshall favored what he considered fair play. He did not condone bigoted racist behavior. Black candidates for officer status must be judged on their merits, he insisted. That meant, however, that the army must select their number only in proportion to blacks in the general population.

He also sponsored a preflight training program at all-black Tuskegee Institute that gave rise to the famous Ninety-Ninth Fighter Squadron, which flew successful missions in North Africa and Europe, and he praised Eisenhower's use of black soldiers in the 1944–45 Battle of the Bulge, though Ike then was perhaps moved more by desperation than by a commitment to equality.

In later years Marshall would often be called the "Organizer of Victory." Did he excel, then, as architect of a well-trained citizen army? The enormous difficulties and challenges he faced—the embedded individualistic American values, the nation's cultural diversity, its provincialism and regionalism, the severe time constraints events imposed—must be kept in mind. And with these very real limitations, his training of an army ground force for combat was not an outstanding success.

Marshall believed in an informed soldier who understood why it was important for him to learn the laborious skills assigned in training. This was commendably democratic, but it did not make for individual GI initiative in battle. Ironically, in North Africa and Europe the Wehrmacht rather than the U.S. Army would excel in small-unit initiative. Between 1939 and the war's end in mid-1945 the American army expanded from some 200,000 men to 8.5 million. Perhaps, considering the task of creating a mass army virtually overnight, the result could not have been different. The American soldier in battle, at least in the early stages, inevitably resembled the product of American mass production in manufacturing. The German soldier, on the other hand, seemed the product of the "boutique" craftsman tradition of Continental Europe.

In fact Marshall delegated much of the actual day-to-day training process—weapons mastery, marching, marksmanship, bivouacking, sanitation, unit maneuvers, small unit and officer leadership, and the rest—to General McNair, his appointee as head of the Army Ground Forces. Early in the war McNair was widely praised for his training programs. An article in the *Saturday Evening Post* in late January 1943 reassured readers that if "our boys, rushed into battle after one year . . . of high gear training" can "outsoldier German troops," the credit "must go to a five-foot-eight soldier" from "Verndale, Minnesota," widely hailed as "the brains of the American Army. . . . If you have a son or husband in uniform," the article noted, "you may owe his welfare or even his survival to 'Whitey McNair.'"[51]

McNair's celebrity did not last. According to the army's own self-examination, he was aware of the American infantry soldiers' failings and sought to rectify many of them. But by the time of his death in France from friendly fire in July 1944, he and his work had come under damaging attack. The publicly aired charges included initially prescribing too brief a draftee-basic-training period (only thirteen weeks), failure to encourage initiative and small-unit tactics, and inadequate training in weapons proficiency. In North Africa, in their first serious encounters with the Wehrmacht, American troops and their commanders would prove both unskilled and unsteady.

The air force and navy did a much better job of creating pilots than the army did creating infantrymen. Only painfully, and often lethally, did American young men learn in actual combat the skills of soldiering, and they probably never equaled man-for-man their counterparts in the Wehrmacht. As for teaching the vital lessons of "combined arms combat"—the integration of infantry, artillery, armor, and air—those, too, were feebly if at all transmitted to officers and men at the training camps. At the Kasserine Pass, in central Tunisia, especially, the failure would detonate like a bomb and shame the American army. Marshall himself recognized the weaknesses of the training process when, a decade and a half after the events, he acknowledged that "some of the divisions" sent to North Africa in the fall of 1942 "were only partly trained and badly trained."[52]

Yet despite Marshall's awareness, the transatlantic failings of the American infantry in battle would be fostered by several of his own policies regarding recruitment and replacement in the army's ground forces.

Raising and training an army, while important, were only secondary functions of the chief of staff. As for grand military strategy, it did not take long for the apparent Anglo-American agreement of early 1942 on future operations to unravel. By May a careful new study of Sledgehammer had reinforced the view of British planners that it would be a very risky venture unless German morale were to deteriorate abruptly—an unlikely prospect. Later that month Vyacheslav Molotov, the Soviet foreign minister, visited London and Washington carrying Stalin's demand that Britain and the United States mount a second front before the start of the Wehrmacht's expected new spring offensive in the East. Any attack by the Western Allies, Stalin directed Molotov to tell Churchill, must force the enemy to withdraw at least forty German divisions from the Russian front to be effective in helping the Soviet Union. Churchill balked. Explaining the necessity of achieving air supremacy over the landing area and the shortage of landing craft to transport troops and equipment, he warned Molotov that any help in 1942 must be limited despite the "best will and endeavour," and any move Britain could make in that year was "unlikely . . . even if successful" to "draw off large numbers of enemy land forces from the Eastern Front."[53] The Russian envoy got a better reception in Washington. Though Marshall sought to keep Roosevelt from too firm a commitment for 1942, the president, in a public statement, gave the Russian envoy a virtual guarantee of an effective second front for that year. "Full understanding was reached," the president told the press, "with regard to the urgent task of creating a Second Front in Europe in 1942."⁵⁴ Churchill quickly dispatched Louis Mountbatten to Washington to undo the damage, and the admiral's discouraging remarks gave the president pause. On second thought, FDR said privately, maybe American troops might be better employed in North Africa after all.

Hoping to bolster Roosevelt's apparent change of heart and reinforce his Gymnast scheme, in mid-June Churchill came once again to America with Brooke and Ismay in tow. To head off the persuasive PM, Marshall, Stimson, and a circle of Marshall's military allies composed a statement strongly endorsing the complete Sledgehammer-Bolero-Roundup sequence and sent it off to Hyde Park, the president's Hudson Valley estate, where, to escape the Washington heat, the two leaders met before going on to the capital. While they conferred in leafy Dutchess County, Brooke and Marshall discussed issues in sweltering pre-air-conditioned Washington, where Brooke's London-weight woolen uniform was a torment. Though they continued to disagree about Sledgehammer, they seemed in accord on Gymnast: The North African campaign would be a wasteful diversion of resources better employed elsewhere. They also shared mistrust of their bosses. Both Brooke and Marshall feared that the military "amateurs" who led their respective countries did not fully understand the nuts and bolts of warfare and were too often moved by political considerations or, in Churchill's case, by an overactive historical imagination and an almost adolescent yearning to recapitulate the military glory of his distinguished ancestor the Duke of Marlborough. Talking of this period fourteen years later, Marshall noted: "We were largely trying to get the President to stand pat on what he had previously agreed to. The President shifted, particularly when Churchill got hold of him. . . . The President was always ready to do any sideshow and Churchill was always prodding him."⁵⁵

But Roosevelt's change of heart had firmer foundations than an admiration of Churchill. As yet the American contribution to any operation in Europe must be limited, and so British wishes must be heeded. Besides, as Churchill had noted, there *was* an acute shortage of landing craft as well as a scarcity of shipping brought on by heavy losses to U-boats in the Atlantic, and by Admiral King's sequestering vessels for the Pacific. At their Hyde Park discussion Churchill had confronted the president with these realities and was soon insisting that the only alternative to a 1942 landing in France to draw off German strength was his North African project. Roosevelt found it difficult to deflect this argument and resolved to hand it over to the military chiefs when he and Churchill arrived back in Washington from Hyde Park. At this meeting Marshall and Stimson continued to support Sledgehammer, but the Combined Chiefs worked out a rather mealymouthed compromise preserving Roundup but sidelining any 1942 cross-Channel attack unless "an exceptionally favorable opportunity" should occur.[56] On the morning of June 21, in the middle of these discussions in the White House, an aide handed FDR a telegram. The president handed it to Hopkins, who then passed it to the prime minister. It read: "Tobruk has surrendered, with twenty-five thousand men taken prisoner."[57]

The news was devastating. The British base at Tobruk in eastern Libya had seemed the last barrier between Rommel's Afrika Korps and the Nile Valley and then the oil-rich Middle East. "This was one of the heaviest blows that I can recall during the war," Churchill later wrote.[58] Not only did the surrender threaten devastating military and strategic consequences; it also reflected badly on the reputation of the British army, which had suffered humiliating defeats in France two years before, followed by the Greek fiasco and then the shameful surrender of Singapore following Pearl Harbor. FDR responded immediately. The United

States, he declared, would send three hundred of the new U.S. Sherman tanks to General Auchinleck, now dug in at El Alamein, less than one hundred miles from Alexandria on the Nile. After observing that the Shermans had yet to be widely distributed to his own troops, Marshall instantly agreed to go along. When they finally arrived the tanks would contribute to Gen. Bernard Montgomery's later success against the supple Rommel, soon to be called the Desert Fox.

Generous to an ally on the ropes, on the larger issues of future global strategy Marshall was offended by the continued British waffling. Their sabotage of Sledgehammer, he felt, was downright duplicitous. Even worse, Bolero, the buildup for a cross-Channel operation, was now also in jeopardy. With Stimson's approval, Marshall resolved on a showdown. If the British insisted on replacing Sledgehammer with Gymnast, he told the Joint Chiefs at a meeting on July 10, the United States should "turn to the Pacific for decisive action against Japan." With Admiral King's enthusiastic endorsement, the suggestion was forwarded in a memo to FDR along with the warning that if adopted, Gymnast would scatter and dilute American forces and thus "curtail if not make impossible" a cross-Channel offensive not only for 1942 but for 1943 as well.[59]

It is not clear whether the Pacific First proposal was serious or pure bluff. After the war both Marshall and Stimson insisted it was intended solely to frighten the British into accepting Bolero and Sledgehammer. But that they both considered a Pacific offensive a real alternative to Europe First is reinforced by a second memo from Marshall to the president on the same day. After noting that it would be "impossible to do BOLERO without full British support," Marshall frankly described his strategy: "My object is again to force the British into acceptance of a concentrated effort against Germany." But "if this proves impossible," he would "turn . . . to the Pacific with strong forces and drive for a decision against Japan."[60] In fact at this moment Marshall was bluffing King as well as Churchill and his staffs. In a letter to Eisenhower of July 30, he noted that the proposed "list of withdrawals for the Pacific" would give the United States "liberty of action though not necessarily to be carried out in full. . . . Of course," he added, "Admiral King would like to have them all in the Pacific," but *his own* "intention" was "to make only the withdrawals that seem urgently required for the Pacific as the situation develops there."[61]

Serious or not, the apparent change of heart deeply troubled the British. Dill warned Churchill from his post in Washington that the Americans meant what they said. The prime minister's response was vividly Churchillian: "Just because the Americans can't have a massacre in France this year," he wrote back, "they want to sulk and bathe in the Pacific."[62] It also angered the president, who did not perceive his own emerging Mediterranean strategy as partial abandonment of Europe First, or at least of its cross-Channel aspect. Roosevelt shot off a reply to Marshall, which he emphatically signed "Commander-in-Chief." The Joint Chiefs' memo was "exactly what Germany hoped the United States would do following Pearl Harbor," FDR wrote. Equally bad, it did not provide for using American troops in combat nor did it help "Russia or the Near East."[63] Keep in mind, FDR continued, that once Germany had surrendered, Japan could be dealt with in a few months.

Though the memo was clearly a gambit in the Anglo-American battle over strategy, unfolding events were willy-nilly forcing some shift of U.S. military planners' attention to the Pacific. And even if official American policy placed Europe first, MacArthur in Australia, Adm. Chester Nimitz, commander in chief of the Pacific Ocean Area, and the Japanese enemy had different agendas. Though they were ferocious rivals for leadership of operations in the Pacific, both American commanders had no trouble agreeing that Japan was the chief Axis enemy and seeing the focus on Europe as excessive. And, in any case, the Japanese did not intend to stand still while the Americans polished off Germany and Italy. In early June. Admiral Yamamoto dispatched a powerful task force of battleships, carriers, cruisers, and destroyers eastward toward American-controlled Midway Island in the central Pacific to provoke a showdown battle that would, he hoped, deliver a crippling blow to the American navy and compel the enemy to accept a negotiated peace advantageous to Japan. The bold strike failed disastrously. Having broken the main Japanese naval code, the Americans were prepared for the assault. In a few furious hours, U.S. Navy dive-bombers sank four large Japanese carriers while Wildcat pursuit fliers shot down one hundred Zeros with their veteran Japanese carrier pilots. Japan's forward momentum in the Pacific was ended. American forces were on the move, too. In early August, in the first U.S. land offensive against the Pacific enemy, U.S. Marines landed on Guadalcanal in the Solomon Islands, triggering a ferocious struggle of ground forces, planes, and ships that for six agonizing months was touch and go for the American navy and its land combat division.

Clearly, then, it was impossible to ignore the Pacific. Thereafter, according to Stoler, the Joint Chiefs, Marshall included, would seek to quietly evade the president's veto and fight at least a partial Pacific war. It would prove to be a bloody, costly, and chancy grind, rather than the walkover that FDR supposed. But in light of later events Marshall was right to invest at least moderate resources in the Pacific war while continuing to focus on the Atlantic.

By now, confronted by British intransigence over Roundup and the inadvisability of the Pacific alternative and prodded by Churchill, FDR had concluded that the North African invasion plan was the best option for 1942. Those young Americans streaming from the training camps should be fighting the enemy, not doing guard duty and listening to patriotic lectures in the United States. Besides, Gymnast would give American troops and commanders vital combat experience and perhaps partially satisfy Stalin that the Western Allies were doing something to stop Hitler. It would also serve as a rebuff to MacArthur, whose grandiose military and political ambitions in the Pacific seriously irked the president.

To help settle the matter Roosevelt once more ordered Marshall and Hopkins off to Britain to meet with Churchill and his military leaders, accompanied this time by Admiral King. Before leaving, Marshall conferred with FDR at the White House. Operations in the Mediterranean region, he warned the president, would delay an Allied cross-Channel attack until 1944. The two, according to Secretary Stimson, had a "thumping argument" and Marshall—incorrectly, as it happened—"thought . . . he had knocked out the President's lingering affection for first GYMNAST and then the Middle East."[64]

The three envoys left for Britain on July 16 armed with a two-page memo from the president designed to clear the strategic air. The envoys should "reach immediate agreement" with the British on "definite plans" for 1942 as well as more "tentative plans" for 1943. It was "of the highest importance that U.S. ground troops be brought into action against the enemy in 1942," the message declared. But if Sledgehammer was "finally and definitely out of the picture, FDR wanted the three "to take into consideration . . . a new operation in Morocco and Algiers designed to drive in against the back door of Rommel's armies." Roosevelt took the occasion to repeat his objections to a Pacific First strategy. "I am opposed to an American all-out effort in the Pacific," he wrote, reinforcing his view with the silly prediction that the "defeat of Germany means the defeat of Japan, probably without firing a shot or losing a life."[65]

But whatever the president preferred, Marshall did not intend to abandon his opposition to a North African operation. Before the Americans left for Britain, Dill wrote to Churchill from Washington to warn him what to expect when they arrived. Either mistakenly or to goad the prime minister, he asserted that Marshall's "first love" was the Pacific theater. He was, moreover, now convinced that the prime minister preferred an attack in North Africa to one in Europe. Marshall had lost confidence in Britain's commitment to Roundup, Dill wrote. He believed that there was "no real drive" in Britain behind the preparations for a cross-Channel landing in 1943. As to how Churchill should respond to Marshall's skepticism, he advised the prime minister to work hard to convince his visitors when they arrived that he was truly "determined to beat the Germans" and would "strike them at the earliest possible moment."[66]

Marshall, King, and Hopkins landed in Scotland on July 17 and went directly to London to confer first with Eisenhower, who, through Marshall's auspices, had been appointed in June primarily to head Bolero, but with the grand title of Commanding General, United States Forces, European Theater. It is a challenge to account fully for this extraordinary honor. Ike had no combat experience; he had never led troops in battle. To warrant his new title he had been catapulted in rank ahead of sixty-six more senior major generals. A recent biographer of Eisenhower believes that the choice was essentially an empty gesture: Neither Marshall nor Secretary Stimson, says Jean Edward Smith, "believed the new operation [the cross-Channel attack] would ever take place," given the president's recent drift.[67] But there was a more fundamental reason for the Eisenhower appointment: Marshall was choosing a general very much like himself: a coordinator, planner, and conciliator rather than a commander. For the conduct of a coalition war, that must have seemed more important than dash and flash, leading offensive operations, and inspiring troops.

But in any case, Marshall still believed Sledgehammer viable. The day before arriving in Britain he sent Eisenhower an eyes only cable asserting his primary purpose was "to ascertain" from him "whether or not it was believed possible to carry out sledgehammer and advise the president accordingly." He also asked Ike to be ready "with searching analysis of sledgehammer situation; [and] also be prepared with specific outline for how sledgehammer might be carried out." He went on to tell the new commanding general that the proposed North African operation seemed "completely out of the question from Pacific naval requirements point of view alone."[68]

Ike, like Marshall, still believed that Sledgehammer should be tried, although, he admitted, a successful 1942 beachhead in France was a long shot. The operation was necessary to keep eight million Russians "in the war," he told his visitors when they arrived in London. Gymnast, on the other hand, would not reassure the Russians and would only scatter Allied strength and probably rule out Roundup in 1943. The president's memo had tilted the pointer toward the Mediterranean; Ike had turned it once more toward France.

Reinforced by his protégé's opinion, Marshall and the American envoys met with Churchill, Brooke, and the leading British military chiefs at Chequers on July 20. The chief of staff argued passionately for Sledgehammer. The Western Allies must not allow the destruction of the Soviet army if they could prevent it, he asserted. And Sledgehammer "was the most effective action that the Allies could take on behalf of Russia."[69] The British remained skeptical. That day, after wrangling with Marshall and King, Brooke noted in his diary: "They [the Americans] failed to realize that such an action could only lead to the loss of some 6 divisions without achieving any results!"[70] Finally, on July 22, the American envoys gave up the fight and informed the president that they and the British had reached a complete impasse. Not surprised at the result, FDR cabled back that their mission now was to agree to some operation in 1942 against the Germans, preferably in North Africa. Several more rounds of intense Anglo-American discussions ensued with Marshall and his colleagues attempting to prevent a final veto of the 1942 cross-Channel attack. But without success. In the end the Americans were compelled to agree that Sledgehammer was dead and instead Gymnast (now labeled Torch) would be launched in the fall. And yet a shard of optimism survived, at least in Marshall's mind. Perhaps the North Africa operation could be whittled down sufficiently to permit Roundup in 1943. The continued irresolution, however small, did not please FDR. On July 30 he ended all doubts with an emphatic ukase: "As commander-in-chief," he directed that Torch "would be undertaken at the earliest possible date." It was "now our principal objective and the assembling of means to carry it out should take precedence over other operations," including Roundup.[71] In the words of the historian Thomas Parish, "Marshall had been completely defeated." The president "had exercised his prerogative as chief strategist."[72]

Marshall may have been miffed at being overruled, but with time he came to recognize the political imperatives. As he told Forrest Pogue in late 1956, he and his colleagues had failed to see that the "leader in a democracy has to keep the people entertained." That might sound like the wrong word, he admitted, but it conveyed the correct thought: "people demand action and the U.S. could not wait until everything was entirely ready."[73]

And so by midsummer the Anglo-American strategic road immediately ahead had finally been determined: Whatever the chief of staff preferred, the Mediterranean it would be. But one more person would have to be convinced—Joseph Stalin in the Kremlin. In Cairo to discuss with his generals the deteriorating situation in Egypt and the Middle East after the fall of Tobruk, Churchill decided he would bring the news of the Allied decision to the Soviet leader in person, a mission, he admitted to Roosevelt, that promised to be a "raw job." The PM arrived in Moscow by air on August 12 with Brooke, Wavell, and other high-level British officers, accompanied by Averell Harriman, representing FDR. They reached the Soviet capital as the struggle at Stalingrad to check the German thrust toward the vital Caucasus oil fields was gathering steam, with the outcome still in doubt. To bring "Uncle Joe" the news that there would be no cross-Channel second front in 1942, Churchill admitted, "was like carrying a large lump of ice to the North Pole."[74] In fact Stalin almost certainly knew what the prime minister intended to tell him, so deeply had Soviet spies in Britain penetrated secret Allied discussions at the highest levels.

At the first of several meetings at the Kremlin, Churchill confessed to Stalin that there would be no cross-Channel attack, no second front, in 1942. "The British and American Governments," he reported in the first meeting, "did not feel themselves able to undertake a major operation in September, which was the only month in which the weather was to be counted on." In effect, he expounded, the Western Allies could not soon mount "an operation which would have the effect of bringing German infantry and tank divisions back from the Russian front."[75] But that did not mean, he hastened to add, that the British and Americans did not intend to help their Russian ally. They were preparing "a very great operation in 1943," and for that purpose a million American troops were scheduled to reach Britain by the spring. Unhappy with this news, Stalin repeated Soviet demands for an attack in the West in 1942. When Churchill described the drawbacks of a premature cross-Channel effort, Stalin brashly questioned the Western Allies' courage. Why were they "so afraid of the Germans?" he asked. His own "experience showed that troops must be bloodied in battle" for their leaders to know their fighting qualities. "A man who is not prepared to take risks cannot win a war," he insisted, and concluded with a remark that the British should try fighting for a change.[76] An outraged Churchill replied that he pardoned the aspersion "only on account of the bravery of the Russian troops."[77] But he also sought to defend the Anglo-American agenda for 1942. "What was a second front" after all? he asked. "Was it only a landing on a fortified coast opposite England? Or could it take the form of some other great operations which might be useful to the common cause?"[78] Britain and the United States were determined to do their part against Hitler before the present year was out, he assured the Soviet leader. The expanding British-based air war against Hitler's cities and factories was contributing to German defeat. But, more important, the Allies were going to launch a major attack that fall in North Africa that would weaken the Axis and help Russia immensely. Operation Torch would free the Mediterranean from Axis control and "threaten the belly of Hitler's Europe." To illustrate his point Churchill pointed to a sketch of a crocodile he had drawn on a blackboard. The Western Allies meant to "attack the soft belly of the crocodile" in 1942 rather than its "hard snout," the cross-Channel assault to be reserved for the following year. Torch, he assured Stalin, would draw off much German strength, especially planes of the Luftwaffe, from the eastern front. At first Stalin professed to be reassured. At least the Western Allies did not intend to sit on their hands through 1942. "May God help this enterprise to succeed," he responded. Several times during the prime minister's exposition, Harriman, as FDR's personal representative, intruded to add that Roosevelt was "in full agreement" with Churchill on the decisions reached.

Stalin's acquiescent mood did not last, and the next day, in an aide-mémoire, he lambasted the British for breaking promises he claimed had been made to Molotov on his recent visits to London and Washington. The "refusal of the Government of Great Britain to create a Second Front in 1942 . . . inflicts a mortal blow to the whole of Soviet public opinion and . . . complicates the situation of the Red Army at the front and prejudices the plan of the Soviet command," the document asserted.[79] Churchill replied the next morning with a brief written defense of the British position that denied any broken promises and repeated the arguments for Torch.

Though Stalin continued to act jovial and personally friendly, the rest of the PM's stay in Moscow was rocky. Military discussions between Brooke and the Soviet generals in the remaining days of the visit never got off the ground. The Russians refused to answer questions about their fighting fronts and simply repeated as a mantra, "A second front now."

Yet as he left Moscow for home on the sixteenth, Churchill remained optimistic. He had, he felt, established a cordial relationship with the man in the Kremlin whose goodwill seemed so vital to ultimate victory over Hitler. The Russians now "knew the worst, and having made their protest are entirely friendly," he reported to his cabinet.[80] But Churchill was deceiving himself. Whatever goodwill the Soviet leader had shown him was merely part of the act. Stalin still needed the Anglo-Americans, however disappointing their material aid had been thus far, and he chose not to jeopardize it.

Most important, Torch was now definitely on track. Yet what remained for Marshall and all the others whose brains and energy would be engaged in the immense, tangled, and complicated diplomatic, logistical, and military tasks in the months ahead could not yet be known. The difficulties and challenges in the end would far exceed even those anticipated by Torch's most determined opponents. As for Marshall, he had been overruled; he could no longer hope to avoid a major operation in North Africa.

CHAPTER 6

"UNDERBELLY"

Whether he welcomed Torch or not, for the next year and a half most of Marshall's attention would be focused on the Mediterranean. He had other concerns, of course. Army troops and airmen would be in the thick of the fight in the Pacific and would be garrisoned on Atlantic islands from the Caribbean to Iceland; under Bolero, American soldiers, with their equipment, were arriving in Britain in force to prepare for Roundup, the cross-Channel invasion. And many thousands of men in olive-drab uniforms would remain at home in training camps or serving in logistical capacities. But in these critical months the chief of staff, while juggling many strategic and administrative balls, remained centered on the problems and events in the "cradle of Western civilization." No more than elsewhere would the Mediterranean theaters be under his command; in July the CCS formally agreed that Dwight Eisenhower, his protégé, would head the Torch landings and the campaign to evict the Axis from French North Africa. Ike was not entirely comfortable with his new responsibilities, and neither, apparently, was his boss. For a time there was talk that he would be coming to Washington for advice and guidance. Ike demurred, however. In late September he wrote to Marshall that nothing would give him "greater mental satisfaction" than a visit to "talk over" with him "the various contingencies that may arise in the early days of the assault" and "discuss [with him] many of the major problems that later may have to be solved on the spur of the moment." But he begged off on the grounds that his British subordinates would not welcome his absence for the week or so a trip home would entail.[1] In the end Marshall would give his protégé almost unlimited leeway to manage the vast new operation as he wished.

But if Torch was not a trial of Marshall's combat generalship, as a first "blooding" for American fighting men the operations on the Mediterranean littoral would put to rigorous test his policies as the organizer and trainer of the new American army.

The test began on November 8 with the Allied landings in Vichy-controlled Morocco and Algeria. To succeed, Torch required diplomatic as much as military prowess. One reason FDR favored the operation was his belief that the authorities in Morocco and Algeria, the western part of France's North African possessions, might be weaned from Vichy and induced to join the Anglo-American Allies if the Americans took the lead. Many Frenchmen despised the British, their former allies. "Perfidious Albion" had betrayed France in 1940, they believed, and soon after, claiming to be keeping the ships from German hands, the Royal Navy had treacherously attacked the French fleet in Algeria, killing more than twelve hundred French sailors and marines. In part it was this jaundiced view that had led to Ike's appointment as commander in chief of Torch rather than some British officer with more combat experience and greater seniority.

As a preliminary to Torch, to avoid hostilities with Vichy forces the American consul general in Algiers, Robert D. Murphy, had contacted leading French officers who seemed willing to defy Marshal Pétain and switch sides. At their behest Murphy, joined by Gen. Mark Clark, a close friend of Eisenhower and one of his top subordinates, slipped into Algeria to discuss the planned invasion with dissident French military leaders. Knowing that the French authorities in North Africa would not accept the leadership of Charles de Gaulle, the proud and irascible head of the British-sponsored anti-Vichy Free French, Murphy had apparently offered command of all Allied military forces in North Africa to Henri Giraud, an anti-German French general whose escape from German captivity after France's 1940 surrender had made him a hero to many of his countrymen. When Ike told the general that the Allies would not put him in charge of the entire Allied invasion force, he decided to remain on the sidelines. In any event the French commanders in North Africa were not enamored of Giraud and had refused to consider laying down their arms.

Once the landings commenced, the figure of Adm. Jean Darlan, supreme head of the Vichy armed forces, entered the complicated picture. Darlan was fortuitously in North Africa when the Allied troops came ashore and began to encounter determined French defenders. Disappointed with Giraud, the Americans concluded that Darlan had the respect of the Vichy generals in North Africa and was the man who would end the threat of having to fight the French as well as the Italians and Germans.

Unfortunately the admiral was a blatant pro-German, anti-British Vichyite, whose selection was certain to stir public wrath in both Britain and America against the Allied authorities who favored him. Churchill called him "a bad man with a narrow outlook and an evil eye."[2] Initially unwilling to treat with the Anglo-American Allies, Darlan changed his mind when on November 10 Hitler renounced the 1940 peace treaty with France granting Vichy autonomy, and Axis troops took over control of the unoccupied zone of defeated France. Freed by this act from his fealty to Pétain, soon after the landings Darlan concluded an agreement with Clark to end the French resistance while guaranteeing continued French sovereignty in North Africa and confirming the independent status of French military authority. He would become high commissioner of French North Africa while Giraud took over as commander in chief of local French forces.

For the sake of sparing American lives, Eisenhower accepted the Darlan agreement and soon came under withering attack in the British Parliament and in the British and American press. The admiral was a French equivalent of Vidkun Quisling, the Norwegian traitor, they declaimed, who, besides his unsavory Vichyite connections, as high commissioner was unwilling to rescind vicious Vichy-imposed, anti-Jewish laws in the French North African colonies. The highly respected CBS radio correspondent Edward R. Murrow, broadcasting from London, succinctly posed the dilemma to his transtlantic listeners: "Are we fighting Nazis or sleeping with them?"[3]

Faced with the uproar, FDR backed away from the agreement. It was a "temporary arrangement . . . justified solely by the stress of battle," he told the American public.[4] The president cabled Ike that the United States did not trust Darlan and the Allies should keep a close watch on his movements. Marshall rushed to his protégé's defense, however, meeting with reporters, congressmen, and the president himself to plead Ike's case. On November 20 he wrote to Eisenhower that he approved of his deal with Darlan and was doing his "utmost to support" him. "Do not worry about this," he wrote. "Leave the worries to us and go ahead with your campaign."[5] A month later he urged Eisenhower "to clear your skirts of all that interferes with your complete concentration on the fighting and let subordinates or us in the rear carry these other burdens."[6]

These responses characterized the overall relations of the chief of staff with his top commanders. Marshall's general rule reflected his overall managerial style: Protect them against criticism and give them a free hand to fight the war as they saw fit. His advice on the occasion of Ike's departure for London to run Bolero was typical: "See what needs to be done, then do it. Tell me about it when you can."[7]

In some ways Marshall's relationship with Eisenhower—catapulted ahead of men with far more seniority and tied to him by both gratitude and deference—was a special case. Particularly during the early months of their friendship, they resembled a father and adolescent son, with Marshall at times questioning his subordinate's judgment and the younger man in turn resentful of his superior's authority. But as is also true in typical families, the son in this case frequently chose to disguise his feelings. In the months of planning for Torch, while still new to the job of high military command, Ike often sounded humble and almost obsequious in his letters to his chief back in Washington. In one message of late October he wrote: "Whenever I'm tempted to droop a bit over burdens cast upon us here, I think of the infinitely greater ones you have to bear and express myself a fervent wish that the Army may be fortunate enough to keep you at its head until the final victory is chalked up."[8] The deference and obeisance were not unlimited, however. When, in September 1942, for example, Marshall criticized his decision to appoint Gen. Walter Frank commander of the Twelfth Air Force, Ike openly bridled. Yet he would eventually repay Marshall's good opinion, though the chief's hands-off policy did not always produce happy outcomes.

The political storm over Darlan quickly dissipated after the admiral's assassination by an anti-fascist French monarchist just before Christmas. Conflict over French military and civilian authority in North Africa and elsewhere continued, but only marginally affected the early military operations.

By the time of the Giraud-Darlan maneuvers, Torch was well under way, but the operation would be marked by hesitation and miscalculation from the outset.

Jittery about the first major transatlantic American military venture, Marshall fought to confine the landings to Morocco, on the easily accessible Atlantic coast of French North Africa. It was a mistake. If carried out, the decision would have been a serious strategic blunder. The British, initially supported by Eisenhower, had urged at least one major landing site in Algiers, closer to Egypt, where Allied troops could help the beleaguered forces of General Auchinleck, commander of the British Eighth Army, defending the Suez Canal and the Middle East against the wily Rommel and his Afrika Korps. The British preference took on added relevance when, shortly before the Torch landings, Bernard Montgomery, Auchinleck's successor, with vastly greater manpower and matériel than his opponent, defeated Rommel at El Alamein, ending the threat to the vital Suez Canal and forcing the vaunted Afrika Korps into a slow, costly retreat from Egypt westward through Libya. Now the predominantly American invasion forces and the victorious British Eighth Army, coming from opposite directions, could meet in Tunisia, potentially crushing the Germans and Italians between them and forcing the final surrender of the entire Axis enemy in North Africa. Eisenhower had partially yielded to Marshall's caution. Some of the initial landings would be within the Mediterranean itself, not just the Atlantic coast. But none would be in Tunisia, closer to Montgomery's forces pursuing Rommel. Events would discredit Marshall's timidity. The failure to land in Tunisia would enable the Germans, reinforced from Italy through Allied delay, to mount an aggressive defense that would postpone the final North African victory until May 1943.

The Torch landings, at nine different sites, commenced on

November 8 when the undetected Allied forces, launched either from Britain or directly from American East Coast ports and transported safely through sub-infested Atlantic waters, converged on the ports of Casablanca, Oran, and Algiers. Though under the overall command of an American general, Torch was a cooperative Anglo-American venture. It consisted of three task forces—West, Center, and East. The first two were commanded by American generals, George Patton and Lloyd Fredendall. The landings at Algiers, the most easterly site, were a joint Anglo-American operation led by British general Kenneth Anderson. The Royal Navy, moreover, had escorted the American forces that originated in Britain, and the RAF had flown cover for troops of both nations.

Both American Torch commanders were Marshall's choices. The showy, pugnacious, spit-and-polish Patton was a longtime friend whose courage, dash, and tactical enterprise the chief of staff admired—but with reservations. Patton presented problems. In Marshall's view the Californian loved violence too much and had a puerile romantic streak along with a tendency to recklessly blurt out his ill-considered opinions, and a foul mouth that at times offended both the chief of staff and his wife. Katherine once told Patton after a bout of swearing in her presence, "You have no balance at all."[9] Fredendall seemed an easier choice. An infantry commander whose name Marshall had inscribed in his rumored "little black book" of top potential leaders, he seemed to be competent and decisive. "You can see determination all over his face," Marshall once exclaimed.[10] Ike had at first resisted selecting Fredendall as a Torch leader but eventually came around. Soon after the invasion he would write Marshall: "I bless the day you urged Fredendall upon me and cheerfully acknowledge that my earlier doubts of him were completely unfounded."[11]

Torch was the first British-American joint military effort, and to Marshall's delight and great relief, the landings had been marked by admirable cooperation between the Allies. The result, he felt, had vindicated his faith in the unified-command principle that he had sold to FDR and Churchill at the Washington Anglo-American meetings in December. Pleased with the outcome, the chief of staff was happy to publicly sing its praises. In a talk to the Academy of Political Science in early November, he called the Allied Torch cooperation a "remarkable success" and claimed that the unity-of-command principle was responsible for the happy result. Indeed, he asserted, it was the basis "for all combined action between Great Britain and the United States" and "the most heartening factor of the War to date."[12]

And there *had* been a relatively smooth meshing of Anglo-American operations in Morocco and Algeria. But what the chief of staff left out of his assessment was the larger frame of coalition strategy: the extent to which Torch, in its inception, promised to favor British desires to preserve their far-flung empire over less sharply defined, but assuredly nonimperial, American war goals. Nor would the smooth Anglo-American cooperation in North Africa last. Before the Axis forces finally laid down their arms, British-American relations would become inflamed by cultural disparities and misunderstandings, mutual contempt, and downright distrust of each other's competence, highlighted on one side by the inexperience and often ragged training of American citizen-soldiers and on the other by the feeble leadership of British forces and the less-than-sterling performance of British Tommies in the Mediterranean theater after El Alamein.

In a narrow sense, however, the Torch landings were a success. After some initial and often costly resistance by the Vichy French army and navy at the West and Center landing sites, American troops, far more numerous and better equipped than the defenders, established firm control. At Algiers, where Darlan's intervention had put an early end to resistance, there were few Allied casualties. And yet, though a useful tryout for the American army Marshall had worked so hard to create, even the landing operations would be deficient in many painful, even embarrassing ways. In getting ashore and taking firm control of port facilities, strongpoints, and administrative centers, the inexperienced, unbloodied American citizen-soldiers performed with a mixture of enterprise and ignorance, valor and poltroonery. At St. Cloud, in western Algeria, they were stopped by ill-equipped Vichyite French Foreign Legionnaires and an undermanned Tunisian infantry regiment—"second- or third-class fighting troops," according to an American intelligence report—and had to bypass the town to move on to Oran.[13] At Port Lyautey in Morocco, when Gen. Lucian Truscott's Sixtieth Infantry attacked the local casbah, manned by fewer than three hundred French soldiers feebly reinforced by three antique Renault tanks, they were sent reeling. "Officers as well as men," one colonel informed the War Department, "were absolutely dumbfounded at their first taste of battle."[14] Nor was the performance of Patton's troops of the Western Task Force superior. At one point in the early combat Patton completely lost patience with the weak fighting qualities of his men. After observing their fumbling efforts at Fedala Beach near Casablanca, he described them "as a whole . . . poor, the officers worse. No drive. It is very sad."[15]

As we shall see, the military gaffes of Torch were not singular; more of the same were to follow. After the landings the whole Allied North African campaign would falter, with unhappy consequences.

Marshall had discounted the strategic importance of the southern Mediterranean coast, but what about the enemy? The Führer's attitude is hard to determine. At times he considered the Allied invasion a major threat to the Reich. "To give up Africa means to give up the Mediterranean," he noted soon after the

Allied landings. It "would mean not only the ruin of our revolutions [the Nazi and Fascist], but also the ruin of our peoples' future."[16] Other German leaders were more skeptical. According to Rommel, the German High Command from the outset considered "Africa . . . a 'lost cause'" and believed that "any large-scale investment of matériel and troops in that theater would pay no dividends."[17] And the Führer's passive acquiescence in their conclusion, Rommel believed, betrayed his true feelings about the North African campaign.

However they rated the attack, the Germans reacted quickly to the Allied invasions. In Europe Torch triggered the German occupation of the part of France under the Pétain government's control. Simultaneously, to prevent a German seizure, Vichy crews scuttled the remaining French fleet at its base in Toulon. Meanwhile, the Germans rushed troops by air and sea to prevent Allied occupation of French Tunisia, where Allied forces coming from both directions had not yet appeared. On November 10 the first German soldiers—paratroopers flown in from Naples—arrived near Tunis, the capital. They were soon reinforced by sea across the Sicilian strait and some weeks later by units of the Italian army and the Afrika Korps retreating from Egypt following El Alamein. The French authorities in Tunisia had not opposed the Axis invaders. Having saved their "honor" by killing hundreds of American and British soldiers in Morocco and Algeria, the Vichy army and navy yielded to the Germans virtually without firing a shot. By January there were one hundred thousand Axis troops in the colony. When the first Allied forces arrived overland from Algeria, full of bravado and misplaced self-confidence, they suffered a rude shock. Within days the Axis troops, now in firm possession of Tunis and the important port of Bizerte, stopped General Anderson's forces in their tracks. The fighting soon settled down to a costly stalemate.

An important component of the Allied problem in Tunisia was leadership. A reserved and cautious Scot commanding predominantly British troops, General Anderson had little faith in his mission—and with good reason. The first encounter of British units and some Americans with Axis troops at Medjez-el-Bab in central Tunisia was an Allied debacle. With the loss of only twenty-two men, the Germans evicted the Allied forces from the key town on the road to the capital. Thereafter, though greatly outnumbered and beset by severe shortages of munitions, vehicles, tanks, and fuel, the Germans made monkeys of the Allies, even after the Americans from Algeria had arrived to reinforce Anderson's troops. Finally joined by Rommel's forces from Libya, in mid-February Gen. Hans-Jürgen von Arnim, commander of the Fifth Panzer Army, outmaneuvered and outfought the British and Americans and fended off for many weeks every Allied effort to take Tunis and Bizerte.

Even more than the Torch landings the bungled Tunisia campaign highlighted the military weaknesses of both Allied commanders and soldiers. During the operation Eisenhower, in overall command, exposed his military inexperience while revealing few of the diplomatic skills that would serve him well months later in Europe. Distracted by the Darlan-Giraud-de Gaulle imbroglio, despite Marshall's continued support and advice the Allied supreme commander, bedeviled by the diplomatic tangles, remained holed up in Algiers, both physically and psychologically distant from the fighting front. In late December the frustrated Marshall finally sent Ike a blunt message: "I think you should delegate your international diplomatic problems to your subordinates and give your complete attention to the battle in Tunisia."[18] Ike himself did not rate his performance in the early stages of the Tunisian campaign very highly. Nor did his superiors. Summoned to Casablanca in mid-January to report on Tunisia to Churchill,

FDR, and the combined military staffs at their major strategy conference, he was raked over the coals, failing to convey the confidence and decisiveness expected of a supreme commander. At a top briefing session with the Allied leaders on January 15 his Satin plan to interpose Fredendall's forces between Rommel's and Arnim's troops already dug in in northern Tunisia was brutally demolished by Brooke. The plan, Brooke told his colleagues, was a seriously flawed scheme that would likely end with the American forces being ground up between the two German armies.

In fact Satin was a weak improvisation thrown together in early January by Ike's staff, and he found it difficult to defend it to his peers and superiors when attacked. Embarrassed, he left the room dejected. He had gotten no help from Arnold, King, or even from Marshall, who would consider Ike's performance on this occasion rather lame. Roosevelt, too, was unimpressed. In a meeting soon after with Marshall, FDR discussed the chief of staff's earlier request that Ike be given a fourth star to bring him to par with the rank of most British field generals. The president declined. He would not promote him, he told Marshall, "until there was some damn good reason for doing it, that he was going to make it a rule that promotions should go to people who had done some fighting."[19]

Nor was British leadership in Tunisia any better than the American. If Ike's was lackluster, Montgomery's was no more effective. After arriving In Tunisia with his victorious Eighth Army, the hero of El Alamein unsparingly displayed his worst military sides: attention-hogging egomania, contempt for Americans, a penchant for unimaginative set-piece World War I–type battles, and insistence on achieving overwhelming preponderance before engaging the enemy. Even Churchill, who worshiped the flair and daring of the historic Nelsons, Wellingtons, and Marlboroughs (including his own ancestor, the first duke), often criticized

"Monty," especially in later phases of the war, and frequently expressed dismay at the pervasive timidity of British military leadership.

As for the Allied rank and file, their performance in North Africa, even after the Torch prologue, was considerably less than dazzling. In more than one engagement untried U.S. soldiers stampeded from the battlefield to safety. In early February, at Sened Station in central Tunisia, units led by Col. Thomas Drake panicked when attacked by Stuka dive-bombers and, when a junior officer shouted that the enemy had achieved a breakthrough, fled en masse toward the rear by foot or hastily requisitioned vehicles. As Drake reported, the men "were wild-eyed as they roared along at full speed." An officer present noted that "all of the infantry soldiers I could see anywhere around were hightailing it to the rear."[20] Clearly these were inexperienced soldiers whose training back home had been imperfect at best. Even Marshall later conceded that "we had some issues in Africa" and that the weak performance of American troops there was primarily "through lack of training." "Their training," he noted, "was only partially completed and Rommel's people came at them in a very vicious way and it rather surprised them."[21]

But their replacements, to fill division and regiment vacancies, under the army G-3's seriously flawed policies, were often worse. When some 450 new men arrived to reinforce the 168th Infantry, a unit of the Iowa National Guard, their commander, Lt. Col. Robert Moore, noted that many had not even received elementary rifle training. When he asked a private if he could operate a Browning automatic rifle, the soldier responded: "Hell, no, I've never even seen one!"[22]

One major engagement—the Battle of Kasserine Pass in mid-February—epitomizes many of the deficiencies of both American combat leaders and rookie American troops in the North African campaign and directs attention to the overarching issue of how well Marshall and his colleagues constructed the American army in World War II.

The Kasserine Pass was one of several through Tunisia's Dorsal Mountains, running northeasterly from the Algerian border in two branches and within the immediate command area of Lloyd Fredendall, head of the Second Corps. Nominally a subordinate of Anderson, headquartered to his north, Fredendall rarely met or communicated with his superior, and the two generals failed to coordinate their moves during the Tunisian campaign. It is no surprise, then, that Anderson had little faith in Fredendall or his green soldiers.

The American general, as we have seen, had met the rigorous test for inclusion in Marshall's merit list, but his actions in the series of bloody clashes labeled "Kasserine Pass" make the reason for his choice an enigma. The general was an eccentric man who issued commands in a private idiosyncratic language that few of his subordinates understood. He also apparently was unusually committed to his own personal survival. He avoided visiting the front lines and had, consequently, an imperfect picture of the terrain on which his men would fight. He established his headquarters at "Speedy Valley," near Tébessa, a major Allied supply depot in Algeria, seventy miles from the front. There, for his personal safety, he had army engineers blast from the rock two tunnels that ran 160 feet into a hillside. He surrounded this command post with an entire antiaircraft battalion. Gen. Omar Bradley, who in mid-April succeeded Fredendall, would call the protective bastion "an embarrassment to every American soldier."[23] News of Fredendall's fainthearted proclivities had reached Ike in Algiers, and he responded with a stern lecture. Writing to him on February 4, just before the encounters that would sully his name, Ike urged him to avoid "the habit of some of our generals in staying too close to their command posts." Speed of movement was essential in battle, and to achieve it required "an intimate knowledge of the ground and conditions along the front." That could "be gained only through personal reconnaissance and impressions." No doubt that entailed personal danger, but generals, he observed, "are expendable just as any other item in an army."[24] Events would soon show that Ike's lessons were not taken to heart.

In central Tunisia, Fredendall faced Rommel, newly escaped from Montgomery's pursuit, who now shared command of Axis forces in the French colony with Arnim, both under the overall authority in Rome of Field Marshal Albert Kesselring, one of Hitler's most competent generals. The Battle of Kasserine Pass— actually a series of hard-fought small engagements—erupted when Rommel sought to drive north toward Bône, in eastern Algeria, to attack Anderson from the rear and then to smash Montgomery moving in from Libya. The Desert Fox had under his command some seventy thousand troops, both Italian and German; he also had a batch of Mark IV medium tanks and a few of the new heavy Tigers, equipped with the deadly 88 mm antitank cannon. These were superior to the American M3 Lees and Grants, with their thin armor, and even to the newer Shermans. In addition the German crews were experienced; the American tankers had never fought a battle. Fredendall's Second Corps was spearheaded by the First Armored Division and troops of the 168th Infantry, many of them recent replacements. These were raw troops never before in combat and inadequately prepared to take on veteran Axis opponents.

As the Allies awaited Montgomery's Eighth Army, moving ponderously toward Tunisia from Libya, Kesselring unleashed Arnim and Rommel against the Allied line, manned in the center initially by a force of ill-equipped Free French. "We are going to go all out for the total destruction of the Americans," Kesselring announced.[25] On January 30 Arnim attacked the French at Faïd Pass and quickly overwhelmed the defenders. The American response to the French calls for help was tardy, and the pass quickly fell into German hands. Seeking to recapture the position, an American counterattack spearheaded by Sherman tanks ran into an ambush and was routed with heavy losses. Further assaults against the Germans by infantry were also repelled with numerous casualties. Faïd remained in enemy hands.

In the next two weeks Fredendall ordered harassing probes against Rommel. Led by Colonel Drake, the American attackers walked into another ambush. To survive, the men frantically sought to scratch out personal shelters against enemy fire with their helmets, but took serious casualties from German artillery, Stuka dive-bombers, and enemy tanks, which crushed many Americans as they huddled in their shallow holes. Drake's troops soon panicked. The men, their commander reported, fled "wild-eyed" in any vehicle available, "anything that would roll." An artillery officer remembered that "a sort of hysteria took hold of everyone."[26]

The mismanaged battles around Faïd and Maknassy created a miasma of dissidence and doubt among the Allies. The French blamed the Americans for the loss of Faïd; the British felt confirmed in their skepticism of the Yanks; Ike began to doubt the competence of Fredendall. To the south of Arnim's forces, the impatient Rommel finally received Kesselring's permission to advance against the Americans, now in full retreat. The Germans were aware of shaky American morale from intercepted radio messages sent in clear, without encoding. Rommel decided to aim at the Kasserine Pass, flanked by two long hills, both weakly held. As he awaited Rommel's attack on Kasserine, Fredendall called urgently for reinforcements. In reality he had sufficient manpower, but the troops were badly placed and scattered. In fact the initial defense of the pass would fall on the backs of the nineteen hundred men of the Nineteenth Combat Engineer Regiment, despite their name a unit still untrained in combat, who, since their arrival at the front some weeks before, had been employed constructing roads and digging Fredendall's tunnels at Speedy Valley.

As Rommel prepared to attack, the Americans were entrenched on the floor of the valley, leaving the hills at either side to the troops of the Afrika Korps, who, once they took the crests, could pour fire directly onto the Americans below. The first light German probes to seize the pass were quickly repelled, but enemy troops, backed by machine gunners, were soon infiltrating American lines. Anticipating an imminent full-scale assault, General Anderson ordered a no-retreat response. "No man," he directed, "will leave his post unless it is to counterattack."[27] His back-stiffening order fell on deaf ears. That evening, as they faced a ruthless German artillery barrage made more terrifying by the first-time use of *Nebelwerfer*, banshee-screaming six-barreled mortars, many of the engineering troops fled their posts. Daylight brought complete collapse as Axis soldiers forced their way through the pass along Highway 13. Defense units soon cracked, and individual American soldiers began bolting to the rear to escape the onslaught. Late in the afternoon Col. Alexander Stark of the 26th Infantry Regiment abandoned his headquarters to avoid capture. With his staff and several hapless army cameramen in tow, at points he had to crawl on hands and knees to bypass enemy troops only a few yards away.

American casualties had not been heavy. But defended by unskilled men and commanded by timid, untalented officers, the Kasserine battle had been lost. Rommel and his lieutenants sought to exploit their victory by pushing farther west and north toward Tébessa. But this time the American defenders were backed by the artillery of the American Ninth Infantry Division, a unit rushed from eight hundred miles away to the front to save the day. And it did. Frequently the most effective branch of the U.S. Army, the artillery gunners checked the German attack, forcing Rommel to withdraw. By this time the Desert Fox himself was wearing out. On March 9, after a miscarried assault on Montgomery's Eighth Army, now finally in Tunisia, with his health failing, Rommel returned to Germany on sick leave. Eastern Tunisia still remained in Axis hands with Arnim, now under the overall command of the Italian general Giovanni Messe. The Anglo-American Allies had not seen the last of Rommel, but the field marshal would never return to Africa.

Though the debacle at Kasserine was mercifully over, the reverberations at home would continue for months. Thirty thousand American troops had been engaged in and around Kasserine. Only three hundred had been killed, but a total of three thousand were listed as wounded and an equal number as captured or missing. The army's performance had been inglorious. As Harry Butcher, Ike's naval aide, noted in his diary: "The proud and cocky Americans today stand humiliated by one of the greatest defeats in our history."[28]

The military censors kept the full grim story of Kasserine from the American public for some time, but the political and psychological fallout among knowledgeable insiders was instantaneous and damaging. The drubbing severely strained inter-Allied relations. The spit-and-polish British general Harold Alexander, chosen at the Casablanca Conference to replace the indecisive Anderson as Ike's chief deputy in North Africa, was dismayed with his Yankee allies when he took over in mid-February. The American troops seemed "soft, green, and quite untrained," he wrote. They lacked "the will to fight." His "main anxiety," he told his superiors in London, was the "poor fighting value of the Americans. They simply do not know their job as soldiers and this is the case from the highest to the lowest," with the "weakest link of all . . . the junior leader, who just does not lead, with the result that their men don't really fight."[29]

Among informed Americans the repercussions of the Kasserine debacle were pronounced and not, overall, salutary. Though he had played no role in the conduct of battlefield operations in Tunisia, Marshall was not able to avoid reacting to the drubbing. He could not have been entirely surprised at the results when fledgling American soldiers encountered Axis veterans for the first time. Even before the Kasserine battles he had learned from Ike, during a side trip from the Casablanca Conference, of the slack discipline among American troops in North Africa. Reporting to Army Ground Forces commander McNair on February 1, soon after he returned to Washington, Marshall noted that Ike had complained that laxness in saluting and observing small regulations was being "magnified many-fold . . . once the troops became involved in the confusion and discomforts of campaign."[30] The events at Kasserine, when they became public, put Marshall on the defensive. At moments he seemed angrier at the press for reporting the fiasco than at his generals for causing it. In a memo to Gen. Alexander Surles, head of the army's public relations office, he complained at the frequent references in the newspapers to "green troops," a label he considered an aspersion on his training policies. Marshall also defended his fighting men against the critics. In response to General Alexander's trashing of American GIs he retorted: "Yes, American troops start out and make every possible mistake, but after the first time they do not repeat [them]." He then turned the tables: "British troops start out the same way and continue making the same mistakes over and over, for a year."[31]

Yet the critics were right to find fault in the performance of the Army Ground Forces in North Africa, and later in other theaters as well. One source of weakness was the limited assigned strength of the army's infantry branch. Soon after Pearl Harbor the War Department had mandated a total ground forces "troop basis" by the end of 1942 of 3.6 million enlisted men and seventy-three combat divisions. By mid-1943 the number of ground combat divisions had been raised to a total of ninety. But even ninety would prove inadequate for the needs of effective combat against enemies whose conquests stretched from the Aleutians to New Guinea. There were simply too few fighting men to do the job, particularly later on the European continent.

The system placed severe strains on the fighting men at the hazardous edge of battle. According to historians Kent Roberts Greenfield, Robert R. Palmer, and Bell I. Wiley, "with divisions so few . . . thorough training" was essential, but also a system that "provided for relief of front line soldiers from constant exposure to the stress and hazards of battle through some arrangement to periodically take bloodied, depleted units off the line." The existing arrangement imposed "a severe mental strain . . . on the individual soldier, especially the infantryman, who felt no matter how long he fought, or how long he survived the dangers of combat, he must remain in action until removed as a casualty." Men "simply became tired and when tired were more easily killed, wounded, or captured."[32]

The problem of army size would not seriously affect the Allied campaign in North Africa, where the Axis forces were limited by Allied control of the air and sea routes across the Mediterranean. But it was to become acute after D-Day, June 6, 1944, when, in northern France and along the Franco-German border, Allied soldiers would confront large formations of seasoned Wehrmacht troops, many from veteran units brought from the Russian front, fighting desperately to keep the enemy from the Reich's heartland.

Early in the war Marshall was a strong proponent of rapid expansion of the army at all costs. In the fall of 1942, he later noted defensively, he had resisted a congressional drive to whittle down draft call-ups. Justified as an attempt to reserve manpower for domestic needs, especially agriculture, this move was actually intended to spare pain to voting constituencies and save Treasury money. At the time he had warned that reduced call-ups would restrict the army's size to 6.5 million by the end of 1943, rather than the then-planned 7.5 million, and seriously cripple operations projected for 1943 and 1944. The War Department understood the need for food and arms production, he wrote, but it seemed to him that "the people are not fully aware of what it means to have too few troops . . . to sustain a battle against enemies of the character of the German and Japanese."[33] Unfortunately, once the army had reached the 1943 "troop basis" the chief of staff would come to defend that limit as if it were holy scripture.

When considering the failings of U.S. troops' combat performance, we are speaking primarily of the ground forces, that is, the infantry. These deficiencies derived not merely from inadequate numbers; training of these divisions was a major part of the difficulty. Initially, during the early "mobilization" phase of the war, when the permanent wartime divisions were still being formed, the infantry training cycle was only thirteen weeks, too little for the mid-twentieth-century version of military combat. Then, too, far too many men were initially trained as tank-destroyer or antiaircraft specialists, services that had been planned for generously at the outset by the Victory Program but proved excessive in practice.

Besides inadequate training, the inferior caliber of men assigned to army units as ground combat troops helped subvert the quality of the American infantry. The U.S. Army as a whole did not get the cream of the manpower crop. Sailors and marines, largely volunteers, were, by and large, better specimens of manhood than soldiers. Within the army, in turn, the quality of the infantry soldier, measured by physique, morale, and intellectual caliber, was inferior to that of men in other branches of the service. Some of this was owing to the pell-mell wartime expansion of the Army Air Corps, which drew off men who met higher physical and intellectual standards; some of it could be ascribed to special programs like the ASTP (Army Special Training Program), that recruited fit and particularly smart recruits who, after learning to march, drill, and fire their rifles, were sent to colleges to train as doctors, engineers, translators, and psychologists. It was also derived from the policy until 1944 of assigning draftees to particular military specialties by their civilian occupations rather than by their physical and mental capacities as measured by military induction tests. Thus the skilled, and presumably smarter, plumbers, carpenters, electricians, and office clerks ended up in army desk jobs or other noncombat branches; the unskilled and, presumably, mentally inferior filled the infantry's ranks.

General McNair recognized the "sub-average" quality of the infantry's personnel. He was particularly alert to the physical inferiority of the typical infantry recruit and ascribed it to "the fact that professional men or skilled workers come from the more privileged classes which are better fed and housed and as a result have better physiques generally."[34] This flaw in personnel policy could be overcome, he believed, if infantry assignment by civilian occupation were abandoned and replaced by physical and health criteria. But whatever the reason—poor implementation or conservative resistance to change—the reform impulse failed to alter the outcome. Describing the situation as of late 1943, the historian Robert Palmer, one of the authors of the definitive and official 1948 work on the recruitment and training of infantry during the war, wrote: "The quality of the manpower in the ground arms when mobilization was nearly completed . . . compared unfavorably with that of other elements of the Army."[35] Max Hastings, a British scholar of World War II, writing in 2005, agrees: "To put the matter plainly," he writes, "infantry . . . reposed at the bottom of the U.S. War Department's barrel."[36]

And the ninety-division limit undermined the infantry arm in still another way. To maintain total infantry fighting strength, rather than create more divisions as the number of men in each dwindled by "attrition," the mandated ones had to be topped off by individual replacements. These men were drawn from mixed sources: excessive air cadet units, overstaffed tank-destroyer and antiaircraft battalions, the ASTP, eighteen-year-olds (draftees late in the war), and problem soldiers not wanted by other units. Assigned to replacement depots ("Repple-Depples" in army slang), these men stagnated, often losing skills and physical fitness. In the words of the army historians Palmer, Wiley, and Keast, "The experience of replacement . . . tended to destroy their morale and undo the effects of their training."[37] It was also inhumane and wasteful of manpower. When they arrived in their new divisions these men were strangers to the veterans, who often refused to treat them as comrades worthy of friendship and help. Lacking experience and combat savvy, they frequently became little more than cannon fodder. Both the British and German armies created new divisions to make up for attrition. Some American critics suggested as a partial solution that, if not whole new divisions, the infantry be reinforced at least by replacement *battalions* that had trained together rather than men added individually to depleted divisions. But G-3, claiming that the suggested scheme would conflict with "our national conceptions as to the sanctity of our divisional organization," opposed it.[38]

Marshall could not ignore the flood of criticism produced by the Kasserine disaster, both of infantry training and the system by which ground troops were assigned to units. In a letter to McNair in early September 1943, well after the Tunisian campaign, he noted that a recent observer had written to him how the men he had just visited at a Casablanca replacement center seemed "flabby" and " ill-trained." They were not young, this observer noted; their average age was twenty-eight. But most of them were "fresh from basic training, "and "they looked exactly what they were—raw recruits." The "frightened and unsure look in their eyes," he reported, "was not heartening."[39] Marshall received similar reports when he consulted trusted generals who had led units in Tunisia or had closely analyzed the campaign after it ended. General Bradley, who succeeded as final battle commander of the American forces in Tunisia, told Marshall that existing processes for training infantry and field artillery were adequate. Instruction of trainees in the use of mines and in deployment of tank destroyers had to be improved, he acknowledged. But in his view one of the chief deficiencies, as revealed in Tunisia, was the weak performance of junior officers who lacked enterprise and initiative. Marshall's old friend Gen. Walton Walker seconded the indictment of the junior leadership and added to the list of deficiencies the unfortunate lack of air-ground cooperation, which at times had allowed the numerically inferior Luftwaffe to dominate the battlefield.

Though defensive about the army's failings, the chief of staff was prepared to suggest ways to improve the combat branches. His proposals, however, seem shallow. On August 4, 1943, "seriously disturbed" by an Army Special Services Division survey that reported a poor state of morale in the infantry, Marshall wrote to McNair to "suggest remedial action." McNair responded with his plan to use mental and physical qualifications as the bases for assigning men to military branches. He also proposed that infantry personnel be awarded special "fighting pay," and that to elevate the prestige of the infantry there be created a new medal specifically honoring infantry service. "My only regret," McNair replied to the chief of staff, "is that we did not start something along this line about two years ago."[40] Yet however "disturbed" he was, Marshall rejected McNair's proposals. The American soldier would ridicule the label "fighter" that the new honor conferred, while the suggested "ground medal" would cheapen decorations generally. In fact his counterproposal, emphasizing improving morale, was only a different version of McNair's scheme. "Men will stand almost anything if their work receives public acknowledgment," he later wrote to General Surles: "They are inclined to glory in its toughness and hazards if what they do is appreciated."[41] Though he feared the approach would probably alarm the families of the men so designated, the army should find a way to dignify the infantry rifleman by emphasizing how tough and dangerous his job was.

It is possible to blame McNair, Marshall's protégé, rather than Marshall himself, for the defects in army personnel policy. But the chief of staff, true to his noninterference principle, never pushed McNair hard enough to alter his personnel and training policies. And overall, Marshall would conclude that McNair had done a good job. Shortly after Germany's surrender in 1945, in a memorial service to McNair, who had died of wounds in France in July 1944, he praised him for his excellent training policies. "Much of our success in battle," he noted, derived from "the training which our units have received" under McNair's aegis.[42]

To what extent does Marshall's role in the shortcomings of American fighting men in North Africa and in later theaters affect our estimate of his career? He was not a combat general; he never led troops in the battlefield against an enemy force. He once described his role as "pick[ing] the right man for the job and back[ing] him up with every resource at our disposal."[43] One historian has described him as "the epitome of the modern military manager," whose "energy was devoted to training and logistics."[44] He had other important functions as well—as a skilled military diplomat and as a strategist, for example. But it is clear that much of his reputation rests on his achievements in creating an army out of virtually nothing and teaching it how to fight. And here, at his presumed forte, he proved at best mediocre.

Besides the failings of the GIs wielding Garand M1 rifles, Kasserine and later battles revealed the failings of the army's ground forces combat leadership. After the Tunisian rout many critics indicted the performance of lower-level officers—the lieutenants, captains, and majors who led the platoons and company units on the battlefield. Returning from a long trip through the Mediterranean theater in May, Hanson Baldwin, the respected military correspondent for the *New York Times*, confirmed the failings of the ordinary GIs he had observed. But "the greatest American military problem," he added, was "leadership." The army, he concluded, had thus far "failed to produce a fraction of the adequate officer leadership needed."[45]

Marshall was not blameless here either. He had wide experience with training junior officers—as head of the Monterey unit of the Officers' Reserve Corps before World War I and then later at Fort Benning, where one of his duties was to teach junior officers small-unit tactics and maneuvers that included officer initiative. Marshall must be praised for advising his Benning pupils to reject the static tactics of World War I trench warfare and for encouraging an "open warfare" approach to combat. But his much-vaunted success at Benning seems to have had little or no effect on the performance of American small-unit commanders when they encountered their first serious enemy.

What about the generals? Thomas Ricks believes that Marshall was often brutal in his dismissal of incompetent generals, but at times he was also slow to recognize the failings of top commanders. He was reluctant, for example, to recognize that Fredendall must go. Unusually sensitive to the personal humiliation of being relieved—at the very time Ike was considering sacking the incompetent commander of the Second Corps—Marshall proposed promoting him! In the end, supported by Bradley, his new deputy, on March 4 the supreme commander told Fredendall that he was being sent back to the United States to be replaced as head of American forces in Tunisia by Patton. He would be reassigned to head a training command in Tennessee, where his Tunisian experience, presumably, might prove valuable. Several staff heads also rolled, but however inferior their performances, the army under Marshall was reluctant to demean incompetent officers publicly, and as Ricks has noted, the chief of staff himself often gave them a second chance at another posting.

When all is said, however, assigning responsibility for the failings of American fighting men in World War II must go beyond the mistakes of administrators and beyond training and replacement deficiencies. More than one observer has noted the inherent tension between orderly democratic societies like 1940s America and the so-called warrior virtues. Despite the historical mythology, America in 1940 was a peaceful and, by contemporary world standards, a prosperous society. Whatever their proclivities in later years, American males were no longer "gun-totin'" cowboys or frontiersmen with rifles displayed over the mantelpiece. They were unused to being shot at or shooting at other human beings. As soldiers they were intent on surviving, not grappling with homicidal enemies. And the problem was particularly acute in the infantry, where the exposure to personal danger and physical maiming was the greatest. Gen. James Gavin, commander of the elite Eighty-Second Airborne Division, inscribed in his diary

in January 1945 his analysis of how unsuited to military life were
the values of young American males as they fought the final battles of the war:

> If our infantry would fight, this war would be over by
> now. . . . We all know and admit it, and yet nothing is
> done about it. American infantry just simply will not
> fight. No one wants to get killed. . . . Our artillery is
> wonderful and our air corps not bad. But the regular
> infantry—terrible. Everybody wants to live to ripe old
> age. The sight of a few Germans drives them into their
> holes. Instead of being imbued with a desire to get close
> to the German and get him by the throat, they want to
> avoid him if the artillery has not already knocked him flat.[46]

Yet despite the deficiencies in training, leadership, and fighting
spirit, the Allies finally prevailed in North Africa. After ten weeks
of hard battling following Kasserine, the Allied forces in Tunisia
overwhelmed the outnumbered, depleted, undersupplied Axis army
under Messe and Arnim. Under Patton the Second Corps regained
the ground lost at Kasserine and began to push from the west
against the remaining Axis forces in Tunisia. Among the American
troops discipline tightened and morale improved, though at this
point the new American commander showed little of the aggressive
flair he would reveal in later battles. As Patton closed in from the
west, the British, under Alexander to the north and Montgomery
to the south, methodically squeezed the Axis troops into an ever-
smaller pocket encompassing Bizerte and Tunis.

In this last phase of the campaign serious new Anglo-American
tensions surfaced. Having lost confidence in the fighting qualities
of his allies, Alexander sought to confine the Americans to "clean-
ing up battlefields," in effect excluding them from the final coup.

A concerned Marshall radioed Alexander asking him to relent. He should "make a real effort to use the II U.S. Corps right up to the bitter end of the campaign. . . . I believe," he reassured Alexander, "that our units are learning fast. Their morale, technique, and physical condition improve daily, and the idea of U.S.-British partnership that is so essential to the final winning of this war essentially grows in strength." Marshall also defended his concern on the grounds that the knowledge garnered by American troops in North Africa would be a valuable learning experience that would help with training at home. He wrote: "We must develop a large number of qualified instructors that can be sent to the U.S., thus insuring that the great forces that must sometime be ferried across the ocean will have the highest possible degree of battle efficiency attainable prior to actual participation in the conflict."[47] But Marshall had nationalistic concerns as well, and radioed Eisenhower in mid-April warning him not to give way to Alexander because of the "unfortunate result as to national prestige . . . and reaction of public."[48] Ike responded by flying to Alexander's headquarters and in effect ordering him to reconsider. He backed this test of the unified-command principle with a version of the Pacific First argument: Unless the American public felt it was fully participating in the struggle against the Germans, it would favor a shift of focus to the Pacific, where presumably it need not worry about supercilious British allies.

In the end American troops were assigned the northernmost sector of the front, and on May 7, under Bradley's immediate command, captured the port of Bizerte just hours after British troops entered Tunis. Squeezed into an enclave on Cap Bon, the remaining Axis forces laid down their arms on May 13. The final prisoner bag was impressive: Some 275,000 Axis troops surrendered to the Allies, along with Generals Arnim and Messe and a flock of other German and Italian generals. The total human haul was more than twice as large as at Soviet-defended Stalingrad just the previous month. But the victory had not been cheap. Allied losses during the North African campaign—Tunisia as well as Torch—were substantial. British casualties numbered 38,000, with 6,200 killed; American casualties were 18,200, including 2,700 killed. Free French losses included 19,500 casualties, with 2,100 dead. The Axis losses were an estimated 8,500 German and 3,700 Italian dead. The depletion of Allied equipment had been appalling, far greater than that of the Axis, but in both numbers and in tanks, guns, and planes, the Allies could far more easily absorb the losses than could their enemy.

And so it was a famous victory, but as we have seen it was not won through superior strategy, soldierly skill, or combat élan. As in so many future successes it was achieved through sheer weight of equipment and fighting manpower against an enemy already depleted by attrition and suffering from serious shortages of fuel and supplies. As one American general would confess in a different venue: "The American Army does not solve its problems, it overwhelms them."[49]

And what had the anti-Axis cause gained? The answer is full of ambiguities. Some scholars insist that the North African campaign provided valuable combat experience for the American army. Omar Bradley would second their views. "In Africa we learned to crawl, to walk—then run," he later wrote.[50] Although imperfect training and replacement policies continued through the war's end in Europe, it is unquestionable that the experience of battle proved valuable for top American leadership when they encountered the Wehrmacht again in France. Assuredly North Africa taught Eisenhower much about military and coalition diplomacy, skills that he would put to good use in 1944–45. Patton, too, would learn valuable lessons in the Mediterranean and display them abundantly on the Continent months later.

It could also be argued that North Africa served at least as a partial second front. Hitler considered his commitment of troops and planes to North Africa a plus for the Axis. In July, after Arnim's surrender, he would contend that the Axis defense had postponed the Allied invasion of France by some six months. The dictator also believed that it had deflected an early Allied invasion of Italy and a thrust into Germany from the south.[51] And his response, of course, confirms the value to the Russians of the Allied North African campaign, a conclusion with which Stalin, if only by implication, agreed. In mid-February, when it seemed that the Allied North African campaign had stalled, the Soviet dictator wrote to Churchill to complain of the impact of the halt. "We have reliable information to the effect that since the end of December, when the Anglo-American operations in Tunis . . . were slowed down, the Germans transferred twenty-seven divisions . . . from France, Belgium, Holland, and Germany itself to the Soviet-German front. . . . It is just because the military operations in Tunis slackened that Hitler was able to throw in some additional troops against the Russians."[52] The Soviets did not consider the North African campaign an adequate substitute for a true second front, but they obviously gave it some credit for helping Russia in its plight.

Was Marshall wrong to oppose the North African operation? As he had anticipated, it certainly delayed the "mother of battles" with the Wehrmacht in France that the chief of staff believed essential for final Allied victory. Overlord was put off until the spring of 1944 by the needs of Torch and the Tunisian campaign. But was this a debit or a credit? In retrospect it seems undeniable that an Allied attack on the Continent, even in 1943, would have been at best a close thing. However dubious their motives, the British were right to steer clear of a major cross-Channel attack when shipping, manpower, equipment, and experience were still inadequate. But finally in Marshall's view, on the loss side of the ledger, the invasion of the former "Barbary States" further fed Churchill's overblown conviction that the "soft underbelly" strategy was the royal road to victory and, to the very verge of D-Day, encouraged his assumption that the Mediterranean was a theater in which to invest valuable Allied resources. In later months the PM would continue to resist Marshall's cross-Channel strategy, agitate for pushing Turkey into the war, and even launch an almost comically inept and unsuccessful all-British assault on the Axis-occupied Dodecanese Islands off the Turkish coast.

The question of the next Allied step after Tunisia had been settled well before the Axis surrender in Tunisia on May 13—and once again not to Marshall's satisfaction. The strategy was hammered out by FDR and Churchill and their staffs at a major conference at Casablanca in Morocco on North Africa's Atlantic coast.

As early as November 1942—restless in the politically contentious atmosphere of Washington, always attracted to a little excitement, and assured by Marshall that Tunisia would fall in just two or three weeks—Roosevelt accepted Churchill's proposal that the three anti-Axis leaders—he, Churchill, and Stalin—meet in North Africa to work out a coordinated strategy for the rest of the war. Stalin declined the offer; his personal presence in Russia was needed now at the beginning of a major Soviet offensive against the German invaders.

In cables to Churchill preliminary to the proposed conference, FDR speculated about operations after the North African campaign. His thoughts ranged widely. The Allies might consider operations to invade Sardinia, or Sicily, or mainland Italy, or Greece, or move against targets in the Balkans, the latter in conjunction with the still-neutral Turks, who Churchill believed could, and should, be brought into the war. FDR qualified his acceptance of any of these by insisting that the Bolero buildup of American forces in Britain to precede the cross-Channel operation continue undiminished.

At a White House meeting in early January between the Joint Chiefs and FDR, the president and Marshall clashed over future strategy. The two men would never be personally close. Though both Marshall and the fighting force he commanded were beneficiaries of administration policies, Marshall avoided too intimate an identification with FDR: For the sake of the army he must appear to be above politics. But temperament also played a role in their personal distance. FDR's legendary charm and habitual bonhomie had little appeal for the chief of staff, a man with limited social give, who was himself all business. His scruples against mixing military issues with politics may have inspired his aloofness, but it also suited his cool temperament, which prevented emotional intimacy with more than a tight circle of people.

At this White House meeting, preliminary to Casablanca, the volatile president seemed to embrace Churchill's preference for further operations in the Mediterranean after the Axis were evicted from North Africa. To Marshall the prime minister's choice was just another version of the British "peripheral" policy and a serious digression from the cross-Channel operation. He reiterated that the Joint Chiefs as a group, while not unanimous, strongly preferred a major attack in northwestern France to additional operations in the Mediterranean. Further actions in the south might take a heavy toll of shipping, he warned, and "completely destroy any opportunity for successful operations against the enemy in the near future."[53] As if to scuttle any successful move by the American planners to counter their British opposite numbers' certain defense of the "soft underbelly" position, however, FDR failed to order the Joint Chiefs to prepare a written defense of a cross-Channel strategy. It is not clear that Marshall could have overcome FDR's inclinations in any event, but there is little evidence that his voice as yet counted decisively with his boss or, for that matter, with all his military colleagues. And yet, as the well-informed John Dill would tell his British colleagues just before the North African conference officially opened, the Joint Chiefs would oppose expanding Torch into other major operations in the Mediterranean that threatened the primacy of the cross-Channel invasion.

The Casablanca Conference opened on Thursday, January 14, 1943. It would be one of eleven "summits" of two or more of the top anti-Axis leaders during the war. It took place when Britain was at the peak of its military power, fresh from Montgomery's victory over Rommel at El Alamein, and still supplying a clear preponderance of men and matériel to the Anglo-American alliance. That timing made it inevitable, perhaps, that its outcome would be a victory for the Churchillian perspective.

The most pressing immediate concern was what to do with the half million Allied troops who would be idle once the Axis were gone from the southern rim of the Mediterranean. But the issues to be debated were broader. The Allies would have to answer the question What next? in virtually every aspect of the war now raging on every inhabited continent and every ocean in the world.

The delegates at Casablanca met at the Anfa Hotel, a resort set idyllically overlooking the Atlantic and surrounded by graceful palm trees and fragrant orange groves, with adjacent villas for the national leaders. Elliott Roosevelt, who accompanied his father to the conference, called the accommodations "unpretentious but very modern, small but very comfortable."[54] Marshall, along with Hap Arnold and Sir John Dill, had left Washington by plane on the ninth, followed by a second plane carrying Admiral King and General Somervell along with army planner Albert Wedemeyer and his navy counterpart, Adm. Charles Cooke. The American

Top: George C. Marshall, Sr.

Bottom: Laura Bradford Marshall.

All photographs courtesy of the George C. Marshall Foundation unless otherwise noted.

George C. Marshall, Jr., about 1885.

Lily Marshall, Fort
Leavenworth, about 1908.

First Classman Marshall in
his furlough coat.

Mrs. Clifton Brown and her children in 1922: Allen *(left)*,
Molly, and Clifton.

President Franklin D. Roosevelt and Prime Minister Winston S.
Churchill aboard HMS *Prince of Wales*, 1941.

The chiefs of the War Department confer, March 1942.

Gen. George C. Marshall at dinner with *(left to right)* Admirals Ernest
King and William Leahy, and Gen. Harry "Hap" Arnold.

Roosevelt and Churchill *(seated)* with their respective chiefs of staff
at Casablanca, January 1943.

Visiting Gen. Douglas MacArthur and his commanders,
December 15, 1943.

President Truman congratulating General Marshall in the courtyard of the Pentagon, 1945.

Gen. Dwight D. Eisenhower and Gen. Marshall at Allied HQ, Algiers, June 3, 1943.

General Marshall sitting at his desk in the Pentagon beneath a portrait of General Pershing, November 1, 1943.

Marshall talks with Lt. Gen. Albert C. Wedemeyer, Commanding General, U.S. forces, China theater, at Chungking in January 1946.

Communist Party member of the Committee of Three, Gen. Chou En-lai *(left)* meets with Kuomintang member Gen. Chang Chun in Nanking, January 10, 1946.

Secretary of State Marshall, congratulated after his swearing-in ceremony.

Secretary Marshall talks with Senators Arthur H. Vandenberg and Tom Connally after a meeting of the Senate Foreign Relations Committee, February 14, 1947.

Dodona Manor in Leesburg, Virginia, where George and Katherine spent weekends during the war, and where Marshall spent his retirement after serving as secretary of defense. (*J. Vandervaart, the George C. Marshall International Center*)

General and Mrs. Marshall in the garden of their home, 1949.

staffers arrived early in Casablanca in order to discuss issues with their British opposite numbers before their respective bosses appeared. There would be three sets of meetings at the conference: separate discussions by the respective British and American military chiefs and their staffs; discussions between the British and American staffs as part of the CCS sessions; and discussions by the Combined Chiefs with Roosevelt and Churchill. The most passionate exchanges would take place at the latter meetings, when British-American differences would often lead to raised voices and scowling faces. More than once Brooke would become alarmed at the contention and anger displayed at these sessions.

Though amply forewarned, from the outset Marshall and his colleagues were once again at a disadvantage with the British, who had arrived with a large, briefed-to-the-gills delegation of military planners and experts. Just offshore was HMS *Bulolo*, a converted passenger vessel, loaded with maps, documents, and prepared position papers, along with Foreign Office and War Office experts and other resources for the British to make their case with their American cousins. Admiral King would later note that he and his fellow Americans at Casablanca "found . . . that every time they brought up a subject, the British had a paper ready."[55]

Though not yet fully prepared to push for Roundup in 1943, Marshall and his colleagues, as Dill had warned, also did not intend to allow Churchill and his staffers to make the Mediterranean the future center of the Allied war effort. The Americans were quickly put on the defensive. Backed up by the deluge of analytical papers and documentation, with many more months of war experience, Brooke and his colleagues could speak authoritatively, as the Americans still could not. The American staffs were also reluctant to openly oppose FDR who, they feared, was too much under the influence of the magnetic British prime minister for his country's good.

The British could make several major points to argue their case for further Mediterranean operations: once again, the waste of manpower if Allied troops after the North African campaign were allowed to remain idle; the opportunity to capitalize on the opening of the Mediterranean to free Allied passage; and the forward momentum already achieved in the North African theater. These realities made it difficult to resist the British plan to invade Sicily after the Axis defeat in Tunisia. But the Americans were determined to prevent any unlimited dispersal of Allied resources to areas Wedemeyer, for one, described as "neither vital nor final."[56]

At the January 16 meeting of the Combined Chiefs, Marshall spoke up aggressively against the British fixation on the Mediterranean theater. Allied planners must decide what the "main plot" of the war should be, he declared. "Every diversion or side issue" from that position acted as a "suction pump" draining energy and substance from the whole Allied war effort.[57] Two days later, at a morning CCS meeting, he clashed with Brooke over a memo of the British Joint Planning Staff that categorically rejected a cross-Channel attack in April 1943 as impractical. Besides its risks as a military operation, it was ruled out as well, the document said, by the perennial landing-craft shortages. Brooke softened the statement by dangling the bait of a cross-Channel operation in the spring or summer of 1944, *if* the Americans agreed to continue Mediterranean operations after a Tunisian victory. Knocking Italy out of the war and tying up German troops assigned to defend its weak ally, he claimed, would actually expedite a successful later invasion of France.

Marshall refused the bait and returned the discussion to the cross-Channel attack itself. The "doubtful" point, he responded, was "whether if the proposed Mediterranean operations were undertaken sufficient forces would be available in the United Kingdom to exploit the situation which the Mediterranean operations might have created." "Thus," he continued, "when the moment to strike across the Channel arrived, we should be unable to reap the benefits."[58]

Many other topics besides the next move in the Mediterranean theater were discussed in the beautiful Moroccan setting: the devastating U-boat war, the troublesome China-Burma theater, the proportionate allotment of resources to the Pacific versus the Atlantic, the possibility of bringing Turkey into the war against the Axis, the vital need to keep Russia fighting, the submarine war against the Japanese, and the Bolero operation. Of these, the issue of the Pacific generated almost as much controversy as the next step to take in Europe. Not unexpectedly Admiral King beat the drums aggressively for a larger allotment of Allied resources to fight Japan. Only 15 percent of the Allies' resources were being set aside for the Pacific, he asserted. Thirty percent would be needed to prevent the Japanese from consolidating their Pacific gains and so making their final defeat more difficult. Marshall, who, like FDR and other American leaders, believed China to be an important player in the war, also wanted a British commitment to take Burma back from the Japanese to help open the overland supply routes to Chiang Kai-shek, China's Nationalist leader. Though reluctant to divert resources to the Far East at this point, the British agreed to consider the American proposal for a Burma campaign that came to be labeled operation Anakim, a name reflecting one of Churchill's fanciful Old Testament allusions.

But the core of the debate remained the Mediterranean and the next Allied move, if any, within its limits. Marshall's impassioned exchange with Brooke at the January 18 Combined Chiefs meeting was the conference's crisis point. Though the British were still contributing a preponderance of men and arms to the Allied military effort, the Americans, Brooke knew, would have to be coaxed to support any action in the Mediterranean after the imminent Axis defeat. He had always assumed that they still favored Europe First. But abruptly that seemed to change, and by lunchtime CIGS was in despair. A new American memorandum declared that they now wanted to amend their concurrence that Germany was the chief Allied foe: Marshall was threatening to play the Pacific card. The British, he noted, seemed uninterested in deploying the troops accumulating in England for further operations against the European enemy. If they did not wish to use them, the Americans could do so in the Pacific. Brooke replied that he did not believe Germany and Japan could be defeated simultaneously, and that if the Allies attempted it they "[would] lose the war."[59] The two sides now seemed at an impasse; no agreement with the Americans seemed possible. The morning meeting had been "very heated," Brooke noted in his diary, and the Combined Chiefs "seemed to be making no headway." In his later amended diary comments, Brooke recalled that when he left the conference room "he was in despair and in the depths of gloom."[60] Fortunately, at lunch, Marshal Dill succeeded in cheering him up. In reality, Dill claimed, the British and Americans were not so far apart as they seemed, and with a little more discussion an agreement might be reached. When Brooke protested his unwillingness to "move an inch" on some of the points of Anglo-American disagreement, Dill responded: "Oh yes, you will. You know that you must come to some agreement with the Americans."[61] And so it proved. Returning to the Combined Chiefs meeting at 3:00 p.m. with a slightly revised version of the British proposal, Brooke was surprised when Marshall and his colleagues approved it.

The accord reached that day was, however, a British victory overall. The Americans agreed that the conquest of Sicily (code-named Husky) would be the next Allied operation with further actions in the Mediterranean, most prominently an invasion of Italy itself, depending on future circumstances. Marshall, in turn, conceded that Roundup was dead for 1943. Echoing his British colleagues' formula, he acknowledged that given Husky's needs, especially for landing craft, unless German morale experienced "a complete crack," operations across the Channel in 1943 would "have to be extremely limited."[62] In effect Roundup would be delayed. But Marshall refused to give in completely. He understood that, if not in 1943, the British had accepted a cross-Channel operation in 1944. And in any case, before undertaking a Sicilian operation it would be necessary "to determine just what part it would play in the over-all strategic plan."[63]

Other matters besides Mediterranean operations were settled that day. The British agreed at some point to launch an offensive to evict the Japanese from Burma. On the allocation of resources between the Atlantic and the Pacific theaters, a rough compromise was reached. The Allies would continue offensive operations against Japan but avoid using resources that might prevent attacks against the enemies in Europe as opportunities might occur. Both sides also agreed, along with other secondary matters, to support a massive bombing campaign against Germany. But the core issue was strategy in the Mediterranean, and here the decision was to proceed, though how far, against which targets, and for how long remained ill-defined. In fact most of the apparent agreements were "soft" and would have to be reargued, renegotiated, and modified several times before finally being translated into actions. But for now it could be claimed that there had been a meeting of minds.

Brooke credited Dill's intercession with Marshall for the agreement, however ambiguous. And he was probably right. Dill would often make the rough places plain on the Anglo-American wartime road. In the preceding months he and Marshall had established a unique rapport that enabled the military leaders of each nation to understand the other's views and helped reconcile disagreements between them. As Marshall wrote to FDR soon after the conference: "It was apparent that . . . a great deal was done by Dill to translate the American point of view into terms understandable to the British, also the fact that in certain matters there could be no compromise."[64]

It has been said that the discussions at Casablanca, however acrimonious at times and however murky the participants' strategic conclusions, did at least allow the military leaders on both sides to take the measure of their opposite numbers. Perhaps. But they did not engender mutual respect. Wedemeyer, for one, saw the conference as showing British guile prevailing over American innocence. Before leaving Casablanca he wrote to a military colleague condemning U.S. acquiescence in the "underbelly" strategy: The British had "swarmed down upon us like locusts," he noted, and while he had "the greatest admiration for them, . . . we lost our shirts and are now committed to subterranean umbilicus operations in mid-summer."[65] For the acerbic Brooke, though his side had won, the discussions reinforced his earlier opinion of Marshall. The American chief of staff, he caustically noted in his diary entry of January 20, "has got practically no strategic vision, his thoughts revolve around the creation of forces and not on their deployment. He arrived here without a single real strategic concept, he has initiated nothing in the policy for the future conduct of the war. His part has been that of somewhat clumsy criticism of the plans we put forward." Brooke had a better opinion of King. The admiral was "shrewd," though completely fixated on the Pacific. As for air corps commander Hap Arnold, his outlook was limited to air strategy policies. On the other hand, he added, "As a team [the Americans] are friendliness itself." Discussions, he acknowledged, were often heated, "yet our relations have never been strained."[66]

And, however unfair, Brooke's estimate of Marshall's performance at Casablanca was not far off the mark. The distinguished American military historian Maurice Matloff, in his 1959 study of World War II coalition warfare, has noted that at Casablanca "General Marshall succeeded in making no real change in the direction of Allied strategy." He had obviously tried to check the forward momentum of Churchill's "underbelly" policy, as seconded by FDR, but had struck out. "The simple terms in which War Department planners had tried to solve the problem of limiting operations in the subsidiary theaters had failed." As for the larger goals of Casablanca, "no real long-range plans for the defeat of the Axis Powers emerged."[67]

The discussions of the Joint Chiefs and the Combined Chiefs, as well as their meetings with FDR and Churchill, were of course secret. But two diplomatic events at Casablanca received wide international publicity. Among the issues hanging over the conference were the relations of the French factions now in the UN camp. After Darlan's assassination Giraud remained in charge of French armed forces in North Africa. But what about de Gaulle, the self-proclaimed leader of the Free French? Supported by the British, who had seen him early on as an alternative to Vichy, his authority had been accepted in a number of the French colonial territories. Neither FDR nor Marshall, however, liked the arrogant, haughty, six-foot-four French general who assumed that he personally incarnated La Belle France. Marshall first met de Gaulle in London during his July 1942 visit. He, like American leaders generally, was careful to avoid any appearance that he accepted de Gaulle's leadership of non-Vichy France. The French, after the war, would have to choose their rulers democratically, they believed. But whatever he felt personally about the lofty Frenchman, Marshall recognized the value of the quarter of a million French troops in North Africa and the French colonies. Ill equipped by Anglo-American standards, they formed a manpower reservoir that, once provided with modern guns, tanks, and planes, could prove valuable especially when the cross-Channel operation was finally mounted. To Marshall, accordingly, the disagreement between the two French generals seemed a petty squabble that was only impeding the war effort.

At Casablanca, FDR sought to force agreement between de Gaulle and Giraud to divide political authority over the former French North African possessions. Convinced that the Americans did not truly respect France's rights as a cobelligerent, and unwilling to accept competing leadership, de Gaulle at first demurred but was induced to sign a statement of unity with his rival just in time for the concluding conference press meeting on January 24. The picture of the two antagonistic generals shaking hands at the outdoor press conference became one of the memorable visual icons of the Casablanca Conference. In fact no real cooperation between the two men was ever achieved. Giraud eventually led a successful French invasion of Corsica but lost out to the politically shrewder de Gaulle as leader of postwar France.

At this same windup media circus, amid the popping flash-bulbs and shouting reporters, FDR slipped in an unexpected diplomatic surprise. As far back as the previous May he had privately endorsed the principle of "unconditional surrender" as Anglo-American final terms for the Axis enemies. The president had a twofold purpose: First, such a declaration would avoid any Axis claim, as the Germans had made in 1919 and after, that their surrender in World War I had come through internal political betrayal, not military defeat on the battlefield. It would also reassure Stalin that the Western Allies meant to provide unlimited support to the Soviet Union; they would not make a separate negotiated peace with Hitler no matter how advantageous it might seem. The statement, then, was not on the spur of the moment, as FDR would claim. The president in fact, it has been said, had promoted the Casablanca meeting in part to serve as a forum for the surrender announcement. Churchill, moreover, was in on the secret, and FDR and the prime minister had agreed at their January 18 meeting to release a statement that the Western Allies intended to "pursue the war to the bitter end."[68]

In later months, and future years, the unconditional surrender formula would be held responsible—probably mistakenly—for prolonging the war unnecessarily, with all the horrific consequences of the Holocaust and further death and maiming of soldiers and civilians alike. For Marshall, however, the announcement was welcome at the time. Given the delay on a second front, it would reassure the Russians, he believed. In later months, when the Allied offensive in France and the Low Countries had bogged down, he would second Ike's appeal for the formula's modification. But with the perpective of time he thought it a boon. The Germans and Japanese, he admitted to Pogue in 1957, "might have conceded the war a little earlier" without it, but overall it had "a great psychological effect on our people, on the British people, and on the Allied people generally, as well as on the Germans."[69]

At Casablanca, well before the final victory in Tripoli, the Anglo-American Allies had made the decision to invade Sicily. The attack, the Combined Chiefs soon decided, should begin at the "period of the favorable July moon."[70] But Casablanca had failed to provide needed detail of further operations in the Mediterranean and elsewhere. The remaining uncertainties seriously worried Churchill. Anxious, as he later wrote, to settle whether the fruits of the now-imminent victory should be "gathered only in the Tunisian tip" or whether the Allies should now "drive Italy out of the war and bring Turkey in on our side," he initiated another top-level meeting of the Allies in Washington.[71] This would take place during mid-May at a conference code-named Trident.

On May 11 Churchill and his entourage of almost one hundred military staffers, civilian experts, and top political advisers arrived in New York aboard the war-converted luxury liner *Queen Mary*. Whisked to the capital by train, they were greeted at Union Station by the president and his military staffers. Once again the prime minister took up quarters in the White House. There the Free World leaders would meet six times during the two-week conference, while the Combined Chiefs convened in the Board of Governors Room at the Federal Reserve Building on Constitution Avenue. This time the British would meet their match in the large and proficient American delegation. Trident would be held in far more favorable Allied circumstances than at Casablanca. There the Anglo-American cause, though looking up, had remained unsettled. Now, in May, the war was decidedly turning around. The day after Trident opened, news arrived of the final Axis surrender in Tunisia. In the Pacific the hard-fought and costly campaigns to evict the Japanese from Guadalcanal and New Guinea were now successfully concluded. On the Russian front, the Red Army's Stalingrad victory the previous January had been followed by the lifting of the siege of Leningrad and the retaking of the important cities of Kursk, Belgorod, and Kharkov. And things were now even less gloomy on and under the tempestuous Atlantic: For the first time since Pearl Harbor the disastrous and unsustainable U-boat toll was finally beginning to fall.

And yet the future of Anglo-American efforts after Husky still remained uncertain. Brooke, for one, still worried that the Americans' "hearts are really in the Pacific."[72] Marshall's was not one of those hearts, however. He agreed with the main thrust of a Joint Chiefs memo of May 8 declaring that the cross-Channel operation and the continued bombing of Axis targets in German-occupied Europe must "not be delayed or be otherwise prejudiced by other undertakings in Europe."[73] But Marshall failed to deflect the Joint Chiefs' proposal that the president hint to Churchill that if the British continued to demand overly ambitious operations for the Mediterranean the United States might consider diverting resources to the Pacific theaters.

At Trident Marshall and his colleagues finally got the president to take an unequivocal stand against further Mediterranean proliferation. Ever since Casablanca the Joint Chiefs had been seeking to woo Franklin away from Winston. In the weeks preceding Trident, Marshall had worked on FDR to assure his support of a strictly limited Mediterranean agenda. The United States must not, he coaxed, allow itself to be entangled in major military operations east of Sicily. Mainland Italy must be avoided. Occupying the Italian boot would be "more of a liability than an asset," he told FDR, draining men and aircraft from any cross-Channel attack.[74] Besides appealing to the president's strategic sense Marshall sought to activate FDR's always-sensitive political antennae. In this communication he reminded the president that a large segment of the American public considered the Japanese, not the Germans and Italians, to be the real enemy. This Pacific First perspective was leading to grumbling in Congress that the United States was doing Britain's bidding, he noted, a charge that leading men on the powerful Senate Foreign Relations Committee were taking seriously and threatening to investigate. Allowing the British to have their way in the Mediterranean would just feed anti-British prejudice and the Pacific First lobbyists. Whether or not Marshall's advice did the trick, at Trident FDR would seek to rein in British plans to attack the Italian mainland after Husky.

Nonetheless, total clarity of goals would still not be vouchsafed the conferring Allies. The conference would witness the same zealous racquet wielders replaying the same tedious tennis match as four months before, with the same serves and volleys by both sides. In his opening statement at Trident, Churchill soft-pedaled the Italy-versus-France issue. He did not reject the cross-Channel attack directly. Like his leading military advisers, he acknowledged the ultimate necessity to invade France—but only if a plan could be devised that had "reasonable prospects of success."[75] Meanwhile, the great goal after Husky must be to eliminate Italy from the war. The historian Andrew Roberts detects a deep emotional side to the prime minister's motives here. Churchill, he writes, despised Mussolini as a tinhorn bully and a "whipped jackal of Hitler."[76] But of course these feelings remained buried under the overt needs of grand strategy. In the White House, at the first plenary Trident meeting on May 12, the prime minister sought to sell the benefits of Italy's defeat. It would have many favorable strategic consequences, he insisted: It would eliminate the remaining threat of the Italian navy; it would force the Axis to abandon the Balkans; it would induce the Turks to join the Allies. In short, it could well mark "the beginning of the doom" of the Germans.[77]

FDR was skeptical. He admitted that it would be tempting after Husky to employ the large Allied armies in the Mediterranean to knock Italy out of the war. But—a better seer than Churchill—he noted that he had "always shrunk from the thought of putting large armies into Italy," for it seemed likely to cost the Allies more than it would the Germans.[78] The president reiterated the need to implement Bolero. It was preferable after Husky to deploy the surplus manpower to build up forces in Britain for the long-proposed cross-Channel assault. And that assault, he declared, should be mounted no later than the spring of 1944.

Needless to say, Marshall welcomed FDR's emphatic support for his cross-Channel priority but feared the continued waffling of the British leaders. He was infuriated by Brooke's observation at a CCS meeting on May 13 that "no major operations would be possible [in France] until 1945 or 1946" since "it must be remembered that in previous wars there had always been some 80 French divisions available on our side." It "appeared that ROUNDUP was still regarded as a vague concept," Marshall angrily responded. "Did this mean," he asked, "that the British Chiefs of Staff regarded Mediterranean operations as the key to a successful termination of the European war?"[79]

Back and forth the opposing arguments between the Allies flew once more. Much of the discussion concerned other theaters besides Europe. But again, two—northwestern Europe and the Mediterranean—occupied most of the Allied planners' time and stirred up most of the acrimony. The Combined Chiefs, in their discussions of Where next? championed the positions of their respective bosses. Marshall and Secretary Stimson, as in the past, considered Churchill's qualifiers for a cross-Channel operation another version of his nibbling-away policy: The invasion would only come, the British were saying, when the Germans had been brought to their knees by bombing and the relentless attrition of their army by the Russians on the eastern front. Marshall was now willing to concede that Sledgehammer back in 1942 would have been "suicidal."[80] For their part, the British did not categorically reject the need for an eventual cross-Channel assault on the German-occupied Continent. But their schedule for Roundup seemed to slip ever further into the future. Much more, they insisted, must first be accomplished in the Mediterranean. At the heated May 13 meeting Brooke claimed that if "we did not continue operations in the Mediterranean, then no possibility of an attack into France would arise."[81] He invoked the plight of Russia to bolster his case. It would be better, he claimed, "from the Russian point of view" that the Allies should "attack Italy now rather than start preparing for cross-Channel operations." As part of his pro-Russian argument Brooke raised once again the valid issue of unused men and equipment after Husky. The Sicily campaign would be brief, he insisted, and it seemed "unthinkable" that so many men and military resources should remain idle for months after it concluded while the Russians were engaging 185 Axis divisions on the eastern front. As for transferring the Allied troops from Africa to Britain to implement Bolero, it would be a difficult operation owing to the persistent dearth of shipping. And yet without the ships "no major operations would be possible until 1945 or 1946."[82]

Marshall and his colleagues lobbed back. The Joint Chiefs, after reiterating the Europe First strategy, once more strongly endorsed "a determined attack against Germany on the Continent at the earliest practicable date." "All proposed operations in Europe," they continued, "should be judged primarily on the basis of the contribution to that end."[83]

From the outset Marshall remained at the forefront of the cross-Channel battle. The Bolero buildup in Britain must not be abandoned, he insisted at the first Combined Chiefs meeting. He was "deeply concerned," he declared, "that the landing of ground forces in Italy would establish a vacuum . . . which would preclude the assembly of sufficient forces in the United Kingdom to execute a successful cross-Channel operation." If "we were ever to get the forces in the United Kingdom, we must begin now."[84] Marshall repeated his warnings at later CCS discussions. Further operations in the Mediterranean, beyond Husky, might well take more resources than anticipated and "thus when the moment to strike across the Channel arrived we should be unable to reap the benefits of our Mediterranean operations . . . and our resources in the U.K. would permit of nothing more than an unopposed landing."[85]

On the post-Husky issue Marshall could count on the navy's support. Whatever his position on the resources balance between Europe and the Pacific, on the cross-Channel operation Admiral King sided with Marshall. Leahy, too, though a navy man, defended Marshall's views. The North African campaign, he reminded members of the Combined Chiefs, had been undertaken "in order to do something this year while preparing for the cross-Channel operations." Little had been done, however, to prepare for that attack, "since all available U.S. resources had been sent to North Africa."[86] Further operations in the Mediterranean would only delay Roundup. But Marshall could not, of course, count on Brooke's support. In fact at Trident CIGS' view that his American counterpart was a military incompetent was confirmed. "It was quite evident," Brooke later wrote, "that Marshall was quite incapable of grasping the objects of our strategy, [or] the magnitude of operations connected with cross Channel strategy."[87]

Hovering over the whole discussion, as it would so often, was the issue of landing craft for amphibious operations. Both Allies had failed initially to understand the vital necessity for vessels that could safely carry men and equipment from ship to shore. The British had designed such ships, but the Americans, despite their industrial might, had been slow to produce them, and both sides in the discussion had used the shortage to bolster their arguments for or against further Mediterranean operations.

On the fifteenth the staffs took a rest-and-relaxation break at nearby Williamsburg, the restored capital of eighteenth-century colonial Virginia. There the Americans, using the good offices of John D. Rockefeller Jr., the restoration's generous patron, served as hosts to their British counterparts. The generals and admirals took tea at the Raleigh Tavern; dined on a lavish dinner of terrapin, fried chicken, fresh asparagus, and Virginia ham at the Williamsburg Inn; toured by candlelight the handsome colonial Governor's Palace; and attended Episcopal services at the eighteenth-century Bruton Parish Church. Ismay would later write that, though the Washington discussions had at times been acerbic, the Williamsburg weekend had been "beautifully arranged, had given them all a chance to get to know one another, and there had not once been a mention of the war."[88] Even Brooke was delighted with the visit.

Back in Washington, the meetings and debates resumed and continued until May 25, but the major decisions between the two Allied staffs were reached on Wednesday morning, the nineteenth. The result was a compromise. Marshall and FDR extracted from the British the promise that Roundup, the landings in northern France, would be launched in the early spring of 1944. But Churchill and Brooke got the green light for the boot of Italy as the next Anglo-American invasion target, the "free hand" in the Mediterranean to last until November.[89] But there was a qualifier here: Eisenhower, the North Africa supreme commander, would plan the additional moves beyond Husky against Italy, with final decisions on the specifics to be reserved for the Combined Chiefs, where of course Marshall would have an effective say. Meanwhile, four American and three British divisions would, in November, be transferred from the Mediterranean to contribute to Bolero. These conclusions were incorporated into a "Final Report to the President and Prime Minister" adopted on May 25, the last day of the meetings.

Though an attempt at balance, all in all, the outcome at Trident must be judged a success from the American perspective, certainly an advance over Casablanca. At the vast new Pentagon Building, to which Marshall had relocated his office in mid-November, there was the sense that the concessions and opacities of the Moroccan conference had finally been resolved. The United States would go for Italy (more or less) if the UK would go for Roundup in the spring of 1944. The Combined Chiefs had also endorsed a number of subordinate operations: to occupy the strategic mid-Atlantic Azores from Portugal as part of the campaign against the U-boats; to reinforce the combined Allied bomber offensive against German targets so as to destroy the enemy's industry and undermine "the morale of the German people"; to improve land communications with China by way of Burma; to evict the Japanese from the Aleutians, the Solomons, and the Marshall and Caroline Islands; and, finally, to launch a massive air attack by American bombers against the important Axis-controlled oil field at Ploiesti, in Romania.

But if Marshall and his colleagues were pleased, Churchill was not. In his view the agreement on further Mediterranean operations, leaving critical decisions on post-Husky strategy to Ike and the CCS, was uncomfortably inconclusive. At the final Trident meeting with the Combined Chiefs and FDR, he proposed that Marshall accompany him to Algeria, where they would meet with Eisenhower and—so the prime minister privately hoped—extract from him irreversible promises to launch an Italian mainland campaign soon after Husky. According to Stimson, Churchill also intended to "work on" Marshall to get him to accept some of his further "desired excursions in the eastern Mediterranean."[90] Later that day the president ordered Marshall to humor the prime minister. Himself reluctant to face "Uncle Joe's" wrath over further delay of the cross-Channel operation, Roosevelt proposed that Churchill and the American chief of staff use the flight to Algeria to compose a letter giving Stalin the bad news that a real second front had been postponed for yet another year.

Marshall balked at the president's plan. He had other things in mind personally for after Trident, including an inspection trip to the South Pacific with King and a much-needed vacation with Katherine. He complained to Stimson that by sending him off to North Africa, the president was treating him like "a piece of baggage."[91] But he was dutifully aboard the Boeing flying boat with the PM and General Ismay when it lifted off from Chesapeake Bay for Gibraltar on May 26. During the transatlantic flight Churchill assigned the difficult Stalin letter to Marshall, whose clear and comprehensive explanation he later praised as a remarkable statesmanlike performance. In any case, Marshall would note, composing the apologia—as well as engaging the prime minister in distracting discussions of historical and current events—had spared him from listening to another pro-Mediterranean Churchillian harangue during the tedious seventeen-hour flight.

At Allied headquarters in Algiers, seconded by Brooke, Churchill prodded Ike to get on with specific plans for invading the Italian boot. Meanwhile, a visiting Anthony Eden, the British foreign secretary, at a meeting with Ike and Marshall, hinted at an invasion of the Balkans as a possible Allied initiative after Italy. Marshall wanted to first see how the Sicily invasion went before committing Allied troops to crossing to the Italian mainland, but was soon worrying that his protégé was not being resolute enough. And Eisenhower in fact was wavering. Whatever his earlier doubts, he now accepted the necessity of ending Italy's part in the war. He also asserted that an invasion of the Italian boot would be an easy operation. Marshall disagreed. At Trident he had warned Brooke that a "German decision to support Italy might make intended operations [against tthe Italian mainland] extremely difficult and time consuming."[92] Along with many others, Ike now made a bad guess that would prove costly in lives and resources. The Sicilian operation, still ahead, he asserted, should "give a good indication of the type of resistance likely to be encountered on the mainland of Italy itself."[93] It would do no such thing. The invasion of mainland Italy would be a bloody twenty-four-month-long slog up the Italian boot that would cost the Allies more than three hundred thousand casualties, including 23,500 American military deaths, and would turn much of central Italy into a wasteland.

Students of events in these months before Allied troops finally landed on the beaches of Normandy in mid-1944 cannot
avoid exasperation at the wavering and indecision of all parties
involved. Despite Churchill's and Brooke's reservations regarding
Roundup, on the other side Marshall remained skeptical, to the
end, of invading mainland Italy. At the Algiers meeting he waffled about the move to the Italian boot but did not directly oppose it. Forcefully reminding Brooke, Churchill, and the others
that they had set a definite date for the cross-Channel attack, he
still failed to make entirely clear his continuing doubts about an
Italian invasion, allowing Churchill to believe that the decision
was solid.

When the meetings adjourned for two days Marshall took the
occasion to make a quick tour of the American-occupied areas of
Tunisia and to observe the holding camps for the quarter million
German and Italian POWs captured in May. When he returned
to Algiers the meetings briefly resumed with a presentation by
General Montgomery, newly arrived from Britain, of his strategic
plan for Husky. Marshall had never met the famous victor of El
Alamein. He liked his plan but not the man. Small, bird-faced,
eccentric in dress, Montgomery was arrogant, self-serving, and
aggressively ambitious. Even Brooke thought he was tactless and
"lack[ed] appreciation of other people's outlook." The Americans,
CIGS accurately observed in his diary, did not like Monty, and,
he astutely predicted, it would "always be a difficult matter to
have him fighting in close proximity to them."[94] At the meetings'
end Marshall agreed to hold a press conference for some thirty
British and American journalists to answer their questions about
the war and its progress. It was a masterly performance that enhanced his reputation for grasping the intricacies and problems of
the war, theater by theater. One correspondent remembered it as
"the most brilliant interview" he had "ever attended."[95]

Marshall returned to Washington soon after, arriving back at his Pentagon office on June 8 and reporting to Stimson. The secretary expressed fear that the persuasive prime minister had unraveled the Trident results on the Algiers trip. Marshall assured him that he had saved the Trident gains—and without offending Churchill in the process. But in fact, as events would soon show, the PM had not taken Marshall's words of caution about an Italian invasion seriously. Indeed, soon after Husky, the entire turbulent issue of Mediterranean versus cross-Channel would, like some old virus still lurking in the body, break out again, requiring further emergency treatment to avoid dangerous consequences. Not until after the landings on the Sicilian beaches in July would the Allied leaders and planners definitively make the Italian mainland the next Anglo-American objective.

At each of the Allied conferences in the year and a half following Pearl Harbor, the strategy and problems of the Pacific had been largely background noise. For Britain the German and Italian danger was the all-in-all; Asia and the Pacific could wait. For Admiral King and the U.S. Navy they were almost the whole game.

CHAPTER 7

PACIFIC WOES

The immense ocean that formed the core of the Pacific theater extends over sixty-four million square miles, one-third of the earth's surface. With its archipelagos, atolls, beaches, gulfs, volcanos, and capes, it stretches from the Arctic Circle to Antarctica, from the cordillera-edged Americas to the teeming mainland of East Asia. Its waters lave a multitude of nations and dependencies, many with ill-defined, overlapping boundaries. It was the spacious domain where the war started, and for many Americans it remained the more valid battleground. From the outset the war in the Pacific deeply engaged George Marshall, but unlike his performance in the Atlantic theaters, where his voice was commanding, his role in the Pacific was often hesitant and constrained.

Several factors explain this unsure grip. First, there was the navy. The Pacific was the navy's realm, and Ernest King was its monarch.

Interservice struggle for predominance in a given theater was, perhaps, inevitable. King and the admirals accepted the army's priority in the Atlantic arena. No doubt the navy had a significant role to play in the Atlantic and Mediterranean. Indeed, the defeat of the German U-boat campaign against Allied Atlantic shipping, to which the U.S. Navy contributed, was the sine qua non of victory in Europe. But the maritime Battle of the Atlantic had to be shared with the British, with the Royal Navy in ultimate charge. King was almost resentful of the Atlantic. He was slow to see the vital need for Atlantic convoys to check the Axis subs, and besides he despised the British, whose turf the narrower ocean was. Having "fought under the goddam British in the First World War," he was reputed to have proclaimed, "if I can help it, no ship of mine will fight under 'em again."[1] The Pacific was the place where the U.S. Navy could truly shine in the war against the Axis.

The army of course could not be denied an important role in the Pacific. The navy had a carrier-based air force and a military arm of its own—the marine corps—trained primarily for amphibious operations, but there were never enough marines or enough navy Wildcats and Corsairs to meet its offensive needs. Though frequently reluctant to do so, the admirals often had to turn to the army and its air arm for support. And then there was MacArthur's command in Australia: With powerful urges to run the Pacific war by himself, the general had his own quasi-autonomous military force and his own small fleet. Finally, since Marshall was a leading voice on the Joint Chiefs, his approval for allotment of overall U.S. resources of men and matériel among the Allied theaters was generally vital for any important strategic decision. This role gave him a voice in the navy's affairs—but not necessarily when it came to MacArthur. The chief of staff could not always successfully challenge his nominal subordinate, who exceeded him in fame, popularity, and thespian flair.

Leaving China aside, the Pacific war presented two major puzzles to the Joint Chiefs' planners in Washington: What proportion of Allied fighting men and matériel resources should be allotted to it compared with Europe and the Mediterranean? And who should run the show? And, as part of this second point, how—or whether—to apply the unified-command principle so basic to Marshall's vision of Allied grand strategy?

For months after Pearl Harbor the American public's anxious attention was riveted on the bitter land, air, and sea engagements to stop the Japanese juggernaut. But to the planners and strategists at the Pentagon, including Marshall, many of the key Pacific issues were jurisdictional. After the collapse of the ABDA under General Wavell, the question of a supreme commander for the whole Pacific area became urgent. Admiral King supposedly favored such a unified command but stipulated that its head must be a naval officer. Marshall of course favored unity in principle but failed to fight for it successfully. Intent on assigning authority to the newly rescued MacArthur, he initially proposed a separate supreme command only for Australia, where MacArthur was now headquartered. In early 1942 the Joint Chiefs hammered out a compromise, but one that violated the principle that Marshall himself had so earnestly defended just weeks before. The vast Pacific theater would be divided into two major divisions: the Southwest Pacific Area (SWPA), with MacArthur as supreme commander in Melbourne (later relocated farther north in Brisbane), and the Pacific Ocean Areas (POA), with Admiral Nimitz as commander in chief, headquartered at Honolulu. For the purpose of combat leadership, the second of these was to be further divided into three geographic subdivisions: South, Central, and North Pacific, the first under Vice Adm. Robert Ghormley and the other two under Adm. William "Bull" Halsey. And the unity principle was violated in still another way: Admiral Nimitz was to retain ultimate control of the modest contingent of second-class naval ships allocated to MacArthur (Seventh Fleet) under Adm. Thomas Kincaid, an authority that would trigger a fusillade of protests from Melbourne and embroil Marshall in incessant struggles to settle interservice disputes. Finally, in the overall war against Japan, there was the British-headed South East Asia Command (SEAC), established in August 1943, encompassing India, Burma, Ceylon, Malaya, and Sumatra, a theater that encroached on China, which Americans, if not Britons, deemed a vital partner in the anti-Axis war.

This arrangement would not resolve the issue of Pacific jurisdictions. There would be constant bickering over service boundaries, particularly those between MacArthur and the navy. The divided authority would also fail in the late phase of the Pacific war to establish clear priority in the final drive to subdue Japan, and at least once, in the waters off the Philippines, produce near disaster. But for the moment it was the best that was achievable.

But besides the interservice disputes over who should run the Pacific war, it was inevitable that Pacific combatants—soldiers as well as sailors—would resent the uneven division of military resources between themselves and the Europe–North Africa theaters. It is true that the navy's own 1940 Plan Dog had proposed a Europe First strategy for the United States in the event of war with the aggressors. But Admiral King would ceaselessly protest the resource disparity between East and West. The Pacific fleet, he insisted time and again, had been consigned meager rations of 15 percent of the manpower and war tools allotted to Europe and North Africa, too little to effectively fight its assigned enemy. Redirecting an additional 5 percent to the Pacific would not harm the Europe First strategy but would enormously accelerate the war against Japan.

Viewed as a whole, the charge of geographic discrimination of military resources was not valid. As one student of World War II military command has noted, almost half of all American servicemen who were sent overseas were dispatched to the Pacific.

But of course many of these were sailors or marines. The army, however, did in fact favor the Atlantic. As the war raged in Europe and the Mediterranean, Marshall and Stimson—their occasional resort to bluff notwithstanding—successfully resisted investing more resources in the Pacific than the 15 percent King cited. Of Marshall's ninety combat divisions, Stephen Taaffe observes, only some twenty-one served in the Pacific theaters, fifteen of them under MacArthur's command.[2] The long delay of the cross-Channel assault in Europe would provide an opportunity, seized on by both MacArthur and King, to expand operations against the Japanese. But the bias remained to the very end of the European phase of the war. One set of figures cited by the historian Samuel Eliot Morison—a reserve admiral—shows a roughly 3 to 2 split of troops and a 2 to 1 split in aircraft in favor of Europe over the Pacific at the end of 1943.[3]

In later years Marshall's most zealous critics would accuse him of harboring malicious prejudice against the Pacific theater. He thought this unfair. Though he obviously put the "German war" first, he always tried for balance, he insisted. When Forrest Pogue remarked to him in 1956 that "a lot of people assumed that you just gave up on the Pacific," he denied the charge emphatically. "My struggle was to see that the main show [Europe] went on," but also "that the later show was not washed out."[4]

In its quest for "more" the navy could usually count on MacArthur as an ally. Almost from the moment he arrived in Australia, fearing that his would be the "forgotten front," MacArthur demanded more troops, more planes, more guns, and more of the other matériel he needed, first to stop the enemy's advance southward toward Australia and then to drive his own forces north toward *dai Nippon* itself. Typically, in May 1942, when naval resources originally assigned to his command were abruptly switched to imperiled Midway Island to fend off Admiral

Yamamoto's massive attack, he cried havoc. If the losses were not made up by stripping other theaters, he warned Marshall, Australia might fall to the Japanese. And if that were to happen, "the United States itself will face . . . a crisis of such proportions as she never faced in the long years of her existence."[5] And the protests resumed even after the decisive Midway naval victory had proved the worth of the additional investment. In late August he once again warned that neglecting the Pacific risked disaster. The Europe First grand strategy must be abandoned, he cabled the War Department, to avoid military catastrophe in the Pacific. "I beg of you most earnestly," he wrote to Marshall, "to have this momentous question reviewed by the President and the chiefs of staff lest it become too late."[6] Nor were the general's complaints confined to official channels; they were broadcast to his wide and influential network of military and political allies and partisans. "Out here," he wrote to his old friend Gen. George Van Horn Moseley, "I am busy doing what I can with what I have, but resources have never been made available to me for a real stroke. Innumerable openings present themselves which because of the weakness of my forces I cannot seize."[7]

MacArthur shamelessly manipulated the press to serve his goals. In early August 1942 he apparently fed the American head of the INS news service in Australia the material for a long indictment of the Joint Chiefs for starving the Southwest Pacific theater of troops and munitions. The article was widely circulated in the United States and angered Marshall, who quickly shot off a message demanding that the general issue a denial of the assertions. But Marshall fudged the issue of discrimination. "The needs of the Southwest Pacific Theater," he asserted, "are weighed against those of all other theaters and once determined they have equal priority with those of other theaters." He went on to say that MacArthur was of course "aware of what has been done and what is being done to supply your theater to meet the needs of the strategy adopted."[8] The response at best was disingenuous. It failed to deny the priority to Europe; it assumed MacArthur accepted that choice, and of course he did not. Other field commanders would complain to Marshall of shortages and supposedly unfair discrimination, but none seemed to suffer so severe a case of "localitis" (to use Marshall's term) as did the commander of the Southwest Pacific Area.

But if MacArthur and King agreed that the United States must pay more attention and provide more resources to the Pacific theater, that did not lessen the ferocious competition between them for control of operations within the theater itself.

In June 1942, following the crushing Japanese defeat at Midway, King proposed a navy-led offensive that, according to MacArthur, threatened the jurisdictional agreement between him and the navy arranged earlier in the year. Nimitz and his forces, according to this plan, would seize the Solomons and adjacent islands, with their eventual goal the occupation of eastern New Guinea and New Britain, the potential Japanese launch points for invading Australia. MacArthur's role would be limited to supplying some land-based aircraft and a few ships from his small naval contingent. Suspecting weak support in the War Department, the general immediately cried foul. MacArthur was no friend of Marshall's. Gen. Robert Eichelberger, one of his most respected subordinates, claimed that he once heard his chief declare, "George Catlett Marshall is the most overrated officer in the United States Army."[9] And Marshall guardedly reciprocated the negative feelings. But whatever his personal reservations about his former boss, the chief of staff in this case rushed to defend him. The navy plan, he wrote to King, was "neither a logical arrangement in accordance with the principles we have adopted for joint action," nor was it "a practical method for directing the operation." By agreement, he reminded King, MacArthur was "in command of the area concerned," and, moreover, his staff had been reconnoitering the target area for months and was better informed of its characteristics than was the navy. "To my mind," he concluded, "it would be most unfortunate to bring in another commander at this time to carry out the operation."[10] In response King reminded Marshall that when it came to Europe he had supported the unity principle in favor of an army supreme commander. In the case of the South Pacific, however, where "practically all the forces used in the first instance will be amphibious and naval in character," the commander of the operation should be a naval officer.[11]

The Army-Navy Pacific rivalry was exacerbated by the personalities of the two principals. Neither King nor MacArthur was a timid soul. The tall, balding chief of naval operations was a hard-drinking, acerbic, aggressive, irascible man afflicted with a strong case of concupiscence, apparently not confined to his wife. Navy lore had it that he shaved daily with a blowtorch. His daughter called him "the most even-tempered man in the world. He is always in a rage."[12] MacArthur was equally prickly and contentious. Marshall managed to preserve a passable working relationship with King, but MacArthur and his staff could not. The SWPA commander did not despise all the navy's leaders; he got along well enough with Admiral Halsey. The two argued, but MacArthur always retained his respect for him as "a real fighting admiral," not one (like so many others, he believed) who sought above all to avoid risking his ships.[13] But as for Halsey's colleagues, especially Nimitz and King, Halsey's chief, they were the enemy, almost as malign as the Japanese foes.

In the absence of a supreme commander, MacArthur's personal defects, like King's, fed the unfortunate Pacific interservice struggle. The general suffered from more than a touch of paranoia. At times in his career he believed himself the target of a conspiracy by men in high places to defeat and humiliate him. These fears tainted his relations with his colleagues in the army itself. The War Department, he was convinced, was run by members of the "Chaumont crowd," the inner circle of AEF staffers around Pershing in 1918, including Marshall, who were not his friends. And he was not entirely mistaken. Many of the staff officers at Pershing's Chaumont headquarters *had* resented MacArthur's brash, daredevil, self-promoting behavior in France. And later, during the twenties, Pershing himself, while chief of staff, had treated MacArthur rather shabbily, owing, many believed, to the romantic entanglement of both men with the same woman, the heiress-playgirl Henrietta Louise Brooks, MacArthur's first wife.

But besides the SWPA commander's suspicious nature, there was his dismaying megalomania. Son of a revered Civil War hero and military governor of the Philippines, MacArthur saw himself as a man of destiny who could rescue the nation from evil and incompetent leaders. He had grand political ambitions—an affliction Marshall deplored in any military leader, including in his lifetime patron General Pershing—and had already begun his persistent campaign to gain the Republican presidential nomination. With such inflated self-regard and grandiose goals, MacArthur inevitably chafed at relegation to a secondary theater and found it intolerable as well to share ownership of that theater with the navy. The interservice feud was personified by the antagonism between the general and Adm. Chester Nimitz, the POA commander in chief. That conflict was "bitter," Marshall later lamented, "the prejudice so great."[14]

The chief of staff often took the side of his fellow general, but he blamed both antagonists for the frequent interservice clashes. Nimitz was essentially a reasonable man, he believed, though King, he agreed, was not. As for MacArthur, he concluded in long perspective, he was power hungry and ambitious. He "wanted to run things. . . . There were no concessions on his part whatsoever."[15] Yet there was an important qualifier: Marshall did not hold him solely responsible for the army's share of the interservice contention in the Pacific. The disagreements were greatly aggravated, he believed, by MacArthur's chief of staff, Gen. Richard Sutherland, a military bully and an unpopular man at Southwest Pacific headquarters, who, through the entire war, carried on a virtual vendetta against the navy.

Yet whatever his true feelings, Marshall tried to avoid an open breach with his Pacific subordinate. He was careful to praise MacArthur and induced the president to stroke his ego by frequent displays of personal gratitude for his military successes. After his escape from Bataan, it was Marshall who recommended that MacArthur be awarded the Congressional Medal of Honor, an award the general's father had also received. At times Marshall also sought to muzzle MacArthur's critics. At one meeting of the Joint Chiefs, when King had fiercely denounced MacArthur, Marshall squelched the admiral with the stinging rebuke: "I will not have any meetings carried on with this hatred."[16]

Meanwhile, on the Pacific battle lines, though starved for men and arms, MacArthur's American and Australian forces in New Guinea checked and then gradually rolled back the early Japanese advances from the north toward Australia. Each gain, however, triggered another round of negotiations over control and resources among the divided Pacific commands and commanders.

By early 1943 the July agreement on Pacific jurisdictions seemed inadequate. In February both MacArthur's joint Australian-American campaign against the Japanese in Papua, in south-central New Guinea, and the navy–marine corps invasion of Guadalcanal in the Solomons, had been victoriously concluded, but both operations had uncovered confusion in command and poor coordination between the services. Now, with further advances against the enemy in prospect, Marshall and King both believed that clarification of Pacific authority was essential. In February the chief of staff convened a conference in Washington for mid-March, which would bring together senior representatives of the army, air force, and navy to consider future Pacific moves, assign resources to the different services, and sort out the lines of authority over future operations. The deficiencies of disunity would be repaired.

The meetings were attended by most of the senior staff officers in the Pacific, with Marshall and King initially stepping off to the side ready to intervene only if necessary. Making the case for the navy was Charles Cooke; for the army, Wedemeyer of Victory Program fame. MacArthur remained in Brisbane; Sutherland would be his voice at the meeting. The immediate issue at hand was MacArthur's Elkton II Plan, aimed at the capture of Rabaul in the Bismarck Archipelago off northeast New Guinea, a goal set by the Joint Chiefs.* The seizure of the heavily manned and fortified enemy stronghold, the chiefs stipulated, must be accomplished with the modest allotment of troops and equipment imposed by existing shortages of shipping and other resources. Back in Brisbane, MacArthur had bridled at the assignment when first proposed. To conduct the Southwest commander's part of the offensive successfully, Sutherland protested, would require more than twenty-two divisions and forty-five air groups, not the niggardly allocation the chiefs had proposed. The navy, too, had its disagreements with MacArthur, but not over resources, and now, at the conference, its spokesmen made it clear that they

---

*This action eventually was incorporated into a joint operation with the navy named Cartwheel, in which MacArthur's New Guinea advance, part of his "go north" strategy, would be joined by Halsey's simultaneous attack toward Bougainville Island.

too wanted more of everything for the Pacific. Admiral Cooke, described by some army planners as even "meaner than King," aggressively presented the navy's case. He had attended the Casablanca Conference as part of the navy's contingent and now denied vehemently that the Allies there had rejected the need for vigorous operations in the Pacific. The planners at Casablanca, he claimed, had only agreed "to employing the maximum means against Germany which will not jeopardize our position in the Pacific."[17] He especially questioned whether the European theater had not received more airpower than needed at the expense of the Pacific.

The interservice debate quickly became heated, with the Army Air Forces overall, though making its own demands for reinforcement, supporting the Europe First line. Though Marshall and the army yielded minimally on the added-resources issue, chipping in a few additional air groups for the Rabaul assault, in exchange they reduced the number of ground troops assigned to the Pacific theater. With help from Admiral Leahy, chairman of the Joint Chiefs, the army also squeezed from the navy an agreement that MacArthur would be placed in charge of all operations in his assigned Pacific sector, including some conducted by naval task forces.

The conference did not solve the problems that had inspired it. It failed to change, except marginally, the existing percentage allocation of resources from Europe to the Pacific. As for the conflict over service jurisdictions, it had been solved for only one operation. Marshall's surviving hope to address the larger problem of divided Pacific command had been ignored and would bedevil army-navy relations to the war's end. All told, according to Maurice Matloff, "the military planning growing out of the . . . Conference was essentially short range and limited in scope."[18]

The inconclusive nature of the outcome perhaps owed something to Marshall's inattention. He had been briefed on the early conference meetings by Wedemeyer, but soon after, nursing a persistent cold, he had gone off with Katherine to Miami Beach for ten days of relaxation. If he expected to enjoy the sea and sand anonymously he was disappointed. At one point, in a local shoe store with Katherine to buy beach sandals, he was recognized by the manager, who, in a loud voice, announced his presence. As Pogue notes, to the general's dismay, the "quiet crowd of shoppers turned into a noisy welcoming committee."[19] Marshall returned to Washington on March 14, but in his absence the interservice divisions had hardened, making the disappointing achievements of the Washington meetings perhaps inevitable.

In the months that followed, the differences between MacArthur and the navy over Pacific strategy sharpened. A year and a half after the Pearl Harbor disaster, the navy's confidence and esprit had returned; moreover, by midsummer of 1943 dozens of new aircraft carriers, battleships, and landing craft were sliding off American construction ways. The navy's wartime expansion would be phenomenal. Unlike its sister service, the navy encountered few obstacles to growth from citizens and politicians. By mid-1944, Max Hastings notes, "warships were coming off the slips faster than crews could be mustered and trained to man them."[20]

Revived confidence and augmented firepower now stirred navy planners to demand a major realignment of U.S. Pacific strategy against Japan. Rather than MacArthur's plan to roll up the Japanese conquests from the south by advancing from his Australian base, retaking the Philippines, and then moving against the enemy's home islands, priority would be given to a navy-led thrust through the central Pacific against the fortified islands mandated to Japan by the League of Nations, bypassing the Philippines. A Central Pacific strategy, then, would become the major thrust against Japan. The navy's new resolve was heralded in February when King proposed an attack against the Gilberts, followed in early June by an assault to seize the Marshall Islands farther north. At the Quadrant Allied summit conference in mid-August in Quebec, the Combined Chiefs would officially sanction the navy's new strategy, though avoiding the issue of the Philippines, whose ultimate fate did not yet seem urgent.

The new Central Pacific initiative obviously put MacArthur and the navy on a collision course once more. For MacArthur, bypassing the Philippines was inconceivable. Strategically, he observed, they lay athwart the most direct route to Japan. Their successful reconquest, moreover, would force the Japanese to rely on limited-range carrier planes while exposing them to more effective Allied land-based aircraft. But for MacArthur retaking the Philippines was more than a strategic issue. The commander of SWPA had promises to keep. After his escape from Bataan to Australia he had solemnly pledged he would "return." This was a matter of sacred honor, he insisted: He could not betray the Filipinos suffering under the brutal yoke of the Japanese enemy. But beneath the surface assuredly there also lay guilt. MacArthur, more than a few observers believed, had saved his own neck by abandoning the Filipinos to their grim fate when he fled to Australia. He and his partisans of course denied the charge, but it is difficult to avoid the conclusion that long after the escape he remained uneasy about his own motives and sought to appease them by his commitment to return.

And on the issue of the route to Japan, MacArthur had reason to worry about his superior's support. Marshall was indecisive. Early in the debate, as in the past, he resisted the navy's attempt to subordinate MacArthur's authority to theirs. Yet he and the army planners finally proved surprisingly accommodating to the navy. Much to King's delight, the new navy Central Pacific strategy was endorsed by the Joint Strategic Survey Committee, a panel of the Joint Chiefs headed by Marshall's Anglophobic friend Stanley Embick. For the navy the new track, the Central Pacific offensive, not only seemed the fastest and least costly road to the enemy's homeland, but it might also compel the Japanese navy to accept battle with the now-superior American Pacific Fleet—which would quickly decide the Pacific war.

But despite yielding to the navy's new strategy, Marshall did not totally abandon MacArthur. At the Quadrant Conference in August 1943 he would argue that both axes of attack in the Pacific must be pursued, even if it meant some duplication of effort. In effect he had once again failed to take a focused position. There is no reason to assume that Marshall's response was based purely on strategic considerations. Whatever its military virtues, the two-pronged strategy also met an important political need. Today historians generally judge deficient MacArthur's defense of the Philippines after Pearl Harbor, but the contemporary media had made the bitter struggle at Bataan and Corregidor into an intrepid epic and MacArthur into a national hero. (As late as 1945 Americans would place him first in a poll of the country's greatest generals.) Now, as the military and naval chieftains debated the future course of the Pacific war, the sovereign American voters demanded that he not be sidelined into a mere supporting role. Whatever Marshall himself actually felt about the general and his plans, it was probably decisive that FDR and his political advisers simply could not ignore the public's yearning for a military savior.

Marshall and MacArthur met face-to-face only once during the war. The meeting was a spinoff from another Allied summit that included meetings with Russia's Stalin and China's Chiang Kai-shek. From late November through early December 1943, the chief of staff attended two meetings in Cairo code-named Sextant, the first devoted largely to Far Eastern matters, the second to tying up the loose ends of the first. Sandwiched between the two would be Eureka, a more consequential meeting in Tehran with the Soviet leader to consider further operations against the European Axis enemies. Following the second Cairo meeting, after sightseeing visits to Luxor and Karnak to inspect ancient Egyptian monuments, Marshall decided to fly home by way of the Far East and the Pacific. Twice before he had considered visits to MacArthur but had changed his mind. Now, he believed, the general needed some reassurance that he was still esteemed and he, his boss, must make the time for it.

Marshall traveled to the Pacific by C-54 army transport provided by General Sutherland. He had intended to visit his stepsons, Clifton and Allen, in the Mediterranean, where they were both serving as army officers, but canceled the side trips as inconvenient. On the way he stopped in Ceylon (now Sri Lanka) briefly and then flew on to Port Moresby in New Guinea, MacArthur's forward headquarters. He had hoped to meet the general at Moresby. But MacArthur rudely chose not to be present, and Marshall had to seek him out on nearby Goodenough Island.

When they did meet, their discussion, held in private, apparently was cordial. There is no official record of what the two men said; only MacArthur's own self-serving account exists. Marshall did have reservations about MacArthur, and disapproved even more of his obsequious staff, which he labeled dismissively as MacArthur's "court."[21] In any event, at lunch that day, according to MacArthur, Marshall was accommodating. But he was also apologetic. After reviewing the decisions regarding the Pacific and the Far East made at Cairo, he acknowledged that the Southwest Pacific was being shortchanged. But it was not his fault, he explained. He had defended the army's role in the theater, but Admirals Leahy and King, both influential with the president, were responsible for the navy's priority, and there was little he could do to rectify it. MacArthur depicted himself as taking the high road. For his own part, he told Marshall, he deplored the interservice rivalry in the Pacific. The army-navy competition must not be allowed to undermine the war effort against Japan, he piously declared.

Marshall left New Guinea on December 16 for Guadalcanal and then flew on to other Pacific sites where American fighting men were engaged or garrisoned. He inspected training camps, visited military hospitals, spoke to assemblies of troops, and observed combat rehearsals and reenactments. On December 19 he arrived in Honolulu, where he attended a demonstration in jungle-fighting techniques. At the end of the presentation he delivered a pep talk to the men who had performed, most of them scheduled to embark soon for the Pacific island fighting fronts. It was a curiously confused and ambiguous speech that lauded American military training while simultaneously acknowledging its deficiencies and, by implication, his own imperfect performance as a trainer. He began with a simplified explanation of the early successes of the Japanese army following Pearl Harbor: The enemy, he noted, had received jungle training while American soldiers had not. And yet, he reassured the soldiers, those advantages were limited. The "Japs" were "restricted and lack variation," while "our great advantage is our enterprise and resourcefulness." This remark undoubtedly played well to Americans' self-image as an innovative, individualistic, democratic people. But Marshall could not ignore the reality as revealed by recent combat experiences in the Mediterranean. He immediately undermined the self-congratulation by praising the enterprise of the Wehrmacht as Americans were now confronting it in Italy, especially its focus on small-unit tactics. He concluded with an improbable summons to the soldiers to imitate the German enemy: "You men have to do the same and better, and you have the initiative and the leadership to do it."[22]

Well into 1944 the rivalry between MacArthur and the navy over jurisdictions and directions continued, with Marshall seeking to smooth ruffled feathers. In March 1944, long after King had consolidated his Central Pacific strategy, the issue of theater boundaries again intruded. King wanted to add the harbor and airfield of Manus Island, just north of New Guinea, to Nimitz's theater. MacArthur once again saw the move—which favored the navy's preference for a more direct approach to Japan over his own cherished invasion of the Philippines—as an attempt to curtail his authority and derail his plans. In fact, the general was right. King doubted the Philippines were strategically important to winning the war against Japan. Formosa to the north, closer to the enemy's home islands, was the better objective.

On February 27 the general sent Marshall a letter, hand-delivered in Washington by Sutherland, shrilly protesting once again the navy's attempt to intrude into his Southwest Pacific command. The letter was full of MacArthurian bluster and half-hidden threats to invoke his popularity with the American public to intimidate his opponents. Not only was this a serious reflection on his capacity to lead, he wrote, it was psychologically demoralizing and would "cause a reaction not only in the soldiery but in public opinion that would be extremely serious." He was particularly alarmed, he said, that the navy intended to prevent him from retaking the Philippines. His personal integrity and honor were at stake, he once more told his chief, and he must be allowed to present his case personally to Stimson and FDR before Marshall decided how to respond to the proposed change. The implication was clear: He would resign if the navy got its way.

Marshall yet again sought to soothe the general: "I am in agreement with the reasons you advance against such a proposal" as the navy's. On the other hand he could not see that "a change in boundary of your area, in itself, could be regarded as a serious reflection upon your capacity to command." Nor could he see that it implied that the navy intended to take from MacArthur's leadership any campaign to invade the Philippines. Still, if MacArthur wished, he wrote, he would arrange for him to see Stimson and the president.[23] In the end MacArthur abandoned the visit to Washington and settled the issue with the navy directly. In a meeting in Brisbane in early March he told the visiting Halsey that he was not going to be bulldozed by the navy. No navy ships would be allowed to use the facilities at Manus except those of Admiral Kincaid's small Seventh Fleet squadron, attached to his own Southwest Pacific command. Halsey protested that the general was hampering the war effort, but to no avail: MacArthur got his way.

Nonetheless the issue of whether to bypass the Philippines to make Formosa, off the Chinese mainland, the launchpad for invading Japan itself remained very much alive. The option preferred by the navy appalled MacArthur on many grounds. His honor and his conscience were deeply involved. But in a mid-June protest to Marshall he made his case against the latest navy challenge on strategic and propagandistic grounds. "It is my most earnest conviction that the proposal to bypass the Philippines and launch an attack across the Pacific directly against Formosa is unsound," he declared. The operation would have to dispense with vital land-based air support and would suffer devastating enemy air attacks on its flanks from the Philippines. "The hazards of failure would be unjustified when a conservative and certain line of action [the Philippines route] is open." MacArthur also dismissed another non-Philippines proposal: launching an attack directly on Kyushu, the southernmost Japanese home island. It was, in his opinion, "utterly unsound." Once more the invaders would be exposed to lethal air assault, and without adequate shipping to transport the troops to boot. But besides these military considerations MacArthur believed that avoiding the Philippines would seriously damage America's reputation at home and abroad. "If the United States should deliberately bypass the Philippines, leaving our prisoners, nationals and loyal Filipinos in enemy hands without an effort to retrieve them at earliest moment we would incur the gravest psychological reaction." Millions in Asia would lose respect for America. It would also, he warned, "cause extremely adverse reactions among the citizens of the United States."[24]

Just returned from Britain and Italy, Marshall replied to his difficult subordinate a week later. His response was not favorable. While MacArthur's position had not yet been discussed by the Joint Chiefs, he wrote, he would give the general his views "without delay." Marshall sought to put the case in a larger frame. The information received from the secret decrypts of Magic indicated a steady buildup of Japanese strength in the Philippines and adjacent areas, he noted. "In other words further advances in this particular region will encounter greatly increased Japanese strength in most localities." By contrast, "It would appear that the number of troops required for a successful operation against Formosa in early 1945 would not be required against the *present* garrison of Formosa." But there was another consideration in favor of the Formosa option. The military picture in China had not been promising since the beginning of the new Japanese offensive. The Joint Chiefs now feared that the Chinese army would collapse and the country's entire Pacific Coast fall into enemy hands. They believed that the United States might well need to occupy that coastal region as part of a successful final campaign against Japan, and the possession of Formosa would keep the Japanese from preventing that operation. Marshall made his endorsement of the Formosa tack credible by noting that an assault on or about November 1 would begin with six divisions, with three more to soon follow.[25]

The exchanges between MacArthur and his Pentagon bosses did not settle the issue of the Philippines versus Formosa. The subject would fester for weeks more before being finally resolved at the highest level.

China, the vital portion of the Pacific theater located on the East Asian mainland, was home to five hundred million people, many of them now suffering under an imperialism far crueler and more exploitive than previous Western versions. American planners could not ignore the Japanese conquests on the Asian mainland, and above all the fate of China. Marshall had no doubt of its importance. If nothing else, he had spent two and a half happy and prosperous years during the 1920s in Tientsin and believed he understood China's strategic value. In this Pacific arena the chief of staff would be less an observer and mediator and more an active agent.

The American preoccupation with China long predated Pearl Harbor. For many years Christian denominations in the United States had labored to bring the message of Jesus and the Gospels to the "heathen Chinee." Millions of American churchgoers had contributed their mites on Sundays to the missionary cause in East Asia, and in the process had come to sympathize with the Chinese people and even to admire Chinese culture, though in fact few understood the appalling inequality, poverty, and pervasive venality that marked its political and social institutions. The brutal Japanese attacks of the 1930s, triggering two prolonged Sino-Japanese wars—the true beginning of World War II—had further stirred American sympathies for the suffering Asian people. Roosevelt reinforced this concern for China by his strong belief—prophetic, though premature—that the vast East Asian nation was destined to become a world power that would vitally affect postwar events and have to be reckoned with in the years ahead.

But besides its cultural and future geopolitical imprint, China counted strategically. On mainland China the armies of the Nationalist (Kuomintang) leader Chiang Kai-shek in the center and the south, and of the Communist leader Mao Tse-tung at Yan'an in the north nailed down almost a million Japanese troops, soldiers who might otherwise be abetting Japan's conquests or defending the Japanese home islands. It was no secret that the ill-trained, ill-led, underpaid, and underequipped Chinese armies, both Nationalist and Communist, though collaborating during the war to fight the common enemy, were incapable of defeating the Japanese and indeed seldom engaged them in full-scale battle. And it was also clear that Chiang's regime was rife with greedy, corrupt officials who siphoned off millions of dollars of Allied aid to line their own pockets while the Communists, though winning the favor of the peasants, rejected the values of Western democracy. Yet unlike the skeptical British, for whom the Pacific war was a sideshow, American strategists could not afford to dismiss Chiang and Mao as irrelevant. At the outset at least, Marshall was one who believed that "keeping China in the war," and if possible bolstering and reforming its military forces to make them effective, was a significant component of victory in the Pacific.

To American strategic planners, this conclusion in turn required that the vast country's land connections with the outside world through the Burma Road, lost when the British abandoned Burma to the Japanese foe in 1942, be restored. Clearly, without easy access to the planes, guns, trucks, food, and ammunition needed by a modern army, China could not become an effective opponent of Japan. Chiang himself craved restored links with the outside world, though within the Nationalist leadership the military supplies from Britain and America more often served to strengthen the regime against its domestic, rather than its foreign, enemies. Marshall's experience in Tientsin twenty years before had exposed him to the early struggles for Chinese unity. Now, after Pearl Harbor, when China had become a potentially important ally in the battle against Japan, the deep division between Chiang's Kuomintang and Mao's Communists threatened to nullify its value as a partner in war.

Marshall had his reservations about Chiang's regime, but the true enigma was Mao and his communists. The stocky, moon-faced son of a prosperous peasant, as a young man Mao had supported the 1911 revolution under the leadership of Sun Yat-sen, which overthrew the Manchu Qing Dynasty and established the Chinese republic. In 1921 Mao became a charter member of the Chinese Communist Party, which, through the early twenties, remained allied with the Kuomintang founded by Sun. Finally refusing to share power with another authority, in 1927 Chiang drove the Communists from the Kuomintang. In response Mao established a virtually independent Communist state in Jiangxi Province in southeast China and was soon engaged in a guerrilla war with Chiang. In 1934–35 the Nationalists forced their rivals to abandon Jiangxi and, following the famous "Long March," resettle in Yan'an, in Shensi Province, in the north-central region. There Mao and his followers reestablished their autonomous regime and instituted reforms favoring the peasants and creating an honest, though harshly authoritarian, administration that evoked wide admiration among visiting observers. In the late 1930s Mao and his associates joined the struggle against the Japanese invaders and, many observers believed, fought more effectively against the enemy than the corrupt and inefficient army of the Nationalist central government in Chungking. In later years Mao and his regime would be equated by many Westerners with the Soviets as part of an international Communist conspiracy, but in fact, at least at the outset, the Russians were skeptical of Mao and his followers. They were not, they believed, orthodox Marxists for they mistakenly identified the peasants, rather than the urban prole-tariat, as the true agents of revolution. And besides, they were potential rivals rather than submissive allies of the Soviet gov-ernment in Moscow. In June 1944 Stalin himself revealed Soviet ambivalence about Mao and his followers. "The Chinese Com-munists are not real Communists," he told American ambassa-dor Averell Harriman. They were " 'margarine' Communists. . . . Nevertheless," he added, "they are real patriots and they want to fight Japan."[26]

At Chiang's request, after Pearl Harbor, FDR agreed to ap-point a high-ranking American officer to serve as the Generalis-simo's military adviser. When consulted, Marshall, seconded by Stimson, recommended Gen. Joseph Stilwell. The general would serve simultaneously as Chiang's chief of staff, as commander of the small contingent of China-based U.S. troops, as admin-istrator of American Lend-Lease, and as commander of Chinese forces deployed in the British colony of Burma.

The choice was an easy one for Marshall. Stilwell and his wife, Winifred, were friends of his from Tientsin days, a friendship reinforced when Marshall brought Stilwell to Fort Benning in the late twenties to help reform the Army Infantry School. Since then Stilwell had visited China several times and spoke acceptable Mandarin. He was also a stubborn, caustic man who earned the sobriquet "Vinegar Joe" at Benning for his harsh tongue-lashing of incompetent students.

Soon after his arrival in Chungking, Stilwell detoured to Burma, China's neighbor to the west. There he witnessed the post–Pearl Harbor British defeat by the Japanese and the hasty, fumbling withdrawal of British forces to India, the retreat that had severed the Burma Road. This inglorious debacle, and later experiences, made Stilwell a vocal Anglophobe who called the haughty British military leaders in SEAC's India headquarters "monocled asses" and worse. Back in China he also developed a deep contempt for Chiang and his regime for its corruption, incompetence, and cowardice. In his most jaundiced view the Chiang-led Nationalists were "a gang of fascists" much like the Nazis but without their efficiency. His opinion of Chiang himself, reinforced by later events, was no better. Chiang was contemptible; the "peanut dictator," or "the little dummy," as he called him.[27] Stilwell had a better opinion of Mao and his forces. The communists in Yan'an, he confided to his diary, "reduce taxes, rents, interest, . . . raise production, and standard of living, . . . practice what they preach."[28] Chiang and his circle soon came to reciprocate Stilwell's disdain. The American commander, they concluded, was an arrogant, overbearing man, a sharp irritant who wielded too much power and expected the impossible of them.

If Vinegar Joe felt only contempt for Chiang and his regime, he respected the Generalissimo's subjects, the Chinese people, and believed them capable of making effective soldiers if properly trained and supplied. To that end he organized in India a five-division elite corps of American-trained Chinese troops. These men would help the Allied campaign, planned at Casablanca, to retake Burma and restore China's connection to the outside world. He also pushed hard for building a new road from northeastern India to restore a land supply route to China to supplement the risky, costly, and limited American-piloted cargo plane flights over the lofty Himalayan "Hump." The Ledo Road, soon nicknamed "Stilwell's Folly," never carried the volume of equipment and supplies transported by the air route, precarious and wasteful though that was, and its construction cost the lives of eleven hundred American service troops, many of them African Americans. The goal of restoring the original Burma Road then remained an Allied objective.

The "China tangle" was further snarled by the presence of

Claire Chennault, an aggressive, leather-faced, retired Army Air Corps officer who had arrived in China in 1937 to serve as Chiang's aviation adviser in the developing struggle against the Japanese aggressors. In April 1941, well before Pearl Harbor, Chennault organized the Flying Tigers, a fighter plane group composed of American mercenary pilots based in Burma that received broad media attention in America, much of it exaggerated puffery, for its success in combat with the Japanese air force.

Chennault and Stilwell soon clashed over the most effective military strategy for the Nationalists to pursue against Japan. By 1941–42 Chiang's forces and the Japanese invaders had reached a stalemate. Avoiding battle when- and wherever possible, the Generalissimo in effect no longer challenged the enemy's occupation of a broad swath of coastal China. Stilwell believed that properly equipped and under his tutelage, Chinese troops were capable of mounting a major land offensive against the enemy that could drive them from the country. Chennault's vision was drastically different. A passionate and uncritical advocate of airpower, he held that China's contribution to the Far Eastern war would be primarily as a giant aerodrome for the Allies. American planes based in unoccupied China would attack Japanese-controlled Chinese cities and Japan's vital maritime commerce; Japan itself would be pounded into submission. As he wrote to Hap Arnold, with five hundred planes to command he could "burn out the industrial heart of the [Japanese] Empire with fire-bomb attacks on the teeming bamboo ant-heaps of Honshu and Kyushu," the Japanese home islands.[29] Secretary Stimson and his writing collaborator McGeorge Bundy would later describe Chennault's view as, in essence: "American air power would defeat the Japanese."[30]

Chiang much preferred Chennault's strategy. Airpower was far cheaper than a large well-trained, well-paid army, and less disruptive of his preferred political and social arrangements for Chinese society. Stilwell's plan would impose heavy costs in manpower and equipment that the lethargic and self-protective Chiang shunned. Besides, the Generalissimo preferred to husband his resources for an eventual showdown with Mao and his forces. And in any case, the high-handed and demanding American was personally resented, and any policy he favored was suspect.

Unfortunately Stilwell had a rare gift for making enemies even beyond Chiang and his circle. His harsh criticism and rancorous relations with the British military leaders in New Delhi would offend Lord Louis Mountbatten, Alexander's successor as SEAC head. At one point Mountbatten demanded that Stilwell be removed from any role in Burma and confined exclusively to his China responsibilities.

Despite the general's personal deficiencies Marshall and Stimson remained staunch Stilwell partisans. The chief of staff and the secretary of war shared the prickly general's desire to reopen the sealed Burma land route for resupply and reequipment of the Chinese army. They also accepted his vision of a reformed Chinese army capable of carrying its weight against Japan. Marshall, moreover, considered the inefficient, and insufficient, air supply route from India over the Himalayas, favored by Chennault, an intolerable drain on overall Allied manpower and equipment. As he would tell an interviewer in 1956, the "extraordinarily heavy expense of planes to carry gasoline to Chiang's air effort was a very costly matter to us in Italy."[31] At Casablanca, Marshall strongly endorsed Stillwell's plan for a British-Chinese campaign to recapture Burma—though not, he cautioned, at the expense of Europe First. As for Chennault's air campaign against Japan from mainland Chinese bases, it would, he believed, merely provoke a major, and probably successful, Japanese offensive against those bases. Responding to an earlier proposal to build up U.S. airpower to protect the Hump route, Marshall noted that "as soon as our air effort hurts the Japs, they will move in on us, not only in the air but also on the ground."[32]

Yet Marshall was not indifferent to Stilwell's personal failings. In March 1943, after a series of press articles describing his protégé's disagreements with Mountbatten, he sharply rebuked him: "You do not appear to have made an effort to establish a smooth working-relationship with the British commander and his staff regardless whether or not you agree with [their] final decisions," he wrote. Stilwell must "seek an immediate personal interview with Admiral Mountbatten" to see if he could "reach a working accord which is essential between two officials in the positions he and you occupy."[33] Stilwell complied and apologized for his offenses, but his resentment of the British and Chiang did not abate.

Unfortunately for Marshall and Stimson, at the outset Chennault had the backing of Roosevelt, who considered the airman's plan a low-cost, low-risk experiment at worst. And with FDR's support the air bases were established in unoccupied China. Looking ahead, in late 1943 Chennault's pilots launched the first air raids against Japanese targets from Fourteenth Air Force bases in southern China. Other raids by the new giant B-29s soon followed. But Marshall was right: The president's gamble quickly failed. The attacks triggered a major Japanese ground offensive (Operation Ichigo) that overran the bases and shut the raids down and then threatened the very survival of still-unoccupied China. B-29 attacks on Japan continued, but only after they were rebased on the Pacific islands of Saipan and Tinian following their seizure from the Japanese in the summer of 1944.

Meanwhile, the Stilwell-Chennault wrestling match raged on. In early September 1943 Chennault wrote to FDR complaining that he had not received promised supplies and implying that Stilwell was responsible. FDR passed the problem on to Marshall, and the chief of staff concluded that the blame lay with Chiang and his wife, the fetching American-educated Mai-ling Soong, who had become Chiang's adviser and most effective advocate in the United States. Soon after, China's foreign minister, Dr. T. V. Soong, Madame Chiang's brother, on a visit to Washington, provoked the president by a set of ill-tempered demands that China's status in the anti-Axis grand alliance be raised to equality with the Big Three and Stilwell's power over China's military affairs be reduced. An exasperated FDR asked Marshall to make the irascible diplomat see reason. Marshall talked soothingly to Soong but rejected any change in the command structure in the Far East. Finally, under persistent bombardment from Soong, in mid-October FDR lost patience with the whole China imbroglio and told Stimson that he had decided to fire Stilwell. Marshall's own faith in his protégé had diminished when, the previous April and May, at several conferences in Washington, a weary Stilwell had made a poor showing defending himself and his policies to the Joint Chiefs. He had been tempted to dismiss Stilwell at that time but had reconsidered. Now, on October 19, at both the president's and Chiang's behest, he composed a telegram informing Stilwell "that in view of the attitude of the Generalissimo it will be necessary to replace you in your present position in the Far East."[34]

Marshall brought this document to Stimson's office for his final approval. However, just as the secretary was reading the message, Stilwell's own cable arrived at the War Department, informing him that the Generalissimo had changed his mind. Apparently Madame Chiang and her sister Madame H. H. Kung had unexpectedly intervened on Vinegar Joe's behalf. Though risking a family schism, the sisters had subverted their own brother's wishes and saved Stilwell's neck. After an interview with Chiang at which he contritely promised to avoid further challenges to the Generalissimo's authority, Stilwell was restored to favor.

Despite this near-beheading, Stilwell's standing with Marshall and the president reached its apogee in mid-1944, when the new Japanese Ichigo offensive, triggered by Chennault's bombing campaign and met by feeble Nationalist resistance, seemed to threaten China's very survival. In early July, Marshall approved a Joint Chiefs memo to FDR that praised Stilwell, took issue with Chennault's reliance on the Hump supply route to support his air campaign, and recommended that the president prod Chiang to accept Stillwell as overall commander of all military forces in China. FDR agreed and sent the proposal to Chiang. To strengthen Stilwell's hand, he simultaneously promoted him to the rank of full general. The Generalissimo's response was negative. Chiang had no intention of letting a foreigner, and a hostile one at that, take over general command of all Chinese forces. He could not adopt the president's proposal, he told Roosevelt. Chinese troops did not readily accept direction from any authority, and the complexities of Chinese politics would make a foreign commander's role unmanageable. He promised, however, to give careful thought to the president's suggestions.

In August 1944, at Chiang's request, Roosevelt chose an interlocutor to stand between the Generalissimo and Stilwell. Patrick J. Hurley, Herbert Hoover's suave secretary of war, would be the new ambassador to the Republic of China. In early 1942, shortly after Pearl Harbor, Marshall had sent Hurley to the Far East to help rescue the besieged Americans at Bataan. Obviously unsuccessful in that impossible assignment, he had nevertheless earned the respect of both Marshall and Stimson, who now helped secure the China mission for him.

In his directive to Hurley of August 18, composed by Marshall, FDR specified that he was to "promote efficient and harmonious relations between the Generalissimo and General Stilwell."[35] Hurley failed. From Stilwell's point of view he was a bad choice. Though he knew little of China, the Oklahoman, despite an initially favorable view of Mao, soon became a zealous anti-Communist who disowned Stilwell when he recommended turning to the Yan'an-based Communists for help against the enemy. Fed up once more with all the sound and fury, FDR now again determined that Stilwell must go. At a meeting with the president on October 15 Marshall defended his friend. But for naught; this time FDR was adamant. Two days later Marshall radioed Stilwell that he was being recalled. He would be replaced as American commander in China by another Marshall favorite, Albert Wedemeyer.*

The Stilwell-Chiang dispute was in many ways a classic tempest in a teapot. It did not vitally effect the outcome of the war. China never became a major contributor to Japan's defeat; the occupiers were evicted from the Asian mainland only when Japan surrendered unconditionally to the Allies aboard the battleship *Missouri* in Tokyo Bay in August 1945. But the wrangle of the two men would foreshadow the poisonous struggle in the minds of Americans over China's postwar fate. Marshall, much to his regret, would, through his role in the "China Tangle," be swept up in the domestic political storm over the "international Communist threat" that enveloped the early postwar years.

The Stilwell affair also contributes to our reservations about Marshall's judgment of men. No one can dispute Stilwell's formidable credentials for his China mission. But like Fredendall, he was temperamentally unsuited to high military command. Could Marshall have known this, or was his personal affection for the Stilwells enough to blind him to Vinegar Joe's damaging personal flaws? In his later years Marshall would deny he had known the

---

*Stilwell went on to serve as commander of the Army Ground Forces and then briefly of the Tenth Army in Okinawa. He died of stomach cancer in 1946.

incompetent Lloyd Fredendall well, but when he selected him as a Torch commander he seemed quite familiar with him. In any event, he could not deny that Stilwell was a close personal friend. In both cases of poor choice Marshall eventually acknowledged his mistake, but meanwhile valuable time, effort—and lives— had been expended needlessly.

China was not the only mainland Asian theater that came into Marshall's ken. Among the many issues considered at the Allied Quadrant Conference in August 1943, held in the Citadelle high above the picturesque French-Canadian town of Quebec, were British-American differences over Burma, the Japanese-occupied British colony adjacent to China's western boundary and its land connection to the outside world. There FDR, Churchill, and Canadian prime minister William Mackenzie King, along with the Combined Chiefs and the usual large cast of supporting military and diplomatic players, plotted the course of Allied military operations for the remainder of 1943 and for 1944.

From Marshall's professional perspective the decisions regarding European operations were the most significant strategic results at Quebec. The highlight of the meetings was the confirmation of May 1, 1944, as the date for Overlord, the cross-Channel invasion. But not without conditions on the British part: The operation would take place only if the German defenders could muster no more than twelve mobile divisions, if German airpower on the Continent could first be seriously eroded, if the artificial harbors ("Mulberries")being prepared for the invasion could be made ready in time. On a personal level for Marshall these decisions highlighted the urgent issue of who should be the supreme commander of Overlord, whenever it should be launched.

Now—two years after Pearl Harbor—the center of military gravity between the Allies had shifted decisively to the larger, richer United States. Churchill and FDR had now agreed that the supreme commander of Overlord must be an American. Yet for CIGS Alan Brooke, whatever his personal doubts about the operation itself, hope lingered that he might be its commander, and he was surprised when the prime minister now told him that the choice would be Marshall. How did Brooke feel about it? Churchill asked. Brooke's outward response was reserved, as his British upper-class code required: He was "disappointed," he told the prime minister. But in fact Brooke was devastated. It was "a crushing blow," he later acknowledged, and he was "swamped by a dark cloud of despair."[36]

Marshall, on the other hand, had made no secret of his hopes. As he had remarked to Stimson sometime earlier, every soldier would prefer a field command. The leadership of the momentous cross-Channel invasion would be the apex of his life as an army officer; it would raise him to the eminence of his hero and mentor, John Pershing. Even before Quadrant he knew of the still-confidential decision to choose an American and assumed that he would be designated. With her husband's change of status apparently imminent, Katherine had packed the family furniture and quietly moved out of the chief of staff's quarters at Fort Myer. The confident Marshall, meanwhile, hinted to several colleagues that he was looking forward to seeing them in London when he took command of Overlord at the beginning of the New Year.

But of course it was not to be. As rumors of the probable appointment began to leak, public opinion turned unfavorable. Not out of disdain for Marshall, however. Most of the demurrers believed him too valuable in place; others held that the choice was a British plot to get rid of a strong defender of American interests. Even General Pershing deplored the possible change: To transfer "our most accomplished officer" to a "tactical command in a limited area," he wrote to FDR, would be to waste his "outstanding strategical ability and experience."[37] In the face of the skeptical response FDR put the decision on hold. To choose Marshall as supreme commander would surely mean bringing Eisenhower to Washington to take his place, and Roosevelt did not feel comfortable with such a switch. As he later said, he could not sleep easily with Marshall away from Washington. At Quadrant, Marshall resigned himself to accepting his fate, whatever it might be. Though he had aggressively fought for advancement in rank during the parched years of the twenties and thirties, now, true to his austere ethic, he refused to push his claim. The final decision was postponed.

For the British the war against Japan was a minor issue at Quebec. Consideration of Pacific matters, they insisted, could well be postponed until after Germany's defeat. But if the Americans demanded major operations against the Japanese before that time, for the sake of preserving resources for Europe, they should be conducted primarily by the U.S. Navy. Any simultaneous thrust due northward by MacArthur would be a costly duplication of effort.

At Quebec the Americans, of course, could not afford to be as blasé about the Pacific theater as their ally. Marshall still put the cross-Channel operation first. But he bridled at British indifference to the Japanese menace. The war with Japan, he believed, must not be pushed aside until some indeterminate time when all the loose ends in Europe had been neatly tied up. Admiral King, as usual, took the lead in advancing the claims of the Pacific theater, once more demanding an increased allotment of resources to defeat Japan. Marshall may not have approved of such a redistribution, but at Quebec he endorsed King's Central Pacific advance, which made the long-planned attack on Rabaul irrelevant. Now, instead of risking the high cost of subduing sixty to one hundred thousand entrenched, battle-hardened Japanese troops, fully prepared to die rather than surrender, the base would simply be bypassed. MacArthur subsequently claimed credit for this "leapfrogging" tactic that promised to spare American lives. In fact it was King who originally endorsed bypassing Rabaul, though MacArthur would employ the tactic to good effect in his advance toward the Philippines in later months. Not until Quadrant, however, was it applied formally, when the Allies decided to skip Rabaul, isolating the enemy forces and leaving them to rot on the vine.

Mainland East Asia, too, got its share of attention at Quebec. To Marshall and his colleagues, Burma's fate mattered, for as China's land connection to the outside world, it impinged directly on the fortunes of the Far Eastern war. For the British, though retaking the region promised to restore a lost portion of the empire and reverse an inglorious defeat, they did not give the operation a high priority. Churchill for one, despised "jungles," which he considered impossible terrain for military success, and did not accept American faith in China's ability to help defeat Japan.[38] Yet under the code name Anakim, early in 1943, the Allies had prepared a plan to recapture *all* of Burma, including the northeast, adjacent to China, which served Sino-American interests, not just the south, adjacent to India and Malaya, which served British imperial goals. Unfortunately several minor military setbacks convinced the British, who resented American pressure, that they lacked the resources to oust the Japanese from the region. At the Trident Conference in May the Allies agreed to a contracted version of Anakim that limited it to the northeastern quadrant of Burma, the part closest to the severed Burma Road. Chinese forces would attack the enemy from Yunnan and from new bases in India, while British and British colonial troops would advance eastward from India and launch amphibious operations against the Japanese along the Bay of Bengal coast, as well as an offensive in Burma's occupied central area.

Neither the British nor the Chinese were enthusiastic about the modified Anakim scheme, and they dithered and vacillated, unconscionably in Marshall's view. At Quadrant in August he badgered his British colleagues for action in Burma, seeking to deflect a Churchillian peripheral scheme to invade Sumatra and once more making the point to the dubious British that China must be allowed to make a major contribution to Japan's defeat. But Marshall simply could not wait for Anakim in any version. For a time he placed his hope for a successful campaign to reopen the Burmese supply route to China in Orde Wingate, a visionary and unconventional British army officer who had served his country ably in Palestine and fought the Italians successfully in Ethiopia. Wingate's early 1943 behind-the-lines exploits in Burma, leading the so-called Chindits, a band of part Indian, part British irregulars, against the Japanese, had caught Churchill's romantic fancy, and the PM had impulsively brought him to Quebec to join the discussions. There the young officer had also impressed Marshall, who endorsed a second Chindit incursion against the Japanese.

Marshall would be disappointed with Wingate. His second "long-range penetration" of 1944 failed when the British refused to deploy further ground forces in support. Revived as an air operation, it failed again. On March 4, 1944, while returning to his field headquarters, Wingate died when his plane crashed.

But while Far Eastern military operations hung fire, larger political issues regarding China came to the fore. FDR was determined, as Chiang had long hoped, to establish the parity of China with America, Britain, and Russia. He also sought to bolster Chinese morale and resolve, and in the fall of 1943, over Churchill's objections, invited Chiang to join the Western Allies at the first Sextant Conference at Cairo. Chiang was delighted to attend. His delegation would include Madame Chiang as her husband's chief translator and back stiffener.

The American delegation flew into Cairo on the afternoon of November 21 after some aerial sightseeing of recent Eighth Army battlefields in Egypt and Libya along the way. Chiang and his entourage reached Cairo a little too early to suit Churchill, who, besides his skeptical view of China's potential, preferred the Western Allies to settle their remaining differences over Europe in private before discussing Far Eastern issues.

Marshall had met Mai-ling Soong in Washington some months before, but never the Generalissimo. Despite Stilwell's and Brooke's caustic estimates he took a liking to the benevolent-miened, scholarly-looking head of the Kuomintang and found reasons to excuse his shortcomings. And his opinion would never change. After the war he told Forrest Pogue: "I was and am fond of Chiang Kai-shek." Admittedly "he had a terrible problem getting good men" and many of his circle were corrupt. But he "was personally no grafter."[39]

At Cairo, Marshall reiterated, over Brooke's doubts, that China could make a major contribution to the war against the Japanese. He acknowledged Chinese failings. True, at first they had resisted deploying ground troops against the enemy. They had also, he agreed, sought to limit Stilwell's inspired scheme to bring Chinese divisions to Ramgarh in India for intensive retraining by American instructors and resupply with American arms. But they had since abandoned their obstructionism, he assured his colleagues at a Combined Chiefs discussion. And so it seemed. At the Sextant meetings Chiang expressed his willingness to accept the modified Anakim scheme to open up an overland resupply and reinforcement route through Burma. But there was a catch: To draw off Japanese troops the British must promise to mount naval and amphibious operations in the Bay of Bengal, a proposal made by Mountbatten and endorsed by Marshall. Despite Chinese qualifiers, Marshall and King both considered this response a breakthrough; the Chinese were actually going to engage the common enemy after years of inaction.

But then Chiang spoiled the favorable effect by demanding that besides the land campaign in Burma the Western Allies continue to deliver ten thousand tons of supplies a month over the Hump. Marshall and the other planners were offended. They not only believed the proposal unrealistic; they resented the arrogant tone of the Chinese negotiators: They had "rights" in the matter, a Chinese general had aggressively announced in defending his country's position. Already worried about starving the military buildup in Europe for lack of air transport, Marshall exploded: "Now let me get this straight. You are talking about your 'rights' in this matter. I thought these were *American* planes, and *American* personnel, and *American* material. I don't understand what you mean by saying we can or can't do thus and so."[40]

Ultimately the first Cairo Conference failed to achieve, as the Americans had hoped, the incorporation of China as an equal partner in the United Nations' anti-Axis coalition. Undoubtedly the reality of China's real weaknesses was a critical factor for failure. But the Nationalists' domestic agenda and Chiang's recalcitrance also played a part in the outcome. SEAC supreme commander Mountbatten summed up Cairo's disappointing results on the China question. Negotiating with Chiang, he noted, had been totally frustrating for the Western leaders and their staffs. "[We] have been driven absolutely mad," he noted in his diary.[41]

And in the end, the Burma theater would never make an important contribution to Allied victory. The Bay of Bengal attack was quickly abandoned. In the spring of 1944, under British general William Slim, an ill-conceived Japanese thrust into India was blocked at Imphal, and finally in early 1945 Slim's forces invaded Burma and, with rare good luck and brilliant generalship, retook the former colony. Coincidentally Chinese troops briefly joined the Nineteenth Indian Division in northern Burma to open the long-severed Burma Road. But once that was attained and supplies flowed freely to the Nationalists by land, they were withdrawn to prepare for the coming struggle for domestic supremacy with Mao and his forces. Slim's victories, then, were achieved without aid from Chiang Kai-shek and his ragged army.

The opening Cairo meetings were followed by an important conclave of the Big Three heads of state and their staffs at Tehran in Iran (see chapter 8) and then a return to Cairo to complete the Anglo-American conference. Chiang and most of the Chinese delegation had now returned home, but Far Eastern issues were not ignored. It was at this second session of the Cairo gathering that FDR decided to cancel the Bay of Bengal operations as a serious drain on the vital LST landing craft essential for Overlord.

By the end of 1943, as the Sextant meetings adjourned, the Pacific and Asian theaters had been placed in perspective. They would remain subordinate to operations in Europe and the Mediterranean. No matter what the pressure on Americans for an early Pearl Harbor payback, the final campaign against Japan would come later. The China-Burma-India theater, particularly, would remain a sideshow. In fact, China itself, even in American estimates, would cease to be regarded as a major player in the anti-Axis war. The Pacific could not be neglected, of course: If nothing else, King and the navy would not allow it. But whatever China's role, the U.S. Army, too, could not avoid a strong commitment. First there was MacArthur to reckon with. He commanded and demanded attention. Despite the Europe First commitment of Marshall and his Pentagon colleagues, the army forces in the Pacific would grow between the end of 1942 and December 1943 from 350,000 to almost 700,000 men. This figure was more than 100,000 greater than the planners had assumed in a March 1943 estimate. Nevertheless MacArthur and his partisans were right;

in the eyes of Marshall and the War Department, Europe still came first.

When Marshall left Cairo for his round-the-world trip in December 1943, Japan was still a formidable foe capable of exacting on land, sea, and in the air a high price for any gains by its enemies. Not until 1945, when it was beaten into submission, was it less than a cornered tiger, a fierce and dangerous adversary. In the Pacific arena Marshall had been a force in the affairs of China but not with notable success. The failure would bode ill for his and his country's postwar relations with China. In the remainder of the Pacific he had been a secondary player, with King and MacArthur running the show. But now the chief of staff's mind was centered once more on events across the Atlantic where the climactic battles against the senior enemy were already under way.

CHAPTER 8

EUROPE AT LAST

Months before Sextant adjourned, the Western Allies had launched the first stage of Churchill's "underbelly" strategy: Operation Husky. On July 10, 1943, two Allied armies came ashore in Sicily, the large, populous island off the toe of the Italian boot. The American Seventh Army, led by Patton, landed near Gela on the island's south-central coast. The British Eighth Army, under Montgomery, came ashore on the east coast, a short distance away. The invasion was the second-largest amphibious operation of World War II, eclipsed only by the Normandy landings a year later. Yet the Sicilian invasion, as well as the drawn-out Italian mainland campaign that followed,* would expose once again serious flaws in American military leadership and failings in American combat performance, now less excusable following the harsh experience gained in North Africa.

Husky was mismanaged from the outset. Eisenhower and his

---

*The Italian invasion as a whole had no code name, though separate operations, as at Salerno, did.

deputy, Gen. Harold Rupert Leofric George Alexander, Churchill's beau ideal of a professional British soldier, failed to provide a coherent overall plan for conquest of the island. Meanwhile, as in North Africa, lacking confidence in his own judgment, Ike dithered and delayed the planning process to the point where a disgusted Montgomery, no speedy facilitator himself, had to step in to end the impasse and allow the operation to go forward. The brief campaign in Sicily that ensued was no better conducted than the operations in North Africa. It repeated the pattern of Anglo-American rivalry, with Patton and Montgomery clashing over military objectives and routes of attack and in the end allowing the crafty German commander, Marshal Kesselring, to evacuate his troops and equipment across the Strait of Messina to fight another day. The conquest of Sicily was not a famous victory. Carlo D'Este, one of Eisenhower's biographers, calls it an operation "beset by military blunders, controversy, and indecision."[1] In the five weeks of battle, notes the historian Douglas Porch, "sixty thousand Germans had managed to hold off eight times their number of Allied troops as they organized a successful evacuation from the island."[2]

Marshall was more positive about the Husky campaign than are the scholars, however. Despite his initial reservations he deplored the badmouthing in the press of American troops' performance and was lavish in his praise for virtually every high officer involved in the mishandled campaign. In a message to Ike from Quebec on August 17, as Patton's troops rolled into Messina just behind the departing Axis soldiers, the chief of staff wrote: "Congratulations and my profound thanks for the brilliant success with which you have brought another tremendous job to a victorious conclusion. You have carried your vast responsibilities in a most impressive manner in the preparation, coordination, and direction of the Sicilian operation." He also had fulsome praise for

Patton. His role, he said, was "a grand job of leadership," and he concluded by even expressing his "admiration" for "the manner" in which Montgomery, Alexander, and their British colleagues had "combined to carry HUSKY through to a triumphal conclusion."[3]

Marshall's tribute was outrageously hyperbolic, but the invasion of Sicily did achieve one undeniably happy result: the fall from power of the brutal Fascist dictator, Benito Mussolini.

The landings in Sicily made a mockery of Mussolini's grandiose promises to Italians that the war would prove the virtues of Fascism, convert the Mediterranean into an Italian lake, and establish Italy as ruler of "a new Roman empire." Disillusioned with Il Duce, whose decision to join Hitler in the war had led to such grief for his people, on July 24 the Fascist Grand Council, with the support of King Victor Emmanuel III, voted to depose him in favor of the Italian chief of staff, Marshal Pietro Badoglio. The aging marshal soon opened negotiations with the Allies for Italy to leave the war, and in September, after Allied troops had landed on the southern Italian mainland, the new government concluded an armistice with Britain and the United States that soon became a formal alliance. In the end Italy as a cobelligerent contributed relatively little to the Allied cause. Still, the downfall of the dictator, Adolf Hitler's close partner, bolstered Allied morale at a time of uncertainty and continuing doubt.

Unfortunately from Marshall's perspective, the surrender of Fascist Italy tipped the balance inexorably toward further Mediterranean operations. With Italy officially out of the war Churchill foresaw a rapid occupation of the Italian boot followed by an attack on the core of Hitler's Europe, either through the Balkans or across the Alps that bordered Italy to the north. But the expectation of Churchill and a few other optimists that mainland Italy would fall like a ripe plum into Allied hands would be cruelly dashed. On September 12 Mussolini was rescued by the Germans from incarceration and set up as the head of the puppet "Salò republic" in northern Italy. Then, rather than abandon the Italian mainland to the invading Allies, the Germans poured veteran combat divisions into the boot and, under Kesselring's brilliant command, fought a tenacious defensive campaign that took advantage of every Apennine peak and valley and every swift-flowing Italian river to keep the Allies from capturing Rome and sweeping into the Po Valley, Italy's industrial and economic heart.

Kesselring's nimble defense of the Italian boot was abetted once more by Allied ineptitude. On September 3 British troops under Montgomery had come ashore on the toe of the boot in the far south of mainland Italy, three hundred miles from Salerno on the west coast, where Mark Clark's American Fifth Army landed six days later. Instead of rushing to join the besieged Salerno invaders, the British Eighth Army, afflicted by Monty's usual timidity and overpreparation syndrome, spent days slogging cautiously up the Adriatic coast while the Americans barely held on to their beachhead on the west coast. Montgomery, however, was Churchill's and Brooke's concern. The feckless Clark was Ike's and Marshall's.

Clark was another protégé of Marshall's, an officer he respected and had slated for future high command. For his part Eisenhower considered Clark "the best organizer, planner, and trainer of troops" he had ever met.[4] But Clark was also a publicity and glory hound, a man ruthless toward subordinates and, during the Italian campaign, a commander obsessed with the capture of Rome, at best a dubious strategic goal. The tall, hawk-nosed general was also an Anglophobe, driven by a ferocious rivalry with Montgomery and the British to reach the Eternal City first. One historian has suggested that "Clark saw the Italian campaign as being fought as much against the British as against the Germans."[5]

Blaming others for his failures, Clark never found a way to overcome the inspired Kesselring. After finally breaking out of the Salerno beachhead on September 19, he tried frontal assaults against Wehrmacht bastions at Monte Cassino and the successive fortified German defensive "lines" across the peninsula. He also launched an end run around the Germans at Anzio, south of Rome. None of these worked, and meanwhile losses among his multinational forces mounted shamefully. Several of the Fifth Army's engagements became bywords for bloody mismanagement. In mid-January, Clark sent hundreds of Texans of the Thirty-Sixth Infantry to their deaths in a fruitless, botched effort to bypass the German "Gustav Line" by fording the Rapido River south of Rome. At Anzio soon after, Clark's subordinate Maj. Gen. John Lucas, another officer favored by Marshall, allowed the enemy to seal off the beachhead, keeping the Allied landing forces from quickly taking Rome. At Monte Cassino, a key spot on the Gustav Line tenaciously held by the enemy, Alexander, supreme commander in Italy following Ike's transfer to head Overlord, ordered the bombing of the revered ancient abbey, a move that only turned sacred architecture into impassable rubble that further delayed the attackers.

Clark's troops finally marched into Rome on June 4, 1944, to be greeted by rapturous Roman citizens shouting "Americano! Americano!"—overjoyed to finally see an end to their war. From Washington, Roosevelt cabled Clark: "You have made the American people very happy. It is a grand job well done."[6] It was a precious moment that Clark had craved for many weary months, but the "American Eagle" was soon deprived of his Roman triumph. Two days later the news of the Eternal City's conquest was wiped off the front pages of the Allied press by D-Day, the long-delayed Anglo-American cross-Channel landings in Normandy. When informed of the landings Clark blurted out: "They didn't even let us have the newspaper headlines for the fall of Rome for one day."[7]

Marshall avoided interfering with the operations in both Sicily and mainland Italy. Though he had opposed the Churchillian "peripheral strategy," in January at a Combined Chiefs meeting held during the Casablanca Conference, he had finally accepted the logic, or at least the inevitability, of a campaign against Italy. Once more the threat of troop idleness proved telling. Given the number of Allied troops left with nothing to do in North Africa after the anticipated victory, "operations against Sicily appeared to be advantageous," he acknowledged.[8] But Marshall never liked the Italian campaign and avoided taking any significant part in its conduct. He was never able to pursue a complete hands-off policy, however. To his credit, during the planning stage for Husky, he proposed—fruitlessly—a preemptive attack to capture Messina before it could be used as an evacuation port for a retreating enemy. At another point during the planning period, when Ike asked for alternatives if the Sicily operations should go awry, he suggested several options but carefully noted that these "are not in keeping with my ideas of what our strategy should be"; the "decisive effort must be made against the continent from the United Kingdom sooner or later."[9] If he intruded at all during these preparatory months he did so diffidently. On March 1, for example, while suggesting how Ike might deal with the fatigue and inexperience of American troops under his command, he concluded with the remark: "I offer this in a purely personal manner and wish you to feel no necessity for explanation of why you do not consider it practical."[10]

Though shunning the day-to-day details of the Italian campaign, the chief of staff could not ignore the fiasco at Anzio. Churchill's brainchild, Marshall had not condoned the operation. He had, however, approved of its ground commander, Major

General Lucas, one of his circle of favorites. Lucas, he believed, was a man of "military stature, prestige, and experience."[11] Now, after the disappointment at Anzio, admitting that "Washington estimates" were "long range and therefore weakly based," Marshall radioed Gen. Jacob Devers, Ike's successor at Algiers, the Mediterranean theater headquarters, that he agreed that Lucas's leadership appeared "below stern standard[s] required in existing situation."[12] With Marshall's approval, Devers relieved Lucas and replaced him with Lucian Truscott, who proved to be a far more able combat officer.

And the Italian operation did not even cease after the capture of Rome. The fighting in Italy would stagger on for another eleven months, not ending until the final unconditional general German surrender to United Nations forces on May 8, 1945.

The butcher's bill for Husky and its mainland successor was appalling. The twenty-month-long campaign to evict the Axis from Italian soil inflicted 312,000 casualties on the Allied forces, about 40 percent more than the far more extensive operation in northwestern Europe that began with the Overlord landings in Normandy. Some 750,000 U.S. troops fought in Italy and would alone sustain 120,000 casualties, including more than 23,000 killed.

Whether the lives of these Americans and Allied troops, not to speak of many Italian civilians', were sacrificed in vain or the campaign in Italy advanced appreciably the destruction of Nazi Germany, and if Marshall was right to have resisted the "underbelly" campaign are issues that have divided both participants and scholars. Looking back on the campaign from the perspective of later years, several historians have denied that the Allied investment in the Italy hastened the defeat of Hitler or helped the embattled Russians. Rather, to appease the juvenile urges of an incurable romantic who happened to head a world empire, it squandered lives, resources, and energies that might have been better deployed directly to defeat the most evil tyranny in modern history. But other scholars have disagreed, though not necessarily along lines of nationality.* As for contemporaries, Marshall apparently considered the entire Mediterranean theater an unfortunate distraction. Churchill, needless to say, gave his ardent support to the Italian operation, even on the eve of D-Day, when its disappointing progress and unexpected costs had already become abundantly clear. Writing to Ike in mid-April, he proposed a revised strategy for the campaign and noted that whatever the setbacks, it was tying down thirty-four German divisions in the "Western Mediterranean Theater" and would "make an immense contribution to Overlord."[13] As for those high-level experts on Axis fortunes, Stalin and Hitler, they agreed the Italian campaign indeed made a difference. Stalin was happy to see British and American troops engaged anywhere on the European continent in 1942 and 1943, though he would eventually cry "Enough!" to the delay it caused for the cross-Channel attack. Hitler, too, apparently confirmed the strategic impact of the Allied operation when, in July 1943, during the ferocious German Kursk offensive in Soviet Ukraine, he would order the withdrawal of two powerful SS panzer divisions from the eastern front to bolster the Axis forces in Italy. But perhaps, on the credit side of the ledger, the

---

*The British historian John Ellis dismisses the Mediterranean theater as little more than "an extended footnote" compared with World War II's eastern front. His compatriot John Keegan sees the Italian campaign as "marginal." Robert Love, an American scholar, calls the entire Mediterranean theater "a wasteful peripheral strategy." Another American, Douglas Porch, however, disagrees. The Mediterranean, he writes, "was the European War's pivotal theater, the critical link without which it would have been impossible for the Western Alliance to go from Dunkirk to Overlord." Moreover, he states, "the Axis decision to open a Mediterranean front was a critical strategic mistake that the allies would have been foolish not to exploit." See Porch, *The Path to Victory* (New York: Farrar, Straus & Giroux, 2004), pp. 661ff.

British historian Max Hastings deserves the last word. All told, he writes, "the Italian front occupied the attention of one-tenth of Hitler's ground forces, which would otherwise have deployed on the Eastern Front or in France."[14]

Marshall seems never to have passed judgment on the entire Italian campaign. But as head of the American army, once under way he inevitably hoped to see it succeed and discovered pluses along with the drawbacks. In late December, after months of stagnation on the peninsula following the fall of Rome, he defended the operation as providing "the containment and attrition of the enemy in the greatest possible numbers." "The issue," he added, was "not one of territory."[15] Yet after Rome the continuing grind came under increasing attack in the press at home, with the emphasis on the deteriorating morale of American troops.

Marshall laid much of the blame for the negative view of Fifth Army morale at the door of Clare Boothe Luce, the playwright-celebrity-congresswoman from Connecticut and wife of the press lord Henry Luce. In early 1945, following a visit to the Italian theater with the House Military Affairs Committee, Mrs. Luce charged that American troops in Italy felt neglected and abandoned. When the American press, prodded by her and similar critics, began to call Italy the "forgotten front," Marshall reacted with anger. As he later noted, these claims were a "dreadful blow" to military morale. But Marshall would confirm Clare Luce's claim that the troops' state of mind was, in fact, negative. "Corps commanders" had told him, he later recalled, that they "didn't know what to do about their troops. They had gotten obsessed with the fact that we had forgotten them entirely."[16] At the time, to reinforce troops' morale, Marshall induced FDR to include a special tribute to the soldiers in Italy in his 1945 State of the Union message, and arranged to have that portion circulated in the Italian theater.

One event that cannot have failed to affect Marshall's view of the Italian campaign as a whole was the tragic death of Allen Brown, his younger stepson, near Rome. Both in army uniform in southern Europe, Allen and his brother, Clifton, had spent three wonderful spring days of leave together before Allen, a "tanker," left for the Anzio beachhead with the First Armored Division. On May 29, 1944, shortly before the Fifth Army finally entered Rome, Marshall received a radio message from General Clark that Lieutenant Brown had been killed in action. The childless Marshall had emotionally adopted his stepchildren and followed their lives and careers with paternal interest. Of the three, Allen was his favorite. Marshall's grief was real and deep. Needless to say he sought to comfort Katherine, but in his own sorrow he also felt driven to speak to friends—Hopkins, Dill, British ambassador Lord Halifax—who had also lost sons in the war. Months later, after D-Day, Marshall made an unscheduled trip to Italy to visit Allen's grave at the Anzio cemetery and spent a solemn, contemplative half hour alone by the grave site.

Sorrow, then, undoubtedly, but it would not be surprising if Marshall also felt guilt over Allen's death. In a sense he had put Allen in range of peril. When Allen prepared to enlist in the army in September 1942 his stepfather had recommended the tank corps and had, after his stepson graduated from the Armored Force School at Fort Knox, facilitated his transfer to North Africa. In the fall of 1943 Allen's division was reassigned to Italy. It was while he was standing on the turret of his tank near the Alban Hills south of Rome to survey the terrain ahead that a sniper's bullet ended his life. Whether or not Marshall made the emotional association suggested here, stoicism and respect for patriotic duty were intrinsic parts of a soldier's values—perhaps Marshall's in particular—and it can be assumed that they served him as comfort on this tragic occasion.

Well before Rome fell, Overlord had eclipsed the Mediterranean as the main strategic concern of the Western Allies. The needs of men and equipment for the Italian campaign had clearly impacted the larger strategy of the war in Europe. In early 1944, as agreed at Quadrant, Marshall was able to withdraw from Italy five combat divisions, three British and two American, along with a collection of scarce LST landing craft, for the Bolero buildup in Britain. Yet he had to fight the disgruntled Churchill all the way. It would not be until the Eureka meetings of the Big Three at Tehran that Churchill finally acquiesced in the decision to launch the great cross-Channel attack, and even then he would try to run out the clock to prevent his rivals from actually getting possession of the ball.

Marshall and the president arrived at Tehran for the Eureka Conference after a seven-hour flight from Cairo, accompanied by FDR's civilian advisers Harry Hopkins and Averell Harriman, along with Generals Arnold and Somervell and Admiral Cooke. The British delegation included the heads and staffs of the senior services as well as Foreign Minister Anthony Eden. Confident that he could manipulate Stalin by his charm and powers of persuasion, Roosevelt was initially lodged at the American legation. Then, warned by Stalin of a plot against his life, he moved happily into the supposedly safer Russian compound. Marshall and the other Allied military personnel settled in with their bags at the headquarters of the U.S. Persian Gulf Command several miles away.*

The Tehran meetings were held against a background of soaring American confidence. Roosevelt and his advisers were now fully

---

*The president's move was a mistake: The Russians had bugged his rooms and probably heard every word he and his advisers uttered, including his ingenuous expressions of trust in Stalin's goodwill.

aware of the shift of resource balance between the two English-speaking nations, and intended to deploy that advantage in the discussions with Stalin. At a mid-November meeting just before the Cairo Conference the president had proposed making whoever headed Overlord the commander of the entire Allied transatlantic theater, including the Mediterranean and the Middle East. This would expand the reach and power of the supreme commander, who, it was by now acknowledged, would be an American. To defend his proposal Roosevelt asked the military planners for the projected figures of total U.S. and British forces on January 1944. The numbers were conclusive. The British Commonwealth would be able to deploy about 5 million men, they told him. The comparable American total was just over 10.5 million. Marshall and Arnold concurred when the president observed: "We are definitely ahead of the British as regards the number of men we have overseas at the present time and will soon have as many men in England for Overlord as the total British forces now in that place."[17] At the conference itself, though never verbalized, this view was clearly detectable: The United States would now have a louder voice than at any preceding conference of the two English-speaking nations.

At this preliminary November meeting Roosevelt also raised the matter of Churchill's fascination with Balkan operations following success in Italy. He would veto it if it came up, he declared. Speaking for the Joint Chiefs, Marshall made his aversion even more emphatic. "We do not believe that the Balkans are necessary," he said. It would prolong the war in Europe and also in the Pacific. The Americans now had "a million tons of supplies in England for Overlord," and it "would be "going into reverse to undertake the Balkans." To block Churchill, Marshall was prepared once again to play the Pacific card. If the British insisted on "any such proposal," he noted, "we could say that . . . we will pull out and go into the Pacific with all our forces."[18]

The Big Three focus at Tehran would be to define the road ahead against the common European enemy. As a secondary goal, the Americans hoped to induce the Soviets to commit themselves to the war against Japan after Germany's defeat. But whatever the agenda, Tehran would expose the new balance of forces. Not only had Britain become the junior partner in the Anglo-American alliance, the Soviet Union, with the might of 330 combat divisions and spectacular victories to its credit at Stalingrad, Kursk, and the Orel Salient, had in some ways become the senior partner in the larger anti-Axis UN coalition. Stalin now possessed enormous leverage over both Western powers and would not be reluctant to deploy it. The discussions at Tehran would expose the persistent differences between the American and British approach to defeating the Wehrmacht and effectively make the Russians the arbiters between the two. At Tehran the Western Allies would allow the Soviet dictator to define their overall European military strategy for the remainder of the war. "Uncle Joe" would, incidentally, also help define Marshall's future role in the war and decide his historical legacy.

FDR opened the first plenary session of the Big Three on November 28 with a jocular reference to his relative youth among the three heads of state and hence his fitting role as the first meeting chairman. "We are sitting around this table," he continued, "for the first time as a family, with the one object of winning the war." Churchill responded that in the hands of the participants rested the "future of mankind." Stalin followed the feel-good remarks with an impatient proposal that they all "get down to business."[19]

FDR started the discussion with a brief description of America's Pacific involvement, but soon moved to the issues of greater concern to the Soviet leader. He apologized for the delay of the second front, blaming it in part on the imperatives of the Mediterranean strategy and in part on the all-embracing excuse: the chronic shortage of landing craft. But Overlord, he promised, would not be postponed beyond May or June 1944 as agreed to by both Western Allies at Quebec. Put on the spot by Roosevelt's pledge, the still-skittish prime minister was now compelled, in Stalin's presence, to second the president. There were "no differences," Churchill insisted, between Great Britain and the United States except in "ways and means"; he, too, hoped to launch a cross-Channel offensive against Hitler's *Festung Europa*. Later in the discussion, with more than a touch of mendacity, the PM claimed that he had never "regarded the Mediterranean operations as more than a stepping stone to the main offensive against Germany." But then he waffled. He "could not, in any circumstance," he added, "agree to sacrifice the activities of the armies in the Mediterranean in order merely to keep the exact date of May 1 for Operation Overlord."[20]

It is not clear whether the Americans had planned to make Stalin the broker of the Western Allies' remaining strategic moves in Europe. But in his remarks that followed, Stalin in effect vetoed further extensive operations in Italy, making the invasion of France the unavoidable course to take. The Soviet leader opened his comments with a promise to join the Americans in the Far East against Japan, after Germany's surrender. He then turned to his chief concern, the war against Hitler. He amiably agreed that the operations in Italy were "of great value to further the war against the Axis" insofar as they opened the Mediterranean to free navigation. But "now they [were] of no further great importance as regards the defeat of Germany." Rather, the "most suitable sector for a blow at Germany would be from some place in France." Stalin endorsed Anvil, an invasion of southern France, first proposed by the Allied planners at the Quadrant Conference and now, at Tehran, reiterated by Marshall as a valuable adjunct of Overlord. Ideally, Stalin stated, the Anglo-American assault on the Continent should be a pincer movement in France from both the Channel in the north and the Mediterranean in the south. Stalin had little patience with the tortuous Italian campaign. He waved off Clark's cherished goal, declaring that Rome could be "captured at a later date."[21]

The next morning, when the military staffs of the UN partners met for the first time, the previous day's amiability was notably absent. In a mid-November secret memo preceding the conference, Gen. Sir John Kennedy, Brooke's Assistant CIGS, had already laid out the British agenda. The "strategy to be advanced in the coming conference," he wrote, must "continue the offensive in Italy," induce Turkey to join the Allies against the Axis, mount various actions to bolster Tito's anti-Axis guerrilla partisans in the Balkans, and "accept a postponement of Overlord."[22] Churchill's obliging remarks at the plenary session had only disguised the British Mediterranean addiction, and at the morning session Brooke ardently defended continuing the Italian offensive until the second front in France was actually launched. CIGS also took issue with Soviet support for an invasion of the South of France to either precede or follow the cross-Channel operation. There would not be sufficient forces left over from Italy, he claimed, to allow two invasions of France.

Mistrustful of the Allied commitment to invade France, Marshal Kliment Voroshilov, Stalin's military mouthpiece, now asked the American chief of staff to explain *his* country's position on land operations in Europe. Marshall responded with a minilecture on American logistical plans to supply the projected invasion. It was the American resolve to bring as many troops into action as possible, he said. Fifty divisions and mountains of supplies and equipment were available in the United States for the campaign; the problem was the shipping and landing craft to get them to the scene of battle. The reason for "favoring

Overlord from the start," he noted, was that it was "the shortest oversea transport route." After the initial landings in France reinforcements could "be sent directly from the United States to the French ports." Not until his concluding remarks did Marshall finally get around to answering Voroshilov's question, and even at this point his response was off center. "If we confine ourselves to reduced operations in the Mediterranean for the next three months," he declared, it would "entail the least interference with OVERLORD." As for the issue of invading southern France, he disagreed with General Brooke. That operation was very important for the success of the cross-Channel operation.[23]

Voroshilov chose to interpret Marshall's remarks as a firm American agreement that Overlord was, as he said, "of the first importance." But seeking further reassurance, he asked Brooke directly whether he too considered the cross-Channel invasion a certainty. CIGS responded with the usual British temporizing. Britain "considered the operation as an essential part of this war." On the other hand, "his majesty's advisors had always stipulated that it must be mounted at a time when it would have the best chances of success." The German "fortifications in Northern France" were "of a very serious character," and German communications in the area where the battles would be fought were "excellent." But then he backpedaled. Conditions, he assured the Soviet marshal, would finally be propitious in 1944.

Reassured or not, Voroshilov hastened to put the full weight of the Soviet leaders behind Overlord. Marshal Stalin and the Soviet general staff attached "great importance to OVERLORD," he pronounced, and "felt that the other operations in the Mediterranean" could "be regarded only as auxiliary." The Soviet marshal went on to predict that Overlord would "be successful" and "would go down in history as one of our greatest victories." "As a military man," he personally thought that Overlord was "the most important operation and that all the other auxiliary operations such as Rome . . . and what not, must be planned to assist OVERLORD and certainly not to hinder it." Brooke was quick to reassure Voroshilov that he "recognized that the Mediterranean operations are definitely of a secondary nature." Yet he refused to surrender unconditionally. Further military action in Italy and elsewhere, he insisted, could help Overlord and have a positive impact on the eastern front.[24]

That afternoon the Big Three leaders held their second plenary session, and after a review of the morning's military discussion took up once more the issue of Overlord. It was during this meeting that, in an almost offhand way, Marshall's future role in the war was decided. However improbably, it was Joseph Stalin who finally forced FDR to choose between Marshall and Eisenhower as supreme commander of the cross-Channel invasion of France.

Stalin had never met Eisenhower and had just been introduced to Marshall for the first time. But he apparently favored the American chief of staff from the outset. The Soviet leader, Marshall later noted, was "agreeable in regard to me and made sort of semi-affectionate gestures."[25] In any event, at Tehran, Uncle Joe had no patience with the Anglo-American failure to chose a commander for Overlord, and during this second plenary meeting pointedly asked who had been designated to lead the operation. When told that it "was not yet decided," he responded bluntly: "Then nothing will come out of these operations."[26] Still uncertain of his decision but recognizing that further delay was not expedient, Roosevelt promised that when he and Churchill returned to Cairo to complete their interrupted conference the issue would finally be settled.

By now, over Marshall's strong dissent, FDR had abandoned his view that the supreme commander, whoever he might be, should lead *all* Allied forces in Europe. Rather, he now agreed, his powers should be limited, as the British preferred, to the operations in France, both Overlord and Anvil, with a separate unified command for the Mediterranean. Reducing the scope of the supreme commander worsened the case for Marshall by strengthening the argument that to take him from his critical Pentagon office to command Overlord would be an actual demotion. The president had more compelling reasons as well to keep Marshall close by. It was perhaps at this point that FDR—observing Marshall in action against Brooke and Churchill at Tehran—that FDR concluded that he could not forgo his presence close to the White House and Capitol Hill. But in any case, after questioning many observers, the playwright and speechwriter Robert Sherwood, a good friend of Harry Hopkins and a man who knew FDR well, concluded that "no one will ever know just what finally went on in Roosevelt's complex mind to determine the decision."[27]

Back in Cairo, before dinner on December 4, the president sent Hopkins personally to sound Marshall out in his quarters on the matter of the supreme commander of Overlord. Like his boss, Hopkins was reluctant to take a point-blank approach and instead left Marshall to make his own case. The president "was in some concern of mind" about the appointment, he told the chief of staff. The statement hung in the air, awaiting a response. But Marshall's pride forbade a self-seeking answer. He kicked the ball back. He would "go along wholeheartedly with whatever decision the president made"; Roosevelt "need have no fears regarding [his] personal reaction."[28] That was all that the emissary could extract from the candidate. Informed of the exchange when Hopkins returned, FDR now had no choice, however uncomfortable it made him: He must personally confront the general. The following day he summoned Marshall to his villa. Which post did Marshall prefer, he asked, army chief of staff or supreme commander in

France? Marshall refused to answer. "I just repeated again in as convincing language as I could that I wanted him to feel free to act in whatever way he felt was to the best interest of the country and to his satisfaction and not in any way to consider my feelings. I would cheerfully go whatever way he wanted me to go."[29] Without any means of escape Roosevelt now made his choice; the chief of staff, he said, would remain at the Pentagon.

Marshall had chosen his own fate. The decision to command Overlord had been his to make; Roosevelt would have gone along if he had made his preference clear and emphatic. But to have done so, as Marshall's biographer Mark Stoler writes, would have violated "his sense of honor and duty" and also have blemished his self-crafted persona.[30] George Marshall could not do it.

Once Marshall was out of the running, the only real choice as Overlord commander was his protégé. On December 6 Roosevelt, still in Cairo, sent a brief message to Stalin: "The immediate appointment of General Eisenhower to command of Overlord has been decided upon." Marshall sent Eisenhower a longhand copy of FDR's telegram with his own endorsement: "Dear Eisenhower, I thought you might like to have this as a momento [*sic*]."[31] In a Christmas Eve radio broadcast the president publicly announced the appointment of Eisenhower as supreme commander, Allied Expeditionary Force. His headquarters would be known as SHAEF.

And so Marshall once more had failed to win a combat command. He would never lead men in battle; he would remain a desk officer, a military manager, and a top administrator to the end of his army career.

Was he deeply disappointed? He never said. His aide, Col. Frank McCarthy, a man who knew him well, claimed, just following the decision, that he showed no outward sign of a setback. Yet on many occasions in his career he had lamented being passed over for troop command and relegated to staff jobs. Commanding troops was a pervasive goal in the professional army. It was why vigorous, adventurous, intelligent young men were drawn to military life in the first place. It was also normally the road to quick advancement. And then there were fame and glory. FDR understood that the supreme command assignment of Overlord would be a kind of military apotheosis. As he would tell Eisenhower while in North Africa, they both knew who had served as Lincoln's chief of staff in the last years of the Civil War, but virtually no one else did, while "every schoolboy" knew the names Grant, Lee, Sherman, and Jackson. He hated "to think," the president mused, "that fifty years from now practically nobody will know who George Marshall was."[32]

Marshall arrived back in Washington from his round-the-world, post-Sextant trip on December 22, tired from his visits to MacArthur and the Pacific troops and the long hours on cramped, noisy planes. After a day in his Pentagon office he and Katherine went off to Dodona Manor to unwind and relax. During their years in Washington they would often seek refuge at the Leesburg house, and on religious holidays they attended services at the town's small Episcopal church. But this year, as in others, they closed it soon after Christmas.

To escape the harsh Washington winter the Marshalls stole a week off in early January to visit Miami Beach. The oceanside Florida city had been taken over by the military as a training camp, with most civilians ousted from the beachfront hotels and replaced by air corps cadets and instructors. Nevertheless, it was, Katherine later wrote, "a delightful week." She and George swam in the warm Atlantic water each day before lunch, took a nap, and then went for another swim, or, alternatively, the general would go deep-sea fishing.[33]

Marshall returned to his office on the sixteenth to resume the business of fighting the war. A later description depicts his routine labors at the new Pentagon Building. The chief of staff sat behind a large antique desk bequeathed to the government by Philip Sheridan, the dashing Civil War cavalry officer who had served in the 1880s as commanding general of the army. On Marshall's office wall was a painting of the critical Meuse-Argonne battle of the First World War, which he had helped plan. In the corner of the room was a grandfather clock; next to it an American flag and his four-star general's banner.[34] To preserve his health and energy Marshall maintained limited hours. He arrived early but also left early, believing that no effective work was ever done much past three o'clock.

Marshall had returned to Washington to find the country suffering from a combination of war weariness and overconfidence. With the Japanese Pacific offensive effectively checked and the Wehrmacht in retreat, many Americans now felt that UN victory was assured and they could relax their vigilance and resolve. One disturbing symptom of the new mood was widespread labor troubles.

As part of the post–Pearl Harbor mobilization effort, the government had extracted a pledge from organized labor to eschew strikes that interfered with vital war production. The inevitable management-labor disputes would be settled by arbitration through the National War Labor Board (NWLB). By and large the unions had kept their pledge. But not the United Mine Workers, led by FDR's opponent John L. Lewis, which had defied the government and mounted a damaging work stoppage in mid-1943 that had outraged the president. Now, as 1944 approached, infected with the new complacency virus, the railroad brotherhoods threatened to shut down train service throughout the nation, an action that promised to strangle the war effort. Two days after

Christmas, Roosevelt ordered the War Department to take control of the railroads. Now, if the railroad brotherhoods struck, the union leaders could be prosecuted for obstructing the war effort. Three of the brotherhood unions agreed to call off the strike, but two remained poised to walk out. Meanwhile, the steelworkers, too, were growing restless at what they considered unfair treatment at the hands of the NWLB and the steel company executives. To many media pundits the once-united country seemed on the verge of turmoil. In Germany the Goebbels propaganda machine, it was reported, was gloating at the anticipated disarray of the American war effort.

Marshall had avoided taking sides in labor disputes, but the actions and threats of the unions now enraged him. He was "sleepless with worry," he informed Jimmy Byrnes, director of the Office of War Mobilization (OWM).[35] Equally dismayed, Byrnes arranged for Marshall to meet with a small group of influential print and radio journalists for an off-the-record session to drive home the dangers of labor unrest to the national interest. At the meeting Marshall uncharacteristically vented his anger at the unions. He "banged his white-knuckled fist on the desk" and called the imminent rail strike "the damnedest crime ever committed in America," an act that could cost America hundreds of thousands of lives.[36]

Despite the reporters' pledge, details of the meeting and Marshall's performance leaked out and brought a storm of criticism down on his head. William Green, head of the American Federation of Labor, called Marshall's attack "irrational, uninformed, and inflammatory."[37] The leftist journalist I. F. Stone scolded Marshall for his "exaggerated" attack and suggested it was intended "to stir popular support for further anti-labor legislation."[38] The mainstream press generally applauded him, as did the Communist *Daily Worker*, always solicitous of Soviet needs, but the adverse publicity chastened Marshall and clearly reinforced his resolve to avoid future political and ideological controversies.

During these months of marking time for the cross-Channel main event, Marshall rescued his friend Sir John Dill from professional decapitation. Dill and Churchill, his boss, had never gotten along; that was why the field marshal had been removed in late 1941 as CIGS and replaced by Brooke. But, exiled to Washington as head of the British Joint Staff Mission, he had become a close friend of Marshall's and an invaluable liaison between Britain and America. Churchill now believed he was too close to the Americans and had grown uncomfortable with his role in the British military delegation in Washington. To save Dill from recall Marshall arranged for Yale University to award him the Charles P. Howard Prize for contributing to improved international relations. A colorful academic procession accompanied the ceremony, photographs of which were duly sent off to London. Churchill was impressed; Dill stayed on in Washington.

As he waited for D-Day, Marshall occupied himself speaking to war bond rallies, addressing the American Legion, deciding the fate of the failed general John Lucas, seeking convalescent accommodations for the ailing Harry Hopkins at White Sulphur Springs following a hospital stay, and proposing to Eisenhower a major airborne operation to accompany the cross-Channel landings. In late February he appeared before the Senate Foreign Relations Committee to oppose a Senate resolution endorsing U.S. support of a "Jewish Commonwealth" in Palestine in light of the "ruthless persecution of the Jewish people in Europe."[39] Though a low level of anti-Semitism was, at the time, pervasive in Protestant America, there is no reason to believe that Marshall disliked Jews. Bernard Baruch was a close friend, and the chief of staff often sought refuge from the cares of his job at Baruch's show plantation in South Carolina. Marshall's objections to the resolution, like those of his War Department colleagues, were that it would upset the Arabs in North Africa and the Middle East, where American troops were stationed and require military reinforcements to retain order. Better to postpone such a motion until the war was over, he told the senators.

During these waiting months a private incident affords a rare glimpse into both Marshall's marriage and personality. Once back from their Florida break, Katherine had resumed her public routine as wife of the wartime chief of staff. In March she came to New York to do her part for the Fourth War Bond Drive. There, on a freezing, windy day in Lower Manhattan, she gave her standard twenty-minute speech and, at the end, was lassoed by the event's promoters into a public display of eating doughnuts from the Doughnut Wagon, whose owner had promised to provide a free doughnut to every bond buyer at the rally. Lashed for an hour by freezing wind, she returned to Washington with a ferocious sinus infection.

What followed at Quarters No. 1 when she reached home reveals an important thread in the Marshalls' marital relations. The general apparently did not exempt his wife from the unbending persona he had cultivated over the years. When George returned from the Pentagon that evening he scolded his wife as if she were a child and he her father. "After taking you to Florida for a week to get the sun, you undo all the good accomplished in one hour—standing on 14th Street in New York for one hour, eating doughnuts! What, in Heavens name, have doughnuts got to do with the War Bond Drive? If you can't say 'No' you ought not to be allowed out alone!"[40] Katherine writes that she laughed at her husband's tirade, but surely she felt undervalued in some way.

If not completely in Katherine's favor for a time following this incident, Marshall was clearly popular with the American media. On January 3 *Time* magazine placed his picture on its cover as

"Man of the Year." The text that followed was blatantly hyperbolic. "Never in U.S. history has a military man enjoyed such respect on Capitol Hill," it announced. The chief of staff had transformed a "worse-than-disarmed U.S. into the world's most effective military power." A list of Marshall's specific accomplishments followed: He had "laid out a program of training and a schedule of equipment that are unmatched anywhere"; he had avoided "hastily planned or ill-advised military operations"; he had insisted on unity of Allied command; he had "refused to be panicked by nervous demands of theater commanders in sending out green and half-equipped troops"; he had early recognized the significance of airpower and promoted the air program; he had been open to the possibilities of new military equipment and weapons. All told, he was the closest thing to the "indispensable man."[41] Many of these achievements were either mythical or half-truths.

However flattering *Time's* accolade, during this period of military stasis and public distraction Marshall was forced to confront once again a serious military manpower shortage. The shortfall most affected the infantry. The three young historians who, at the war's end, wrote the *Organization of Ground Combat Troops* volume for the army's Official History series concluded, with some judicious restraint, that "the ground forces of World II proved to be none too large." In 1918, they observed, American troops were "needed only in France," but in "1942–45 they were needed on opposite sides of the globe."[42]

The shortage, though first noticed in 1942, had become acute as forces were being assembled in Britain for the cross-Channel operation. As General McNair, the head of G-3, wrote to Marshall in early January 1944: "At no stage in our operations, including the present, has the supply of replacements been adequate." In his opinion "the most serious aspect of the replacement situation" was "not the replacement agencies [that is, the Repple-Depple arrangement], but . . . lack of manpower. . . . Units of the Army Ground Forces today," he explained, had "a net shortage of 56,000 men."[43] Marshall acknowledged the shortfall. Later that month he sent an urgent message to theater commanders asking them to economize on the use of manpower by abandoning rear bases no longer essential, by employing civilians in rear areas to replace service troops, and by other means. "Worldwide requirements for forthcoming operations are creating service and combat troop demands which are becoming increasingly difficult to meet," he wrote. "It is necessary," he continued, "to make drastic revisions in the troop bases of all theaters."[44]

Despite these efforts to conserve, by mid-1944 the manpower dearth was being felt with increased force on the fighting fronts and promised to seriously weaken operations in the battles still to come.

The infantry deficit in the last year of the war had several causes. First, casualties in Italy and the Pacific had run high, higher than expected. Then, after D-Day, the grinding battles in Normandy and in the Hürtgen Forest (on the Belgian-German border) and the Ardennes (which took in parts of Belgium, Luxembourg, France, and Germany) would make losses far worse. But Marshall and Stimson also believed that part of the blame rested with the Selective Service System. Run by civilians and sensitive to the needs of industry and agriculture and the pressures of influential politicians and anxious parents, local draft boards handed out wholesale deferments for "essential skills" and 4-F ("unfit for service") classifications. At one point in late 1944 the secretary and the chief of staff would seriously consider forcing the Selective Service head, Gen. Louis Hershey, to resign, and replacing him with a more compliant man.

In these months Marshall also worried about the fighting

quality of the American infantry. But he refused to change one of its causes—the flawed replacement system so misused in the North African and Mediterranean campaigns. Writing to Ike in mid-May he acknowledged the mediocre "effectiveness of the infantry in combat" and admitted that "many suggestions" for change had "been considered." These included "special replacement companies in regiments; special replacement battalions in divisions; overstrength to be used for mandatory furloughs and separate regiments for relief purposes." But all of these, he insisted, were "unsatisfactory for one reason or another." His rejection of reform, when parsed, relies on arbitrary precedent. "The magnitude of our world-wide tasks and the limitations of manpower," he claimed, "require the specific assignment of every man we are authorized and all are so assigned on the Troop Basis."[45]

Yet Marshall was not totally unyielding. Recognizing some of the replacement policy's failings, he suggested shortly before D-Day that Eisenhower place a single officer in charge of the system in northern Europe. This commander would see to it that replacement candidates did not stagnate in depots but would be quickly reassigned to new posts. However, he still insisted that it was more important to keep the existing divisions up to strength than to add to their number. What the fighting army needed, he wrote, was not more divisions, but a robust supply of vigorous, well-trained replacements. Ike responded that "the procedures we adopt should be perfected before the attack so that we can depend upon the greatest economy and efficiency in the use of manpower." Nonetheless it would be difficult to find the right man for the job, for "he must be tough but understanding and broadly experienced but still full of energy."[46]

Though he and Marshall agreed that the Selective Service System under Hershey was deficient, Stimson did not concur with his chief of staff about the overall size of the Army Ground Forces.

In the weeks before D-Day, worried that too few troops were available for the imminent cross-Channel invasion, he strongly recommended that additional divisions be created. Marshall resisted. The chief of staff, Stimson noted in his diary, "takes quite a different view." He was "more optimistic" in a way that Stimson believed "rather dangerous." Stimson was apparently tempted to bring the matter to FDR to adjudicate but did not want to provoke an open struggle with Marshall when "he was in fundamental agreement [with him] on so many issues."[47]

To be fair, Marshall had sought periodically to alleviate the dearth of fighting men by tapping new sources. He sought to shift to combat units many soldiers in training for noncombat roles. One of his targets was the Army Specialized Training Program (ASTP), created by Stimson in late 1942 to educate especially qualified draftees to meet the army's needs for doctors, dentists, translators, engineers, and psychologists, and incidentally to keep in operation colleges and universities, their enrollments severely depleted by the draft. Assigned to colleges and universities for programs paid for by the U.S. Treasury, these academically talented young men, numbering as many as 140,000 in 1944, received army wages and attended classes in uniform but were unavailable for combat service. Marshall never liked ASTP. Smart, educated men, he believed, should lead infantry units, not be shunted off to the sidelines. By 1944, as serious military manpower shortages mounted, such men, he concluded, could not be spared as riflemen and infantry squad leaders. In February Marshall told Stimson that unless the War Department ended the program he would be forced to disband ten combat divisions. The secretary reluctantly complied, cutting ASTP in half and shifting its members to regular training divisions for basic combat training. Many of these men deeply resented what they considered the army's breach of faith.

Early in the war Marshall had also concluded that one large unutilized personnel pool was the nation's women. The chief of staff was scarcely a modern feminist; in fact within his marriage he was a patriarch of the old school. But when a group of activists proposed creation in May 1942 of the Women's Army Auxiliary Corps (WAACs, later shortened to WACs) to replace male soldiers in noncombat positions with uniformed women, he—unlike many of his military colleagues—had enthusiastically embraced it and helped guide the authorizing measure through Congress. The chief of staff personally selected the efficient Oveta Culp Hobby, a socially prominent Texan, as the corps' first head. By the end of the war 150,000 women had served as WACs, relieving as many as seven divisions of men for combat duties.

As the war wound down, Marshall and his boss also worried about the nation's *future* wartime manpower needs and actively supported the National Service Bill introduced early in 1945 by Representative James Wadsworth of New York, mandating that all men eighteen to sixty-five and all women eighteen to fifty in times of national crisis perform services for their country either in uniform or as civilian war-connected workers, the assignments to be determined by a director of national service. Though supported by Secretaries Stimson and Knox and by both Marshall and King, it was strongly opposed by organized labor and by some segments of industry management and, to Marshall's regret, never reached a final vote in Congress. In the years ahead, painfully aware of Americans' initial unpreparedness in two wars, Marshall would continue to fight for some version of universal service for the country's young men.

Meanwhile, in London, during the relatively quiet months preceding D-Day, final planning for an invasion of northern France was being completed under Cossac, the cross-Channel planning staff headed by British lieutenant general Frederick Morgan. As early as

August 1943 Morgan and his staff had prepared an invasion plan that became the basis for discussion between the Allies. His original proposal had provided for three Allied divisions for the initial landings on the French coast. With Overlord finally in place, Montgomery, chosen to lead the initial land combat operations, objected. This was too weak a force to overcome German resistance on the beaches. This time Monty was palpably right, and the proposed Anglo-American landing force was increased to five divisions.

Marshall's role in the stupendous cross-Channel operation would be limited and largely confined to the planning phase. Repelling British attacks on Anvil was one contribution to Overlord. Churchill believed that an invasion of southern France would weaken, rather than strengthen, the cross-Channel assault. Writing to Ike in mid-April before the operation, the prime minister announced that his support for Overlord had now "hardened very much." But for that very reason he opposed the Anvil operation. "I do not believe an advance up the Rhone Valley . . . will [favorably] influence our main operations this summer." The Germans, he noted, would fight a minor holding operation in southern France and save their strength to repel the Normandy invaders.[48] For a time even Eisenhower thought that, for the sake of Overlord, the Anvil operation should be contracted. Marshall fought to retain Anvil. The Allies, he said, had promised Stalin at Tehran to conduct such an operation; it was also, he insisted, a profitable way to utilize the growing number of Free French divisions coming online. In early February he scolded Ike for his doubts, but concluded characteristically that *he* must nonetheless be the ultimate judge. "OVERLORD, of course is paramount," he wrote to the supreme commander, "and it must be launched on a reasonable secure basis of which you are the best judge."[49] In the end, renamed Dragoon, the invasion of the French Mediterranean coast was postponed until mid-August, two months after

Overlord, and proved a success primarily by providing the intact port facilities of Marseille to supply the Allied armies by now fighting hard in northern France.

During this early stage of Overlord planning Marshall sought to help Eisenhower find the best battle commanders for the operation. Writing to him in late March, he noted his "special effort," with McNair's advice, to give him "a few more men" who had demonstrated in the United States "that they are in an aggressive mood and have developed well in the [officer] training program." He had told McNair that he wasn't "so much interested in . . . their tactical skill" as he "was in having sturdy, aggressive fighters who would stand up during moments of adversity. . . . The point I wish to make," he concluded, "is my desire to provide for you all the skill that we can muster for the first four weeks of your battle and you will not be involved in quibbles with G-1 for personnel."[50] But Marshall's role in selecting combat leaders for Overlord was largely advisory. "Commanders in the American Army," Ike would write, "were all of my own choosing. Ever since the beginning of the African campaign there had existed between General Marshall and me a fixed understanding on the point."[51]

But there were several notable exceptions to the self-denying policy: top combat commanders Omar Bradley, Mark Clark, and George Patton.

Marshall had met Bradley at Fort Benning in 1929, where, as an instructor at the Infantry School, the homely young Missourian became one of "Marshall's men."[52] Though not known for his élan, and probably undeserving of his popular reputation as the "GI's general," Bradley was a sound, steady leader, and when Marshall suggested him to command the American combat forces in Normandy under Montgomery, Ike accepted the recommendation with pleasure. He also accepted without demur Mark Clark, another Marshall favorite.

Patton was a more problematic Marshall choice than either of the others. The swashbuckling, profane, ill-tempered general had disgraced himself during the Sicilian campaign by slapping, for supposed malingering, two battle-stressed American soldiers he encountered at army field hospitals. On one of these occasions he unguardedly shouted: "There is no such thing as shell shock. It's an invention of the Jews."[53] Ike made him apologize to the victims of these outbursts but did not send him home. Marshall, as we saw, already recognized Patton's propensity for outrageous behavior and expression, but apparently not until the Washington columnist Drew Pearson published the story in November 1943 did he learn of the slapping incidents. Then, in late April, while in England awaiting assignment for service in France, Patton blundered again. Speaking to a small luncheon meeting on the occasion of an American "Welcome Club" opening for troops, he remarked that since it was the "evident destiny of the British and Americans, and, of course, the Russians, to rule the world, the better they knew each other the better job [they would] do."[54] No doubt many Americans would have agreed with the general, but to the British and American governments, struggling to present the UN as an altruistic champion of liberation from tyranny, it was infuriating. This time Marshall learned about the indiscretion before Ike and warned him that Patton had endangered the whole army promotion list then before Congress for approval. In an exchange of cables with the supreme commander he acknowledged that Patton was a scrapper who had "actual experience in fighting Rommel and in extensive landing operations followed by a rapid campaign of exploitation." But if Ike believed that another general would do for the job lined up for Patton in France, he should feel free to replace him. Eisenhower was personally disgusted with Patton's behavior. "I am exceedingly weary," he wrote to his chief, "of his habit of getting everybody in hot water through the immature character of his public actions and statements."[55] He apparently interpreted Marshall's message as a recommendation to fire Patton. But for some tense days he dithered, uncertain whether keeping him would offend his boss. In the end Marshall firmly reassured Eisenhower that the decision was his to make, and after an appropriate dressing-down, Ike wrote to Patton that his faith in him "as a battle leader" had overcome his chagrin at his personal indiscretion. He would be allowed to retain his command.[56]

If Marshall occasionally forayed into the choice of top commanders, at one point in this preparatory stage he also intruded into a major tactical issue: the use of airpower in the cross-Channel campaign. Marshall's proposals for the use of the army's air arm warrants a mixed review. Though scarcely a fanatic, he was a firm believer in airpower and could not resist urging the augmented use of the Allied air arm in the approaching Continental operations. When, in the run-up to the Normandy landings, fearing high French civilian casualties, Churchill had objected to the saturation bombing of French railroads and train marshaling yards to keep the Germans from reinforcing the invasion beachheads, Marshall insisted that Ike and the air commanders be allowed a free hand in deciding vital strategy. That decision proved astute. By D-Day the French railroads serving the Channel ports had been made virtually unusable. German reinforcements for the beachhead defenders were crucially delayed; the Allied invasion forces were not thrown into the sea.

But Marshall's air campaign proposals for France were not always wise. In early February he suggested that Ike seriously consider a massive airborne operation, deploying parachutists and glider troops, to accompany the cross-Channel seaborne landings. In fact on D-Day two American airborne divisions *would* descend on the Cotentin Peninsula, where they managed to confuse the German defenders and probably contributed to the successful landings farther east in Normandy. But Marshall's February plan, seconded by Hap Arnold, went beyond these operations. As an opening move of the cross-Channel attack, he proposed that several airborne contingents be dropped near Évreux, close to Paris, where they would attack the German forces from the rear as they raced to repel the Allied beachhead landings in Normandy. Besides aiding the landings, such a "true vertical envelopment," he told Ike, "should be a complete surprise" to the enemy as well as a "rallying point for considerable elements of the French underground." The operations would open "another front in France" and "tremendously increase" the speed of the Allied buildup. Fearing that such a novel move would be rejected by Ike's conservative planners, he urged the supreme commander to consider the plan carefully before his staff "tears it to ribbons."[57]

Ike's response was a judicious no. He "agreed thoroughly with the conception," but disagreed "with the timing," he wrote to his chief. "Mass in vertical envelopments is sound," but since the airborne force is initially "immobile on the ground," the time for such an envelopment "is *after* the beach-head has been gained and a striking force built up!" It would be difficult early in the Normandy campaign to defend these lightly armed airborne troops against heavy German attack. He, too, "instinctively" disliked upholding "the conservative as opposed to the bold," he assured Marshall, but perhaps large-scale airborne operations would be more useful later in the campaign.[58] And Ike was right. As Gen. James Gavin, the astute leader of the Eighty-Second Airborne Division, would later note: "Washington never seemed to understand how vulnerable airborne was to tanks unless we were reinforced immediately."[59] Those limited airborne landings that actually accompanied D-Day would prove costly in lives and were ultimately as futile as those employed by the Market Garden operation in occupied Holland conducted by Monty later in the year.

On June 6, 1944, at 1:30 a.m., thousands of American, British, Canadian, and Polish troops stormed ashore on the beaches of Normandy in northern France. D-Day, for which Marshall had labored for two and a half years, had finally arrived.

Back in Washington, Marshall had remained cool, seemingly almost indifferent, during the tense final countdown to the landings. The night before, he was at the Soviet Embassy to receive a decoration, the Order of Suvorov. He escaped to Quarters No. 1 soon after the ceremony and simply went to bed. As he later explained his composure, "Well, there was nothing I could do about it anymore. It was much better to get a good night's sleep and be ready for whatever the morning might bring."[60]

For the rest of the eleven-month campaign to destroy the German Reich, Marshall remained on the sidelines while the European Theater of Operations (ETO) generals engaged the Wehrmacht in mortal combat. At times he lost touch with the details of Ike's battle plans. At one point, after the initial landings had been stabilized but the breakout from the beaches not yet achieved, he seemed mystified by Eisenhower's intentions. At the end of July he complained to the supreme commander, "We had not received recently any information on your thoughts concerning the situation and your probable course of action." For instance, he went on, "we received no information of Bradley's present offensive except an unexplained reference in a radio [communication] from Mr. Stimson referring to COBRA, whatever that was."[61]

Though he left active command of the campaign to Ike, Marshall could not resist visiting the Allied landings soon after the Normandy beaches were secured. On June 8, after a brief stop in Britain, he was ferried to Omaha Beach, where the American troops had gained a toehold by the narrowest of margins. Af-

terward the chief of staff reported optimistically—too optimistically—to FDR and Stimson: "Conditions on the beachhead are
generally favorable with but minor difficulties or delays." He was
especially pleased by the fighting spirit of the American troops.
Morale was "high," he noted, and "our new divisions as well as
those which have been battle tested" were "doing splendidly." As
for the commanders, "Eisenhower and his staff are cool and confident, carrying out an affair of incredible magnitude and compli-
cation with superlative efficiency."[62] On the way home Marshall
stopped over in Italy and took the occasion to visit the military
cemetery at Anzio where Allen was buried. Back home he wrote
to Madge Brown, Allen's widow, to describe the grave site and to
tell her that all her husband's fellow soldiers spoke of him in "very
high terms."[63]

Marshall made one more trip to the front in France before
the final defeat of Germany.[*] In early October, accompanied by
Byrnes of the OWM, he flew to Paris, freed from German occupation in August, to see again for himself how the war was
progressing.

Much had changed, of course, since those anxious days of early
June when the success of the Normandy landings was still at risk.
For weeks after the Allies consolidated their hold on the beaches
they had struggled to breach the successive walls of impenetrable
hedgerows that imprisoned them in the shallow Norman landing
enclave. Then, in late July, Bradley launched Cobra, the operation that Marshall had complained that he knew nothing about.
At Saint-Lô his First Army, preceded by Sherman "Rhino" tanks
armed with steel plows in front, punched through the hedgerows,
broke out into smooth, tank-friendly country, and raced toward

---

[*]He was also briefly in southern France in late January 1945 to visit Ike prior to the
Big Three conference at Yalta.

the German border. Meanwhile, led by Patton, now arrived in France as commander of the newly activated Third Army, American troops overran Brittany, captured the port of Brest, and then joined the First Army in its dash toward the Rhine. The breakout at Saint-Lô offered the chance for Bradley and Patton to encircle much of the German army on the western front and perhaps end the war in a matter of weeks. But neither Eisenhower nor Bradley was willing to accept the risks to the American flanks and refused to authorize the wide sweep needed to close the trap. The bulk of the German army escaped, though badly mauled and in headlong retreat. The Allies now began a fast sprint across France, led by Patton's troops. In mid-August, as part of Anvil-Dragoon, American and Free French forces landed along France's Mediterranean coast to weak opposition. Vital supplies and munitions were soon pouring through Marseille to the Allied armies to the north. A month later the Dragoon invaders from the south had linked up with Patton. On August 25, reinforced by Free French troops, a largely undamaged Paris fell to the Allies. By early September, with the Americans and British hot on the heels of the Wehrmacht's retreating Army Group B, the war in the West seemed almost won. As Churchill would note in mid-September, since Sextant "everything we had touched had turned to gold."[64]

The surge of confidence was misplaced and damaging. At this point "an unhealthy aura of overoptimism and self-deception swept through the ranks of the Allied high command," Carlo D'Este has written.[65] Though distant from the scene of battle, even Marshall was infected by the "victory disease" and believed the war would be over by early November.[66]

Though the summer of 1944 brought Marshall professional satisfactions, it was also an anxious time for him personally as his role in the Pearl Harbor disaster came under renewed scrutiny. Americans understandably sought answers to the debacle of December 7, 1941. Shortly after the catastrophe, FDR had appointed Supreme Court Justice Owen Roberts to investigate the attack. The second of nine official investigations, the Roberts Commission inquiry condemned General Short and Admiral Kimmel for dereliction of duty, and they had been removed from their commands. But the results had not satisfied skeptics, especially FDR's political enemies. Seven Pearl Harbor investigations would follow the Roberts proceedings, including the one conducted by the Army Pearl Harbor Board in June 1944 and another—the most exhaustive—in 1945 after the war ended, by a Joint Congressional Investigating Committee whose sessions would last for weeks.

In the case of the army board inquiry, all three of the members, it was said, were officers who had reason to resent the chief of staff for decisions he had made that adversely affected them and their careers. Marshall naturally brooded about the inquiry's personal impact, but he and Stimson also worried that it might reveal the existence of the still-secret Magic code decipherments and squander a vital American intelligence asset. They particularly feared that, in the course of the 1944 presidential campaign, the Republican candidate, Thomas Dewey, would reveal that the commanders at Pearl Harbor had access to the secret Japanese codes.* The hearings, lasting through the early fall, accordingly, were held in secret and no mention was made of Magic in the official record.

Marshall's one-day interrogation took place in his own Pentagon office on August 7. His testimony was somewhat offhand. He admitted to lapses of memory and to mistakes in judgment but blamed the disaster ultimately on General Short. The army

---

*To prevent that from happening Marshall would approach candidate Dewey and, appealing to his patriotic instincts, ask him not to use the information against FDR. Dewey complied.

commander in Hawaii, he noted, had been given orders "to put his command on alert against a possible hostile attack by the Japanese," and "the command was not so alerted."[67]

Marshall was shaken by the final army board report submitted in November 1944, soon after FDR's reelection to a fourth term. The board ascribed the "Pearl Harbor disaster . . . primarily to two causes." First, as Marshall had attested, was General Short's failure "adequately to alert his command for war." But second was the War Department's failure to keep Short "adequately informed as to the developments of the US-Japanese negotiations," information that "might have caused him to change from the inadequate alert to the adequate one."[68] Marshall himself came out bruised. He was not branded a conspirator or a traitor, as extremists then and later believed was warranted. But according to the board, the chief of staff had been remiss in a number of significant ways. He had failed to keep General Short fully informed in the weeks before December 7 of how severely strained relations were with the Japanese; he had failed to send additional instructions to Short when it became clear that the general had misinterpreted his warning of November 27 to mean that he should guard primarily against sabotage in Oahu, not against a general attack; he had failed on the evening of December 6 and the early morning of December 7 to warn Short of an imminent break with Japan; and, finally, he had failed to investigate fully the state of readiness in the Hawaiian army command between November 27 and December 7.

In other words, the assessment of Marshall's actions was harsh. It challenged the image that he had planted in the minds of the nation's leaders and the public at large. When Roosevelt, a strong Marshall partisan, read it he remarked, "Why, this is wicked! This is wicked!"[69] Though the board's conclusions remained secret, when he learned of them from Stimson on November 11, Marshall seriously considered resigning. Discussing the findings with his boss, he lamented that "his usefulness to the Army [might well have] been destroyed." Stimson sought to reassure him. "I told him that was nonsense," the secretary wrote in his journal. Dismayed by the report himself, Stimson ordered an additional study of the Pearl Harbor circumstances along with a review of the conclusions by the judge advocate general. Based on these efforts, in a private written statement, the secretary absolved Marshall of all responsibility for Short's failures on December 7. None of these, he wrote, could be "attributed to the Chief of Staff." On the contrary, he wrote, "throughout this matter, I believe, he acted with his usual great skill, energy, and efficiency."[70] The secretary of war's support revived Marshall's spirits; there would be no more talk of resignation.

Stimson favored release of the army board report along with a word-for-word refutation of its conclusions, but the president ordered the document sealed until after the war. In fact enough of the overall conclusions seeped into public consciousness to confirm the suspicions of the isolationists and other administration enemies. In the words of Marshall's biographer Ed Cray, the report would be "a political time bomb ticking away under Marshall's reputation through the rest of the war."[71]

It was in mid-September, during the brief fall euphoria, that the Anglo-American Allies met for their last bilateral summit conference, code-named Octagon. Once more the site was Quebec, the picturesque Francophone town on the St. Lawrence River.

Marshall himself saw little reason for another Anglo-American meeting, but Churchill was uneasy at the nine-month delay since the last summit and considered several important issues between the Allies still unresolved. Foremost, he feared the Americans intended to transfer Mark Clark's Fifth Army from Italy to France. He had a better plan for these troops: Once they had defeated

Kesselring, send the Allied forces in Italy northeastward through the so-called Ljubljana Gap in Croatia and then push on to Vienna, where they could meet the Russians moving west from Ukraine. The American planners had no intention of joining in any Churchillian Balkan adventure, and at Quebec Marshall made their objections clear. But the chief of staff also promised not to withdraw American units from Italy until the Germans there surrendered. At Octagon, Churchill also sought to assure a British role in the Pacific after Germany's defeat. Such a role, he felt, could redeem the humiliating post–Pearl Harbor British debacles in Burma, Malaya, and Singapore, and help Britain recover the occupied portions of its Far Eastern empire. He did not offer British ground forces to the Far East—there were none to spare; but the Royal Navy, still a force to be reckoned with, surely could expect to join the final push against Japan. Neither Marshall nor FDR had any desire to help their ally regain past imperial glories. Nor did they feel they needed substantial British help to finish off the Pacific enemy. King especially did not wish to share credit for Japan's final defeat with the Royal Navy, and glared at the president at a session when he verbally accepted Churchill's offer. In the end Marshall proved more willing to accommodate the British than did the Anglophobic chief of naval operations. At one point he and the hard-nosed King "nearly had words."[72]

More significant than the arguments at Octagon over Allied military operations were the discussions of postwar German issues. At Quebec the Allies amended a provisional agreement among the Big Three on separate occupation zones in Germany after victory to shift the U.S. zone to the southwestern portion of the country, leaving the northwest to Britain. Churchill and FDR also signed on to the draconian Morgenthau Plan, which promised to strip postwar Germany of its industrial base and make it into a pastoral, deindustrialized, almost medieval economy. Both

Marshall and Stimson had vivid memories of the faulty peace-making arrangements following the First World War, and both opposed a draconian peace. In discussions prior to Quebec, they had agreed that the Morgenthau scheme was likely to foster resentments akin to those after Versailles and encourage similar toxic political responses. Marshall did not speak up against the plan at Octagon, but the discussions with Stimson undoubtedly helped influence his later policies as secretary of state.

In some respects Octagon also marked the early rumblings of the Cold War. By the fall of 1944 Soviet armies had pushed past the prewar boundaries of the USSR and were about to cross into Poland and the Baltic states, with the Balkans not far beyond. It was Churchill's fear that the Russians, and Communism, would occupy and completely dominate postwar Eastern Europe that fueled his interest in an Allied thrust toward Vienna. But Americans, including Marshall, were not yet as alert to Soviet ambitions as the prime minister and refused to go along.

Taken together the results of the Octagon meetings were minor. The grand military strategies of the Allies were already in place and seemingly proceeding satisfactorily. Though postwar problems were cropping up, they had not yet become urgent. The American military staffs at Quebec were by now practiced in the ways of their "cousins," and could parry them effectively. At previous Allied conferences Marshall had been a stubborn and often aggressive partisan. At Quebec in the late summer of 1944 he could relax, confident that he had contributed abundantly to the blueprint for victory.

But the optimistic mood of late summer 1944 did not last. During the fall and winter the Allied advance in France, rather than a milk run to Berlin, became a frustrating and costly slog; the war in northern Europe degraded into a virtual stalemate. Hitler had no intention of allowing the hated enemy, led by the Jews, to destroy his "thousand-year Reich." New secret weapons—buzz bombs, V-2 rockets, jet-propelled pursuit planes—would come to Germany's rescue and destroy the enemy's air fleets and undermine the morale of the British people. With 3.4 million troops still left in its ranks, the German army, stiffened by Hitler's fanatical resolve, was a long way from surrender. Behind the barrier of the Maginot-like Siegfried Line it would halt the Allied offensive in its tracks, the Führer believed. The Western Allies, by now alienated from the Bolshevik Asiatic Russian hordes, he predicted, would accept a negotiated peace; Germany, and its conquests, would be saved.

Hitler's generals, though skeptical of the dictator's inflated hopes, were encouraged by Anglo-American logistical problems to continue the fight. In the sweep across France, as their supply lines stretched out, the Allied armies, denied undamaged Channel ports, were being compelled to leave much of their gasoline, fresh equipment, and ammunition behind them. Anvil-Dragoon helped alleviate the supply problem but not enough. On September 4 the British had captured the Belgian port of Antwerp, one of the largest in Europe, but, despite Ike's persistent pressure, had failed to clear enemy forces from the Scheldt Estuary connecting it to the sea. By late summer the tanks and trucks of Patton, Montgomery, and Bradley were running out of fuel and could not go farther.

The military stasis fomented stresses within the Allied coalition, with Montgomery, commanding the Twenty-First British Army Group to the north, serving as the lord of discord. The prickly British general was dissatisfied with his role in the European theater. After the cross-Channel landings the British-Canadian units under his immediate command had failed to show much enterprise in capturing the important Norman port town of Caen. Then, after the breakout from the beachheads by

Bradley and Patton, the Americans had garnered all the head-lines. To regain the spotlight Monty had sought to turn his temporary Overlord field command into a permanent arrangement but was frustrated when, acting on Marshall's advice, on September 1 Ike decided to take direct charge of the battlefront himself. Many of Montgomery's discontents echoed his nation's: Britain was now the junior partner, unable to match the American military cornucopia—human and matériel. It had also failed to acquit itself in combat. With the exception of El Alamein, time and again British troops and generals had lost battles even on occasions when the odds were clearly in their favor. But Montgomery's divisiveness also derived from personal qualities. He was monumentally egocentric and overconfident. He scorned the supreme commander's military abilities. Ike's "ignorance as to how to run a war," he wrote to Brooke in August, "is absolute and complete." Eisenhower was essentially an amiable figurehead, though "such a decent chap" that it was "difficult," he admitted, "to be angry with him for long."[73] But he should devote his energies to where his talents lay—inter-Allied relations, military government, and the like—leaving to others, namely himself, the actual land battles.

Eisenhower was aware of his subordinate's disdain. But, in the spirit of Allied amity, he refused to reciprocate, at least publicly. In late July, after a series of American press articles criticizing Montgomery was called to his attention, he wrote to General Surles, the army's chief public relations officer, expressing his concern and proposing a way to squelch the controversy. "My only concern . . . is that criticism directed against any one of my principal subordinates . . . is certain to disturb the spirit of teamwork that I have so laboriously worked for during the past two years."[74] Would Surles, in replying to the press, emphasize that any attack on one of his subordinates was an attack on him? Marshall could not have been more pleased with the response; it was exactly the one *he* would have made.

Ike may have ducked a rivalrous public confrontation with Montgomery, but he could not avoid a battle with him within the highest command levels over how to clinch the campaign against Hitler's Germany. During the summer, with the Wehrmacht in general retreat and Allied forces able to "advance almost at will," Eisenhower had concluded that once the Rhine's west bank had been cleared of enemy troops the Allies would push rapidly into Germany, marching abreast, as it were. "We must immediately exploit our success," he cabled Montgomery on September 5, "by promptly breaching the Siegfried Line, crossing the Rhine on a wide front and seizing the Saar and Ruhr." He denied that he was indifferent to the "northern route of advance," but that should wait until the ports of Le Havre and Antwerp were fully open to use.[75]

Monty begged to differ. The broad-front approach was a colossal mistake. Instead, a "powerful and full blooded thrust toward Berlin," from his position to the north, on the Allies' left flank, was preferable.[76] A narrow, concentrated drive through the Ruhr Valley, he was sure, would slice like a knife through the German defenses, allow the Allied armies to take Berlin in advance of the Russians, and quickly end the war. Equally frustrated with the broad-front strategy was Patton. He, too, favored a focused push, predominantly by armored forces, though to Monty's south, by his own Third Army.

Ike's veto of Monty's strategic plan as a "mere pencil-like thrust," vulnerable to flank attack and too wasteful of resources, set off an explosion when, at a meeting in liberated Brussels on September 10, the British commander, newly elevated to field marshal by Churchill, fired back rudely at the supreme commander.[77] Monty called the broad-front strategy "balls, sheer balls, rubbish!"; it simply would not work.[78] He apologized for his outburst when Eisenhower reminded him that he was Monty's boss, but clearly the ill will between the two continued. In fact, however, both strategies were flawed, Monty's for the reasons that Ike suggested; his own for failing to take into account manpower limitations. The ninety-division army that Marshall had mandated simply could not supply the number of combat troops for a front of six hundred miles, strung out from the North Sea to the Mediterranean. In late December, Ike and his lieutenants would learn how shaky their own troop dispositions were in the face of strong German attack.

Though still wary of meddling in combat operations, Marshall could not entirely avoid being drawn into the dispute over the endgame European strategy. The chief of staff was no admirer of Montgomery. He had been unimpressed when he first met him in Algiers in May 1943. Now, when he dropped in on Monty at his Eindhoven headquarters in the Netherlands during his October 1944 European visit, he was deluged by the British commander with complaints about Ike. According to the new field marshal the supreme commander lacked "grip and operational direction." Operations in eastern France and the Low Countries had "become ragged and disjointed," and the Allies had now gotten themselves "into a real mess." The attack angered Marshall, who "came pretty near," he later reported, "to blowing off out of turn." Monty, he was convinced, was driven by "overwhelming egotism," but in any case, he concluded, it "was Eisenhower's business not mine" and he "had better not meddle."[79] As for the question of broad front versus narrow thrust, though there is no evidence that Marshall was Ike's inspiration, the chief of staff sided with the supreme commander. As he declared in his postwar interviews, he was skeptical of "very dashing action" of the sort recommended by Patton and now by Monty. It had worked in Patton's favor after the Normandy breakout, but "that is not always the case."[80]

Despite the mutual animus, as a sort of consolation prize, and perhaps to indulge Marshall's misplaced taste for airborne operations, the conciliatory Eisenhower in mid-September authorized Monty to launch Operation Market Garden, a modified version of the field marshal's narrow-front strategy. This would be a multinational push, by both ground and airborne troops, to capture the Dutch bridges over the Rhine and its tributaries, turn the enemy's right flank, and, it was hoped, finally envelop the Ruhr region, Germany's industrial heartland.

The operation was a disaster. Monty's staffers were warned by the Dutch underground of two German panzer divisions present at Arnhem, at one of the bridges. As revealed by their Ultra code intercepts,* the British had learned of the presence of hidden German forces in the area. Monty's staff ignored both. The airdrops were ineffective; most were too far from the bridge objectives. The lightly armed parachute and glider troops—British, American, and Polish—sent to seize the river bridges and canal crossings met with ferocious resistance, with many either killed or captured. Meanwhile, British infantry under the overrated general Sir Brian Horrocks, coming from the south to consolidate the presumably captured water crossings and then strike westward into the Ruhr Valley, were subjected to a withering gauntlet of German fire. Fighting their way along a congested two-lane highway, they failed to show much dash and resolve and allowed the Allied airborne troops to be slaughtered by the enemy. Market Garden, when it finally shut down on September 29, had been a

---

*"Ultra" was the name the British gave their successful code-breaking operation directed at German intelligence. It was the equivalent to the American "Magic," aimed primarily at Japanese codes.

costly and embarrassing failure. Even Montgomery, a man not given to self-criticism, admitted he had made some mistakes. On the other hand, he claimed, the operation had been "90% successful," and would, he asserted, have succeeded totally if it had been better backed—presumably by Eisenhower.[81]

After Market Garden the dispute over how to regain the momentum of the summer resumed. Increasing German resistance halted the Allied broad-front advance before it could breach the fortified Siegfried Line and the Rhine barrier to Germany. The fighting along the Reich's western borders proved savage and bloody. The confrontation between Courtney Hodges's First Army and the Wehrmacht in the frigid Hürtgen Forest in November typified the futility of the autumn Allied campaign. The grinding battle sent 24,000 Americans to hospitals or their graves for virtually no gain. Nor was Patton's September drive to take the fortress city of Metz in Lorraine much more successful. Metz did not fall until late November after the Third Army had suffered 45,000 casualties. And at that, the soldiers' lives were wasted. The campaign liberated some five thousand square miles of French territory, but it delayed the American advance for three months and allowed the enemy to retreat intact to stronger positions farther east.

The fighting on Germany's western borders revealed once more the failings of American troop training and manpower replacement policies. The performance of American infantry in eastern France often disappointed their leaders. Lt. Colonel William Simpson of the Second Division's Tenth Infantry acknowledged in a September report that the soldiers he observed had been afflicted with excessive caution. "We lost time because of lack of boldness and aggressiveness on the part of our scouts."[82] The troops, he added, were too ready to withdraw if they encountered resistance. The enemy, too, remarked on the weaknesses of

American troops under fire. The Americans, observed Capt. Walter Schaefer-Kehnert, with the German Ninth Panzer Division, "operated by the book. If you responded by doing something not in the book, they panicked. It usually took them three days after an attack to prepare for the next one. . . . It took a ridiculously long time to get into Germany."[83]

Some of the critics once again pointed directly at the training process as the cause of the deficiencies. The writer and cultural critic Paul Fussell, then a twenty-year-old rifle platoon lieutenant deployed along the western German border, disparaged the infantry training he had received at Fort Benning, where Marshall's "fire-and-movement" doctrine had been promoted. The tactic had been drilled into his fellow rookie junior officers for six months, and "we all did grasp the idea," Fussell later wrote. "But it had one signal defect, namely the difficulty, usually the impossibility, of knowing where your enemy's flank is. If you get up and go looking for it, you'll be killed."[84] Nor were the training deficiencies limited to the foot soldiers. The historian Stephen Ambrose quotes a nettled tank commander at the Battle of the Bulge in December: "I spent long hours in the [tank] turret when I was literally showing men how to feed bullets to the gun. Could they shoot straight? They couldn't even hold the gun right!"[85] Another tanker wrote of the new three-man crew for his light tank that they were all eighteen years of age and that only one had ever even driven a car.

And the flawed troop replacement policy once more, on the German border as in the Mediterranean, contributed appreciably to the deplorable results. One American replacement soldier assigned to the campaign confessed that he had never fired directly at the enemy. In his new battalion "nobody had time to teach you anything, you just had to pick it up for yourself." Pvt. Red Thompson, a scorned replacement, learned to take care of

himself, but, he noted, "I knew I was just cannon fodder."[86] Officers confirmed the problem. A company commander serving with
Patton complained to his superiors that it was foolish to carry out
operations like those at Metz with depleted units filled with raw
replacements. "I knew . . . [such units] were not trained [or] hardened." "All the leaders," he wrote, "were lost exposing themselves
at the wrong time. . . . The new men seemed to lose all sense
of reasoning. They left their rifles, their flamethrowers, satchel
charges and what not laying [*sic*] right there where it was. I was
disgusted."[87]

The deficiencies of training and replacement in the eleven
months between D-Day and the Third Reich's surrender in May
1945 were understood by both the Pentagon and by the leaders at
SHAEF. So why were they not corrected? As noted above, Marshall, McNair, and others poked at the existing system but neither
hard nor effectively enough. In fact Marshall was one of the more
ardent defenders of keeping inviolate the existing divisions, a position that nurtured the crippled replacement system. As for Eisenhower and his lieutenants, Ambrose claims that they were obsessed
with "an ever greater flow of replacements" for the final battles and
did "precious little to insist on improving the training."[88]

Adding to his disappointment with the slowdown and the
costly battle of attrition that followed along Germany's western
borders, the last months of 1944 were not a happy time for Marshall generally. At the beginning of November his friend, Field
Marshal Dill, the man whose role as honest broker between the
English-speaking Allies had so often smoothed the way to needed
compromise, died of pernicious anemia. It was both a personal
and a professional loss that deeply affected Marshall. Overcoming
precedent and some jingoist American Legion officials, he was
able to arrange for Dill, a foreign soldier, to be buried with honors
at Arlington National Cemetery.

Marshall's sorrow may have been eased by his appointment soon after as a five-star general, but it probably was not. Disturbed that the top American officers were outranked by the field marshals of the British and other foreign armies, FDR had decided that the United States should create a new, higher rank than four-star general. Marshall disagreed. He had never felt inferior to Brooke or Montgomery because he was just a "general," he noted. And besides, he believed, a five-star rank, if created, should be reserved as the ultimate honor for a commander after final victory in war, as in the cases of Grant, Sherman, and Pershing. He also deplored conferring the honor on any man while Pershing was alive, and, though now confined permanently to his bed at Walter Reed Hospital, the World War I leader was still breathing. To create such a rank, Marshall felt, would subtract from the honor accorded his revered mentor after 1918. Despite Marshall's objections Roosevelt pushed a bill through Congress, and on December 15, along with MacArthur, Eisenhower, and Arnold, Marshall became a "General of the Army."

Hoping to save the Third Reich from final destruction, in mid-December the Germans launched a major offensive through Belgium's thick Ardennes forest. The last spasm of German offensive power, the attack was a desperate move that Hitler believed might recapture now-functioning Antwerp, split the Allied armies, weaken the Anglo-American coalition, and force Britain and America to accept the negotiated peace he craved. Despite mounting intelligence of a German buildup and the precedent of the German breakthrough in 1940 in the same place, the attack through the tangled Ardennes came as a complete surprise to Ike and his lieutenants. Launched in snowbound, bitterly cold, overcast weather that kept Allied planes grounded, for the first few days the offensive made remarkable early progress against thinly spread American forces, and severely jolted the unsuspecting supreme commander.

Back in Washington, Marshall and Stimson initially dismissed the German Ardennes assault, soon labeled the "Battle of the Bulge" by the media, as a feeble last gasp. Their confidence quickly turned to alarm, but the chief of staff could only urge Ike to do his best. He had given orders, he wrote to Ike on December 24, that the supreme commander be spared all the usual distractions to pursue the single goal of stopping the enemy drive. "I kept down the messages to Eisenhower," he later noted. "I made them recall one they sent during the Bulge; I said 'Don't bother him.'"[89] When the tide of battle finally turned decisively in the Allies' favor, he cabled Ike: "You are doing a fine job and go on and give them hell."[90]

But in fact the top American commanders at European theater SHAEF headquarters in Versailles had *not* done such a "fine job." Ike and Bradley had disregarded the accumulating information from Ultra and other intelligence sources of the German buildup in Belgium. More telling, perhaps, Ike's broad-front strategy, combined with Marshall's ninety-division manpower limit and the heavy casualties in the late fall campaigns at Hürtgen and Metz, had mandated the sparse distribution of forces in the Ardennes.

Alerted to the manpower problems in the Ardennes and fearful of future difficulties down the road, Stimson sought to revise American military recruitment policy. As news of the German successes flooded into Washington, the secretary grew anxious. Selective Service, he demanded, must accelerate the draft call-up so that the army could create ten additional divisions in time for the fighting ahead in both Europe and the Pacific. The chief of staff objected, claiming that an acute shortage of experienced junior officers prevented such expansion. In a session with the secretary that Stimson described in his diary as "very stormy,"[91] Marshall said that he would resign rather than yield and "asked him [Stimson] to tell the President this."[92] Stimson conceded but Marshall did, too—in a minor way. Realizing that perhaps he had gone too far, he wrote to Eisenhower soon after that the "Army ceiling" would be increased by taking into account the number of soldiers in hospitals and "some other ineffectiveness." But, he warned, "this action would not help the flow of replacements for nearly six months."[93] It was a standoff: The American combat army would remain lean and stressed until the final Axis defeat.

By late January, finally, with cloudless skies for Allied aircraft and the arrival of U.S. airborne reinforcements, the Wehrmacht was checked, its gains erased, and the Allied front line in the Ardennes painfully restored and readied for advances into Germany. The enemy had suffered one hundred thousand casualties, but even more than their manpower losses, the Germans had used up their last reserves of tanks and other heavy equipment. From now on only Hitler's fanaticism, and savage repressive measures to put down civilian dissent and defeatism at home, kept Germany in the excruciating and futile war.

The Ardennes offensive would widen the gap between the British and American Allies. Churchill and British opinion makers seized on the Bulge setback to argue again for a greater British role in the final drive into Germany. During these last months of the European war, though usually careful to accommodate British complaints for the sake of coalition unity, Marshall supported Ike's refusal to cave in to British pressures to share troop command with Monty during and after the Bulge. Writing to Ike just before the New Year, the chief of staff called his attention to British press demands that he hand over battlefield authority to a British deputy commander, certain to be Montgomery. Marshall apologized for bothering Eisenhower while he was in the midst of containing the Ardennes offensive, but he felt he had to comment. "Under no circumstances make any concessions of any kind whatsoever," he wrote. Ike not only had his "complete confidence," but there "would be a terrific resentment in this country following such action."[94]

British pressure to favor Montgomery continued into the last months of the European war in the form of demands that the main Allied advance into Germany be in the north, where the bulk of the British forces were concentrated. It was a version of Monty's narrow-thrust strategy and received no better reception from either Marshall or Eisenhower.

The issue of national priority in the final battles in the West carried over to Argonaut, the last wartime conference of the Big Three. The main event was a set of tripartite Allied-Soviet meetings held at Yalta in the Soviet Crimea, but these were preceded by four days of British-American military staff meetings at Malta, the British island redoubt in the Mediterranean just south of Sicily, now finally safe from devastating air attack and invasion.

Marshall played an active role in these preliminary staff deliberations. On January 28, on the way to Malta, he met with Eisenhower at the Château Valmont outside Marseille. Arriving feeling somewhat skeptical of his protégé after the near-disaster in the Ardennes, he would leave reassured. The two men considered Ike's plan for final defeat of the Germans. The general reiterated his broad-front intentions. The final assault would be "a series of concentrated and powerful attacks along the Rhine" and then, after clearing the river's west bank of the enemy, "hurl[ing] some seventy-five reinforced divisions against the Germans in great converging attacks" that would carry the Allied armies to final victory.[95] Brooke had already complained that Ike was about to commit that classic military blunder—dispersing his forces. Backing Montgomery without reservation, he had again proposed instead one vigorous thrust on the Allied northern flank across the Rhine. Now, at their Château Valmont meeting, Marshall emphatically rejected the British scheme and endorsed Ike's plan. To reinforce it he suggested that the supreme commander send his trusted chief of staff, Walter Bedell Smith, to Malta to defend his strategy. As for the British push to take over command of all Allied combat operations, he promised at Malta to beat back the continuing demands of Monty and Churchill.

The following day Marshall left for the scheduled Anglo-American staff discussions. As expected, these focused on Ike's proposed endgame strategy and on the supreme commander's role for the remainder of the European war. On Tuesday the thirtieth, at the Combined Chiefs' session, Bedell Smith and Gen. Harold Bull, his assistant, defended a modified version of Ike's final-offensive plan. Once across the Rhine, Smith explained, the Allies would launch two thrusts into Germany, one to the north, but another from the south. He was careful to highlight the role that Monty would play in the three-phase operation. But Brooke nevertheless objected. The British Chiefs of Staff, he said, "felt that there was not sufficient strength available for two major operations," and "of the two, the northern appeared the most promising."[96] The Combined Chiefs' discussion the following day concerned routine matters and was followed in the evening by a festive, good-humored dinner for the CCS hosted by British admiral Andrew Cunningham at Malta's Admiralty House.

But the surface amiability of Tuesday and Wednesday did not foretell the atmosphere of Thursday. There is virtually nothing in the official records to disclose the passionate disagreements between the Allies on the third day of the meetings. But passionate—and angry—they were, British feelings fueled by their loss of leadership, American by the constant British carping against Ike and pressure to expand Monty's role in the final victory push.

At the Combined Chiefs' afternoon meeting on February 1,

Marshall criticized Montgomery and Churchill for seeking to cripple the supreme commander and apparently disparaged Montgomery's generalship. He clashed once again with Brooke over the plan to invade Germany. The British did not object so much to the American proposal as stated by Smith and Bull, but were upset, they said, by an amended outline by Eisenhower that seemed to retreat from the northern aspect and to muddle the whole issue. When Marshall asked Brooke to approve Ike's broad-front strategy, he refused. This is the sanitized bare-bones written record of events. But the reality was more vivid. The meeting on the first, Harry Hopkins would write, produced one of "the most violent disagreements and disputes of the war." The "arguments reached such a point" that Marshall, "ordinarily one of the most restrained and soft spoken of men," announced that if the British plan were adopted "he would recommend to Eisenhower that he had no choice but to be relieved of command."[97] According to Brooke, Marshall also expressed his "full dislike and antipathy" for Montgomery.[98]

That evening, hoping to calm the waters, Smith came to Brooke's quarters for further discussion of the invasion plan for Germany. He failed. Instead, the meeting became acrimonious. Brooke demanded that Ike be directed to supply more troops to Monty's sector of the advance. At this the American blew up: "Goddamn it! Let's have it out here and now," he shouted. If Ike were to accept these terms it would amount to a vote of no confidence, and he might well ask that the Combined Chiefs relieve him of command. Brooke responded that Ike was a fine chairman of the board and denied that he had any intention of having him dismissed.[99] According to Brooke's diary, despite the acerbity, "the talk did both of us good."[100] But apparently it did not, and on the following day, at the Combined Chiefs' meeting, the battle resumed. This time Marshall evicted the staff members from the room, leaving only the chiefs themselves. He now sought to browbeat Brooke into accepting Ike's amended plan. All Brooke would agree to was to "take note of" Ike's conclusions, and there the issue remained until FDR himself arrived at Malta's Valletta harbor aboard the USS *Quincy* on February 2, the next day.

Roosevelt's physical appearance shocked both King and Marshall when they saw him. The president looked frail and worn. He had lost weight, had dark circles under his eyes, and his emblematic dark navy cape hung loosely on his frame. Churchill would observe that he no longer seemed interested in military strategy, but in fact, at a two-hour session aboard the navy cruiser that same day, FDR had enough energy to settle the Anglo-American military differences in favor of the supreme commander. As a pacifying gesture FDR accepted the British request that Field Marshal Alexander, one of their own—and more compliant than Ike—be appointed his deputy in the European theater. In the end, as personified by the president, American numbers and sheer military preponderance had prevailed over British pride. And apparently the British soon came around to accepting the American strategy. According to Eisenhower, some weeks later, as he and Brooke stood on the banks of the now-unobstructed Rhine, CIGS turned to him and said: "Thank God, Ike, you stuck by your plan. You were completely right and I'm sorry if my fear of dispersed effort added to your burdens."[101] In fact Brooke repudiated the quotation. As he later wrote: "I am still convinced that he was completely wrong."[102]

The Malta meetings were quickly followed by the epoch-making political discussions of February 4–11 among the Big Three at Yalta. In the Cold War years of the fifties Marshall would be accused of collaborating in a betrayal of America's vital interests at Yalta. But in fact the meetings only marginally engaged him. At the opening session he contributed a concise review of the state of ground force battle on the Anglo-American western front. He also described the battering of Germany by the Allied air forces. In a year it had cut enemy oil production by 80 percent. One of his few serious concerns was the Russian role against Japan. At Tehran, Stalin had said that the Soviet Union would join Britain and the United States in the Pacific war after Germany's defeat. But Marshall had remained unconvinced. At Yalta he got a reassuring pledge from Gen. Alexey Antonov, the Soviet chief of staff. But that, too, was not enough. To be convincing, he believed, the decision must be confirmed by evidence of specific mutual advantages. And they were. At an afternoon meeting on February 8 Stalin and FDR put together a plan for Soviet participation in the Far Eastern war that included transfer of marginal Japanese territory to the Russians and a number of minor territorial concessions the Soviets demanded. In return the Soviet leader promised to argue for intervention against Japan before the Supreme Soviet, the rubber-stamp Soviet parliament.

Marshall had gotten what he had come to Yalta for and played no part in the decisions regarding Europe's postwar fate that right-wing enemies of FDR and Harry Truman, his Democratic successor, would later excoriate. He returned to Washington by way of Italy, where he hoped his presence would help counteract Congresswoman Luce's skeptical view of troop morale. Mark Clark, ignoring Marshall's orders, arranged a resplendent honors ceremony that included reviewing troops from all the UN units fighting Marshal Kesselring.

He arrived back at the Pentagon on February 16 and flew down to Liscombe Lodge in Pinehurst, North Carolina, near Fort Bragg, the cottage that Katherine had just bought. Visits to the lodge in winter would soon become part of Marshall's annual schedule. During the week George would remain in the capital, close to his office, while Katherine, her grown children, and assorted grandchildren escaped from the damp, flu-inducing weather of Washington to the dry North Carolina sandhills. Marshall would fly to Pinehurst on weekends "when possible." According to Katherine, George adjusted comfortably to this regimen. Together, Dodona Manor and the house at Pinehurst, she wrote, "were a God-send to an over-burdened and tired man."[103] Marshall actually seemed to like the commuting, considering himself "fortunate" to "[be] able spend my weekends" at the North Carolina resort.[104]

Meanwhile, though the German Ardennes offensive had been turned back and the Allied advance resumed, the relentless fighting in Europe dragged on. In March the Allied armies finally crossed the Rhine at several points and raced toward the heart of Germany. The relative ease of the crossings, Ike believed, had been made possible by his disputed strategy of first defeating the Wehrmacht forces along the river's west bank. Yet lashed on by their fanatical Führer, the Wehrmacht, with increasing futility and growing despair, continued to resist. As the Allied armies advanced into the *Vaterland* itself, they continued to face ferocious resistance, though from depleted forces often consisting of tired old men and fanatical young boys in ill-fitting uniforms. They also uncovered the horrors of the death camps that revealed the true evil of the Nazi regime. In these last days Hitler would grasp at straws. When Roosevelt, visibly haggard and sickly at Yalta, died of a cerebral hemorrhage in Georgia on April 12, the dictator's hopes revived; the American president's demise, he announced, would undermine the enemy's alliance and save Germany. But of course it did not.

On April 25 Soviet and American troops coming from opposite directions met at Torgau on the Elbe River. The Allied armies would go no farther east. The question of pushing on all the way to Berlin before the Russians arrived had already been decided. Patton, whose bellicose right-wing political instincts were by now fully awakened to the postwar Soviet threat, strongly advised driving through to Berlin. More tellingly, Churchill had warned Ike in late March that if the Anglo-Americans failed to "cross the Elbe and advance as far eastward as possible," the Russian army would take Vienna and "overrun Austria." Abandoning Berlin to their tender mercies "may strengthen their conviction, already apparent, that they have done everything."[105] Eisenhower was not naive about Soviet intentions, but considered Berlin "nothing more than a geographical location"[106] and thought there was no good military reason to snatch the trophy from the Russians. Capturing Berlin would unnecessarily offend the Soviets, and for no good tactical reason. Besides, it would force the Americans to take on the heavy logistical burden of caring for additional thousands of hungry, homeless German civilians. He would only reconsider, he said, if the Combined Chiefs of Staff ordered him to do so. There is no record of Marshall's view of the specific Berlin issue. He was indeed aware of the points of conflict with the Russians but hoped that after the war these frictions would not endanger a lasting peace. He also feared jeopardizing the Russian pledge to join the war in the Pacific. It must therefore be assumed that he was not likely to endorse snatching the city from under the Russians' noses. Moreover he was reluctant to incur further American casualties. As he wrote to Ike on April 28 regarding suggestions that advancing Allied forces push into Czechoslovakia, he was "loath to hazard American lives for purely political purposes." Czechoslovakia would undoubtedly "have to be cleared of German troops," but by the Russians, not the Americans, though "we may have to cooperate with the Russians in so doing."[107] Events would vindicate Ike's and Marshall's conclusions about the cost of taking Berlin: In the battles to capture the German capital the Red Army would suffer more than 350,000 casualties, including 78,000 deaths.

On April 30, at his underground *Führerbunker* in Berlin, Hitler and his new bride, Eva Braun, committed suicide. On May 7, at SHAEF headquarters in Reims, the German chief of staff, Alfred Jodl, signed unconditional surrender terms with the Western Allies, a ceremony repeated the next day in Berlin between Gen. Wilhelm Keitel and the Russians. The unholy war in Europe was over!

Marshall was jubilant. Though this private man never made public his joy at victory, it reverberates in his congratulatory radiogram to Eisenhower on the day of Germany's surrender. "You have completed your mission with the greatest victory in the history of warfare," he declared. "You have made history, great history, for the good of all mankind and you have stood for all we hope and admire in an officer of the United States Army."[108]

Whatever his personal response to victory, Marshall could bask in the accolades that now rained down on him. Ike responded to his chief's praise with his own tribute. Marshall had an "unparalleled place in the respect and affections of all military and political leaders with whom I have been associated, as well as with the mass of American fighting men," he wrote. "Our army and our people have never been so deeply indebted to any other soldier."[109] On May 8—the official American "VE-Day"—Secretary Stimson called Marshall to his office, where he had gathered the leading members of the Army General Staff. Positioning Marshall in the middle of the group, he acknowledged his own and the country's "great debt" to the general. He had personally "never seen a task of such magnitude performed by man" as Marshall had accomplished, he said. Looking directly at his friend and cherished wartime accomplice, he declared: "I have seen a great many soldiers in my lifetime, and you, sir, are the finest soldier I have ever known."[110] Churchill, who had already called Marshall "the true 'organizer of victory,'" also lavished praise on the American chief of staff. Ignoring their many disagreements in the flush of victory, the PM composed an encomium carefully matched to Marshall's role in the war. "It has not fallen to your lot to command great armies," but "to create them, organize them, and inspire them," he wrote. Under Marshall's "guiding hand the mighty and valiant formations which have swept across France and Germany were brought into being and perfected in an amazing time." The prime minister concluded with a glowing personal tribute: "There has grown in my breast through all these years of mental exertion a respect and admiration for your character and massive strength which has been a real comfort to your fellow-toilers, of whom I hope it will always be recorded that I was one."[111]

Marshall undoubtedly enjoyed these tributes—and the many others bestowed by friends and colleagues—but he was painfully aware that the job was only half done. Back in September, with German defeat looming, he anticipated the reluctance of American fighting men, especially weary veterans of Europe and North Africa, to accept the additional sacrifices and risks needed to defeat Japan. As before, he turned to Hollywood's Frank Capra for help. Capra produced a short documentary film, *Two Down and One to Go*, that explained to the troops why the Pacific enemy must now be vanquished. Sent under seal to hundreds of military posts, it was not to be played until the end of fighting in Europe.

The finally unveiled thirty-minute film shows Marshall at his desk, in full uniform, with Pershing's portrait on the wall behind him. In a calm and even voice, between clips of heroic Allied wartime military and naval actions, the chief of staff reads his text. Europe had been first, he declares, because the Pacific enemy had not been accessible and, after Pearl Harbor, the United States had initially lacked the naval resources to challenge it. But the war, east and west, was one war, and now that Germany was defeated, "we will not have won this war until Japan has been totally crushed."[112] On VE-Day Marshall delivered the same message to the wider American public by radio: "Let us celebrate the victory and say our prayers of thanksgiving and *then* turn with all the power and stern resolution of America to destroy forever and in the shortest possible time every vestige of military power in the Japanese nation."[113]

In the short Capra film Marshall appears animated and robust. But like many other Allied war leaders he was now tired. His wartime labors had exacted an appreciable personal toll. As he would write to Secretary Stimson several years later: "In all my Washington posts since 1938 I never seem to have [had] a day of restful existence." He expressed a similar view to Ike: "This is not an easy world to live in for people like you and myself."[114] Besides his fatigue, over the years his health had suffered. Though six feet tall, lean, and still vigorous-looking, Marshall had endured several chronic illnesses, including a heart murmur and an inflamed kidney. He had spent time at Walter Reed Hospital. He was now sixty-five and looking forward to retirement. But the Pacific conflict now awaited him. Personal ease, like final world peace, would have to be postponed.

CHAPTER 9

JAPAN-CHINA

The three months between the two "V-Days" were fraught with challenges for Marshall. But foremost, of course, was how to defeat Japan. By mid-1945 the end was already foreshadowed, yet much effort, risk, and loss remained before the tenacious and zealous Japanese leaders and people would allow foreign troops to occupy the precious soil of Nippon and the despised *gaijin* (foreigners) to dictate the affairs of the sacred empire.

By V-E Day, Japan was under ferocious attack on multiple fronts and from all dimensions.

Advancing from the south were MacArthur's ground forces under the plodding Walter Krueger, a Marshall choice as combat commander. For months Marshall had wavered over whether the best course was to invade or bypass the Philippines on the way to Japan. He understood MacArthur's attitudes and loyalties and to some extent shared them. But the chief of staff warned the general not to allow "personal feelings and Philippine political considerations" to distort his judgment. The defeat of Japan must be the primary goal, always kept in view.[1] Yet when it came to

adopting a definite strategy for the military push northward toward Japan, Marshall vacillated and dithered.

All through the first half of 1944 Marshall had continued to
send mixed signals about MacArthur's Philippines-first plans. In
late January, General Sutherland, his chief of staff, appeared in
Washington to present his boss's case to the War Department and
the Joint Chiefs. Marshall reassured him that the planners were
leaning toward MacArthur's views. Soon after, however, Admiral
King descended on the Joint Chiefs to defend the navy's emphasis
on the Central Pacific thrust. Rather than directly oppose the
admiral's plans, Marshall called for further study. Annoyed by
the wavering of his professional superiors in Washington, MacArthur made a personal appeal to Stimson for greater authority
generally over operations in the Pacific, including control of the
naval forces he needed for a Philippine campaign. In defense of
his drive from the south he noted the costliness of the island-by-
island investment in the Central Pacific thrust. "These frontal
attacks by the Navy . . . are a tragic and unnecessary massacre of
American lives." He was appealing directly to Stimson, he said,
because FDR was "Navy minded. . . . Give me central direction
of the war in the Pacific," he declared, and he would "be in the
Philippines in ten months' time."[2]

In the following months MacArthur and King, either directly
or through their surrogates, would continue to tangle over final
Pacific strategy, and in the end Marshall avoided taking responsibility for the result. It would be the president himself who settled
the issue of where army troops would be deployed next in the
Pacific.

The setting for the decision was Hawaii, far from mainland
U.S. shores. In late July 1944 FDR met with MacArthur in Oahu
accompanied by Admirals Nimitz and Leahy while Marshall remained behind in Washington attending staff meetings and con-

ducting routine business. Though commander in chief by constitutional mandate, Roosevelt had often deferred to Marshall and the Joint Chiefs, especially toward the war's end. True, he had vetoed Marshall's Sledgehammer plan in favor of North Africa, but he did not normally claim the driver's seat when specific military strategy was at stake. In late July 1944, however, though in ill health, FDR had just been nominated for a fourth presidential term and was openly seeking to bolster his political capital by a public display of presidential vigor and by identifying with the voters' Pacific hero. MacArthur had no illusions about FDR's motives for his visit. The only reason *he* had been called away to Hawaii from his essential duties in the South Pacific, he was certain, was to provide Roosevelt with "a political picture-taking junket."[3]

And a plenitude of picture taking there would be. On his first day in Hawaii, accompanied by reporters and photographers, the president darted around Oahu in a Packard convertible with MacArthur, Leahy, and Nimitz in tow, inspecting military installations and observing weapons demonstrations. But that evening he got down to business. After a small private dinner with his commanders overlooking Waikiki Beach, FDR asked MacArthur a blunt question: "Well, Douglas, where do we go from here?" MacArthur was equally forthright: "Leyte, and then Luzon, Mr. President." The operation would be easy, he added; the enemy was widely scattered across the islands and could not resist very long; the battle would be over in six months at the most. Finally, he noted, "promises must be kept"—his own and the American government's—to the oppressed but loyal Filipino people. There is reason to believe that Nimitz saw the value in a Philippine invasion, but serving as King's surrogate, he fought back. He acknowledged that the navy would find Manila Bay a useful anchorage, and taking Formosa more difficult than a Philippine campaign. But Luzon, the islands' center, had little military value, he insisted. Nimitz, however, could not equal the general's eloquence and, according to Leahy, got the worst of the debate.

Some scholars believe that it was at this point that the priority issue was settled. But there is a more colorful version of how the decision was reached. According to MacArthur's biographer William Manchester, it was not until the following day after lunch that MacArthur clinched his argument in a brief private exchange with FDR. The general, he notes, brazenly exploited the president's political insecurities. The nation would "never forgive" him, MacArthur declared, if he approved "a plan which leaves 17 million Christian American subjects to wither in the Philippines under the conqueror's heel." Roosevelt might choose King's scheme for reasons of strategy or tactics, "but politically it would ruin you," he asserted. Having boldly spoken truth to power, MacArthur reportedly now declared that he had other urgent duties to perform and unceremoniously walked out of the meeting. It is not clear whether in his remarks to FDR MacArthur was merely describing a reality or was making a threat to directly oppose the president's reelection bid, but FDR was supposedly shocked by his disrespectful comments and his rude departure. By one account, that evening before going to bed, he asked for an extra aspirin. "In all my life," he supposedly told his doctor, "nobody has ever talked to me the way MacArthur did."[4]

Whatever the reality, MacArthur returned to his Southwest Pacific headquarters apparently convinced that he had gotten the green light from the only man who truly counted. And the president would soon confirm his conclusion. Referring to MacArthur's blueprint, on August 9 FDR wrote to the general: "I will push on that plan for I am convinced that as a whole it is logical and can be done. . . . Some day there will be a flag raising in Manila—and without question I want you to do it."[5]

FDR's promises notwithstanding, within the Joint Chiefs' corridors the debate continued. Indeed, not until Nimitz convinced him in September that the Formosa option was not feasible did the obstinate King yield. The decision to invade the Philippines was finally confirmed at the second Quebec Conference (Octagon) in mid-September. One omission from the plan was the role of an overall commander. The army and navy would remain under separate commands.

MacArthur finally got his long-sought vindication on October 19, when a vast armada of battleships, carriers, cruisers, destroyers, and military transports carrying 175,000 U.S. soldiers appeared in the waters off Leyte in the central Philippines. The island was not by itself of great strategic importance, but once equipped with airfields it was expected to serve as a launch point for invading Luzon, the archipelago's cultural, economic, and political heart. Whatever its strategic worth, the Leyte landing would have great symbolic resonance. It was there, on Red Beach, as his troops fought their way inland, that the general waded ashore and, with his acute sense of theater, delivered his famous, media-deluged line: "I Have Returned!"

Unfortunately it would be months before Luzon, with Manila its handsome capital, fell to the American Sixth Army. Excessive rain and poor soil drainage prevented Leyte from becoming the great air base envisioned by the military planners. MacArthur and his lieutenants also underestimated the Japanese overall defense of the archipelago. Tokyo assigned many more troops to defend the islands than the Americans had anticipated, and to lead them chose Gen. Tomoyuki Yamashita, the formidable conqueror of British Malaya. They also gambled much of their naval strength on the Philippine game. They lost in both cases, though barely.

No event of the Pacific war so starkly reveals the drawbacks of failure to create a unified theater command than Adm. Bull Halsey's actions in October 1944 at Leyte Gulf. Assigned initially to protect MacArthur's Philippine landings against naval attack, Halsey was simultaneously ordered by Admiral Nimitz's Hawaii headquarters to engage Adm. Jisaburô Ozawa's main Northern Force battle fleet, steaming toward the Philippines to confront the American navy in a showdown battle. While Halsey was off chasing Ozawa's main flotilla, a powerful Japanese navy squadron of five battleships and ten heavy cruisers under Vice Adm. Takeo Kurita entered the gulf, where MacArthur's troops were disembarking from their transports. Halsey had left protection of the troop transports off Leyte, with their thousands of vulnerable soldiers, to MacArthur's small Seventh Fleet, composed of destroyers, old battleships, and weak auxiliary carriers. The disposition of naval forces was a formula for disaster. Fortunately the timid Kurita miscalculated his odds of success and turned back after brief indecisive engagements with Thomas Kincaid's scrappy small navy. But it was a close and scary thing.

And who was responsible for the frightening near-miss? As the naval historian James Drew tells it, Marshall was in part to blame. It was the failure of the Joint Chiefs to create a unified army-navy command for the Philippine campaign that had led to the near-disaster, he writes. "Great strategists like George C. Marshall and Ernest J. King fell to the temptation of divided command for expediency's sake," and "the cost of this decision was paid for in men and material in the battle off Samar."[6]

Fortunately, having narrowly avoided catastrophe in Leyte Gulf, the U.S. Navy was able to finish off its adversary. Following a series of ferocious surface and air engagements that dwarfed every other naval confrontation in history, by the fall of 1944 Japan's surface fleet had virtually ceased to exist. But the enemy would exact a high price from the U.S. Navy in the battles off the Philippines. Especially costly was the new, devastating Japanese weapon, the kamikaze—suicide attacks on American war vessels and transports by bomb-laden planes piloted by barely trained aviators willing to die for the emperor. These fanatical young men would take a frightening toll of American sailors and Allied ships, and their successes would help determine the remaining strategies of the Far Eastern war.

On land, despite fierce resistance, Krueger's troops finally blasted their way into Manila in late January. For almost a month they, and Filipino partisans, fought to evict the tenacious and brutal Japanese from the city. The enemy took cruel revenge on the capital and its people. The battle, which resembled the epic battles at Stalingrad and Leningrad, left Manila in ruins. Some one hundred thousand civilians died from American artillery bombardment, even more from the crazed vengefulness of the Japanese defenders. Along with the kamikaze attacks, the ferocious urban struggle was a lesson that would resound as Marshall and his colleagues considered the final rounds of the Pacific war.

With MacArthur's forces advancing from the south, Nimitz's amphibious forces pushed from the east. Marshall had little say in the navy's massive Central Pacific campaign. Except for the air assault in which land-based Army Air Corps planes and crews were engaged as supplements to planes from the navy carrier force, sailors and marines bore the brunt of the fighting. But back home Marshall could not ignore the human price of the navy's campaign. At Iwo Jima, a strategically located but barren volcanic island, the casualties would be truly appalling. The tiny island was defended by more than 22,000 Japanese soldiers, whose mission was to delay the American juggernaut rolling toward the sacred homeland. In the torturous thirty-five-day battle all but 216 of these men died. Total U.S. Marine casualties, including wounded and missing, were even greater, though the death roll itself was shorter.

But more agony was yet to come. The invasion on April 1 of

Okinawa, with its thousands of civilian inhabitants, turned into an even more horrifying bloodbath for both sides. Just 350 miles south of Kyushu, Japan's southernmost main island, it proved to be the worst killing field for American forces in the whole Pacific war. In the eighty-two-day land battle American casualties totaled 62,000, with more than 12,000 killed in action. The Japanese military lost one hundred thousand men, their entire garrison. This combat-casualty ratio of about 2 to 1 was far worse than usual in the Pacific, exceeded by the 1.25 to 1 of Iwo Jima. And Japanese civilian casualties reached into the tens of thousands, more than one-third of the total civilian population. At the end of the brutal campaign, at the island's south end, "the bodies of many thousands of . . . civilians lay scattered in the ditches, the cane fields, and the rubble of the villages, or were sealed in caves."[7] At Okinawa once again the Japanese air force deployed its kamikazes to spectacular lethal effect. In some fifteen hundred suicide attacks the fanatical pilots damaged over 360 Allied ships, sinking 28 and killing almost four thousand U.S. sailors, the worst navy battle casualty list of the entire war.

But the attack on Japan was not only horizontal, from different points of the compass. As MacArthur's and Nimitz's forces moved ever closer on land and sea, from overhead the Army Air Force under the truculent, iron-souled Curtis LeMay set about creating a holocaust for the Japanese people. Having been driven from their bases in China by the formidable Japanese Ichigo offensive of 1944, the United States had relocated its new B-29 superbombers in the newly conquered Marianas Islands. LeMay adapted these enormous machines to low-flying area incendiary attacks that turned Japanese cities into infernos, incinerating thousands of flimsy Japanese houses along with thousands of Japanese civilians. A 334-bomber raid on Tokyo on March 9, 1945, burned out almost sixteen square miles of the city, killing 84,000 civilians and injuring another 41,000. LeMay later boasted: "We scorched and boiled and baked to death more people on that night of 9–10 March than went up in vapor at Hiroshima and Nagasaki combined."[8] In the next eight days the Twenty-First U.S. Bomber Group attacked four more Japanese cities, reducing to ashes thirty-two square miles of their centers. In all, by one estimate, American air force raids in late 1944 and 1945 killed between 240,000 and 300,000 enemy civilians and destroyed 2.5 million homes. Only five Japanese cities, of the more than seventy targeted, escaped major damage. An estimated eight million Japanese civilians were turned into homeless refugees in their own country.

Meanwhile, from beneath the ocean's surface, the U.S. Navy's submarines had thrown a taut economic noose around the Japanese home islands. The initial performance of U.S. subs after Pearl Harbor had been disappointing, but by 1944 ruthless winnowing of captains, improved torpedoes, new radar-equipped vessels, and upgraded tactics had made the American undersea fleet a devastating tool of blockade. Japan imported much of its rubber, iron, and aluminum ore and above all its petroleum from its conquered overseas dependencies. In 1942 these vital goods had been transported by a merchant fleet of almost 6 million tons. By 1945, despite aggressive Japanese wartime ship construction, the American navy had reduced this total to 2.8 million tons. In 1944 alone American submarines sent to the bottom 2.7 million tons of enemy cargo vessels and tankers. By early 1945 the island nation's fighting ability had been severely impaired. Especially crippling was the shortage of petroleum to the point where Japanese refiners were experimenting with gasoline made from potatoes.

Did this three-dimensional assault mean that Japan was on the verge of surrender? Both the "air boys" and the sailors—

and their ardent partisans—believed that their services' devastating campaigns could by themselves bring Japan to its knees. Both Admirals King and Leahy insisted that naval operations would soon starve the enemy into submission if they had not already done so. For his part, Army Air Corps commander Hap Arnold was convinced that massive bombing would finish off the Japanese. Marshall doubted both views. The Navy and Army Air Corps' blows might eventually prevail, but not before 1946 or later and that delay, he feared, would severely strain the patience and firmness—and the pocketbooks—of the American public. The Japanese people, he felt, were too willing to accept stoically any sacrifice and punishment to avoid defeat. And Marshall was probably right about Japanese resolve. When an official U.S. Strategic Bombing Survey report of June 1947 examined the attitudes of the Japanese people under the merciless 1945 rain of death from the sky, it acknowledged that the air raids were "the most important single factor in causing them to have doubts of victory." But it also determined that there were other potent elements reinforcing the will to fight on, including fear of defeat, faith in the "spiritual strength and invincibility of the nation," obedience to the emperor, and ignorance of the extent of the disasters their forces had suffered in battle. All told, then, it concluded, though the raids and the blockade had shaken the nation's morale, "the people were not able to organize for revolt; they simply became more obsessed with finding individual solutions to their own severe and urgent personal problems."[9]

Marshall brooded over the costs to America of bringing Japan to the surrender table. At the end of May, as a gauge of his anxiety, he seriously proposed using mustard gas or some other chemical weapon against suicidal pockets of Japanese military resistance and selected enemy manufacturing centers (from which the civilian population would be warned to leave).

Truman vetoed this scheme as a violation of the 1925 Geneva Protocol, but army planners would seriously propose a massive poison gas attack against Tokyo as preliminary to Operation Downfall, the plan to invade Japan's home islands sometime in late 1945.

As developed in the autumn of 1944 by the planners from the Army Joint Chiefs of Staff, Downfall was an ambitious and risky blueprint for assaulting and occupying Nippon itself. It provided for a two-step attack. On November 1, 1945, an armada of carriers, battleships, destroyers, and troop ships would land fourteen U.S. combat divisions on the southern coast of Kyushu (Operation Olympic). The following March, Kyushu would become the launch pad for Coronet, the invasion by twenty-five Allied divisions of Honshu, the largest Japanese home island and site of the densely populated Kanto Plain and Tokyo itself. Many of the American troops for both assaults would have to come from redeployments from other theaters of operation, including Europe and North Africa. Under pressure from Churchill, King agreed to allow the British a small part in the naval action, but the campaign would be virtually all American.

Marshall initially approved of Operation Downfall. It was "essential to a strategy of strangulation [of Japan] and appears to be the least costly worth-while operation following Okinawa," he declared at a June 18, 1945, White House meeting with Truman, the secretaries of war and navy, and several others. The plan "offered the only way the Japanese could be forced into a feeling of utter helplessness." The operation would be difficult, he conceded, but so too had been the Normandy invasion. As for the costs, he estimated that Olympic would inflict 31,000 American casualties in the first thirty days, about the same as MacArthur's Luzon campaign, and a total of some 70,000 for the whole operation.[10]

Marshall's optimism was completely unrealistic. He was being far more hopeful than were the men who had developed the plan. The military planners themselves had no illusions about the bill for Downfall to be paid in lives. Besides the still-formidable regular Japanese army and air services, the enemy, they anticipated, would turn the entire nation into a kamikaze force. Allied invaders, both on land and sea, would face suicide attacks on a scale far greater than even those at Okinawa. And their guess was probably right. Japanese strategists had deduced the broad outlines of the American invasion scheme and devised their own strategy to foil it. According to the military historian D. M. Giangreco, "Their defense plans were both comprehensive and chillingly prescient."[11] They would launch suicide attacks that would destroy one third of the American Kyushu invasion force even before it reached the beaches. And once ashore, if the Americans breeched this defense, they would face the "Patriotic Citizens Fighting Corps," some twenty-eight million Japanese civilians, virtually untrained and admittedly armed only with obsolete rifles, swords, bamboo spears, and even stones, but willing to expend their lives for the emperor. The whole country would in effect be prepared to commit seppuku (ritual suicide) to destroy the hated and feared invaders.

These grim tactics, if actually applied, translated into horrifying mortality statistics. A Joint Chiefs' estimate in April suggested that a ninety-day campaign on Kyushu would cause 456,000 Allied casualties, including 109,000 dead. Add another projected ninety days of fighting for Coronet, and the total military casualty list, it was suggested, would reach 1.2 million, with more than 260,000 fatalities. A study authorized by Stimson (probably composed by former president Hoover), which also assumed wide-scale hostile participation by enemy civilians, predicted much higher losses than even these figures. In such a situation, it stated, the Allies would suffer between 1.7 and 4 million casualties, with some 400,000 to 800,000 dead. As for Japanese military and civilian casualties, the report estimated that there would be between 5 and 10 million fatalities.

We must assume that Marshall's ludicrously low casualty estimate for Downfall was prompted by his initial sense that it was unavoidable. But it seems clear that he felt deep misgivings, and by late summer he had found another option to bring the fanatical enemy to its knees.

Besides the likely butcher's bill, another deterrent to a massive invasion of Japan was the persistent American military manpower situation. The heavy casualties in Italy, France, and Belgium at the end of 1944 had aggravated the army's overall problem and spilled over to the Pacific theater. In late December, as the Battle of the Bulge was winding down, Marshall wrote urgently to MacArthur: "The latest requisitions from overseas theaters indicates [*sic*] that we are faced with a potentially dangerous situation and that prompt and vigorous action is needed to correct the situation." The War Department had already "completed the process of withdrawing able-bodied men from fixed installations and service units; we have inactivated all surplus units and have made large forced drafts on both the Service and Air Forces. In spite of this," he noted, "we have been unable to supply sufficient replacements to meet world-wide needs, and consequently all theaters will have to produce some of their own replacements." He went on to suggest several ways that MacArthur could accomplish this goal on his own front.[12]

As the Pacific war ground on, the frightening examples of Okinawa and Iwo Jima and the early military discharge policy— all on top of the basic ninety-division commitment—added to the crisis and revved up Selective Service call-ups. As a result, as Giangreco notes, "the capacity of Army Ground Force replacement training centers reached a wartime peak of 400,000 in June 1945," some two months after the advance into Germany had ended.[13] Yet despite the expedited draft figures, the question remained: Would the U.S. forces be numerous enough to do the job of Downfall at an acceptable price?

The controversy over Downfall also raised the issue of who would lead the final assault on Japan. The failure of King and Marshall to agree on a single commander for the Philippine campaign had produced a near-disaster when Halsey's Third Fleet had abandoned the army troop transports at Leyte to chase after the surviving Japanese naval force. MacArthur of course saw himself as the rightful supreme commander, pitted against the navy. But besides the threat to his own ambition, he charged the sister service with having a larger secret agenda. After the war, he claimed, the admirals intended "to control all overseas positions . . . using the army as a sort of home guard."[14] The question was decided after an extended wrangle between King and Marshall that in the end Marshall won. In early April, shortly before Roosevelt's death in Warm Springs, Georgia, a new command structure for the Pacific was established, making MacArthur chief of all army forces in the Pacific and, in effect, commander of Olympic and Coronet.

During these weeks before Japan's surrender Marshall also worried about the Russians. Already there were ominous signs that the structure of cooperation between the Soviet Union and the Western Allies was crumbling. In Eastern Europe, where Soviet armies now occupied a wide swath of geography until recently under the heel of the evil Nazi empire, the Soviets had installed puppet regimes that called themselves "democratic," but were actually Communist dictatorships on the Soviet model. Especially egregious was the Soviets' refusal to allow, as promised at Yalta, the pro-Western Polish government-in-exile to establish its authority in Soviet-occupied Poland. At the expense of Turkey and Greece, Stalin was also probing for that long-coveted Russian holy grail, a foothold in the Mediterranean; he had even expressed interest in bases in the former Italian colonies in North Africa and enhanced influence in Korea.

None of this as yet seemed urgent or unresolvable; full consciousness by American leaders of the Soviet threat was still months ahead. But it raised concerns about Soviet cooperation against Japan. Stalin had promised that the Soviet Union would join the Pacific war in August. Marshall still had doubts that they would finally come through. But increasingly the question was becoming not "Whether?" but "Why?" Why would Russia's intervention be needed? By early summer some military planners were certain that the war against Japan was as good as won; there was no need of Soviet help. The chief of staff was less sure, and he waffled on the issue. On the one hand he was skeptical of Soviet ambitions and wished to avoid providing the Soviets with opportunities to expand their reach and influence in East Asia. On the other, despite doubts among army planners and his own worries about Soviet ambitions, he still preferred the Russians to enter the war. Their veteran divisions, he believed, would certainly help against an implacable enemy, while excluding the Soviets from the Pacific war would not, if they insisted, limit their ability to extract concessions and exert postwar influence in the Far East.

The question of Russia's role in the Pacific war lurked beneath the surface at the last Big Three conference, held from late July into early August at Potsdam, outside rubble-strewn and occupied Berlin. The original personnel of UN summit conferences had changed. Churchill was now gone. In the British general election of July 5, following VE-Day, the Labour Party, led by Clement Attlee, had defeated the Conservatives. Attlee would replace Churchill as prime minister and occupy the British seat at the conference table. FDR, of course, was absent, too, replaced by Harry Truman, a man Marshall had gotten to know well during the war when he headed the Senate Special Committee investigating waste and corruption in military procurement. Both outspoken, both autodidact historians, they would forge a strong bond that would soon transform American foreign policy. Truman would come to believe Marshall "the greatest man of World War II."[15]

The Potsdam Conference was devoted primarily to issues of European political settlements and jurisdictions. The conferees defined questions and produced agreements regarding Germany and Europe that would later engage Marshall as secretary of state. But with the fighting over in the West, it had not initially been clear that the Allied military leaders even needed to attend. In the end, however, the limited Far Eastern agenda was deemed sufficiently important to justify their presence.

At Potsdam the Combined Chiefs took the occasion to consider Britain's role in the final campaign against Japan. Marshall was willing to accept a modest British contribution, primarily naval, but made it clear that if the British did not wish to participate in the chancy Downfall, they were free to bow out with no hard feelings. At Potsdam too Truman confirmed the selection of MacArthur for full command of operations in the final military assault against Japan. In the president's mind, as in Marshall's, the conference was also a test of Soviet involvement in the Far East. The new secretary of state, James Byrnes, Cordell Hull's successor, feared the Russians would demand a share in the occupation and control of defeated Japan and now preferred to exclude them from joining the conflict. Truman disagreed with Byrnes about the importance of Soviet entry into the Pacific war. Soviet participation in the final assault against Japan was essential, he believed, and he pushed hard to clinch the Soviet pledge. He was overjoyed when the Russians complied. "I've gotten what I came for," the jubilant Truman wrote to his wife, Bess, from Potsdam on July 18. "Stalin goes to war [against Japan] August 15 with no strings attached." "I'll say that we'll end the war a year sooner now," he added, "and think of the kids who won't be killed. That is the important thing."[16]

In midconference, at Alamogordo, New Mexico, five thousand miles from Berlin, an event occurred that would permanently alter international relations in the postwar world and shape Marshall's future career. There, on July 16, American scientists successfully activated a plutonium bomb with the incredible power of twenty thousand tons of TNT. Truman informed Stalin that the United States had developed a "new weapon of unusual destructive force," but provided no details. In fact he did not need to. The Russians had been fully informed of the clandestine Manhattan Project by secret agents and were already working industriously on their own version of a fission bomb. The Soviet leader politely congratulated Truman on having such a powerful device to use against Japan but seemed otherwise unimpressed. However dismissive, Stalin assuredly understood that "the Bomb" deeply impacted future Soviet relations with the Western capitalist democracies. From where Marshall sat, it was more immediately relevant to Soviet entrance into the Pacific war: With such an implement of war in their possession, did the Allies need Russian help in the Far East?

Well before Potsdam, during the weeks of Allied debate over how to defeat Japan, there had hovered the specter of the yet untested new weapon based on atomic fission. Marshall himself was fully aware of the massive program to develop an atom bomb. Indeed, he was one of its architects. Since before Pearl Harbor he had served as a member of the policy committee assigned the task of exploring how to develop and use the potential explosive energy of the uranium and plutonium atoms. The army had guided the physical development of the Manhattan Project, and it was Marshall who had recommended Col. Leslie Groves, of the Army Corps of Engineers, as manager of the vast construction program required. Despite his deficient scientific education, Marshall had kept abreast of the project's progress. When the gargantuan bills began rolling in, he helped lobby Congress for the secret sums required to pay them.

In late 1944 Groves's report to the War Department that a working weapon would soon be ready for testing set off rounds of earnest discussion within the administration and among the military planners of how and when—or even whether—it should be deployed. The discussions accelerated after Germany's defeat in early May, when the prospect of confronting an intransigent Japan on its home islands became more urgent. Marshall was in the thick of the debate and once more seemed indecisive. At a late May meeting of the "Interim Committee" appointed by Truman to advise him on the bomb, he expressed his ambivalence about its use. He too yearned for a quick end to the war, he said, but at the same time, using such a destructive weapon raised "primordial considerations," by which he apparently meant questions of a moral and humanitarian nature. In a meeting with Stimson and Assistant Secretary of War John J. McCloy on May 29, Marshall suggested, in mitigation of the bombs' indiscriminate destructiveness, that "they might first be used against straight military objectives" and then, "if no complete result was derived from the effect of that, . . . we ought to designate a number of large manufacturing areas from which the people would be warned to leave."[17] But he remained unsure. When asked if he would order dropping the bomb under any circumstances, he responded: "Don't ask me to make the decision."[18] And Marshall's uncertainty extended to whether the bomb affected Soviet participation in the Pacific war. At Potsdam the president had asked him if the new weapon now made Russian intervention irrelevant. Marshall's answer was delphic. We had asked the Russians to enter the war for the sake of tying down the Japanese army in Manchuria, he replied. But the mere Soviet military presence on the Manchurian border was by itself enough to do the job of restraint. On the other hand, even if the United States "went ahead in the war without the Russians, and compelled the Japanese to surrender to our terms, that would not prevent the Russians from marching into Manchuria . . . thus permitting them to get virtually what they wanted in the surrender terms."[19] Whatever this response was intended to convey, Stimson chose to interpret it as a no. In his diary the secretary noted: "Marshall felt, as I felt sure he would, that now with our new weapon we would not need the assistance of the Russians to conquer Japan."[20]

One final event engaged Marshall's attention as the conference prepared to adjourn. On July 26 Britain, the United States, and Nationalist China issued the Potsdam Declaration, laying out the terms for Japan's surrender. The enemy, it said, must withdraw from all its conquests; the Japanese military must be disarmed; those responsible for Japan's expansionist policies must be punished. The future Japanese government, moreover, must guarantee to its citizens the normal personal freedoms of democratic nations. When these requirements had been met and a peaceably inclined Japanese government installed by the free choice of the people, UN occupation forces would be withdrawn.

Marshall had no reason to object to any of these initial provisions. But the final paragraphs of the declaration bothered him. This coda avoided specific mention of the new atomic weapon, as yet unknown to anyone but a handful of political and military leaders and scientists. Instead it called upon the Japanese government to announce the "unconditional surrender" of all its armed forces, with "prompt and utter destruction" as the price of refusal.

To avoid further fighting and further casualties, many voices in the administration, and in Congress and the Allied press, had urged modifying the unconditional surrender formula adopted at Casablanca. In early June, Marshall himself had endorsed the formula as likely to bolster the public's resolve to accept serious losses in the final battles against Japan. But at Potsdam he relented. To expedite the war's end he would allow Emperor Hirohito, universally depicted by American propaganda as an evil influence, to remain.

In the end Marshall not only accepted Hirohito; he also accepted the bomb. In the weeks following the June White House meeting with Truman, he had come to appreciate better the probable human costs of invading Japan. When asked by Forrest Pogue in early 1957 whether he felt using the bomb was needed to push Japan to surrender, he responded unequivocally: "I . . . felt [that] dropping . . . the bomb . . . would end the war possibly better than anything else, which it did." At this point he dismissed claims that Japan would have surrendered without the attack as "rather silly." The devastating B-29 incendiary raids had failed to bring Japan to its knees, he noted: "We had had those terrific destructions and it hadn't had those effects." As for the assertion that he had disagreed with Secretary Stimson's support for using the bomb, he told Pogue: "I was just as responsible as he was. Because my arguments were very much for using the bomb."[21] Whatever it said about the chief of staff's personal qualities, such vacillation could not seriously have affected the final decision that led, in early August, to the devastation of Hiroshima and Nagasaki.

In preparing for the endgame Marshall also had to grapple with the issues of demobilization and the related problems of military and civilian morale. He remembered the political pressure to quickly discharge servicemen after the Armistice in 1918 and its dreadful impact on the nation's later military readiness. As early as 1943, when the tide in Europe had just begun to turn, he envisioned a thunderous chorus of "Bring the boys home!" as soon as the fighting stopped.

On the demobilization issue, military planners had already decided that, unlike in World War I, discharge from further military service would now not be by unit—division, squadron, regiment, wing, and so forth—but by an individual "selection-out" process. Almost two million men—the ones with the highest number of "points" based on combat duty, length of service, region of service, injuries or wounds, military decorations, and parenthood—would be brought home, and, after suitable display and feting as heroes in their hometowns, honorably discharged. Many of the rest—including thousands still in training—would be transferred to the Pacific to finish the job of defeating the remaining Axis foe.

Though the scheme seemed simple and logical, in practice it could not satisfy the powerful urges and feelings of GIs, their families, their state governors, and their congressmen. For every soldier, sailor, and airman whose points assured an early discharge and return to blessed civilian life, there was another who must remain at the beck and call of drill sergeants and duty officers—and face the enemy. Following VE-Day, redeployment to the Far East with its attendant hardships and dangers would be a knotty problem; resistance was sure to be formidable. Between May and August, despite Marshall's and Stimson's disapproval, some 450,000 men from army ground combat units were released from service though the war still raged in the Pacific. Many of these men were, in Marshall's view, part of the "first team," including seasoned noncommissioned officers, "the men who [made] a unit dependable in battle." Whole divisions, he later reported to Congress, were being gutted and "made almost unfit for combat."

Compounding the demobilization difficulty, among the men designated for redeployment from other theaters, morale had deteriorated. Officers reported that they had observed in some units slated for transfer "a very disturbing situation approaching open sedition."[22]

One shudders to think of how untested American units, stripped of their best men, would have fared on Kyushu and Honshu against suicidal and fanatical opponents. But of course they were spared the experience. Having rejected the Potsdam ultimatum, the Japanese leaders learned what the promised "prompt and utter destruction" meant when, at 8:15 a.m. local time on August 6, the B-29 *Enola Gay* from Tinian, piloted by Col. Paul Tibbets, released above Hiroshima, on southern Honshu, a uranium bomb. In microseconds "Little Boy" discharged the equivalent of thirteen thousand tons of TNT, killing between seventy and eighty thousand people, 30 percent of the city's population, and wounding another seventy thousand. On August 8 the Soviet Union declared war on Japan; thousands of Soviet troops swept across the border into Japanese-held Manchuria. The next day another American B-29 dropped a plutonium bomb, "Fat Man," on Nagasaki with lesser, but still appalling, physical destruction and loss of life. On August 15 Hirohito, in an unprecedented radio broadcast to his people, announced that Japan had agreed to cease fighting. The greatest, most costly, war in human history was over.

Needless to say, Japan's surrender elated Marshall, though in many ways the victory over the Wehrmacht still seemed to him the more significant achievement. Letters of congratulation and appreciation from the humble and the mighty poured in after VJ-Day. Churchill sent a spare but eloquent message: "Thank you very much."[23] Marshall would have been happy to retire from the army after VE-Day, but the president had asked him to stay on until Japan's defeat. With Eisenhower slated to succeed him in November, Truman finally allowed Marshall to resign as chief of staff. But retirement from the army itself was still delayed and not until a week later did Marshall become a civilian. On the occasion of his resignation the president publicly described him as "the greatest military man that this country ever produced—or any other country for that matter."[24] And the American public probably agreed. If he chose, Marshall could now have included himself in the same pantheon as Washington and Lee.

As Katherine would write, the resignation transformed her husband. "A great load seemed to roll off [his] shoulders. At breakfast he was carefree, the heavy lines between his eyes began to disappear, he laughed once more."[25] Katherine herself felt a mighty lift in spirits as the moving van with their furniture and other possessions left Quarters No. 1 at Fort Myer for Leesburg. She had never liked the fall season, but this time she looked forward to enjoying the brilliant reds and yellows of the Virginia countryside's turning leaves.

Her repose did not last very long. Marshall was relieved to have shed his wartime duties and responsibilities; he was bone tired and glad to limit his activities. But this did not preclude promoting his cherished cause of peacetime universal military service. He appeared before Congress to push unification of the army and navy to save money and avoid the infighting and duplication of efforts that he felt had marred American military performance during the war. He also defended the army's demobilization policies against critics who condemned it as unfair and too leisurely. Truman considered appointing him head of the American Red Cross, a well-paid sinecure, but the deal fell through. All told, these were minor matters. Then, on November 27, his relative ease was abruptly ended by a phone call from the White House.

That sunny late fall afternoon the Marshalls had just driven down to Dodona from Washington. After briefly contemplating the beauty of the day from the house's portico, Katherine decided to take a nap before dinner. As she climbed the stairs to her room she heard the telephone ring and George pick it up. Without preamble the president said: "General, I want you to go to China for me." Marshall immediately answered yes and, lest his wife's rest be spoiled, abruptly hung up on Truman. Without knowing the call's content, Katherine slept for an hour, and when she came down from her bedroom found George stretched out on the chaise longue listening to the afternoon news on the radio. At the doorway she heard the announcer say that Patrick Hurley, U.S. ambassador to China, had resigned. Then came the announcer's words: "President Truman has appointed General of the Army George C. Marshall as his Special Ambassadorial Envoy to China. He will leave immediately." Katherine was thunderstruck. Her husband approached her apologetically to explain. "That phone call as we came in was from the president. I could not bear to tell you until you had had your rest."[26] Katherine accepted the inevitable but was not appeased. The president, she wrote to Col. Frank McCarthy, Marshall's former secretary and a close family friend, should not have called on her husband for such an assignment so soon. It was a "bitter blow." If Marshall "could have had even a few weeks' rest, . . . I would not have had such fears about his going."[27] Katherine was not wrong: Fatigue would play a part in Marshall's experience in China.

Truman had summoned Marshall to help bring unity and democracy and, above all, stability, to postwar China. But why Marshall? The president may have been influenced by his experience as a soldier in Tientsin during the 1920s and by his involvement with Stilwell and the China-Burma-India theater during the war. But probably more important, the president had come to know and respect Marshall during his own leadership of the wartime Senate's "Truman Committee." And then of course there were also Marshall's successes as a negotiator with prickly military allies during the war and his adept handling of Congress. All told, as Truman later explained, he could "think of no one who would be better qualified for a difficult mission to China."[28]

The China mission would launch a new and unexpected public phase of Marshall's life. And yet for him World War II was not quite ended. In September, just after Japan's surrender, pressured by Republicans and FDR's enemies, Congress decided to finish the already drawn-out process of investigating Pearl Harbor. Under the terms of congressional Joint Resolution 27, Senate Majority Leader Alben Barkley of Kentucky, a Roosevelt loyalist, chose five senators and five representatives divided by party—six Democrats and four Republicans—to serve on the Joint Committee on the Investigation of Pearl Harbor of the Seventy-Ninth Congress. The committee's sessions would last from November 15, 1945, to May 23 of the following year.

The purpose of this last formal Pearl Harbor inquiry,* Marshall claimed, was not really to uncover the facts or even to "get" *him* but, as he told Forrest Pogue in 1956, "to crucify Roosevelt. . . . There was no feeling in the War Department" itself, he added, "that we had anything to hide."[29] But that was at the friendly Pentagon, where Secretary Stimson revered Marshall and refused to acknowledge virtually any army blame for Pearl Harbor. But what about Marshall's own feelings?

The committee sought to accommodate Marshall's need to leave soon for China on his new assignment and scheduled his appearances for early December. But the minority committee

---

*Actually, in 1995, pushed by the families of General Short and Admiral Kimmel, Congress authorized another inquiry into the Pearl Harbor debacle, one limited to the guilt or responsibility of the family forebears. It ended inconclusively, without full resolution of guilt or innocence.

members, at least, led by Republican senators Homer Ferguson of Michigan and Owen Brewster of Maine, were unobliging. Indeed, they *were* out to "get" Marshall—along with other prewar interventionists, not merely FDR—and plied him with hostile questions regarding his role for more than twenty hours of testimony. This time, with the war over, the secret Magic decrypts, with whatever information they may have transmitted to the Pearl Harbor commanders and their Washington bosses, became available to the investigators.

For a man renowned for his effective testimony before influential groups, Marshall did not acquit himself well on this occasion, when his conduct and judgment concerning Pearl Harbor were once again being questioned. He was now one of the most revered men in the country. His "entrance" into the congressional committee room, the historian Gordon Prange has written, "resembled an ancient Roman triumph in miniature," with every seat filled and spectators standing three-deep in the aisles.[30] Marshall was now a man of sixty-five who, second only to Franklin Roosevelt, had carried the heaviest burdens of America's world-encompassing war. Those who saw him in these months would note how worn he looked. Yet the chief of staff's testimony betrays more than fatigue. It discloses a tentativeness and an uncomfortable defensiveness that he had seldom displayed when testifying many times previously before congressional committees dealing with other issues.

Even Prange, who rejects the "revisionist" indictment of FDR for conspiring to draw America into World War II "through the back door," is skeptical of Marshall's testimony on December 6, his first day before the joint committee. He "was not," he writes, "a good witness. He had a rather rambling style and did not express himself well." He gave many one-word answers and replied frequently with "I-do-not-recall."[31] It should be noted that a sim-

ilar quality had colored Marshall's testimony to the Army Pearl
Harbor Board the previous summer. It is possible that his hesitant tone merely reflected his weariness or the normal erosion of
the years. Or did the irresolution derive, perhaps, from a buildup
of anger and annoyance at having his judgment questioned so
harshly by the minority committee members and their equally
adversarial staffs? Or might it have revealed his skepticism of
President Roosevelt's policies toward Japan during 1941? Marshall had in fact hoped to delay war in the Pacific until the army
was better prepared to fight. But the tough, even punitive, actions
toward Japan by FDR and Secretary Hull during the fall and
early winter before Pearl Harbor would, he had feared, precipitate
a premature crisis. And yet now, at the hearings, he found himself
forced to take the administration's line that no blame attached
to the White House for the disaster; General Short and Admiral
Kimmel alone, this view asserted, were at fault on December 7.

"Perhaps" applies to all these speculations. But Marshall's
demeanor may also reveal a degree of self-doubt—indeed pangs
of conscience—at his own imperfect performance in the events
leading to Pearl Harbor. In his own testimony some days later,
General Short would defend himself in part by accusing Marshall
of having failed to provide the information necessary to prepare
for an attack.

In the end the majority and minority reports, released on July
20, blamed both army and navy commanders in Oahu for the
decisions made—or not made—at Pearl Harbor but differed in
their assignment of responsibility to the top command in Washington. The majority criticized both Marshall and Stark for insufficient vigilance in overseeing their subordinates in Hawaii.
They also deplored Marshall's failure on the morning of the
attack to send his warning message to Short "on a priority basis."[32] But Marshall was absolved of blame for the weakness of his

warning message of November 27. It should not have led Short
to continue routine military exercises and assume that he need
guard only against sabotage. It had provided, the majority said,
"ample notice to a general in the field that his training [program]
was now secondary—that his primary missions had become execution of the orders contained in the dispatch and the effecting
of maximum defense security."[33] The minority report advanced a
more general indictment. Stark and Marshall were both lumped
together with FDR and Secretaries Hull, Stimson, and Knox as
the "authorities and agents of the United States" who failed "to
perform the responsibilities indisputably essential [to] the defense
of Pearl Harbor." In Marshall's case he was one of the "authorities" who fell short by poorly transmitting the true state of affairs
to their Hawaii subordinates. Revealing their isolationist roots,
the minority denounced the "Washington authorities" for undertaking "a world campaign and world responsibilities [that is,
World War II] without first making provision for the security of
the United States which was their prime constitutional obligation."[34]

In sum, though Marshall had escaped sharp personal censure,
he was not held blameless, certainly not by the erstwhile isolationists. Yet it is clear that he had not lost the broad esteem and affection of many Americans. When, on December 13, he finished
his testimony, however flawed, the audience in the committee
hearing room had loudly applauded. But the ordeal of blame was
not yet over. In the decade ahead the suspicions and resentment
that infused the Pearl Harbor indictment would, in the shape of
panicky anti-Communism, metamorphose into a toxic cloud that
would envelop Marshall along with the rest of the nation.

But meanwhile, there was the urgent mission to China.

China's postwar troubles were immense and labyrinthine.
Its contribution to Japan's defeat had not been impressive. Its

poorly performing armies had managed to immobilize the more than a million soldiers of the Japanese mainland Kwantung army, the force that occupied China. But beyond this passive role, the country had failed as an ally in the Far East, its troops avoiding engagement whenever and wherever possible and, when forced to fight, were seldom effective. Aside from military incompetence and official corruption, a fundamental component of that failure was internal disunity, the deep divisions between Chiang Kai-shek's Nationalists and Mao Tse-tung's Communists, which had impaired—though not totally prevented—wartime cooperation and discouraged hopes for China's postwar future. Japan's surrender had not, moreover, solved China's other afflictions of poverty, venality, ignorance, and autocracy. But that did not mean that American policy makers after VJ-Day could dismiss it and its troubles. Rather, they continued to hope, as had FDR, that in the postwar world China could become a bulwark of Asian stability and a beacon of Far Eastern progress and even of democracy. They also feared that only a strong Chinese government could successfully resist Soviet influence that would otherwise quickly fill any power vacuum in east Asia. But such desirable goals required unity; the immense nation could not fulfill its destiny if it were to collapse into civil war between Nationalists and Communists. The goal of Marshall's mission, then, was to reconcile the forces of Mao and Chiang to achieve a united, prosperous, democratic nation—a daunting if not impossible task indeed. Meanwhile, there were fifty thousand U.S. Marines in north China charged with helping to disarm and repatriate surrendered Japanese troops and aid the Nationalist government to reoccupy Chinese territory formerly under Japanese rule. What role, if any, should they play in the reunification process? Certainly not too much; American troops must not seek to impose a settlement on China. As Truman later wrote: "I was always aware that there were two enormous land masses that no western army of modern times had ever been able to conquer: Russia and China. It would have been folly . . . to attempt to impose our way of life on these huge areas by force!"[35]

As Marshall prepared to leave for China, American policy makers themselves remained at odds over the issues and the personalities that afflicted and divided it. In China itself, General Wedemeyer, Stilwell's successor as Chiang's American chief of staff, was becoming an active partisan of Chiang and the Kuomintang. Wedemeyer worried about Chiang's limited military resources and doubted his ability to suppress corruption and selfish ambition among his own Nationalist officials and military leaders. But he also feared Soviet meddling in the affairs of the troubled and impoverished nation and saw no alternative to the Nationalists as a bulwark against Soviet Far Eastern ambitions. Meanwhile, in the State Department, a contingent of high-ranking foreign service officers, including John Paton Davies, John Stewart Service, and others, expressed doubts about Chiang and his regime. They insisted that Mao and his colleagues were not true Communists but rather agrarian reformers independent of the Soviet Union and its policies. The cause of Chinese disunity was primarily Chiang's intransigence, not Mao's, they said. These "China Hands," so American ambassador Hurley had come to believe, had no intention of allowing a unified government under Chiang's aegis to prevail. Initially Hurley had sought to bring Chiang and his Communist opponents together on a platform of unity and democracy. Though neither side trusted the other, these negotiations produced a written agreement between the adversaries to work for national unity. But soon after, previously sporadic fighting between the two forces escalated. At this point, strongly convinced that he was being undermined by the State Department left-wingers, the impetuous Hurley, while visiting at home, had resigned his post in disgust and at a press conference, apparently without warning, publicly denounced the State Department, much of American foreign policy, and President Truman personally. From the outset neither Marshall nor the president doubted that the United States would have to favor Chiang and his Nationalists whatever their failings, but everything possible must be attempted to prevent chaos in China. When Marshall arrived in China, then, he would have to sort out and reconcile not only the disputes between the Chinese antagonists but also those within his own government.

Marshall carried with him to China instructions meant to guide his negotiations. In a memo of December 15, the president summed up American goals as "a cessation of hostilities, particularly in north China," and the "unification of China by peaceful, democratic methods." To achieve these ends the special envoy must "persuade the Chinese government to call a national conference of representatives of the major political elements." Secretary of State Byrnes added to Truman's instructions a policy statement noting that the Chiang regime should be considered "the most satisfactory base for developing democracy" but must "be broadened to include the representatives of those large and well organized groups who are now without voice in the government of China."[36]

Some observers of Marshall's mission have noted that he came to China armed with little besides the "influence" growing out of America's wartime friendship and aid and his own personal prestige and powers of persuasion. True, the president had promised "favorable consideration to Chinese requests for credits and loans under reasonable conditions" for compliance.[37] He also promised to provide military advisers to improve and reform the decrepit Chinese military forces. But this bait provided only modest leverage. Under no circumstances, it was understood, would American troops intervene to coerce either side to accept a settlement. The

U.S. Marines were to remain for only limited operations and for a limited time.

Further weakening the American bargaining position was an implicit pro-Nationalist bias. Though his official instructions sought to project a rough neutrality toward the major contending parties, beneath the surface—notwithstanding the China Hands—most American officials, as Acting Secretary of State Dean Acheson later acknowledged, believed that the Chinese Communists were a Trojan horse for the Soviets. There was simply no possibility, Acheson was certain, that the United States would accept a pro-Communist outcome.[38] In fact Marshall himself would detect few signs of Soviet intervention to favor the Chinese Communists, yet the American fear of Soviet intentions remained potent and inescapably affected the outcome.

Marshall arrived in Shanghai on December 20 after a one-day stopover in Tokyo to see MacArthur, now Supreme Commander for the Allied Powers and, in effect, the American viceroy of occupied Japan. The general had not seen his former boss since late 1943 and was surprised at how drawn he appeared. "The war," he observed, "had apparently worn him down to a shadow of his former self."[39] The next day Marshall met with Wedemeyer and Walter Robertson of the U.S. Embassy staff, both of whom, in Wedemeyer's words, told him that "he would never be able to effect a working arrangement between the Communists and the Nationalists." Chiang was still far more powerful than his opponents and would "not relinquish one iota of [that power]," while for their part the Communists "were equally determined to seize all power with the aid of the Soviet Union." Marshall was offended by these skeptical remarks. The special envoy, Wedemeyer later reported, responded curtly: "I am going to accomplish my mission and you are going to help me." Knowing Marshall as a polite man, Wedemeyer was startled at this blunt retort. Apparently unaware of Marshall's bouts of illness, he concluded, as had MacArthur, that his friend and former boss was showing signs of wartime fatigue. Four years of engagement had clearly "exacted a heavy toll both on his physical condition and his nerves," he later wrote.[40]

On December 21 Marshall flew to Nanking (now Nanjing), along with Wedemeyer and Robertson, to discuss with the Generalissimo and Madame Chiang the twin issues of democracy and reconciliation. Marshall assured Chiang of America's cordial feelings for his nation and denied its intention to interfere in China's internal affairs. But he also noted that the United States would not continue to keep its troops and planes in China to help with disarming the remaining Japanese troops and the transfer to China of the former Japanese-occupied regions unless the Chinese government made definite moves toward peace with the Communists. Nor would the United States be favorably inclined to provide economic aid for the vast task of postwar China's reconstruction unless steps were taken toward reconciliation. As for the Communists, if they did not cooperate "they would lose very quickly any vestige of sympathy in the United States."[41]

Chiang responded with some skepticism. The existence of an autonomous Communist army made a unified government impossible to achieve, he said, a statement with which Marshall said he agreed. Chiang then went on to blame the Soviet Union for whatever success Mao's forces had had in recent clashes with the Nationalist army. Here Marshall demurred. He did not believe the Soviets intended to undermine Chiang's regime. In his own direct dealings with Stalin during the war he had found the Soviet leader trustworthy, though not, he acknowledged, most Soviet diplomats.

Soon after this preliminary meeting Marshall and his staff moved on to Chungking, China's provisional wartime capital, to establish headquarters for the mission. There he met with the Communists' chief negotiator, Chou En-lai, an urbane and skillful diplomat with knowledge and experience of the West, who, though an avowed Marxist, did not always agree with Mao, his diehard superior. Chou voiced his concerns that the National Assembly already called by Chiang to write a new constitution for China would be a Kuomintang-packed body, not truly representative. But he agreed to a truce between Communist and Nationalist armed forces and yielded in principle to Marshall's insistence that the Chiang government be recognized as sovereign over all of China.

On January 10 the two sides agreed to stop the recent internecine fighting. To supervise the cease-fire agreement the United States would provide representatives to three-man local teams in the various trouble spots. Marshall also succeeded in arranging for integrating Communist troops into the Kuomintang-run Chinese army. After much hard bargaining on February 25 Chou and Chiang signed an agreement to integrate one Communist soldier to each five Nationalists into the nation's military forces. Meanwhile, to reinforce the cease-fire agreement, Marshall set out on a three-thousand-mile tour by plane through northern China to inform local Nationalist military field commanders of the goals and value of the truce.

Thus, by late February, the special envoy had made substantial progress toward the American goal of bringing peace and unity to China. At this stage of the negotiations Marshall felt that the Communists, with greater faith in their political than their military prowess, were more flexible than their opponents. Unfortunately the agreements were not popular with hardliners on either side and, it would soon become apparent, could not be enforced. But besides, there still remained the major issue of creating a democratic coalition government. This was to be solved by the Political Consultative Conference that convened in Chungking in January to draft a new frame of government for China. To retain his independence of action in a politically sensitive area, Marshall refused to participate in its deliberations, though he offered to serve as an intermediary between the two sides.

Publicly Chiang strongly endorsed the avowed goals of the conference. At its opening session he promised to support freedom of speech, association, and assembly; equal status for all political parties; and popular elections. But privately he and his more conservative colleagues in the Kuomintang seriously feared Communist knavery and deception and suspected Marshall of naïveté in his expectations. In early February Chiang wrote in his diary: "Marshall has been dealing with the Communists for over a month now. Can it be that he has not yet understood the deceptive nature of Communist maneuvers?" A few weeks later he expressed certainty of the special envoy's innocence. "More and more he is being taken in by the Communists. The Americans tend to be naive and trusting. This is true even with so experienced a man as Marshall."[42]

Whatever Chiang's reservations, in three months the special envoy had put in place the framework of a grand China settlement, though clearly many of the individual components remained fragile. So, too, was Marshall. Once again, it seems likely, his health—probably his defective thyroid—would intrude into his life and performance. He had started his mission already worn down both physically and mentally; now, after endless travel and negotiations, and countless conferences and banquets, he was more tired than ever and needed to return home for rest. His presence in Washington, moreover, was essential, he would argue, to consolidate what had already been accomplished. At the end of February he asked the president to allow him to return for a brief visit ostensibly to discuss various matters, but especially the issue of loans to the Chinese government. Before leaving for Washington, Marshall made a trip to Communist headquarters in Yan'an to consult with Party Chairman Mao, the Communist leader. At their meetings Mao agreed to abide by the agreements achieved, but in fact he had deep reservations that would soon surface.

Marshall left Yan'an believing that the gains achieved thus far were reasonably secure. Before leaving China, while in Chungking briefly, he learned that new disagreements between Chou and Chiang had emerged. These made him uneasy, but he was still confident that he had made progress. And others agreed. At this point in the mission Wedemeyer, for one, concluded that he had "done a fine job, winning the respect and admiration of all with whom he came in contact."[43]

The special envoy arrived back in Washington on March 15, to be greeted by the media as a hero. Henry Luce's influential *Time* magazine featured him on its cover once again, and inside the write-up lauded him as a "great citizen soldier" who, "in a totalitarian war, had assembled and directed an army without deviating an inch in the direction of totalitarian practice."[44] Though Luce would soon emerge as a leading member of the pro-Nationalist "China Lobby" that would depict Marshall as a Soviet dupe, or even a Communist "fellow traveler," for the moment the powerful publisher was his unqualified admirer.

Marshall had looked forward to some deserved rest, but the six weeks he spent in Washington proved to be arduous. With the help of Dean Acheson he was able to put together an aid package for Chiang of U.S. and Import-Export Bank loans, cotton credits, and revived Lend-Lease awards. He also completed his interrupted testimony before the Joint Congressional Committee on Pearl Harbor and was able to squeeze in visits with the now-retired Secretary Stimson and with his revered, aged mentor, General Pershing, now residing permanently at Walter

Reed Army Hospital. Marshall had sorely missed Katherine. Her presence had always been a comfort, and he determined to bring her to China when he returned. In part to oblige her, he planned to move his mission headquarters from the insalubrious Chungking to Nanking, the former Chinese capital. There she would be more comfortable and could continue to work on the memoir of their marriage she had begun to write.

In early March, before Marshall left Washington, Wedemeyer had written to Eisenhower that the "permanence of [Marshall's] accomplishments" was "contingent upon his physical presence."[45] And he was right. Marshall's absence on sick leave undermined the mission. He returned to China in mid-April to a deteriorating situation. In his absence the Nationalists were backsliding on their promises and making it difficult for the three-man teams supervising the cease-fire to do their work. The Soviets, for their part, were blocking Nationalist access to Manchuria, Chinese sovereignty over which had been confirmed by the recent agreements, and were looting the province of its industrial equipment. And then, when the Russians finally did leave, Mao's forces rushed in before the Nationalists could arrive, exacerbating animosity and distrust between the rivals. In mid-April at Changchun, the Manchurian capital, Communist soldiers, in clear violation of the recent agreements, drove their adversaries from the city. The easy victory convinced the Communist generals that the Nationalists were pushovers and they need not abide by the truce. They were soon attacking Nationalist towns in China proper. On the other side it strengthened the hands of the ultraconservatives in the Kuomintang, who could now say that Mao and his colleagues had never intended to take the agreements seriously. By the time Marshall arrived back in China, nothing further could be accomplished. Though the Communists claimed they were still willing to consider negotiations, the Nationalists, convinced that the for-

mal cessation of hostilities had given the government in Nanking
the right to send its troops anywhere in Manchuria it wished,
were not.

And Marshall himself had become discouraged. He now believed there was "a complete lack of faith and a feeling of distrust
on both sides." Each "saw behind all proposals from the other an
evil motive."[46] Yet over the next months Marshall's confidence
in the possibility of a settlement of China's divisions fluctuated
widely. For a time the prospects of peace improved. When the
Nationalist military outlook in Manchuria turned temporarily
for the better, Chou advised Mao to agree to another cease-fire.
Chiang remained skeptical, but the two sides pieced together a
three-month truce while negotiations for a more permanent arrangement continued. As the truce expiration date approached
Marshall sought to convince Chiang that it was hopeless to expect a total victory over his adversaries; they were simply too numerous and too powerful. Chiang at first would not listen but,
lectured sternly by Marshall, on June 30, just before the cease-fire
officially lapsed, he agreed to order his commanders to end their
attacks unless attacked first. Pressured by Chou, Mao issued a
similar edict. For a brief period the fighting once again subsided.

Meanwhile, Marshall's personal life in China, as he hoped,
had improved somewhat. He and Katherine moved into the former home of the German ambassador in Nanking. When the
city's weather grew torrid Katherine accepted Madame Chiang's
invitation to join her and the Generalissimo at their summer residence at Kuling in the cooler mountains. There the two women
would become fast friends and remain so even after the Marshalls
returned home.

At this point Marshall inadvertently made an enemy of his
protégé Albert Wedemeyer. Since Hurley's resignation the post
of U.S. ambassador to China had remained unfilled. Wedemeyer

thirsted for the position, but Marshall believed he was too closely associated with Chiang and his regime to be an honest broker between the adversaries. Instead he recommended John Leighton Stuart, the president of the Protestant-sponsored Yenching University, a man born in China of missionary parents who spoke fluent Mandarin. Supported by publisher Luce, himself a son of a China missionary father and a strong ally of Chiang, Stuart was quickly confirmed. Wedemeyer had been deeply impressed by Marshall's initial successes and had praised him glowingly to Eisenhower and Hurley. He now turned sour and skeptical.

Meanwhile, the situation in China worsened, with imminent economic collapse soon joining the growing military turmoil to torment the country's already sorely tried people. In early August, Chiang publicly denounced the Communists for the multiplying troubles and for refusing to "change into a peaceful, law-abiding political party and follow the democratic road to reconstruction." If they persisted, he announced, the Nanking government "must put down [the] rebellions."[47] Marshall and Ambassador Stuart rushed back and forth between the adversaries trying to restore a cease-fire and prevent a Nationalist drive on Kalgan, a major town northwest of Beijing taken by the Communists. Marshall saw the offensive as a complete repudiation of Nationalist promises and, in effect, a deal breaker. On October 2 he cabled the president that "further participation by me in protracted or time consuming message-carrying would inevitably be judged as participation in negotiations which were a cloak to the continued conduct of a military campaign." He had therefore told the Generalissimo that unless the fighting were ended "without further delays" he would "recommend to the President" that he be recalled "and that the US Government terminate its efforts at mediation."[48] Truman later observed that at this point he considered Marshall's mission "at a complete impasse."[49]

For a brief moment after Marshall threatened to return home, Chiang, describing such a move as "unthinkable," offered several concessions to Communist demands.[50] But these did not include abandoning the campaign against Kalgan and were not accepted by Chou and his colleagues. On October 5 the special envoy told Chiang that the "U.S. Government was being placed in a position where the integrity of its action could be successfully questioned and therefore [he] must recommend to the President [his] recall." That same day he radioed Truman requesting him to formally ask for his return. He wished to avoid offending the Generalissimo, however, and asked him to include in his message to Chiang that it was "with great regret" that Marshall had decided to leave and that he did so "with a full realization of the great consideration and distinguished courtesy" with which Chiang and the Chinese people had "welcomed and received him."[51]

By this time Marshall knew that he would soon be taking over the State Department from James Byrnes. As chief of American foreign policy Byrnes, though affable and outgoing, had been unpredictable and inept. He had offended Truman by his frequent insubordination, and the president was glad when the South Carolinian decided to resign in early 1946, though intending to stay on to finish negotiations on several pending minor treaties. Truman, of course, was aware of the slow progress in China, but he did not blame Marshall, whose aura still enthralled him. He seemed the ideal choice to take over at State and guide the nation's increasingly beset foreign policy. Marshall learned of the president's intentions in May when Eisenhower, now army chief of staff, came to China on a visit. He jumped at the offer. "Great goodness, Eisenhower," he exclaimed. " I'd take any job in the world to get out of this one."[52]

Not until the New Year did Truman make public his decision to recall Marshall, and the Marshalls did not leave China until

January 8, arriving in Washington two weeks later after several U.S. stopovers. Just before their C-54 lifted off from Nanking Military Airport the State Department issued Marshall's "personal statement," summarizing and explaining the disappointing outcome of his mission. The "greatest obstacle to peace," the document read, "had been the complete, almost overwhelming suspicion with which the Chinese Communists and the Kuomintang regard each other." Marshall did not fault Chiang, but within the Kuomintang, he declared, there was "a dominant group of reactionaries" who had "been opposed . . . to almost every effort . . . to influence the formation of a genuine coalition government." These men considered cooperation with the Chinese Communists "inconceivable." The Communists in turn "frankly state that they are Marxists and intend to work toward establishing a communistic form of government, though first advancing through the medium of a democratic form of government of the American or British type." Though these conclusions implied irreconcilable differences as the cause of the impasse, Marshall denied that a modus vivendi had been impossible. Describing the most recent breakdown of negotiations, he excoriated the extreme Nationalists but was easier on their Communist opponents. Marshall had little use for the "dyed-in-the-wool" Communists. These men were indifferent to anything but overturning the Nationalist government "without any regard to the suffering of the people involved." He also deplored the poisonous propaganda spewed out by the Communist media intended to "mislead the Chinese people and the world and to arouse bitter hatred of Americans." "Most certainly," he continued, "the course which the Chinese Communist Party has pursued in recent months indicated an unwillingness to make a fair compromise." But on the Communist side, he noted, there had been "liberals as well as radicals," though this view was rejected by those who believed that the Communists were too disciplined a group to permit "such differences of viewpoint." He then went on to describe the "liberals" as predominantly young men who had turned to the Communists out of "disgust at the corruption evident in the local [Nationalist] governments—men who would put the interest of the Chinese people above ruthless measures to establish a Communist ideology in the immediate future."

So what was to be done now? Marshall's solution to the impasse was perfunctory and neither logical nor convincing given his previous characterizations. The Kuomintang, too, apparently had moderates in its ranks and, he believed, with their counterparts in the liberal minor Chinese political parties, must somehow seize the reins from the reactionaries. He was careful to absolve Chiang himself from the charge of intransigence. "Under the leadership of Generalissimo Chiang Kai-shek" they could then, he declared, somehow achieve "unity through good government."[53] In other words, though by what process the result would be achieved was never described, the reasonable men on both sides might come together and reach a solution. It seems a rather lame conclusion.

Why had the Marshall mission failed? The personal statement was a fair summary of Marshall's own views: Ultimately the responsibility for failure rested with both sides, or at least the extremists on both sides. In effect Wedemeyer had been right at that initial encounter with Marshall in Shanghai at the beginning of the mission: The differences between the two were simply irreconcilable. But it is also true that the special envoy had been denied sufficient leverage. Use of American military power to force the issues had been kept off the table. In light of Korea and Vietnam this was surely wise, but nonetheless a handicap. A modest amount of economic aid was simply insufficient to change participants' frozen minds.

But this estimate is not enough. However weak a hand Marshall held, and however intransigent and nearsighted the Chinese opponents, the special envoy had not been blameless. He had been too optimistic about the power of goodwill and sweet reason to bring together the adversaries. He relied too much on his recent wartime experience negotiating with America's European allies. But what had worked with adversaries like Brooke and Churchill, and even Stalin, during the war would not work with Mao and Chiang. Marshall had not been forceful enough to shift the balance in favor of concessions on both sides.

Marshall's imperfect performance as mediator can also be explained in another way: He was simply too tired, too personally stretched, to do the job effectively; the assignment had come too soon after he finished the immense task of managing America's greatest war. Wedemeyer and MacArthur both had noted his fatigue at the outset of the mission. It undoubtedly affected his judgment through the long months of negotiations, but more specifically it had induced him to leave China for home before the early successes had solidified. The six-week visit in March and April, intended primarily as a personal restorative, clearly damaged the fragile agreements he had left behind. His good friend Madame Chiang certainly believed so. Writing to him in Washington from Nanking on April 2 she noted that the political situation in China was becoming hazardous. "I feel that I should tell you frankly that your presence is vital if further deliberations take place. I hate to tell you 'I told you so' but even the short time you have been absent proves what I have repeatedly said to you—that China needs you. . . . And so hurry back."[54] The visit home, even Marshall's laudatory biographer Forrest Pogue concedes, was a mistake.

Marshall's performance in China had many defenders. Harry Truman, deploying Marshall's own argument of irreconcilability, absolved him of blame for the mission's collapse. "If General Marshall returned from his mission without results," he later wrote, "it was because neither of the parties really wanted to live up to the agreement to form a coalition government to unite China."[55] But Marshall has also had detractors who believe that his efforts to achieve an effective compromise were seriously wanting. Wedemeyer, for one, following his rejection as ambassador, harshly blamed his former boss for the mission's failure. In his 1958 memoir, *Wedemeyer Reports!*, he attacked Marshall as few except the neo-isolationist extremists after Pearl Harbor would ever do. "General Marshall," he wrote, "was primarily a military man who had little knowledge of the complexities of the world conflict and no conception of the skill with which the Communists pervert great and noble aspirations for social justice into support for their own diabolical purposes." Besides his naiveté, Wedemeyer wrote, Marshall "was not immune from the besetting sin of most human beings who rise to the heights of power or influence." By the war's end "his reputation was so great and his political influence . . . so overpowering that he thought he could accomplish the impossible." In a word, in Wedemeyer's view, his former chief was afflicted with hubris.

Wedemeyer went further. Marshall's failure derived not only from his defective character; he was also, to use a common phrase of the day, "soft on Communism." He had tilted much too far against the Kuomintang. He would still "esteem General Marshall as one of the great men of our generation," Wedemeyer observed, but he had failed to understand the "Communist menace" and blamed the Nationalists excessively for the failure of his mission. In his final report of January 7, 1947, just as he left China, Marshall had condemned extremists on both sides. Yet Wedemeyer believed Marshall's attack had focused on Chiang's followers as "the dominant group of reactionaries" who had opposed "almost every effort" he had made to create a coalition government. On the contrary, these men, Wedemeyer insisted, had simply been "frank in publicly stating their belief that cooperation by the Chinese Communist Party in the government was inconceivable, and that only a policy of force could settle the issue."[56] In effect they had agreed with Wedemeyer.

Wedemeyer, of course, was not alone. By 1945–46 there had emerged the powerful "China Lobby," a loose coalition of pro-Chiang politicians—mostly conservative Republicans—as well as conservative businessmen, academics, clergy, and army and navy officers, who would condemn Marshall, both during his mission and afterward, for failure to support Chiang with sufficient zeal. Their charge would later be reduced to a pithy, politically effective phrase: Marshall and his like had "lost China."

Not all Marshall's critics were right-wingers, however. In the late summer of 1946 Henry Luce asked Henry Van Dusen, the ecumenical president of the liberal Union Theological Seminary in Upper Manhattan, to write an article for *Life* magazine praising Marshall as a man of "integrity . . . and wisdom," but questioning his actions in China. A recent visitor to China, Pastor Van Dusen noted the oft-mentioned hurdle to a coalition Chinese government: the irreconcilability of the two sides. He also reached the surprising conclusion for a liberal clergyman regarding the only realistic course to pursue: Defeat the Communists on the battlefield while the Nationalists were still better organized and better equipped militarily than their opponents.[57]

The Marshall mission would become part of the emerging Cold War drama, with Marshall cast by the political Right in the role of dupe, if not villain. His adversaries' charges were preposterous, but there was some fuel for the fire. By late 1944 worrisome tensions between the Soviet Union and the West were already apparent. Marshall, of course, was aware of endemic Soviet suspicion, inflexibility, and truculence but had favored doing everything possible during the months following the 1941 Nazi invasion, however risky, to help the Russians survive, and for a time after 1945 he retained faith in the possibility of West-Soviet compromise. In China he had refused to accept the views of American hardliners that the Maoists were little more than Soviet puppets and had declared that he knew Stalin to be a reasonable man who kept his word. Months later, at the frustrating Moscow foreign ministers' conference in the spring of 1947, Marshall would suffer a rude awakening regarding Soviet goodwill. But that eye-opener occurred after he had left China. Though Wedemeyer and Marshall's other critics surely exaggerated his tilt toward the Yan'an Communists, and though Marshall never considered Chiang himself corrupt or duplicitous, he seems to have had less patience with men like the Nationalist archconservative Chen Li-fu than with their sworn enemies. The polished and worldly Chou En-lai, especially, had charmed and perhaps disarmed him as well. This tilt, by magnifying the suspicions and objections of the conservative extremists among the Nationalists, may have helped undermine the promising March agreements.

But the mission was now over, and for the moment the former special envoy could forget China. The Marshalls arrived back in Washington on January 21, 1947, after a brief vacation in Hawaii followed by a train trip from Chicago, one of their stops on the way home. On January 8, in his absence and without hearings, the Senate had unanimously confirmed Marshall's appointment as secretary of state, and the day he arrived in Washington he was sworn in by Chief Justice Fred Vinson with President Truman, Byrnes, and various White House officials present at the brief ceremony. A week later the State Department announced that all remaining U.S. forces would be withdrawn from China and American mediation efforts officially ended.

Now Marshall would face directly, rather than through surrogates, the rapidly evolving, world-shaking crisis of postwar American foreign policy. Managing relations with the Soviet Union, rather than China, would be his new, more consequential, and even more difficult mission.

CHAPTER 10

AFFAIRS OF STATE

George Marshall served as secretary of state during the momentous postwar realignment of international relations. They were not personally his best years. He was now in his late sixties, and time and health problems had exacted a toll, draining his strength and imposing a reduced work regimen. Never a workaholic, the secretary of state included in his daily schedule an afternoon nap and departure for home at 4:30 p.m. As he noted in a July 1948 note to Stimson, he also assigned the "principal burden" of the office to his second in command, Robert Lovett, and continued to insist, as he had as chief of staff, that subordinates not trouble him with minutiae but reach conclusions on their own.[1] This arrangement could be seen as an efficient managerial style—one much needed in a red-tape-encumbered office. But whatever its advantages, in his new post, some observers believed, it impaired his ability to perform at the highest level.

Marshall's experience seemed clearly to fit him as the administration's top foreign policy adviser. A dozen international conferences where the vigorous thrust and parry of military leaders differed little from the debates of foreign ministers and heads of state over treaties were no bad preparation for his new post. Yet, as he admitted at the outset, he was not current on many foreign policy issues. In February, before leaving for an important foreign ministers' meeting in Moscow, he told reporters at a press and radio conference that he still had "a mass of information of transactions and discussions regarding the various problems that I have to absorb here in a very brief time."[2] But Truman had not chosen him for his profound diplomatic knowledge or, for that matter, for his skills as a negotiator with foreign leaders or ambassadors. Like many other Americans, the president had fallen under Marshall's spell of unrivaled rectitude. Also in February, shortly after Marshall was sworn in, the president noted: "The more I see and talk to him the more certain I am that he's the great one of the age." On another occasion he called him "a tower of strength and common sense."[3] But it was his talents as a lobbyist, before both Congress and the American public, that truly counted with the president. As Truman later noted in his memoirs, "his many years in wartime Washington had endowed Marshall with a knowledge and appreciation of the role of Congress."[4] And the president had good reason to believe he would need Marshall's skills on Capitol Hill. It is no accident that Marshall's tenure at the State Department coincided almost exactly with the reign of the Republican-dominated Eightieth Congress, the infamous "Do-Nothing Congress," that sought to frustrate every domestic initiative of the administration and at times would threaten to subvert its transformative foreign policy actions as well. And in the defense of the administration's international and defense positions the president would get his money's worth. Marshall's dignity, rectitude, nonpartisanship—his very austerity—commanded respect from Congress. Except for a small circle of erstwhile isolationists and professional red-baiters, his views were usually accepted as disinterested and irreproachable.

His skill as a lobbyist notwithstanding, Marshall was probably less suited temperamentally for his new role than his old. His two-year incumbency at State had a military stamp not always appropriate for the job. Clearly he brought to his office at Foggy Bottom—the department's brand-new Washington location— many of the habits and practices he had pursued as army chief of staff. At times War Department precedent served the State Department well. He succeeded in reducing the department's endless duplication of effort and its descent, over the years, into a version of what Charles Dickens had called the "circumlocution office." One of his earliest innovations was creation, soon after being sworn in, of a Policy Planning Staff, a version of the army's War Plans Division that he himself had briefly headed. The new division would be charged with detecting emerging foreign relations problems and proposing long-term solutions. Out of its deliberations would come some of the department's most important initiatives.

But there were also drawbacks to the military style. Dean Acheson, the debonair undersecretary of state, described his chief's management approach as that of "the commanding officer." "He said to me," Acheson later reported, "that I was to be the chief of staff and that I was to run the Department and that all matters between the Department and the Secretary would come to the Secretary through me with my recommendation, whatever it might be, attached to the action proposed." Even Acheson, who believed the secretary's directive clarified the lines of department authority, thought the process "had its drawbacks."[5] For one thing, too many decisions for his personal comfort devolved on him. But beyond Acheson's own convenience, at times it also led to weak guidance and poor results.

Marshall could count on talented help in his new post. Besides Acheson, who left in July 1947 to repair his tattered family finances and then returned after a brief hiatus, he had as his chief lieutenant Robert Lovett, a former corporation lawyer who had served Stimson as assistant secretary for air and would be Marshall's alter ego in many of the department's most difficult negotiations. Others included Will Clayton, another business executive, as undersecretary of state for economic affairs; Dean Rusk, a Georgia-born lawyer and wartime reserve army colonel, as chief of the department's United Nations "desk," and Charles "Chip" Bohlen, a foreign service officer with Russian experience and Russian-language skills whom Marshall kept on at State as a close adviser and translator. To head the new Policy Planning Staff he chose George F. Kennan, the knowledgeable—though volatile and temperamental—foreign service officer who in February 1946 had sent from Moscow the incisive "Long Telegram" about Russian policies and characteristics that Marshall had received while in China, and was now back in Washington lecturing at the National War College.

The international landscape during Marshall's months as secretary of state would be defined by two pivotal realities of the immediate postwar world. First was the overwhelming economic primacy of the United States. America had been the richest country on the globe since at least the early twentieth century, but before the war, with its puny army, its isolationist aversions, and its parochial citizenry, it had counted for little (the Western Hemisphere excepted) in the broad affairs of the powers. Now, after 1945, physically intact; its annual output of goods and services almost equal to the rest of the world's combined; its people, and especially its elites, at least partially enlightened by the experience of World War II, the United States was a colossus among the nations.

America's wealth and power conferred on it world leadership, or at least leadership of what would later be called the

First World—that is, the non-Communist industrial countries of predominantly European-derived culture. But there was one major impediment to deploying American power in the immediate postwar years: the nation's military impotence. To his great dismay, Marshall was forced to witness the chaotic disintegration after 1945 of the American military. Under enormous pressure from families, politicians, and rebellious servicemen themselves to "bring the boys home," the military services had virtually collapsed after VJ-Day. Between May 1945 and June 1947 the size of the American army, including the air corps, shrank from eight million to under one million—troops largely equipped, moreover, with outdated, outworn equipment. The navy and marine corps suffered equally damaging cuts in budget, equipment, and personnel. Marshall, with Truman's somewhat reluctant support, sought to persuade Congress to create a system of peacetime universal military training (UMT) to avoid the crises of unpreparedness that had afflicted the nation in both 1917 and 1940. To some, on the political left, the UMT proposal seemed another effort to confront the Soviet Union and a further expansion of the emerging Cold War. But the effort failed primarily because Americans were unwilling to bear the expense of a large peacetime army and navy. Congress did extend the wartime draft, though insisting on drastically cutting military appropriations. When considering military spending in the months after August 1945, American policy makers would invoke the atom bomb as part of the nation's arsenal. But America's sole possession of the bomb lasted only until September 1949. Nor could the U.S. advantage in atomic weapons be readily brandished in international relations thereafter. Using the new destructive weapon was simply too fraught with serious moral and strategic implications. And besides, the bombs were scarce. In the critical year 1947 the United States had fewer than fifteen.

But Marshall faced a second new international reality and the only real challenge to American ascendency: the growing power and assertiveness of the Soviet Union. Just emerging from the war with human losses of as many as twenty-five million citizens and incalculable physical damage, it also had been the primary savior of Europe from German hegemony and had reaped a harvest of respect and gratitude from many of the Continent's people, particularly its intellectuals. With its immense army, still formidable after 1945, it easily dominated the lands in Eastern Europe formerly under Hitler's rule or allied with the Third Reich. Given its age-old envy and suspicion of the West, as well as its acquired Leninist conviction that ultimately capitalism and socialism could not coexist, Russia would emerge as the powerful international rival of the United States. Growing tensions between the former anti-Axis partners had begun emerging as the war wound down. But by early 1947, as Marshall took up the reins of office, the strains between the Soviets and the Western Allies were reaching a critical point.

In recent years revisionist historians have sought to even the balance of blame for the Cold War between the two great international rivals, but Marshall, like most of his countrymen, had little doubt that Soviet expansionist zeal sufficiently explained the conflict. Influenced perhaps by FDR's optimistic view of Soviet-American relations, for a time he retained crumbs of hope that, as during the war, the Soviet Union was amenable to negotiation and compromise. He would soon be swept up in the Cold War consensus, however, and seldom thereafter questioned the conventional American premise that the effort to hedge in the Soviet Union was a struggle for a freer world, one that fulfilled universal human aspirations. Yet unlike the Soviets' allies, and many Western intellectuals, he never perceived U.S. foreign policy as a campaign for American hegemony. In a mid-1947 talk to the Women's National Press Club he expressed indignation at the charge. "There could be no more malicious distortion of the truth," he declaimed, "than the frequent propaganda assertions . . . that the United States has imperialist aims or that American aid has been offered in order to fasten upon the recipients some sort of political or economic dominion."[6] In their quest for mid-American support, Marshall and his internationalist Cold War colleagues were not averse to underscoring the economic advantages to American business and agriculture of generous public funding of defensive measures against the advance of foreign Communism. But the secretary of state himself had no ulterior capitalist motives. His goal of bolstering the devastated European nations after 1945 combined sympathy for human suffering and sincere concern for preservation of free, autonomous government. It had little to do with expanding American commerce and international economic advantage.

While on his failed mission in China, Marshall had lost touch with evolving postwar U.S. European policy. Like many high American officials he had read George Kennan's eye-opening Long Telegram, asserting the inevitable antagonism toward the West of the Soviet Union and the Communist Party, analyzing the sources of Soviet suspicion and intransigence, and proposing that the United States and the American people confront the "malignant parasite" of international Communism by active diplomatic and cultural combat.[7] As secretary of state he later read Kennan's famous "Mister X" article in *Foreign Affairs* reiterating the embedded Soviet hostility and proposing patient but resolute "containment" as the way to check Soviet and Communist expansionism. For months, however, he remained uncertain of the inevitability of East-West conflict, for during the war Russia and the Western Allies had managed to resolve differences and develop successful strategies to defeat the common enemy. Why, he wondered, could this cooperation not be sustainable in the postwar era?

A cascade of jarring events would soon transform his outlook. Among the first was the crisis that erupted in late February 1947 when Britain informed the United States that it no longer could financially underwrite the governments of Greece and Turkey, both struggling against growing Soviet pressure for territorial and other concessions. The message from London jolted the foreign policy establishment in Washington. Few decision makers denied that something must be done to prevent Russian expansion into a region hitherto outside the Soviet orbit. Marshall agreed with his colleagues. On February 27, in a White House meeting called by Truman with congressional leaders and foreign policy advisers, the new secretary read a proposal assembled by his staff laying out a plan to meet the crisis. The Marshall-approved scheme was limited in scope and moderate in tone. Without question the United States must take over from Britain, it read. But warning that failure to provide American financial aid to Greece and Turkey would open the door to Soviet expansion in Europe and into the Middle East and Asia was not being "alarmist," he insisted. And, in fact, there was nothing in the statement about defending democracy everywhere or mounting an anti-Communist world crusade that other "Cold Warriors" had pressed for. And Marshall seemed uncomfortable even with this restrained proposal. In Acheson's words, he "flubbed" the statement he read to the representatives and senators, prompting Acheson to restate the administration's case more forcibly to the assembled bigwigs.[8]

Marshall left Washington for Moscow soon after this meeting to attend the scheduled Foreign Ministers' Council meeting. The fourth in a series of Allied ministerial conferences initiated by the Big Three leaders at Potsdam, its preliminaries fully occupied his mind and he had little input into President Truman's formal request to Congress in early March for $250 million for Greece and $150 million for Turkey, which announced that the United States must "support free peoples who are resisting attempted subjugation by armed minorities or by outside pressures" and "assist free peoples to work out their own destinies in their own way."[9] Critics attacked this "Truman Doctrine" as an open-ended commitment to confronting the Soviet Union and its allies everywhere in the world. To many informed contemporaries the Greco-Turkish aid bill, signed into law in May, marked the end of hope that the wartime cooperation with Russia could be preserved. Yet as he and his staff left for Europe. Marshall still remained unconvinced that the doors to compromise had slammed tightly shut.

In Moscow, Marshall would be driven to a more intransigent anti-Soviet position in what was now being widely called the Cold War. The secretary, his staff, and colleagues arrived in Moscow by plane on March 9 after brief stopovers in Paris and Berlin for consultation with French leaders and with Gen. Lucius Clay, the military governor of the American occupation zone in Germany. The Soviet capital still revealed the awful depredations of the war. Though the Soviet authorities had sought to burnish its appearance for the foreign visitors, beyond the major avenues the city was decrepit, squalid, and cold, with few people visible on its grimy, snow-covered streets.

The chief items on the conference agenda were peace treaties for Germany and Austria along with the subordinate issues of German reparations, future German self-government, and German unification and economic revival. The participants—France, Britain, the United States, and the Soviet Union—were at odds on many of these subjects. Britain, represented by Ernest Bevin, generally agreed with the United States. Both English-speaking nations, having already merged their occupation zones politically, supported a self-governing future German state, but one limited in power; they opposed a united Germany with a strong central government as a potential danger to Europe's peace. Rejecting Treasury Secretary Morgenthau's plan to strip Germany of its heavy industry and convert it into a giant farm, they strongly favored its accelerated economic revival to spare their own nations the need to provide extended support. For that same reason they also endorsed a lenient interpretation of the extent and timing of German reparations. France's foreign minister, Georges Bidault, fearful of a revived aggressive Germany, agreed with the British and American negotiators regarding German unity, but was chiefly concerned with detaching the coal-rich Ruhr from the future Germany to make its resources accessible to impoverished France. As for the Soviet Union, its case, presented by Marshall's old sparring partner, the dogged Vyacheslav Molotov, was overtly focused on collecting immediate reparations from Germany out of current German output, but sub rosa, Bevin and Marshall came to believe, the USSR ultimately intended to convert the former Nazi state into a Soviet dependency. The Russians supported a fully unified Germany with a strong central government. To achieve this, they knew, would take time and, they hoped, would provide the local Communists with an extended opportunity to impose a stranglehold on the occupied country, converting it into another Soviet satellite.

In the end little was accomplished by the conference. For six dreary weeks and forty-four frustrating meetings the negotiators wrangled over details, with stalemate facing them at every turn. But Marshall was not yet prepared to concede defeat, and as the negotiators prepared to adjourn, he requested a personal interview with Stalin, a man he believed had been willing in the past to compromise and whose word, once given, could be trusted. On the evening of April 15, accompanied by Bohlen as translator, Marshall was admitted to Stalin's private office in the Kremlin.

For an hour and a half, while the Soviet dictator doodled wolfs' heads on pads of blue paper, Marshall expressed his concern and depression at "the extent and depth of misunderstandings and differences which had been revealed" at the still-ongoing conference.[10] He described the American people's wartime esteem for the Soviet Union and their growing dismay over recent Soviet behavior. He recounted his differences with Molotov over Germany's future governance, emphasizing the dangers of the revived German power that would accompany centralized unification as the Soviet Union preferred. Foreshadowing later policies, he told Stalin that the American government "was frankly determined to do what [it could] to assist those countries which are suffering from economic deterioration which, if unchecked, might lead to economic collapse and . . . the elimination of any chance of democratic survival."[11] He ended his discourse with an upbeat picture of wartime Soviet-Allied cooperation and expressed hope that it might be restored.

Still wearing his wartime generalissimo's uniform, Stalin assured Marshall "that current differences between the two sides should not be taken too seriously."[12] After all, he said, these were only the first skirmishes in what would surely be a drawn-out set of negotiations. The participants must be patient. Despite the conciliatory words, as the Americans left the Kremlin they concluded that Molotov's obstinacy had derived from the chief himself and they now had little reason to expect progress in the stalled negotiations.

The remaining few days of the conference were as pointless as the earlier ones. On April 24 the ministers held their final meeting, capped by the usual opulent, bibulous Soviet banquet. Two days later Marshall and his colleagues flew home in an atmosphere of gloom and grim failure.

It is generally assumed that Marshall performed well in Mos-

cow, and that disappointment was inevitable given the underlying Soviet agenda. Perhaps. But not all contemporaries, even
supporters of the Truman administration's foreign policy, agreed.
The prestigious *New York Times* diplomatic correspondent, James
"Scotty" Reston, who had praised Marshall's appointment to head
the State Department, in a caustic piece on April 30 reviewed
Marshall's performance at Moscow in less than glowing terms.
Reston had an unusual grasp of Marshall's personality, including
his limitations and strengths. Like so many others, he was taken
in by Marshall's pose as a "Virginian," though in his case to the
secretary's detriment: "The overall impression [Marshall] seems
to have conveyed [at Moscow] is one of moral grandeur," Reston
conceded. "He was severe and aloof, courteous in manner, but
with none of the Virginian's love of people and capacity for humor," he wrote. "Inevitably," he was being compared unfavorably
with his predecessor, James Byrnes, "a warm, happy man with a
rare capacity for political manipulation and a wonderful stock
of illustrative anecdotes." By contrast, in the entire six weeks in
Moscow, Marshall "did not unbend." He "was as rigid as the Washington Monument." He was also an enigma. The other Americans at the conference were still "trying to define what manner
of man he is." Removed from his colleagues and fellow ministers,
Marshall had also seemed strangely indifferent to results. As Reston described them, his work habits resembled those depicted by
Acheson in Washington. Each day he met briefly with his staff at
Spaso House, the American Embassy building, to listen to their
advice and suggestions. These he accepted "without significant
changes," and then retreated to his room until it was time to drive
to the daily ministers' meetings. When these concluded "he was
usually first out of the Conference chamber." Apparently, wrote
Reston, he avoided opportunities to discuss informally major issues with both the Russians and the British. To some observers at

Moscow, the *Times* correspondent concluded, Marshall's behavior "represented an admirable tidiness of mind," but "to others . . . a lost opportunity."[13]

Not every observer agreed with Reston's take, nor does it precisely fit the description of the Moscow sessions by Col. Marshall Carter, an aide assigned to take notes on the meetings.* As usual most of the media praised the secretary's performance. One favorable view is especially interesting for its estimate of Marshall's personality by a high-level American participant in the conference. The economist Charles Kindleberger, the State Department's chief of German and Austrian Economic Affairs, in later years expressed great admiration for his boss and his performance in Moscow. He was an "odd man," a "humorless man," Kindleberger acknowledged, but—in words that would have pleased Marshall—he was also "a great . . . man who was Olympian in his moral quality, a man of who [*sic*] one stands in awe," a "man apart from most men."[14]

Two days after arriving home Marshall reported to the nation on the Moscow Conference in a radio broadcast. The brief talk was upbeat. The conference had dealt with the "very heart of the peace for which we are now struggling," he told his listeners. He described the specific issues at stake and in each case acknowledged little or no progress. But he refused to end on a sour note. He repeated Stalin's observation that "compromises were possible" between the West and the Soviets, and it was "necessary to have patience and not become pessimistic." He concluded that "despite the disagreements . . . and the difficulties encountered possibly greater progress towards final settlement was made than

---

*Carter agrees that his boss worked unusual hours but credits him with more extended effort. See Larry Bland, Mark Stoler, and Sharon Ritenour Stevens, eds., *The Papers of George Catlett Marshall*, vol. 6 (Baltimore: Johns Hopkins University Press, 2013), p. 72.

is realized."[15] But this final affirmative rhetoric was hooey. In fact Marshall was deeply discouraged. As he later reported, he now realized that the Soviet Union "could not be negotiated with."[16] Something more was required to check Russian ambitions. Other observers gave the failure at Moscow even more weight. Robert Murphy, Lucius Clay's adviser in Germany, would write that it was the event "that really rang down the Iron Curtain."[17]

If nothing else, the experience in Europe underscored the connection between the Continent's economic recovery and a successful response to the Soviet challenge. In May 1945 Winston Churchill had famously described Europe as "a rubble heap, a charnel house, a breeding ground for pestilence and hate." By 1947, some scholars believe, recovery was already under way —there was no need for American intervention—and they ascribe the American response to Europe's postwar plight to expansionist American economic policies dating back to the 1920s. But to contemporaries the prostrate nations of Europe did not seem in much better economic shape in mid-1947 than they had on VE-Day. But beyond the purely humanitarian realities, by the time Marshall moved into his new Washington office the political fallout of cold, hunger, lawlessness, and despair had grown ominous. Everywhere within the still-free nations, but particularly in France, Italy, and the Western occupation zones of Germany, the Communists and their allies, playing on desperation and drawing on Soviet prestige, were making deep inroads into the support of conservative, centrist, and even socialist parties, with their goal of converting the free societies into subservient Soviet allies if not de facto Soviet puppets. In early March, before he left with Marshall for Moscow, Will Clayton had sent an urgent memo alerting the State Department to the consequences of failing to grapple with Europe's predicament. "Feeding on hunger, economic misery, and frustration," he wrote, attacks to undermine independence were multiplying, and these "had already been successful in some of the liberated countries." They were imperiling America's security and must be countered with generous American largesse.[18]

The roots of the European Recovery Program (ERP) in the political dangers of Europe's slow postwar rebound are clear. But was George Marshall its father? It is called the Marshall Plan, of course, but it was so named in part for political reasons.

In fact the plight of Western Europe and the need to remedy it were very much in the national air in the early months of the Truman administration. It was, as Kindleberger wrote, "widely discussed during the winter of 1946–47."[19] As he and others have noted, the topic of Europe's dire needs and their likely political consequences was debated by the prestigious Council on Foreign Relations and considered in prominent articles by the pundit Walter Lippmann and the syndicated columnists the brothers Joseph and Stewart Alsop.

One prominent claimant to authorship of ERP was Dean Acheson, and his role was indeed significant. The undersecretary of state had little doubt that without substantial American aid in these difficult months, European democracy could collapse. But he also knew that after three and a half years of war, Americans were weary of further obligations to Europe and reluctant to pay for its seemingly endless needs. His task, then, as he conceived it, was to make the nature of the growing crisis comprehensible to ordinary Americans, and he found the occasion in a talk he delivered in early May 1947 to an influential Southern business group, the Delta Council of Mississippi.

Acheson's remarks at Cleveland, Mississippi, were in fact tailored to the interests of American businessmen, specifically those who managed the extractive agricultural exports of Dixie. He laid out the economic difficulties being experienced by Europe, with emphasis on the devastated Continent's need for American supplies of food, fuel, fiber, and raw materials generally, but without the means to pay for them. With a severely unfavorable balance of trade, the damaged European economies would need large American loans or gifts to make up the deficits—funding beyond the sums for relief already expended or lent through the International Monetary Fund (IMF) and the Export-Import Bank. Such new grants, he told the Mississippi planters, bankers, and merchants in his audience, would make up for Europe's dearth of American dollars and revive markets for American exporters. But Acheson did not ignore the humanitarian, political, and ideological benefits of American generosity. Human beings, he concluded, existed "on narrow economic margins," but so too did "human dignity, human freedom, and democratic institutions." It was "one of the principal aims of [American] foreign policy today to use our economic and financial resources to widen these margins." It was "our duty and our privilege as human beings."[20]

Acheson believed his words to the Delta Council were a "trumpet note" that awakened complacent Americans to the crisis in Europe.[21] He exaggerated their importance, however. The perceptive Kindleberger, for one, doubted their significance. "I have had a hard time," he wrote in a July 1948 memo, "seeing how the Acheson speech at Delta . . . was the midwife to the Marshall plan [*sic*]."[22] Nonetheless their impact, especially on an important economic sector of the public, cannot be dismissed.

Meanwhile, Clayton and Kennan were making their contributions to Europe's revival. In late May, in a second memo to his colleagues at State, Clayton proposed a six- to seven-billion-dollar three-year grant from the United States with the specifics to be drawn up by the principal European nations themselves. "Without further prompt and substantial aid from the United States," he warned, "economic, social, and political disintegration will overwhelm Europe." But, he emphatically cautioned, "*the*

United States must run the show."[23] Kennan's offering, in the form of PPS/1, the State Department's first important Policy Planning Paper, was, like Kennan himself, both professorial and inspirational. It called for "effective and dramatic action" to demonstrate that "we mean business, to serve as a catalyst for their hope and confidence, and to dramatize for our people the nature of Europe's problems and the importance of American assistance." Though it lacked specific economic details, PPS/1 also recommended that the beneficiaries themselves be charged with drawing up the plans. But, differing with Clayton, it also prescribed, significantly, that they, rather than the United States, administer it. The "formal initiative," it stated, "must come from Europe; the program must be evolved in Europe; and the Europeans must bear the basic responsibility for it." Kennan also suggested that any rescue plan include the Soviet Union to avoid blatant, and incendiary, anti-Communist partisanship. The paper ended with a plea that the United States eschew the open-ended commitment of the Truman Doctrine to confront the Soviets' challenges, even when no vital American interest was at stake.[24]

In late May Marshall entered the debate, though rather feebly. On the twenty-fourth he convened a meeting of State Department officials, including Acheson, Clayton, Bohlen, and Kennan, to consider PPS/1. He listened carefully to the discussion, but apparently said little beyond asking Kennan what would happen if the Russians accepted the invitation to join the plan. PPS/1 had already noted that if the Soviets rejected it the onus would be on them. Now, responding to Marshall's query, Kennan pointed out that the United States could put the Russians on the defensive by asking, as a major raw material producer themselves, that they contribute resources to the shared pool. Marshall expressed no overt conclusions. His last advice was a warning to the group against information leaks.

Acheson always felt that his Delta Council address had received less attention than it deserved when first delivered. But the same could be said of the talk by Marshall at Harvard University's 286th commencement, where, along with Gen. Omar Bradley, the poet T. S. Eliot, the atomic physicist J. Robert Oppenheimer, and other prominent Americans, he came on June 5 to receive an honorary doctor of laws degree.

His brief speech, of course, would become famous. There, on a sunny Cambridge morning, following the traditional academic procession, the audience of graduates, faculty, dignitaries, and friends and family watched as university officials conferred degrees on two thousand Harvard seniors and graduate students and listened to selected students deliver the time-honored Harvard commencement addresses in Latin. President James Bryant Conant next awarded the honorary degrees, with suitably florid language. Marshall could not have been more pleased with the citation to him—a validation of his own lifelong personal quest—that Conant made in his award. In both Latin and English, Conant intoned: "An American to whom freedom owes an enduring debt of gratitude, a soldier and statesman whose ability and character brook only one comparison in the history of the nation."

After the conferring ceremonies the dignitaries, honorees, and new graduates and their guests adjourned for a catered lunch followed by a round of brief speeches. It was here that Marshall sought to alert Americans to Europe's quandary and their government's need to cope with it. The text of the ten-minute speech was still incomplete when the secretary left Washington for Cambridge. He had not told the president of his intention, nor had he provided the State Department with a copy of its final form. The address, Marshall later said, drew on the thoughts of Kennan and Bohlen, plus his own ideas, and was hastily cobbled together while he was on the plane from Washington.

Marshall's actual words had little passion or music. (The distinguished diplomatic historian Bradford Perkins, then a fresh-faced new Harvard graduate in the commencement audience, later told his diplomatic history students at Ann Arbor that at the time the speech had not made much of an impression on him.) The "world situation" was "very serious," Marshall declared, but then, borrowing from Clayton, he described the circumstances of Europe's plight primarily as an imbalance between city and country: The city factories were not producing the goods that farmers wanted and so they would not provide the food that urban dwellers needed. He then noted Europe's dearth of dollars to buy necessities from the United States. "Aside from the demoralizing effect on the world at large and the possibilities of disturbances arising as a result of the desperation of the people concerned, the consequences to the economy of the United States should be apparent to all." Adopting the Kennan view that American policy should avoid overt attack on the Soviets, he suggested that it should "not be directed against any country or doctrine but against hunger, desperation, and chaos." Marshall also agreed with the consensus, Clayton perhaps excepted, that the United States must not act "unilaterally. The beneficiaries of American aid must agree among themselves as to the requirements of the situation and the part these countries themselves will take in order to give proper effect to whatever action might be undertaken by this government."[25]

Though the *New York Times* printed the speech on its front page, the American public scarcely noticed the occasion. For Acheson and others in Washington, however, it was an opportunity to start the process of rallying the European nations themselves to the planning process. Acheson had already alerted British diplomats and journalists in Washington and New York of American plans for Europe's rescue. In London, the brief address caught

Bevin's immediate attention. Described to him by a BBC journalist as a speech that proposed "a totally new continental approach to the problem of Europe's economic crisis," a scheme that recalled "the grandeur of the original concept of Lend-Lease," Bevin "grabbed the offer with both hands," as he later told an American audience.[26] Joining with France's Bidault, he and his fellow foreign minister summoned a conference in Paris of other interested European nations to consider how to comply with the American proposal.

The Committee of European Economic Cooperation (CEEC), composed of sixteen nations, set to work in Paris in mid-July to design a program that met the American criteria. Though invited, the Soviets and their allies refused to join the meetings. Several of the satellite nations were initially bedazzled by the American proffer of aid but, bullied by the Russians, joined them in denouncing the meetings as an anti-Soviet maneuver intended to promote American hegemony. The State Department sent Clayton to Paris as observer and adviser; Kennan and other State Department officials visited the conference to contribute to the deliberations. Marshall himself kept in touch with the proceedings by telegram. But the secretary of state played little direct part in the late summer meetings, where the European nations hammered out their detailed response to the American proposal for reconstructing the continent's economy. Once the European nations had drawn up and submitted a recovery proposal, however, his role in persuading Congress to appropriate the necessary funds became vital.

The CEEC plan, completed on September 12 and formally delivered to Washington on October 9 by a small European delegation, followed the general outlines provided by the American planners. It laid out a four-year program costing $22 billion and called for a limited integration of the European economies that foreshadowed the later multinational European Economic

Community and the European Union. The CEEC delegation in Washington discussed the plan with State Department officials, specifically with Lovett substituting for Marshall, who was then busy with meetings of the UN in New York and preparing for another foreign ministers' conference in Europe scheduled for the later fall. One of the chief stumbling blocks between giver and takers was the size of the financial request. Twenty-two billion dollars was far more than Congress would approve, and the White House and State Department quickly cut it to $17 billion to be doled out over four years. Another problem was the pressing need for immediate emergency aid to tide the Europeans, especially the French and the Italians, over the interval until the planned assistance could arrive. To meet the crisis, in late October, Truman called Congress into special session. Marshall temporarily dropped his other activities and, testifying before a joint House-Senate committee, urged passage of the interim rescue measure as part of the larger proposal. The president himself appeared before a joint session to push adoption of the emergency appropriation. Despite the high-powered support, congressional Republicans fought the legislation and mauled the State Department for its supposed past multiple sins. The attacks foreshadowed the dissent ahead when authorization of the full plan was brought up for debate. Yet despite the rancor, just before the Christmas recess, Congress appropriated $522 million for distressed Italy, France, and Austria.

Shortly before this the administration introduced the bill to authorize the full European Recovery Program. As Forrest Pogue notes, it was at about this time that Truman began calling the ERP the "Marshall Plan." The name was frankly expedient. Truman was running for president in his own right, and his ratings with the public were low. He sought to avoid too close a personal connection with the scheme. As the president told his friends:

"Can you imagine [the bill's] chances of passage in an election year in a Republican Congress if it is named for Truman and not Marshall?"[27]

Marshall's major contribution to the plan that acquired his name came with his return from the fifth Council of Foreign Ministers' meetings in mid-December. The conference, held in London between November 25 and December 16, was, as Marshall later reported, "a dreary repetition of what had been said and re-said at the Moscow conference."[28] Once again virtually nothing was accomplished. The secretary spent the Christmas holidays, as usual, with his family, but returned to Washington in early January to add his voice to the debate in Congress that soon swirled around final passage of ERP. Appearing before the Senate Foreign Relations Committee on January 8, he made his case for the measure. He and the committee chairman, the Republican Arthur Vandenberg, had long worked together on issues of foreign policy. A late convert from Midwestern isolationism, the intellectually ponderous, bespectacled Michigan senator had been instrumental in forging a bipartisan internationalist postwar foreign policy. Now, once again, he came to the aid of a law to involve the United States in the affairs of the overseas world. The precise details of the collaboration of the two men are not known, but Marshall would later recount frequent meetings with Vandenberg at Blair House, near the White House, to plot strategy. He would later tell Pogue that Vandenberg "was just the whole show when we got to the actual movement of the thing."[29]

Actually Marshall himself now contributed substantially to the "show." His testimony to the Senate Foreign Relations Committee on January 8 was widely viewed as effective. This time, Scotty Reston of the *Times* gave him high marks: "He was clear. He was calm. He was patient and courteous. And yet," Reston wrote, "he acted like a man who was determined to get substantially the Marshall Plan he wanted or, as already rumored in the capital, retire at last to Leesburg."[30] In his testimony Marshall noted the careful studies made of Europe's needs and of available American resources to meet them. He promised that the government would guard against waste and make the programs work effectively. In the question period following his presentation he sought to reassure the senators that the State Department could manage the program by itself; there was no need for a separate group to oversee it. He denied that the Europeans would use their recovery to injure American business interests. And, he assured the senators, Congress would be frequently consulted in the day-to-day operations of the program. His biggest problem, perhaps, was overcoming congressional parsimony. Seventeen billion dollars, after the many billions of the war itself, seemed outrageous to many frugal Republicans. Marshall defended the size and timing of the requested appropriation.

In his appearance before the House Foreign Affairs Committee several days later Marshall shifted ground. If to the Senate he had emphasized prudence, before the lower chamber he deployed fear, his words reflecting his now-full-blown certainty of Communist evil and aggressive Soviet intentions. "Left to their own resources there will be," he pronounced, "no escape [by Europeans] from economic distress so intense, social discontents so violent, political confusion so widespread, and hope of the future so shattered that the historic base of Western civilization . . . will take a new form in the image of the tyranny we fought to destroy in Germany."[31] The European nations had done what they could to restart their war-devastated societies, but they now urgently needed dollars that the United States alone could supply. To administer the recovery program he urged an executive agency with a single administrator. In response to questions from skeptical representatives, he also played the economic-benefits card. If

Europe collapsed the United States would confront serious trade barriers abroad and would also be compelled to spend far more than otherwise on national security.

By mid-January, Marshall and the other high-level supporters of ERP had effectively presented their case to Congress. But in a presidential election year it was vital that the American voters also be convinced. There already existed a national committee under former secretary Stimson, formed to rally public opinion in favor of the recovery program. But Marshall's participation in the selling job was indispensable, and, setting aside his infirmities, he campaigned for ERP as vigorously as a much younger man. Marshall toured the entire country spreading the ERP gospel, with special emphasis on places where the "opposition" was expected to be strongest, including the Chicago area, where the archconservative publisher Robert McCormick and his isolationist, xenophobic *Chicago Tribune* reigned supreme. The secretary spoke before scores of groups: the Federation of Women's Clubs, university faculties at Berkeley and UCLA, the National Association of Manufacturers, the CIO, Pittsburgh industrialists, Iowa corn farmers, Southern cotton and tobacco planters. Even more than before he focused on the dangers of Communist triumph in the weakened nations of Western Europe. His words at times invoked an almost Manichaean battle between good and evil: "This is a world-wide struggle between freedom and tyranny," he told a California audience, "between the self-rule of many as opposed to the dictatorship of the ruthless few."[32] But he was also more pragmatic, often emphasizing the economic gains for America of a recovered and prosperous Europe. Generally, he later reported, he was well received, but it was often "a hard fight."[33]

The definitive bill incorporating the Economic Recovery Program—the Economic Cooperation Act—was officially introduced in Congress in late 1947. During the debate over its passage, it encountered opposition from both the political Left and Right. Midwestern Republicans, with Ohio's scholarly and dour Robert Taft their leading spokesman, fought to cut the funding and even to replace the whole bill. Outside Congress, former vice president Henry A. Wallace, a man of the idiosyncratic Left, who had been fired from the cabinet by Truman in 1946 for his pro-Soviet views, attacked the legislation as a sellout to American big business and a provocative act against America's former Russian allies. Fearing its warlike consequences, Wallace labeled the program the "Martial Plan." His views, of course, were seconded in the country at large by other domestic partisans of the Soviet bloc. The long debate in Congress was overshadowed in late February by the Communist seizure of power in hitherto democratic Czechoslovakia, abetted by the suspicious death of the pro-Western Czech foreign minister Jan Masaryk. Raising new fears of Soviet expansionist goals, the coup communicated a new urgency to the debate that helped the plan's supporters.

As passed by Congress in April 1948, the ERP measure authorized a total of $13.3 billion to be doled out, in the form of loans and gifts (often of commodities rather than cash) in yearly installments, the first one of $5 billion. Though some critics have demurred—claiming its size was too small to have jump-started Europe's economy and that the physical repair of Western Europe had already been achieved by the time of its passage—its effects, both economic and political, have generally been applauded. During the years when American funds and goods were crossing the Atlantic the aggregate output of Western Europe leaped by 32 percent, with agriculture up from prewar levels by 11 percent and industrial levels by 40 percent. The Marshall Plan, it is said, also checked incipient European inflation, helped modernize European economic accounting systems, and launched the Continent's process of economic unification. Most prominently, defenders of the West's liberal capitalism have celebrated its political effects. Its psychological impact, they say, probably checked a potential Communist victory in Italy's parliamentary elections that May. In the longer view, everywhere outside direct Soviet control, though it remained a formidable force in European political life, Communism as a threat to democratic institutions retreated, with the shift most visible in Germany, France, and Italy. In brief the Marshall Plan, according to mainstream Western opinion, was an extraordinary achievement that checked the Communist threat and solidified the West's struggle to prevail in the Cold War.

It has been said that "success has many fathers." Clearly, in this case, George Marshall was one. In most of the liberal Western world, he would be acclaimed for the plan. His presumed parental role would inspire *Time's* second occasion to proclaim him "Man of the Year." The European Recovery Program would also be the basis for his being awarded the Nobel Peace Prize in Oslo in October 1953. Moreover, as the present authors have personally observed, in the twenty-first century, even among well-educated Americans, Marshall's historical reputation rests almost exclusively on his association with ERP; virtually all his other roles and accomplishments have been forgotten.

And, of course, he deserves kudos for the program that took his name. He hired George Kennan to plan for the State Department and encouraged him to express his views frankly on the European recovery issue. He absorbed the contributions of Acheson, Clayton, and Bohlen and melded them into a roughly coherent whole. Most important, however, he placed his reputation for objectivity, integrity, and independence behind the program both before Congress and the American public. Still, putting it bluntly, he did not author the Marshall Plan. Marshall acknowledged the contributions of many in Congress to the final result. He was particularly generous in his praise of Senator Vandenberg, who worked undauntedly for ERP's passage. But he never claimed personal authorship of the plan and always refused to call it by its common name. Yet he was proud of his labors to get ERP enacted into law. "I worked on that as hard as though I was running for the Senate or the presidency," he later told Pogue. "That's what I'm proud of, that part of it."[34]

But there was other important business besides the fate of Western Europe clamoring for the secretary of state's attention. One of his most challenging, if unexpected, dilemmas was the future of Palestine and the fate of Europe's surviving Jews.

This ancient people, stateless and widely dispersed since the Roman-Jewish wars of the first Christian century, had a long, calamitous history of persecution and lethal abuse by their gentile neighbors, whether Christian, Muslim, or pagan. After 1945 thousands of Jewish survivors of the European Holocaust—part of the vast contingent of postwar "displaced persons" who roamed the Continent desperately seeking safe, permanent homes—looked to Palestine for refuge. But for Jews the quest was often for more than an immediate secure haven. Over the centuries, for many in the world Jewish Diaspora, a return to the land of their forebears, to "Zion," was a yearning that transcended immediate problems and even when not overt, often lay beneath the surface of consciousness.

For many of Europe's Jews the political and intellectual revolutions of the eighteenth and nineteenth centuries had provided an alternative to Zion. Rejecting the narrow bigotry of both traditional Catholicism and Protestantism, the apostles of the secular Enlightenment sought to end the many civil and economic disabilities imposed by the churches and governments of Europe on the Jewish minorities. In Western and Central Europe, though not in benighted imperial Russia, Jews became full citizens in this period, for the first time able to vote, own land, choose their occupations, live where they pleased, marry whom they wished, and attend universities. The lifting of past burdens unleashed a wave of Jewish secular creativity that produced a disproportionate number of men of talent and genius in science, government, business, and the arts.

And yet, even in the post-Enlightenment world, hatred of Jews remained, especially in Eastern Europe but also to lesser degrees in Germany, France, and Austria. Even democratic Britain and the United States were not entirely free in the nineteenth and twentieth centuries of disdain for, and suspicion of, Jews and of humiliating half-hidden social and economic discrimination that hung like a pall over Jews' lives and hopes.

The continued scorn and bigotry of Christians disillusioned a segment of Jewish intellectuals with the new liberal regimes. Some turned to socialism as an alternative. But others turned to Zionism. The Jews, Zionists claimed, would find their salvation not in a state supposedly founded on egalitarian social principles, but in a nation of their own established on the sacred soil of ancient Judaea, now part of Palestine, a province of the Ottoman Empire. There Jews could finally become a majority and be transformed into a "normal" people with the full range of modern social and cultural life that had been denied them even in post-Enlightenment Europe.

The father of the modern Zionist movement was a charismatic Austro-Hungarian journalist, Theodor Herzl, whose 1896 book, *Der Judenstaat* (*The Jewish State*), awakened the dormant Zionism of Jews around the world and led to the creation in 1897 of the World Zionist Organization. The movement appealed initially to the oppressed Jewish masses of Eastern Europe though it also won adherents among German and Western European Jewish intellectuals. It even attracted a group of gentile philo-Semites, especially those whose Christianity was strongly imprinted with Old Testament biblical culture. In 1917, Britain's foreign secretary, Arthur Balfour—prodded by the eminent Russian-British scientist Chaim Weizmann and seeking the support of world Jewry for the Allied cause in World War I—declared in a public letter to Baron Walter Rothschild of the eminent Jewish banking family that the British government viewed "with favour the establishment in Palestine of a national home for the Jewish people." This "Balfour Declaration" contained an important qualifier, however. "Nothing shall be done," it declared, "which may prejudice the civil and religious rights of the non-Jewish communities" in the then-part of the enemy Central Powers. In 1920, after the dissolution of the Turkish empire, Britain accepted trusteeship of Palestine as a League of Nations "mandate," with authority to govern the land until it was ready for self-rule. For some years afterward the Palestine mandate included the territory east of the Jordan River, the region that eventually became the independent Arab nation of Jordan.

What followed was a substantial migration of zealous working-class Jews, and a sprinkling of Jewish intellectuals and idealists, to Palestine determined to create a new society that would provide refuge for Jews, fulfill the prophets' predictions, and refute the stereotype of Jews as parasites on gentile society. In the 1930s they were joined by thousands of German Jews driven out of their homeland by Nazi persecution. By the eve of World War II the Yishuv—the Jewish community of Palestine—had grown to almost half a million and had won broad international admiration for creating egalitarian agricultural communities and flourishing modern towns and cities in an impoverished land long neglected under Turkish sovereignty. Speaking for the community's relations to Britain, the mandate authority, was the Jewish Agency, a body established in 1929.

But there were daunting obstacles in the way of the Zionist dream. The non-Jewish Arab population of mandate Palestine, initially twice the size of the Yishuv, supported by Muslims throughout the Middle East, strongly resisted the Jewish intrusion into what they perceived as *their* nation. During the 1920s and 1930s Arab Palestinians launched numerous savage attacks against Jewish settlements. Jews fought back. In response to the turmoil, in 1939 the British government issued a White Paper restricting Jewish immigration to Palestine to a total of 75,000 during 1940–45. Thereafter the Arab majority would determine the number of new Jewish immigrants, a sure formula for zero. The paper also limited the rights of the Jews to buy land from Arab owners. Soon after the document's issuance, World War II, with its catastrophic impact on Europe's Jews, enveloped the European continent. At the very moment the Jewish community of Europe most needed a safe refuge, it was denied all but a trickle of opportunity to escape the disaster. It did not take long for Zionist and Yishuv leaders to defy the mandate authorities and organize ways to smuggle refugees into Palestine. The mandate authorities in turn imposed a harsh blockade to keep them out, a response that undoubtedly worsened the evolving humanitarian disaster in Europe.

The fate of the Jews in Europe and Palestine inevitably concerned their American coreligionists. In the twentieth century the American Jewish community, with more than four million members by the late 1930s, was the largest in the world, but on the question of Zionism it was divided. Many assimilated German-American Jews dissented from the notion of separate statehood for Jews. It would, they felt, raise the uncomfortable issue of divided loyalties. *They* were, they insisted, Americans of the Hebrew faith, not just Jews who happened to live in America. The Zionist appeal was especially strong among the more recent, and much larger, cohort of Eastern European Jews predominantly from former czarist lands, the Balkans, and Austria-Hungary.

The Holocaust, the systematic mass murder by the Germans

and their allies during World War II of more than six million of Europe's Jews changed the picture of Palestine's future dramatically. At the war's end almost a million Holocaust survivors, physically and emotionally broken by their horrific ordeal, remained in Europe. Few Jewish displaced persons from Eastern Europe wished to return to their former home countries, where in many cases their gentile neighbors remained hostile and even homicidal toward them. Few Western nations, including the United States, suffering either from lingering anti-Jewish feelings or concerned with their own limping postwar economic recoveries, wished to admit as residents more than a trickle of these beaten people.* In 1947 many thousands were still cooped up in squalid camps, barely surviving on Allied or UN largesse. The only hope, it seemed to many Jews and their gentile friends, was for them to join the Yishuv in Palestine, now six hundred thousand strong.

But the Palestinian Arabs and the far larger Middle Eastern Muslim community remained bitterly hostile and promised to fight every attempt to foist the Jewish problem on them or their coreligionists. And though disunited, and still without the political clout of later years, they could not be ignored in the calculations of Western leaders. First there was the emerging Cold War to consider. British and many American policy makers feared that supporting the Jews would propel the Arabs of the Middle East into the arms of the Soviets. Moreover, the Zionists' Middle Eastern Arab enemies sat on the largest pool of underground oil in the world, a cornucopia that gave them enormous influence. Rec-

---

*Marshall was one American who favored a liberal policy of admitting refugees, including Jews, to the United States as a partial solution to the postwar "displaced persons" problem. See his testimony to Congress of July 16, 1947, in Bland, Stoler, and Stevens, *The Papers of George Catlett Marshall*, vol. 6, pp. 176–81. As he noted on another occasion, the position was opposed by "persons whose only reason for opposing the measure was that they did not like Jews." See his March 2, 1948, memo in ibid., p. 390.

ognizing this asset, on the way back from the Yalta Conference in early 1945, President Roosevelt had met with King Ibn Saud of Saudi Arabia to consider issues of mutual American and Arab concern and asked the king what should be done about the plight of the surviving Jews of Europe. Saud answered that the refugees should be forced to return to their homelands and that the defeated Germans should pay the costs of their presence. In fact Ibn Saud harbored even harsher views of the Zionist enterprise than he expressed to FDR. At one point, according to a later American ambassador to Saudi Arabia, the king had told him that "if America should choose in favor of the Jews who are accursed in the Koran as enemies of the Muslims until the end of the world, it will indicate to us that America has repudiated her friendship with us."[35] In any case Roosevelt promised Ibn Saud to do nothing that "prove[d] hostile to the Arab people."[36]

Americans of many persuasions, religious and political, disagreed with Saud about the postwar "Jewish problem." The Republicans Robert Taft and Thomas Dewey, as well as many Democrats—southern conservatives as well as northern liberals—sympathized with the brutalized Jews of postwar Europe, as did most American Christians, especially, perhaps, those of conservative Protestant faith. But this did not mean they invariably favored nationhood for the Jews in Palestine. Many saw the problem as essentially one of providing a haven abroad for Jewish refugees; nationhood was another matter. As for American Jews, few doubted that the survivors of the death camps must be helped and, by 1945, most favored Jewish autonomy or nationhood status for the Yishuv. Especially adamant on statehood was a group of American Jewish religious leaders, including Rabbis Stephen Wise and Abba Hillel Silver, and prominent and influential secular Jews such as Supreme Court Justices Felix Frankfurter and Louis Brandeis, and the world-renowned scientist Albert Einstein.

Within the Truman administration the Zionists could count on White House aide David Niles and Clark Clifford, the president's trusted legal counsel. But these men were outnumbered in administration and executive circles by the doubters and dissenters. Especially skeptical of Zionism, and even of Jewish refugee concerns, was a group of officials within the State Department, particularly those responsible for overall planning for specific Middle Eastern matters. These included, most prominently, chief planner Kennan, Loy Henderson of the Near Eastern and African Affairs Division, and Dean Rusk at the department's UN desk. The anti-Zionists of State were seconded by many officials in the newly formed Defense Department and the armed forces, including the secretary, James V. Forrestal.

Zionists would often accuse these men of anti-Semitism—of disliking Jews as a race or as members of a religious community.

But it was not that simple. Indeed they were not philo-Semites; as a group they did not share the emotional identification of Christian Zionists with the Jews as the onetime "chosen people," and perhaps among themselves they may even have displayed the casual anti-Semitism of the upper-class WASP society of the day. But their opposition to the Zionist agenda derived primarily from their view of America's interests in the Middle East. As a Joint Chiefs of Staff paper of 1948 noted, the creation of a Jewish state would certainly trigger violence between Arabs and Jews, curtailing American influence in the area and requiring American military intervention to prevent disaster. The Joint Chiefs and others also worried about the loss of the oil resources of the Middle East if the United States offended the Arabs. Others in the administration feared that supporting the Jews would benefit the Russians, who would opportunistically rush to the Arabs' defense. It was therefore of "great strategic importance to the United States," concluded the Joint Chiefs' paper, "to retain the good will of the

Arab and Moslem states."[37] These feelings were echoed in several State Department policy-planning papers and in Kennan's diary in late January 1948. There Kennan concluded that Americans could not afford to be "the keepers and moral guardians of all the peoples of the world."[38] In short, favoring the Jews would offend the Arabs and their millions of Muslim supporters and create dangerous risks and turmoil in a part of the world where the United States had a substantial stake.

Marshall himself was free of the casual disdain for Jews that colored the attitudes of his class and was strong as well among the professional military caste. As noted, Bernard Baruch was one of his closest personal friends and later, as secretary of defense, he would resolutely defend Anna Rosenberg, his choice for assistant secretary of defense for manpower, when her nomination came under fire in the Senate and in the press from right-wingers and anti-Semites. Yet, though he recognized the humanitarian aspects of the Palestine issue, Marshall did not share the sentimental affinity for Zionism of the avid Christian Bible readers. To him, as to the pro-Arab officers of the State Department, the Palestine issue ultimately boiled down to expediency: The United States must choose what was best for the United States; the rest was irrelevant.

But in the end it was the president who really counted. As a liberal humanitarian, Truman deeply sympathized with the plight of Europe's displaced Jews. As senator, in 1943, even before the worst horrors of the Nazi genocide had been revealed, he declared that everything "humanly possible" must be done to provide a safe haven for Europe's Jews.[39] He was also a traditional Midwestern Protestant who read and knew his Bible. He was, then, by and large a Christian philo-Semite who admired not only Moses and King David and Isaiah, but also the venerable Zionist leader Chaim Weizmann and American Zionist moderates like Reform rabbi Stephen Wise. As a senator, even before his elevation to the presidency, he had joined fellow members of Congress in support of free immigration of Jews to Palestine and the eventual establishment there of a Jewish homeland. And whenever his resolve slipped, American Zionists could often rely on the president's good Missouri Jewish friend and former Kansas City haberdashery partner, Eddie Jacobson, to stiffen his back. Yet Truman was capable of losing patience with zealous Jews and their barrage of importunings. Early in his administration, exasperated by a raft of Zionist petitions opposing a compromise plan for Palestine, he burst out at a cabinet meeting: "Jesus Christ couldn't please them when he was here on earth so how could anyone expect that I would have any luck?"[40] At one point in the long international debate over Palestine he confided to his diary: "The Jews, I find are very, very selfish. They care not how many Estonians, Latvians, Finns, Yugoslavs or Greeks got murdered or mistreated as DPs as long as the Jews get special treatment."[41] Yet to the end he remained the Zionists' best and most powerful friend and, on the Palestine issue, resented the "career officials" in the State Department who believed that it was *they*, not the "elected officials," who "really make policy and run the government."[42]

The policy struggles within the Truman administration to ease the plight of Europe's Jewish survivors and cope with the Zionist dream for postwar Palestine proceeded in a series of small contentious, controversial steps. The first was the effort to rescind the restrictive British immigration policy and allow large numbers of Europe's displaced Jews entry into Palestine. In August 1945 Truman read the State Department report compiled by Earl G. Harrison, dean of the University of Pennsylvania Law School, vividly describing the sordid, oppressive refugee camps where many Jews were lodged. The report, he said, sickened him. The situation there was "practically as bad as it was under the

Germans." The solution, he concluded, was to improve the way the American military was running the camps and then open the doors of both the United States and Palestine to the afflicted people.[43] At the end of August, Truman sent a copy of the Harrison Report to British prime minister Attlee along with a letter asking him to lift the immigration quota for Jews and admit one hundred thousand refugees to Palestine. But meanwhile the president took care to inform zealous American Zionist leaders that their demand for a Jewish state was "not in the cards now." Its creation, he warned, might "cause a Third World War."[44]

Truman's letter and the Harrison Report angered British officials. Palestine was a British mandate. The American government and president, they said, were putting their noses into other people's business. Although previously friendly to Zionism, the Labour Party also balked at further offending the Arabs. In October, British foreign minister Bevin proposed a joint Anglo-American Committee of Inquiry as a way of directly involving the United States in the resolution of the Palestine issue. Truman and Secretary of State Byrnes accepted, though Chaim Weizmann, now ailing and elderly, along with other Zionists, denounced the further delay. Several of the most militant, including Rabbi Silver, a Republican ally of Robert Taft, attacked Truman for reneging on his earlier position on statehood. Truman responded by repeating his reservations. He did not intend, he told a friend, to go "to war for Palestine."[45]

The joint Anglo-American committee formed following Bevin's suggestion, after extensive hearings and careful investigation in Europe, the Middle East, and in Palestine itself, submitted its report in April 1946. It proposed major changes in the anti-Zionist mandate policies: The British authorities, as Truman had suggested, should immediately admit one hundred thousand Jewish DPs to Palestine and repeal the White Paper's restrictions on

Jewish land purchases and the overall limit on immigration. On the issue of statehood, however, the committee held back. Having encountered adamant and militant Arab protests in the course of its investigation, it recommended against either a Jewish or Arab state, proposing instead an eventual binational entity where both groups could express their legitimate national aspirations.

Truman found the report praiseworthy. But the British government and the ardent Zionists did not. By now, desperate Jewish extremists in Palestine—members of the Stern Gang, the Irgun, and other militant Zionist groups—had begun violent attacks on British targets, including mandate property and British military personnel. The mandate authorities in return imposed harsh punishments, including arrests of Yishuv leaders and hangings of captured terrorists to reestablish order. The violence disturbed Truman, who now worried that the United Stares would be forced to send troops to Palestine to help Britain, and requested the Joint Chiefs to consider the issue. Their June 1946 report decried any use of American soldiers in the Middle East. Such a move might induce the Soviet Union to increase its presence in the region, and that in turn would vitally affect the Western nations' access to its oil resources. Marshall was, of course, no longer an active member of the Joint Chiefs, but their views undoubtedly influenced his own thinking on the subject of Palestine.

With Britain and the Arabs still adamantly opposed to admitting a substantial number of Jewish refugees to Palestine, the debate shifted to its partition into two political entities, one Jewish, one Arab, with Britain either abandoning the mandate entirely or continuing as trustee in a loose federation of the two autonomous statelets. In October 1946, on the eve of Yom Kippur, the Jewish holy Day of Atonement, and only a few weeks before the midterm U.S. elections, Truman issued a statement supporting a version of partition, excluding the unsettled southern Negev

Desert, as the solution of the Palestine problem. The proposal got nowhere. Britain refused to accept partition, and spokesmen for the Arabs were even more intransigently opposed, King Ibn Saud sending two royal princes to Washington to protest personally to Truman. On the other side the most militant Zionists rejected any plan to surrender any part of the Holy Land, including the desert area, but the more moderate Jewish Agency, the voice of the Yishuv, accepted it as promising Jewish sovereignty, however limited, to a part of Palestine. Meanwhile, battered by widespread violence in Palestine and admitting its inability to settle the question, on April 2, 1947, Britain requested that the issue be put on the general agenda of the United Nations, then holding its sessions at Lake Success on Long Island. The UN General Assembly quickly appointed an ad hoc committee (UNSCOP*) made up of eleven member states, chosen to represent all continents, to consider the status and future of Palestine and to submit its report on September 1.

The administration welcomed the development; if nothing else the UN's intervention would provide a needed breathing space. Meanwhile, the president and Marshall believed they should avoid any attempt to influence the General Assembly's decisions. When ardent American supporters of the Zionist position protested against this hands-off policy, Marshall replied that the United States wished to avoid hobbling the General Assembly investigation and deliberations. But, he promised, the United States would respond when the committee made its report. One development that the Americans could not have anticipated was the abrupt change in attitude toward the Palestine issue announced by the Soviet delegate to the UN in mid-May. Until then the Russians, seeking to court the Arabs, had been hostile to the Zi-

---

*That is, "United Nations Ad Hoc Committee on Palestine."

onists. Now, however, they saw the advantage of a split between Britain and America, their two major Cold War adversaries, to be achieved by endorsing Truman's position and defying British opinion. Accordingly, in his May 14 UN statement, the Russian representative, Andrei Gromyko, announced that the Soviet Union considered the British mandate bankrupt and favored Jewish aspirations for statehood. If a united Arab-Jewish state could not be created, then the USSR would endorse a partition of Palestine into two autonomous countries.

Though Marshall agreed with the president on avoiding U.S. pressure on the General Assembly, he disagreed with Truman on the partition issue. One explanation for his stand is that he was seeking to blunt Gromyko's strategy of dividing Britain and America. We know that he was deeply concerned about the anti-American effect in Britain of the flood of pro-Zionist views and propaganda by prominent and influential Americans and wished to tamp it down. But the influence of his colleagues at State was even more potent. According to Jewish Agency spokesman Eliahu Epstein, the fault lay with the rabidly anti-Zionist Loy Henderson. Marshall, he pointed out, was still new to his job and inexperienced. This made him particularly vulnerable to views flowing from the veteran hands at Foggy Bottom, and also receptive to the positions of the War and Navy Departments where the large American oil companies, he noted, wielded enormous influence.

UNSCOP began its work in mid-June 1947, conducting hearings and investigations in both Europe and Palestine. Hostile Arab groups either boycotted the committee or demonstrated against it; by contrast, wherever the UN delegates went they were wooed and cheered by the friendly local Jews. The committee's report, submitted on August 31, presented the General Assembly with two proposals, both written by Ralph Bunche, an American UN official of African descent. Both agreed that the British mandate should be ended and Palestine be given autonomy. The minority scheme, however, endorsed by delegates of three nations, rejected partition and suggested instead a federal state with separate Jewish and Arab divisions. The majority plan, signed by delegates of seven nations, proposed creation of separate, fully independent Arab and Jewish states—the partition version favored by the Jewish Agency and even those ardent Zionists who had reluctantly abandoned their plan for a Jewish state coterminous with all of mandate Palestine.

The proposal came before the second meeting of the UN General Assembly in mid-September 1947. During the six weeks of debate that followed, American Zionists, backed by the Jewish Agency, strongly endorsed the majority partition scheme. As for the Yishuv, as the U.S. consul ceneral in Palestine reported to Marshall, they were "elated." By contrast, Arab leaders denounced both reports virtually without exception. The Arab Higher Committee, the Arab counterpart of the Jewish Agency, insisted that their people "would never allow a Jewish state to be established in one inch of Palestine." Any attempt "to impose any solution contrary to the Arabs' birthright," they threatened, would "only lead to trouble and bloodshed and probably to a third World War."[46]

During the weeks that followed the UNSCOP report, Zionists, both in America and abroad, worried about the American response. Despite all the indicators, the State Department's official position remained in doubt, yet American approval was essential to the success of partition plus statehood. At the UN the American delegation, headed by former senator Warren Austin and including Eleanor Roosevelt, Gen. Matthew Ridgway, and John Foster Dulles, kept in close touch with the president and Secretary Marshall over the issue before the General Assembly. On September 15 Marshall came to New York to speak to the General Assembly. Before the speech he consulted members of the U.S. delegation on the Palestine issue. The secretary still seemed uncertain where he stood. He listened to differing views regarding the position the United States should take on the majority report. He told the American delegates that the Zionists were pushing him hard, but he feared that if the United States adopted the majority report the Arabs would react with violence. The United States must avoid provoking the Arabs and "precipitating their rapprochement with the Soviet Union," as would happen if he took a clear stand in favor of the partition proposal. Yet Marshall was uneasy with his own equivocation. If he avoided a clear position, he acknowledged, he would be accused of "pussyfooting."[47] Marshall left the meeting without expressing his decision, and the evasiveness was reflected in his speech to the General Assembly two days later. The United States, he said, gave "great weight" to both reports but would await the outcome of the General Assembly's debate before deciding how to vote its final recommendations.[48] In effect, whatever his discomfort, he was indeed "pussyfooting."

On November 29, 1947, by direct order of the president and to the dismay of Henderson and Kennan, the U.S. delegates voted with a majority of the General Assembly, including the Soviet Union, to accept the partition plan. In the end Marshall had apparently acquiesced in the decision to establish two separate entities in mandated Palestine, though with serious misgivings.

Meanwhile, the president wavered. In February of the new year, the U.S. ambassador to the UN, Warren Austin, delivered a speech that seemed to withdraw American support for partition in favor of a trusteeship arrangement for Palestine. Truman, in turn, seemed to acquiesce. Zionist were horrified and vehemently protested. Annoyed by what seemed like endless Zionist importuning, until fervently implored by his old Kansas City friend Eddie Jacobson the president initially refused to see Zionist elder statesman Chaim Weizmann who, in an earlier visit to the

White House had persuaded the president to support the Zionist inclusion of the undeveloped Negev Desert in the Jewish portion of the partition. Now Weizmann clearly sought to change Truman's mind on the trusteeship issue. The soft-spoken scientist apparently got Truman to modify his view and so to instruct the U.S. delegation to the UN. Unfortunately, however, Ambassador Austin did not get the message. To the president's dismay, on March 19 Austin spoke to the Security Council proposing that the partition resolution be suspended in favor of a temporary trusteeship. The president took no blame for the gaffe; the "striped-pants boys" at the State Department, he insisted, were to blame. As for Marshall, he was now firmly on the side of the State Department's core members who favored a trusteeship over independence and wished the Zionists would just go away. Besides fearing that America might be dragged into a Middle East war, he deplored the political pandering to the Jewish vote, which he believed governed much of the administration's pro-Zionist posturing.

By now violence had replaced diplomacy as the decisive factor in Palestine's fate. Within hours of the UN vote Arab forces attacked Jewish settlements in Palestine; Jewish paramilitary forces counterattacked. In December the British announced that they would be abandoning their mandate in mid-May, leaving the contending forces in Palestine to fight it out for themselves. With Palestine now a battleground, Marshall thought the Jews' position hopeless. As he would tell the Jewish Agency's Moshe Shertok on May 8, his people were surrounded by millions of hostile Arab neighbors and had their backs to the sea. As a military man he must warn Shertok to avoid false optimism even though the Jews seemed initially to be repelling their attackers. The State Department having the previous December embargoed all arms shipments to the Middle East, if the Jews thought that the United

States would come to their rescue, they were mistaken, he added. They had chosen a risky course.

But if the United States would not provide military aid, would it support the Jews diplomatically? Would the administration recognize an independent State of Israel, whose declaration of which the Yishuv was about to announce? Would it support the new nation in its expected application for diplomatic recognition and admission to the UN? In the world's view American recognition seemed essential to establishing both Israel's de facto and de jure statehood, the latter presuming the formal exchange of ministers.

On May 12, two days before the final British departure from Palestine, Truman assembled his foreign policy advisers, including Marshall and Lovett, in the White House to consider the crucial recognition issue. The meeting was essentially a performance. The president had already made up his mind: He would support recognition in some form and had instructed his counsel, Clark Clifford, to come to the meeting prepared to defend his position. The handsome, debonair Clifford was a willing presidential agent. He was a Zionist, not by birth but by education, with Federal Judge Samuel Rosenman, FDR's adviser on Jewish matters, his chief mentor. The brash young lawyer, like the president himself, had little respect for the State Department's regulars, who, he believed, constantly sought to undermine the White House. He sometimes felt, he later wrote, that the Loy Henderson group "preferred to follow the views of the British Foreign Office rather than those of their president."[49] But would Marshall support the anti-Zionist Henderson faction of his department? Truman thought he knew in which direction the secretary would tilt. In a note to Clifford before the meeting he had observed of the recognition issue that "General Marshall is probably opposed to it."[50] The president was right, except there was no need for the qualifier.

As Clifford later described it, the White House meeting on May 12 was like the famous confrontation at the "OK Corral" in Western history: a "Showdown in the Oval Office."[51] Foreseeing an angry exchange if Henderson and Rusk were present, the State Department had them replaced by two less controversial junior representatives. But the attempt to keep a lid on the discussion did not work. Starting calmly with Undersecretary Lovett's neutral report on the recent conversation with Shertok, and a brief interruption by Marshall confirming his own warning to Shertok, the discussion became heated. As Clifford recalled, it evolved into the most "confrontational and hostile" meeting he had ever attended during the years he spent in the Truman administration.[52]

Marshall's response to Lovett's report set the tone. The Jews could not win militarily no matter how well the early skirmishing was going, he declared. He warned about the dire economic consequences of encouraging the Zionists. America needed oil lest, in Forrestal's recent vivid phrase, it be forced to accept only "four-cylinder cars from Detroit." And there was also the possibility that, deprived of a stable oil supply, the U.S. Army would be unable to carry out its missions around the globe. Clifford replied bluntly. He dismissed State's effort to achieve a military truce between the adversaries. It had been tried and had failed, as had State's recent proposal to establish a trusteeship in a divided Palestine. Turning to the president, seated at his desk, he pleaded with Truman as if he did not already know his preference: "I strongly urge you," he said to his chief, "to give prompt recognition to the Jewish state immediately after termination of the British mandate." This step should be taken before the Soviets got there first. Clifford went on to invoke the moral dimension of the Zionist case. He recounted the baleful distant and recent history of the Jews. Recognition of the Jewish state would be an act of humanity, "everything this country should represent."[53] He continued: "The Jewish people the world over have been waiting for thirty years for the promise of a homeland to be fulfilled." There was no reason "to wait one day longer." The United States had "a great moral obligation to oppose discrimination such as that inflicted on the Jewish people."[54]

As Clifford spoke Marshall's face grew redder. The secretary deeply resented Clifford's very presence at the meeting. Addressing the president, he exclaimed: "I thought the meeting was called to consider an important and complicated problem in foreign policy. I don't even know why Clifford is here. He is a domestic policy adviser, and this is a foreign policy matter."[55] When Truman confessed that Clifford was in the Oval Office at his behest, Marshall shifted to more substantive matters. Clifford's arguments were political in their implications, he insisted, a view that implied that the moral plea was intended to appeal to the American voters, presumably Jews and philo-Semites. To use American support of the Zionist position for this purpose, he would note later that day, would seriously diminish "the great dignity of the office of President."*[56] But whether it was the presumed intrusion by this young untried lawyer onto the State Department's turf, or what seemed his base appeal to domestic political concerns that incited his wrath, Marshall lost his temper. Addressing the president directly, "with barely contained rage" he exclaimed: If he followed "Clifford's advice, and if I were to vote in the election, I would vote against you!" Shocked silence followed Marshall's point-blank statement. It was an extraordinary rebuke of the president. It was also a serious threat to Truman's already shaky chances for nomination and election as president. As Clifford later wrote, everyone present understood that if the

---

*These words of Marshall are recorded in the official State Department account of the meeting. They did not become public until the 1970s.

secretary's position became public it "could virtually seal the dissolution of the Truman Administration" as well as jeopardizing the
president's November bid for another four years.[57] Before they left
the room Truman sought to appease Marshall: "I understand your
position, General," he remarked, "and I am inclined to side with
you in this matter."[58] But as they filed out, in a whispered aside to
his counsel, he also praised Clifford for his presentation. "That was
as rough as it gets," he acknowledged. "But you did your best." He
urged Clifford not to assume that he had "lost it." But "let the dust
settle," he urged. He still wanted to recognize Israel's statehood, but
they must be careful. "I can't afford to lose General Marshall."[59]

Though their paths often crossed in later years, Marshall never
spoke another word to Clifford; apparently he never mentioned
Clifford's name again. Yet over the next few days both sides
sought to avoid a public rupture. The evening of the Oval Office
meeting Lovett phoned Clifford to tell him how worried he was
that Truman and Marshall might "have an open break." Clifford
agreed that such an outcome would be dangerous and came to
Lovett's home to consider possible options to prevent a political
disaster. Might the president be persuaded to change his mind if
Clifford presented State's views to him? Lovett asked. Clifford
said that there was simply no chance that he would. If anybody
was "going . . . to give in" it would "have to be Marshall."[60]

Some observers privy to the confrontation feared that Marshall had made up his mind to resign. But calmer feelings quickly
took over. Truman agreed to postpone the announcement of his
intentions regarding recognition until the Jewish Agency officially
requested it. On the other side, Marshall and his department allies realized that to allow a public clash between the president
and his highest-level official adviser in the midst of an emerging
crisis over access to Berlin would be disastrous. A more composed
Marshall now relented. On May 14 Marshall called the president

and promised that while he could not support Truman's intention to recognize the new nation, he would not oppose it. His motive here was loyalty to the civilian authority as befitted an American soldier. According to Dean Rusk, when asked whether he intended to quit if the president went through with his plan, Marshall responded: "No, gentlemen, you don't take a post of this sort and then resign when the man who has the constitutional responsibility to make decisions makes one you don't like."[61]

On May 14, the day before Britain officially abandoned the mandate and withdrew its troops from Palestine, the State Department issued a press release, drafted by Clifford and Lovett, announcing that the United States intended to recognize the Jewish state. The next day at 10:00 a.m. Washington time, the Yishuv leaders declared the independence of the State of Israel.* A few minutes later the White House announced that the United States was according de facto recognition to the new entity.

In the months that followed, during the heat of the presidential campaign, relations between Marshall and Truman, roiled by the Palestine issue, remained somewhat distant. The president respected Marshall's aversion to the bitterly partisan politics of the moment, and when necessary to consider the political implications of foreign policy, called at times on Undersecretary Lovett, rather than his boss, for advice. The months—and years—following recognition would show that the struggle of the Jews of Palestine for secure nationhood was far from over. Further steps to independence included the UN General Assembly's vote, supported by the United States, that Israel be admitted as a member nation, and a fierce drawn-out struggle to survive the military assault launched against it by powerful Arab enemies. During the final UN discussion of the new nation's boundaries,

---

*Not yet officially named "Israel," however.

Marshall favored the conciliatory proposal by the Swedish UN mediator, Folke Bernadotte, which was protested by the Israelis for giving away the Negev to the Arabs. He fretted over what he considered the blatant political pandering over the Jewish state during the 1948 presidential campaign. But Truman and Clifford now largely ignored him, and he would have little further influence on the Palestine issue during his remaining weeks as secretary of state. On January 31, 1949, the United States finally agreed to exchange ambassadors with Israel.

When all is said, Marshall had failed to mold the Palestine issue to his liking. But it is difficult to deny his insight. Truman's and Clifford's compassionate views on Jewish statehood had prevailed, and the United States would have to live with the long-term unsettling results.

And there was the still-unfinished business of China. The final scenes of the China tangle were played out during Marshall's tenure at the State Department. In those two years the government of Nationalist China, its currency debased, its people disillusioned and rebellious, fell apart. The country descended into full civil war, with the Communist forces under Mao, better organized and motivated, gaining both territory and popular support. By mid-1947 the Truman administration was fast losing faith that Chiang and his regime could survive. But not the powerful members of the China Lobby. During the debate over the ERP they had managed to induce Congress to include some $400 million in technical and military support to the Nationalists as part of the aid bill. Marshall himself was reluctant to repudiate the Kuomintang and remained personally cordial toward Chiang and his charming wife. For a time, in fact, Madame Chiang stayed as a guest at Dodona Manor, waiting for a chance to plead her Nationalist cause to President Truman. But Marshall's confidence that the Kuomintang government could survive was waning. Responding to a request in early 1947 for increased arms for the Nationalists from Wellington Koo, Chiang's ambassador to the United States, the secretary retorted that Koo's chief was "the worst advised military commander in history" and that he was already "losing about 40 percent of his supplies to the enemy." If the proportion should reach 50 percent the United States would have to consider cutting off further military aid. In June, in response to a recommendation by the Joint Chiefs for continued aid to Chiang, he confessed his inner conflict: "I have tortured my brain and I can't see the answer."[62] Soon after, he radioed the American ambassador in Nanking: "We are keenly aware of China's needs," but "in the final analysis the fundamental and lasting solution of China's problems must come from the Chinese themselves."[63] This self-help formula would be successful for ERP; it would fail for China.

The continued China Lobby pressure compelled the president and Marshall, despite their serious doubts, to make a final gesture to save the Chiang regime. In early July Marshall asked General Wedemeyer to head a fact-finding mission to the fast-faltering regime at Nanking. The mission was a stopgap that would give the administration some political breathing space to consider how much additional support to give Chiang and his circle. Probably neither Truman nor Marshall any longer believed there was much hope for the Kuomintang government.

The choice of Wedemeyer is a puzzling one. He had already been passed over as ambassador to China in favor of John Stuart and had become identified with the pro-Kuomintang position. Perhaps his selection was a concession to the China Lobby partisans, who respected him more than did the State Department regulars. In any event, after a month of travel, talks, and interviews throughout China, while proposing broad reforms of Kuomintang policies and behavior, in his official report Wedemeyer attacked Soviet-aided Communist subversion and recommended allotting significant additional funds and material backing, as well as moral support, to the Chiang regime. In his conclusions the general warned against allowing the Communists to prevail in China and noted that "a program of aid, if effectively employed, would bolster opposition to Communist expansion and would contribute to a gradual development of stability in China."[64]

One recommendation of the report—a proposal to sever Manchuria, China's loosely held northern province, from Nationalist control and give it either to a "guardianship of five nations including the Soviet Union" or to a UN trusteeship—was certain to offend the government in Nanking. Marshall and the president accordingly decided to keep the report secret. This was a mistake. The zealous spokesmen for the China Lobby immediately charged that the administration was arranging a cover-up to avoid an endorsement of the Nationalists. The accusation would become an item in the indictment for "losing China" that would soon be leveled against both Marshall and Truman.

The end of the Kuomintang's reign in mainland China now came quickly. On January 1, 1949, Chiang resigned as president of the Chinese Republic, supposedly in the interests of peace. Nationalist troops, poorly led though professionally advised by American military officers and bolstered by superior American equipment, were soon in headlong retreat. By April 1949 the southward-sweeping Communist army had crossed the Yangtse River and were advancing on major Nationalist cities. On April 24 they occupied Nanking; on May 16, Hankow; on May 25, Shanghai. In October the surviving Nationalist government, along with two million civilians and remnants of the Nationalist army, abandoned the mainland and fled to the offshore island of Formosa, soon renamed Taiwan. (Many Nationalist officials carried with them caches of U.S. dollars from the $275 million extracted from Congress by the China Lobby as part of the Marshall Plan appropriations.) There, in their new home, Chiang and his colleagues would claim to be the legitimate government of the Republic of China and promised someday to return to the mainland to oust the Communist usurpers. Refusing to recognize reality, until 1978 the United States would accept the regime in Taiwan as the legal government of China and deny the legitimacy of the Communist People's Republic in Beijing.

It is difficult to see in these months of Nationalist retreat and final exile any sign that Marshall had accomplished much good for his nation or for its friends in China.

During Marshall's twenty-four months at State no issue raised such frightening prospects of military confrontation between the Soviet and American superpowers as the status of Berlin. In a shambles after the Soviet forces had crushed its Nazi defenders, the city was deep in the Soviet sphere of occupation, detached geographically from the Western zones. Like the rest of Germany initially, it was divided into four districts, each under the jurisdiction of one of the victorious powers of World War II, including liberated France. To the Russians, Berlin seemed an ideal hostage in the struggle over the eventual fate of Germany, for they alone controlled land access to the city—and therefore the food and fuel needed by its 2.3 million Western zone inhabitants.

Meanwhile, in the spring of 1948, U.S.-Soviet tensions elsewhere in Europe escalated. In February, the Soviet leaders consolidated their ascendency in Eastern Europe by instigating a political coup in Prague that converted the government of Czechoslovakia, the one remaining democracy in the region, into another Soviet puppet regime. Like other Americans, Marshall was alarmed at this further evidence of Soviet aggression. But as so often, he urged a cautious response. When, in March, Truman's speechwriters prepared a bellicose address for the president to deliver to Congress on recent Soviet iniquities, Marshall strongly objected. The president's language was "too tough," too warlike, too belligerent, he declared. He should be calmer, more businesslike in stating the facts. While in Pinehurst for the weekend he composed a more restrained alternative and submitted it to Bohlen and Clifford for their comments. The two advisers were not impressed. Clifford rejoined that the president's message, to be effective, had to be blunt. At a later session of the foreign policy group George Elsey, Truman's Harvard-educated speechwriter, rudely reported that all those present thought Marshall's draft "stank."[65] Truman himself rejected Marshall's proposal as too timid, and on March 17 delivered a tough network-broadcast speech to a joint session of Congress that accused the Soviet Union of destroying "the independence and democratic character of a whole series of nations in Eastern and Central Europe" and deliberately sabotaging all efforts to achieve international peace. The president also used the occasion to plug the ERP, still working its way through Congress and—to underscore American resolve to defend "the free nations of Europe" from "communist control and police-state rule"—recommended enactment of UMT for the United States.[66]

The Prague coup was soon followed by a much more incendiary Soviet provocation. For months the Russian military governors in Berlin had been tightening access to the Allied zones of the city, stopping Western trains, inspecting freight shipments, closely checking the credentials of personnel. But the decision to force the Western powers out of Berlin completely by shutting down all surface traffic into and out of the city was triggered by the American-British-French decision in early June 1948 to unify their German occupation zones as a step toward creating a future West German state. The new "Trizonia" would become the nucleus of that state, while simultaneously, to help revive the German economy, there would be a new German currency to replace the existing devalued and distrusted prewar reichsmark.

The Soviets saw these moves, understandably perhaps, as threats to their status in Germany and their continued domination of Eastern Europe. They reacted decisively. After warning that they would apply economic and administrative sanctions to force exclusive circulation in Berlin of their own Soviet-issued currency, on June 24 they halted all passenger trains and all motor traffic on the autobahn into the city, leaving untouched only the air corridors, which they considered incapable of supplying its people with sufficient food and coal.

What should the Western powers do? Faced with the growing Soviet truculence over Berlin, Marshall was initially resolute, more resolute than in March. In late April, as the Russians began to tighten the noose, he and Lovett announced publicly: "We intend to stay in Berlin and will meet force with force."[67] The full stoppage of Allied traffic into the city in late June caught Marshall during a health crisis. In a visit to Walter Reed Hospital for a medical checkup the doctors discovered a greatly enlarged right kidney and recommended its removal. Marshall refused the operation but was out of action for several days while Lovett served as his voice at the urgent meetings at the Pentagon and the White House that followed the full Russian ground blockade.

Despite his initial resolve, during the course of the evolving Berlin crisis Marshall played a secondary role. Since war was a possibility, his military experience counted, of course, but the major players were the president himself and Gen. Lucius Clay, military governor of the American occupation zone. One option for the Western powers—the choice favored by General Clay—was to defy the blockade and send supplies by road to the city under military escort. The questions were: Would the Russians meet the convoy with blazing guns, and would the confrontation be the trigger for World War III?

In the course of the blockade crisis Marshall's was again the voice of caution and prudence. He dismissed the dire predictions of imminent war by Secretary Forrestal and other alarmists. He was painfully aware of U.S. military weakness following the precipitous post-1945 demobilization and doubted the country's preparedness for a full-scale war if one should erupt. Besides the manpower dearth, the United States, though still the only nation possessing atom bombs, lacked the ability to deliver them to an enemy target. Yet when, at a White House meeting in early May the nervous and excitable Forrestal proposed a whopping increase in the defense budget to meet the escalating crisis, Marshall supported the president's negative. The policy "of this country," he told the group, "was based on the assumption that there would not be war and that we should not plunge into war preparation which would bring about the very thing we are taking these steps to prevent."[68] Yet the secretary was not totally opposed to a little saber rattling himself, giving his approval to sending two squadrons of B-29 bombers to Britain and Germany to show that the Western powers meant business, but stipulating that these not be equipped to carry atom bombs. As for Clay's proposal of the military convoy option, Marshall strongly advised the president against it, and Truman took his advice.

Despite his caution Marshall fully supported the massive Allied airlift of food and fuel to the Western sectors of Berlin devised as an alternative to an armed challenge on the ground. On June 30 he issued a press release announcing that the United States was in Berlin as the result of agreements with the occupying governments and "we intend to stay." He added that "maximum use of air transport would be made to supply the civilian population."[69] In mid-July, with the air traffic system under way, he told a cabinet meeting that refusing to yield to the Soviets had been essential to prevent "the rest of our European policy" from "failure."[70] And, of course, he was right. The heroic Berlin airlift ("Operation Vittles") would last almost a full year and save the city from starvation at an easily tolerated cost. Meanwhile, the Americans would win the lasting gratitude of millions of former German enemies.

During these jittery days, when a clash with Soviet forces—whether accidental or deliberate—still seemed a real danger, Marshall and his State Department assistants and overseas diplomats conducted earnest negotiations to conclude a peaceful settlement of the crisis. In mid-July, Marshall's attention was drawn away from pressing international concerns to memorialize his revered mentor John J. Pershing, who had died at Walter Reed Hospital at the age of eighty-seven. Marshall's eulogy reflected his own values as a military man. "A great soldier, devoid of political and personal ambitions," he intoned, "his influence went far toward shaping the destinies of our Armies in two great wars."[71] Pershing had asked that Marshall make the funeral arrangements at his death, and the secretary dutifully followed his chief's orders with a state funeral with all the trimmings and interment at Arlington National Cemetery.

Meanwhile, the negotiations with the Russians over Berlin produced scant results. In late July, Soviet foreign minister Molotov agreed to see the American, French, and British ambassadors to discuss the Berlin situation. Stalin himself met with them two days later. The Russian leaders seemed interested in a settlement, Walter Bedell Smith, now U.S. ambassador in Moscow, cabled Marshall soon after. Both Stalin and Molotov, he said, were "literally dripping with sweet reasonableness and desire not to embarrass."[72] Stalin denied that he had ever intended to eject the Western powers from Berlin but then made it clear that lifting the blockade required the end of Western plans to establish a West German government and the adoption by all Berlin of the Soviet-backed "Ostmark" currency. Smith was inclined to a compromise on both issues; the French and British seemed receptive. But Marshall and the president both demurred. To yield even minimally to Soviet conditions, they believed, was a form of appeasement that would alienate non-Communist Europeans and encourage further Soviet aggression. Smith, Marshall cabled, should remind the Russians that the Allies were in Berlin by right, not sufferance, and that they would not suspend their plans for Germany, economic or political, as preconditions for negotiation.

The Berlin issue remained unsettled by the time the third meeting of the UN General Assembly convened in Paris in mid-September. By now the airlift was performing well. Supported by streams of British and American C-47s and C-54s arriving, with bare minutes of clearance, at Tempelhof and Gatow airfields, the people of Berlin were managing to survive. But winter was coming, and the burden of meeting the increased fuel needs of Berliners threatened to severely tax the already strained delivery system. At the Paris UN meeting Marshall prepared to confer with America's partners as well as the Soviets on how to resolve the dispute peacefully and, if the Russians remained adamant, to ask for a UN Security Council resolution condemning the blockade.

The new negotiations with the Soviets at Paris proved no more successful than those that had preceded them. Yet Marshall remained hopeful about America's effort to restrain Russian aggression. Speaking to the French and British foreign policy leaders at the Quai d'Orsay, he remarked that everywhere the Russians were in retreat. American policies had "put Western Germany on its feet" and the Western powers could now "really say that we are on the road to victory."[73] Soon after, the Western Allies submitted a statement to the Security Council condemning the Soviet action on Berlin "as a threat to international peace and security" and asking for a UN censure resolution against the Russians.

Meanwhile, back in Washington, while Lovett and Kennan were urging the Western powers to avoid too precipitous an action that might further provoke the Soviets, Truman was losing patience. Hoping to fend off his left-wing opponent Henry Wallace's charges of "warmonger," he decided to end the Berlin deadlock before the approaching presidential election by bypassing the State Department and intervening directly in the negotiations. On October 5 he informed the department that he would send Chief Justice Fred Vinson to see Stalin in person to explain to him his deep desire for a peaceful settlement of the Berlin issue. Seeing disaster ahead, Lovett rushed to the White House to interdict the scheme. If he proceeded, he told Truman, he risked Marshall's resignation. Marshall himself directly intervened. He had discussed the Vinson plan with the president by teletype while in Paris for the UN meeting on Berlin and managed to get Truman to reconsider the move. The press, however, reported that he and the president were at loggerheads and that Marshall might indeed resign rather than approve the Vinson ploy. Marshall returned to Washington both to reinforce the president's new resolve and to disavow the rumor that he and the president remained at odds. In an off-the-record press conference he told the reporters that he had advised Truman from Paris to avoid any appearance of U.S. unilateral action on Berlin as certain to offend our airlift allies. In any case, by the time Marshall returned to Paris the uproar had subsided; the Vinson mission never took place.

Thereafter the Western powers' resolution wended its slow way through the UN with no action taken. In fact the Berlin airlift crisis would not end until early May 1949, when the Russians, convinced that they could not starve the city out, finally agreed to lift the land blockade. Marshall undoubtedly cheered, but four months earlier, as he had planned, he had submitted his resignation as secretary of state and was not at Foggy Bottom to celebrate the victory with his colleagues.

One of Marshall's contributions to the diplomacy of the early Cold War was his role in launching the North Atlantic Treaty Organization (NATO). Linking the United States and ultimately twenty-eight European* countries, including Britain, France, Germany, Italy, Spain, and several lesser powers, in a treaty of mutual defense and military cooperation, it would be a cornerstone of American foreign policy for more than sixty years and, with modifications, still is today. Its adoption was a momentous break with the "no entangling alliances" precedent established by Washington and Jefferson more than a century and a half previously and confirmed America's leadership of the anti-Soviet "free world" bloc.

Marshall was not NATO's father; Ernest Bevin of Britain fits that role far better. But he had, during the war, contributed to the principle of Western military cooperation that it epitomized. He also helped undermine the wall that the United States had erected around itself from the days of Washington more than 150 years before when, in September 1947, at an inter-American conference in Rio, he supported a mutual defense pact with the Latin American nations of the Western Hemisphere. Yet if the Rio agreement violated the Washington-Jefferson precedent, it did not violate the Monroe Doctrine of U.S. hemispheric defense, and was an allowable exception to it. Not so the NATO treaty, which extended the American protective cover primarily to Europe and committed the United States to the ultimate "entangling alliance."

NATO's germ was the mutual defense treaty, aimed primar-

---

*The recent list includes another North American nation, Canada, and one country that straddles the European-Asian border, Turkey.

ily against a future resurgent Germany, that Britain and France signed with the smaller Benelux nations at Brussels in March 1948. Instigated by Bevin, both Marshall and Truman gave it their verbal support. But it still left the British foreign secretary dissatisfied. The United States, he felt, must be drawn into the collective defense of Europe against the greater Soviet threat now looming. After the Communist coup in Czechoslovakia, a resurgent Germany no longer seemed the most serious danger to the free world.

The State Department was of two minds on the issue of American participation. On the side of caution was Kennan. Whatever his role in launching the Cold War, Kennan now opposed any action that further encouraged it or, rather, threatened to turn it into a hot war. A military alliance with the Western European nations would mean, he wrote, "a final militarization of the present dividing-line through Europe." It would, he said on another occasion, make the division of Europe "insoluble by any other than military means."[74]

Marshall and Lovett were more receptive. At first skeptical of Bevin's proposals, but egged on by John Hickerson of the department's Office of European Affairs, they soon embraced the need for a joint American-European military commitment against Soviet aggression. But they had reservations about too visible an American sponsorship. As in the case of the European Recovery Program, the initiative must come from the European nations themselves, not the United States.

In the succeeding months—the closing stretch of Marshall's State Department tenure—exploratory talks among the Western nations on a mutual defense treaty proceeded apace. Marshall and Lovett played leading roles in the discussions but, acknowledging the American public's aversion to permanent overseas promises, avoided publicity. In October the conferees agreed on a basic outline for a mutual Western defense treaty to include the United States. During this interval, inflamed by the Berlin blockade and the Prague coup, Marshall—though not publicly—made one of the most heated attacks on the Soviet Union of his career. Discussing with the foreign minister of Sweden that traditionally neutral country's possible membership in the pending agreement, he called the Soviet Union "utterly ruthless and devoid of all the basic decencies of modern civilization." It "had seized and used every expediency to serve its particular ends without regard for ethics." If not "opposed," this "ruthless force" could lead to "a gradual establishment over the world of police states." The United States believed, he forcefully stated, that it "must be met by a unity of such states as are willing to accept the challenge."[75]

Marshall's participation in these and other department negotiations was limited by his growing infirmities. In late July he wrote to the retired Stimson: "The fact of the matter is that Lovett bears the principal burden as I get away whenever possible . . . on the weekends in order to get a little relaxation so that I can be clearheaded for the difficult days that are constantly developing and will be with me I suppose until my retirement in June."[76]

Marshall was not present as the NATO conferees hammered out the treaty's final provisions in Washington. He was staying at the U.S. Embassy in Paris with Katherine for meetings of the UN General Assembly and Security Council to consider the Berlin crisis and other matters. On October 9 he flew back to Washington to help Lovett stop the president from sending Chief Justice Vinson to Moscow to confer with Stalin over Berlin. He returned to Paris soon after, when Truman abandoned his lame-brained plan. Though busy with international issues, he and Katherine took time off in Europe for tours of U.S. military cemeteries and sightseeing in France, Italy, and Greece. One of their trips was to Anzio, where Katherine visited Allen's grave. They were pleased to find the cemetery and the town itself, both badly damaged in the war, well along in the repair process. On October 19 the Marshalls met Pope Pius XII at his country estate outside Rome. The secretary was pleased with the pontiff's favorable view of ERP.

He was still in Paris when, defying all the negative polls, Truman won election to a full presidential term over Dewey and brought with him Democratic majorities in both houses of Congress. Marshall cabled Truman his congratulations: "You have put over the greatest one man fight in American history." He graciously added: "I am thinking more of Mrs. Truman's and Margaret's [the president's daughter] pride and joy than of your own satisfaction."[77]

The Marshalls returned to Washington in late November. The secretary went immediately to Foggy Bottom, Katherine to Leesburg. They had Thanksgiving dinner in the private car of the vice president of the Southern Railroad near Roanoke, where they had gone to see VMI's football team play Virginia Polytechnic Institute. Soon after, Marshall entered Walter Reed for his postponed kidney operation. The procedure went well. The lesion was a benign cyst, and the surgeons removed the right kidney to play it safe. Recuperation was slow, however. Marshall was not released from the hospital until the very end of December and missed the traditional Christmas festivities with his stepchildren and their families. He was still in pain when he finally got to Pinehurst, his North Carolina winter home, and recovered his strength only gradually. Hoping to accelerate the healing process, Truman arranged for him to spend time in warm and sunny San Juan, Puerto Rico, at the headquarters of the wartime Caribbean naval command. Marshall's recuperation was further assisted by a stay during Mardi Gras week at the guesthouse near New Orleans of his old VMI classmate Leonard Nicholson, now owner of the *New Orleans Times-Picayune*.

Marshall's absence from the foreign policy stage in late 1948 had political as well as medical sources. From the beginning he had decided to leave office after the presidential election. He had signed on for a limited term, understanding that he was to serve as an advocate for Truman's foreign policy in a politically divided nation. Though the conclusion to resign was independent of who won the election in November, it was clearly made easier by Truman's remarkable upset victory and the return of Congress to more internationalist control. In Marshall's view he had served his allotted time and purpose and could now return to private life. Most Washington insiders knew of the secretary's plans, but when they were announced at the UN meetings just after the election returns reached Paris, the foreign delegates were taken by surprise.

Three days into the new year Marshall submitted a short letter of resignation to Truman. It thanked the president for his personal kindness and expressed his "affectionate regard and great respect."[78] He would leave office on January 20, the day Truman was inaugurated for his full term. The usual flood of congratulations poured in to mark the end of Marshall's foreign policy career and what was assumed to be his working life in general. British foreign secretary Bevin paid generous tribute to his American ally as one of the great American secretaries of state. "I personally, and the British people, will not forget all that you did for victory and in your present office for peace and world recovery."[79] Dean Acheson, already Marshall's designated successor, marked the occasion with a handwritten note. Significantly, Secretary of State Acheson emphasized his predecessor's persona, not his accomplishments. Among the men he had personally known, he wrote, Marshall ranked with the revered Justice Oliver Wendell Holmes of the Supreme Court as a man endowed with "greatness," which Acheson described as "a quality of character," not "the result of circumstances." It had "to do with grandeur and with completeness of character."[80]

Expressions of rhapsodic esteem from colleagues, friends, and professional supporters are inevitable on the occasion of retirement from prominent public life. But the less sentimental historian must bluntly ask: Was Marshall's tenure as secretary of state a successful one? What had he accomplished? Had he been a strong motive force in the events of the early Cold War? Had he helped lead the nation along wisely chosen paths?

First, it has to be said that it was not Marshall who had driven U.S. foreign policy during his two years in office: Truman himself was chief motor force. As clearly shown by his aggressive response to the crisis in Greece and Turkey and the decision to support the strong Zionist position on Palestine, the president had been the pivotal figure. In both cases Marshall had advised cautious action. One might argue that the consequences for the world if his voice had been heeded would have more desirable than the actual outcomes, but that is another matter. Truman's aggressive activism had prevailed over his secretary's caveats. But what about the Marshall Plan, probably the most important policy achievement during his months in office? He had not conceived it; he was not its parent. Its naming had been virtually fortuitous.

And another issue: Had he managed his department effectively and efficiently? As in the case of the army, he has been praised for his tenure at Foggy Bottom as an antibureaucratic reformer. But it is known from both Dean Acheson and Scotty Reston that he often seemed more interested in conserving his own time and energies than in making the agency's workers more productive.

Marshall's most effective role as secretary of state had been as the Truman administration's chief foreign policy lobbyist. Confronting dangerous political uncertainties for internationalist foreign policy initiatives, Truman had hired him for the job of selling them to Congress and the public, and he had done so successfully. Standing above the bitter partisan political fray of those years, in collaboration with Senator Vandenberg he had helped forge an American foreign policy consensus that, for good or ill, would last through the rest of the century. In the most important instance, though he had not fathered the Marshall Plan, his defense and support before Congress and at venues around the nation had been essential to its final adoption and funding.

And now he could leave public life and literally cultivate his private garden in the Virginia countryside. Or could he?

CHAPTER 11

ENVOI

After leaving Foggy Bottom, Marshall spent much of his time at Dodona Manor, in Leesburg. In the mornings he would plant his cabbages, radishes, peas, beans, and flowers and launch his aggressive campaigns against Japanese beetles. Until his death the handsome two-story dwelling and its surrounding four acres would be his permanent home, his time there interrupted by stays at the winter cottage in Pinehurst, North Carolina, and occasional vacations in the Adirondacks and in Michigan.

In late June 1949 the *New York Times* Washington reporter William S. White came to Leesburg to see how the retiree was faring. White was impressed by the dwelling. It was "old and . . . beautiful," though "in an impersonal way." But that suited the man it sheltered, for he seemed to the reporter to be a "remote great gentleman," who appeared more "British" than American, by which he meant, White explained, "laconic and honorably strong and distant." White noted that in their interview Marshall avoided any talk of battles. In none of his remarks about the past was there any "war drama." The war to him was, rather, "an enterprise almost inhumanly complex and exasperating, primarily an enterprise of so many million tons of munitions, so many hundreds of miles of inertly resisting terrain, so many temperamental subordinate commanders to cajole." However tight-lipped, Marshall uncharacteristically complained at length about the burdens public office had imposed on him. Selling the ERP to businessmen had been truly irksome. But he reserved his bitterest complaints for the grilling over Pearl Harbor he had endured from the congressional joint committee in December 1945. That experience he summarized in one sarcastic phrase as "a *charming* week." "The net impression," White concluded as he left to return to Washington, "is of a man to whom duty and honor are as real as the oak trees that stand with such sure strength about him here, a hard just man with an inner life which, surely, few have ever really known."[1] All told, White's was as frank and accurate a portrayal of the essential Marshall as any in his lifetime.

Marshall may have found it easy to leave public life, but Truman found it hard to let him go. Yet if he had to leave, the president felt, he would ease his retirement financially. Marshall had severed his official connection with the army when he accepted the post at State. Now the president arranged to restore his formal five-star military rank, providing him with considerably higher pay as a retiree than he would otherwise have received.

Truman and Acheson also continued to turn to him for advice and help. As a private citizen Marshall continued to speak to influential groups on policy matters. On May 6 he addressed the Foreign Policy Association in New York on the subject of public education in the field of international affairs. His speech to ninety prominent business leaders at the Waldorf-Astoria acknowledged the difficulty of awakening Americans to the importance of overseas events to their safety and prosperity. He recalled the isolationist excesses of the years preceding Pearl Harbor that had ill fitted the nation to face the threats and dangers, including the military hazards, from abroad. The war had of course helped break down Americans' sense of insulation from foreign events, he noted. "In the last ten years, public opinion . . . has progressed a long way toward maturity," as reflected by support for the UN, the Berlin airlift, ERP, and other programs and acts.[2] Although his role in creating NATO had been secondary, Acheson urged him to appear before the Senate Foreign Relations Committee to help push for final adoption of the treaty, signed on April 4. Marshall accepted but the secretary of state, deferring perhaps to his predecessor's infirmities, soon informed him that his help for passage would not be needed. After considerable debate the Senate approved the treaty on July 25.

In the fall of 1949 Truman found a civilian job for Marshall as president of the American Red Cross to replace its embattled head, who was preparing to resign. Enthusiastically seconded by Katherine, the offer seemed congenial. It was not full retirement; there was real work to do; and confined to accepting speaking invitations, receiving awards, answering his mail, and practicing microagriculture, he was restless. In any case, he pledged, it would be his "last public effort."[3]

As president of the disaster-relief organization Marshall untangled its overcomplicated lines of authority and pushed for better funding for its blood-bank system and enhanced medical support for the families of servicemen. Though it left him relatively free of the pressures of the past, the job proved worthwhile, and he performed it successfully. But he could not help following events abroad with intense interest. And there was much to follow.

In China the months of late 1949 and early 1950 witnessed the final flight to Formosa of Chiang, his entourage, his treasury, and his remaining Nationalist troops, leaving the mainland uncontested to Chairman Mao and his Communist forces. On

October 1, 1949, the victorious Communists announced creation of the People's Republic of China, with its capital at Beijing and the Chinese Communist Party as its "vanguard." This "loss of China," the world's most populous country, fanned the fury of the China Lobby. The evil outcome cried out for explanation; it could not be Chiang's and his colleagues' fault, the lobbyists insisted. Behind it must lie the mistakes—nay, the betrayals and treasonous acts—of high-placed Americans. Their outcry soon merged with the overwrought, sensational charges of the junior senator from Wisconsin, Joseph McCarthy, who in February 1950, in Wheeling, West Virginia, attracted national attention when he notoriously claimed that more than two hundred men in high positions in the State Department had betrayed their country to the Communists.

Marshall was no longer secretary; his successor, Dean Acheson, would bear the brunt of McCarthy's reckless Wheeling charges. But Marshall had not been able to avoid totally the loyalty panic that seized the nation during the Truman administration. In June 1947, while still in office, he had been forced by the growing anti-Communist surge to establish within his department a Personnel Security Board to ferret out suspected spies and traitors. Under Conrad Snow, a department lawyer, in its first six months the board detected, and presumably fired, all of ten State Department employees out of thousands. Eventually the Wisconsin senator would take aim directly at Marshall, but even before the Wheeling speech, Senator Owen Brewster, one of the unfriendly Republican committee members on the joint congressional Pearl Harbor investigation, was accusing Marshall of responsibility for Chiang's defeat.

Meanwhile, elsewhere in East Asia, another dangerous and divisive storm was brewing, one that would also draw Marshall into its vortex. The place was Korea, a large populous peninsula attached at its wide northern edge to both Chinese Manchuria and Soviet Siberia. A harshly exploited colony of imperial Japan from 1910 onward, following Japan's defeat in 1945 it was occupied by Soviet forces in the north and by American troops in the south, with the border between the two jurisdictions set at the thirty-eighth parallel. As the Cold War emerged into the open, it proved impossible to unite the peninsula by peaceable means, and by 1948 two political entities had evolved—in the north a Communist regime, with its capital in Pyongyang, led by Kim Il Sung; in the south the Republic of Korea (ROK), led by Syngman Rhee, an authoritarian politician and determined anti-Communist, with its capital in Seoul.

In January 1950, in a speech to the National Press Club, Secretary Acheson made a point of excluding both Nationalist Formosa (Taiwan) and South Korea from the boundaries of a strategic defense perimeter in East Asia that the United States pledged to protect with its military forces. Kim Il Sung may well have seen this as an opportunity to forcibly unite the two Koreas under Communist rule, safe from U.S. intervention. Stalin gave Kim's move his reluctant approval and on June 25, 1950, the North Korean army crossed the thirty-eighth parallel and thrust into South Korea intent on conquest and forced unification. With far superior numbers and equipment, it quickly overwhelmed the ROK defenders, including a few hundred American military advisers still garrisoned on the peninsula.

The American reaction was swift and vigorous. At home in Missouri when the news broke, Truman was swept by outrage. It was, he concluded, a case of naked aggression, an act that America and the non-Communist world could not tolerate. If left unchallenged it would assuredly lead to further Communist aggression, perhaps even in Europe. Even before he returned to Washington the president told his daughter, Margaret: "We are going to fight."4 But in addition to his moral indignation and Cold War fears, the president was propelled by domestic politics. The China Lobby, led by McCarthy, had been screaming that he, and the Democrats in general, were "soft on Communism." Whatever the diplomatic and moral dimensions of the Communist attack, then, the health of the party and the administration required that the United States not take it lying down.

Back in Washington, Truman called a meeting at Blair House of his chief State Department and Pentagon advisers. Their conclusions were unanimous: The United States must act promptly and decisively. The Soviet Union was undoubtedly behind the invasion; the Russians were testing America's Cold War resolve. South Korea must be defended to show Stalin and the free world that the United States would not be intimidated. A second Blair House meeting determined that U.S. air and naval forces would be deployed to stop the invaders, but, with the weakness of the South Korean army not yet apparent, it was decided that no ground forces would be sent. MacArthur, from his proconsular base in nearby Japan, would be placed in overall command of all U.S. forces to be engaged.

The catastrophic rout of the ROK army quickly ended the ban on U.S. ground forces. American infantry combat units from Japan soon landed in Korea to help the faltering Republic of Korea troops. Meanwhile, the American military operation received the sanction of the United Nations. In the temporary absence of Soviet representatives, who could have vetoed the resolutions, the UN Security Council ordered an immediate cease-fire and withdrawal of all North Korean forces from the south and urged UN member nations to assist militarily efforts to restore peace to the peninsula. Soon after, the UN endorsed MacArthur as a single commander for the forces to defeat the invaders. The UN's actions made it possible thereafter for the United States to depict the intervention as a joint UN-U.S. operation and call it a "police action" rather than a war. And in fact seventeen nations ultimately sent troops to defend the beleaguered South Koreans, though the major military punch was always American.

The arrival of American forces changed the course of the military struggle. But not at first. The initial units were composed of ill-trained, out-of-shape occupation troops from garrisons in Japan who were unable to stem the Communist advance. By early August the North Koreans had captured Seoul and crowded their adversaries into a pocket around the southeastern port of Pusan. There, reinforced by new, better-trained army and marine units, the ROK and the Americans beat off strong enemy attacks. On the North Korean side, meanwhile, losses had been high, many times the American casualty list, though their weakening effect was not yet apparent and the survival of an independent South Korean entity seemed doubtful.

It was at this point that Truman once again sought Marshall's help. With his enthusiastic support, in July 1947 the president had succeeded in inducing Congress to pass the National Security Act, creating a new Department of Defense to replace the separate War and Navy Departments that had coexisted—and squabbled—since the early days of the republic. His choice as first secretary of the unified services was James Forrestal, the neurotic former secretary of the navy, whose differences with Truman over Palestine and the military budget triggered clinical depression and his suicide in March 1949. His successor was Louis Johnson, who had been assistant secretary of war when Marshall became deputy chief of staff in 1938. Johnson was a combative and unstable man, and he and the president did not get along. In early July, just days after the North Korean army crossed the thirty-eighth parallel, Truman motored down to Leesburg and told Marshall of his dissatisfaction with the West Virginian. Would he be willing to succeed him? He was content with his present status, Marshall responded, but he was a soldier and would obey the president's wishes if so ordered. On September 6, 1950, after the Marshalls returned from a vacation in northern Michigan, the president directly offered him the post and he accepted, with the sole condition that Lovett be simultaneously appointed his deputy.

The Senate confirmed the new appointment, but this time not without dissent. Times had changed since 1947. Marshall retained a substantial reservoir of goodwill but was no longer beyond attack. The tensions and setbacks of the Cold War had created resentments and frustrations that now spilled over onto the appointee-designate. In the Senate confirmation hearings Indiana senator William Jenner, a right-wing Republican, blasted Marshall along with Truman and Acheson. Referring to a wide range of his actions as chief of staff and China negotiator, Jenner declared he was "not only willing" but actually "eager to play the front man for traitors." It was no new role for him, Jenner insisted, for rather than being "the greatest living American," as Truman had said, Marshall was "a living lie."[5] Shocked by Jenner's venom, Democrats and several moderate Republicans came to Marshall's defense. Massachusetts Republican senator Leverett Saltonstall, for one, denounced the charge that Marshall's life had been a lie. Indeed, if "ever there was a life spent in the interests of our country . . . it is the life of George C. Marshall," he declared.[6] Despite Jenner and his supporters, the appointment was confirmed by a Senate vote of 57 to 11, with the support of fifteen Republicans, but Marshall had been wounded, and in later months more blows would follow.

Marshall moved into his Pentagon office on September 19 just in time to see the tide turn in Korea. For six weeks the fighting at besieged Pusan had raged on. Then, on September 15, UN forces under MacArthur's command made a risky but successful end run, landing at Inchon, far to the north on the peninsula's west coast, opposite Seoul. Soon the Pusan defenders to their south broke out of the besieged perimeter. The North Koreans, now outgunned and outnumbered, failed under the combined assault and retreated in panic northward toward the thirty-eighth parallel, whence they had come. On September 26 MacArthur announced the reoccupation of Seoul. UN forces were soon approaching the old border between the two Koreas and facing the problem of whether to cross the line and occupy Kim Il Sung's Communist domain. Anticipating a successful outcome, on the day of the Inchon landing the Joint Chiefs told MacArthur to look ahead "for a possible occupation of North Korea." On September 27, with the approval of Truman, Marshall, Acheson, and Bradley, they directed him to "conduct military operations . . . north of the 38 Parallel" for the purpose of destroying the North Korean armed forces.[7] Three major constraints were imposed, however: He must not cross either the Manchurian or Soviet borders, order American planes to fly over Russian and Chinese territory, or allow UN—as opposed to ROK—troops to reach the Yalu River on the Korean-Chinese border. If either the Soviet Union or Red China introduced troops into Korea, he should immediately refer the matter to Washington.

Marshall's reactions to the tumultuous events in the Far East before his return to office are unknown. Korea had seldom won his attention in the past. During the closing months of his China mission he had become aware of difficulties with the Soviets over establishing a trusteeship for the former Japanese colony. He was also, of course, conscious of political differences between the opposing Communist and anti-Communist camps within each part of the divided country. As secretary of state, at the Moscow foreign ministers' conference, he had clashed briefly with Molotov over the future disposition of the peninsula. Marshall disagreed

with his State Department policy planners, who believed Korea
of no strategic importance to the United States and advised that
it be abandoned. Such a course, he feared, would lead to a Communist takeover. But later, as a civilian between posts, like most
other Americans he thought little of the issues so far away, in such
an obscure corner of the world.

As he moved into his new office at the Pentagon, Marshall
was painfully aware of problems he now faced. Besides Korea,
the first to confront him was the dearth of military manpower
to fight the hot war now raging in the Far East and to make
credible U.S. foreign policy in the new era of superpower rivalry.
His plan for universal military service in peacetime had already
been rejected by Congress, but he hoped that he could meet the
country's needs by better management of the manpower available
under the now-renewed wartime draft law. It was at this point
that Marshall asked the president to appoint Anna Rosenberg, an
expert on human resources, as assistant secretary of defense for
manpower, and it was on this occasion (see chapter 10) that he
fought successfully for her confirmation in the face of opposition
that included a substantial dose of anti-Semitism.

In fact the postwar military manpower shortage may have
been Marshall's fault, or at least it so seemed to retired admiral Arthur Radford, a military-preparedness zealot. According to
the admiral, Marshall's fight for UMT, however wise for the future, had ignored immediate short-term American defense needs.
"In the years," he declared, "when General Marshall might have
tried to convince the president that our military strength was so
dangerously low that it might invite attack, he elected not to do
so."[8] In any event, like many other Cold War planners, Marshall
changed his mind when confronted by Korea and signed on to
the recent National Security Council Report 68 (NSC-68), calling for aggressive American rearmament to meet Communist

challenges. The report, written under the direction of Paul Nitze, Kennan's successor as head of the State Department's Policy Planning Staff, extended his predecessor's notion of containment to embrace a wider range of places considered essential for American security. It also called for an aggressive expansion of U.S. defense spending to meet the new commitments, to as much as $35 to $40 billion a year, three times the amount under current plans. Marshall would remain a voice of caution in the Cold War chorus, but as secretary of defense not by very much.

In his new post Marshall could count on the help of one of his favorite generals, Omar Bradley, now head of the Joint Chiefs. J. Lawton Collins, another successful ETO general, would be presiding as his deputy. He would also have the services of his good right hand, Robert Lovett, who now, as scheduled, returned to government as deputy secretary of defense to his old chief at State.

Marshall arrived at the Pentagon soon after the Inchon landings and the headlong northward retreat of the Communist invaders. He congratulated MacArthur on his brilliant stroke at Inchon in a handwritten letter on September 30. MacArthur responded with the false bonhomie that often characterized the public exchanges between the two men. "Thanks George, for your fine message," he wrote. "It brings back vividly the memory of past wars and the complete coordination and perfect unity of cooperation which has always existed in our mutual relationships and martial endeavors."[9] The issue of what to do when the rapidly advancing American and ROK forces reached the thirty-eighth parallel had presumably been addressed by the Joint Chiefs' directive of September 27. But how would the Chinese respond when the UN's forces reached the Yalu, their border with Korea? Would they and/or the Russians perceive the advance as a threat and massively intrude, transforming the UN police action into a great-power war? Marshall had approved the September Joint

Chiefs' directive that placed limits on MacArthur's actions. But he soon muddied the issue. On September 29, having heard that ROK divisions would halt at the thirty-eighth parallel "for regrouping," he cabled MacArthur: "We want you to feel unhampered tactically and strategically to proceed north of the 38th Parallel."[10] Ten days later the Joint Chiefs warned the general against taking any action on actual Chinese territory without prior authorization from Washington. But whatever the Secretary of Defense and his colleagues intended, MacArthur chose to interpret the Pentagon's position as releasing him from the Joint Chiefs' restrictions and would cite Marshall's September 29 directive in his later defense following his removal from command.

In fact, during the whole cacophonous controversy over Korea between MacArthur and his superiors in Washington, the secretary of defense would waver and delay and generally fail to take firm positions on his subordinate's actions. As his most scholarly biographer, D. Clayton James, has noted, MacArthur was indeed "guilty of insubordination toward his commander in chief," but "his guilt must be mitigated by the imprecision and contradictory nature of his orders."[11] And James has a point. If the general's actions after Inchon were the record of a would-be "American Caesar"—a man with dangerous political ambitions—they were nourished and fortified by the hesitations and vacillations of his bosses, including Marshall and the Joint Chiefs.

Why was Marshall's voice so tentative and ambiguous? In part his dithering reflected his long-standing command philosophy: Choose the best men as local commanders and give them free rein. But as in the past, it also represented fear of MacArthur's stature in the public mind, and the power and influence of his many political friends.

Be that as it was, by the early fall the possibility of uniting the entire peninsula under a pro-Western regime seemed to MacArthur an irresistible option. Arguing that there were not enough effective ROK troops available to do the job alone, on October 17 he informed the Joint Chiefs that he intended to ignore their limit on which UN forces would be allowed to advance to the Yalu border. Neither the Joint Chiefs nor the Defense Department protested at first, and when the chiefs finally did, their response was a feeble admonition: "Your action is a matter of some concern here."[12]

MacArthur's decision would awaken a sleeping tiger. By early October UN observers were detecting suspicious movements of Manchurian-based Chinese troops along the North Korean border. Yet at the meeting with the president and his military and civilian advisers at Wake Island in midmonth, a confident and cheerful MacArthur brushed aside the dangers of Chinese intervention. The Korean War was won, he declared. Formal Communist resistance would end by Thanksgiving; American troops would be back in Japan by Christmas. As for the Chinese Communist troops, they would not cross the Korean border, he said, because they lacked the airpower to protect their forces against UN attack should they invade. The Russians *did* have the airpower, but, he believed, they could not coordinate it with the Communist troops on the ground. In his impressive performance MacArthur praised the president and the Defense Department for their unstinting support: "No commander in the history of war has ever had more complete and adequate support from all agencies in Washington than I have."[13]

Marshall did not come to the Wake Island meeting. It had been arranged by the president ostensibly to impress the Korean commander with the administration's views of the war as a limited conflict. But Truman obviously had political motives as well for the long trip across the Pacific. The Democrats faced a chancy midterm congressional election in November, and at Wake Truman hoped to demonstrate to the voters his party's command of events. In the event, the meeting revealed the clash of personalities among the men leading the first hot war of the Cold War era. Resentful of Washington's efforts to hold him back, MacArthur, in the view of some of Truman's party, was rude to the president. Like Marshall, Truman in turn seemed wary of MacArthur. Deservedly or not, he was a war hero. His reputation as a masterful proconsul in Japan, dragging the defeated nation from the Middle Ages into the modern, democratic world, was formidable. Public opinion on Korea, moreover, was on his bellicose side, making it difficult to defy him. During the war Marshall himself had found his relations with the commander of the Southwest Pacific theater a distasteful balancing act, and in the end had often been forced to defer to his wishes. The two men had always been vivid contrasts in military type, and Korea highlighted the differences. According to William Manchester, MacArthur's popular biographer, the commander in Korea had "a warrior's mind," and "preferred the warlike spirit to the military spirit." Marshall, on the other hand, "was more of a martial administrator."[14] Marshall's absence from the weekend mid-Pacific conference was excusable on the grounds of his brief time in office. But it was probably also rooted in his desire to avoid the stigma of political partisanship. Perhaps, too, as Army Secretary Frank Pace would claim, it was out of disdain for MacArthur or, alternatively, in the opinion of a hostile MacArthur partisan, it was because Marshall's "fine Virginia [sic] patrician nose does not tolerate the daily smells of Asia."[15]

In any case the meeting at Wake Island settled nothing; MacArthur had become, and would remain, the proverbial loose cannon. No one, it seemed, could tell him what to do. The military historian Russell Weigley writes of a Pentagon meeting that included the Joint Chiefs, along with the president, Secretaries Acheson and Marshall, and others, where Gen. Matthew Ridgway, then deputy chief of staff, asked why MacArthur could not be bluntly told to do what his superiors demanded. His question was greeted, Ridgway reported, by "a frightened silence." Then, on leaving the meeting with air force head Hoyt Vandenberg, Ridgway asked why the chiefs did not give MacArthur categorical directions. The general responded: "What good would that do? He wouldn't obey the orders."[16]

The crisis of Korea came to a head as UN troops approached the Chinese border. In late October advancing South Korean and American units encountered soldiers of the People's Republic. Judged at first as "volunteers," it soon became apparent that they were regulars from Mao's vast army. To check further infiltration, MacArthur ordered his air arm to bomb the bridges across the Yalu. Fearing that the enemy was planning to launch a full-scale Asian war to distract the United States from potential aggressive Soviet moves in Europe, the alarmed Joint Chiefs directed MacArthur to cease all air attacks within five miles of the border, including raids on the Yalu bridges. MacArthur, who would later blame Marshall for the order, predictably protested. To cease such attacks would threaten the "ultimate destruction of the forces under my command," he wrote the chiefs. He agreed to suspend the raids this time but refused to "accept the responsibility" for the consequences without assurance that the president understood the circumstances.[17] At this point Marshall and the Joint Chiefs backed down. The secretary remained skeptical of MacArthur's tactics and troop dispositions, but displayed what Acheson later characterized as a "curious quiescence." On November 7 he sent MacArthur a conciliatory, if uncandid, letter reassuring him that Washington still had confidence in him. "Everyone here, Defense, State, and the President, is intensely desirous of supporting you," he wrote. But expressing the administration's fears of triggering a world war with the Soviet Union, he warned: "We are faced with an extremely grave international problem which could easily lead to a world disaster."[18]

Still not convinced that the Chinese intended a full-scale intervention, in late November MacArthur launched a major offensive designed to end remaining North Korean resistance and, as phrased in the popular press, to bring "the boys home by Christmas." Instead he brought the full weight of the People's Republic army down on his head. On November 25, 260,000 Chinese troops, led by Gen. Peng Dehuai, counterattacked across the frozen Yalu, hitting hard at Walton Walker's Eighth Army and Edward Almond's Tenth Corps. On the twenty-eighth the president called an emergency session of the National Security Council to consider the dangerous turn of military events and how to prevent it from exploding into a full-scale world war. At the meeting a grave Marshall declared that America must not get "sewed up in Korea" but find a way to "get out with honor."[19] He endorsed the views of his three undersecretaries and the Joint Chiefs, whom he had consulted before the NSC meeting. These men had argued that the Chinese invasion was "dictated in large measure by the [Soviet] Politburo." To get "involved in a general war with China," Marshall announced, "would be to fall into a carefully laid Russian trap." To avoid such a possibility, he continued, the recent proposal by Chiang Kai-shek, seconded by MacArthur, that the United States deploy three hundred thousand Nationalist troops from Taiwan against the enemy in Korea, should be categorically declined. Finally, in light of the Chinese Communist intrusion, the United States must beef up its military budget and war preparations. Congress should be urged to pass a supplement to the 1952 budget to meet the increasing costs of the police action in Korea.[20]

Meanwhile, the massive Chinese offensive proved devastating.

Caught flatfooted, UN and ROK forces retreated southward in disarray after suffering painful losses from both bitter cold and Chinese bullets. In January the Communist army retook Seoul and pushed south with every prospect of ejecting their UN enemies entirely from the Korean peninsula and making good Kim Il Sung's original goals of uniting it under Communist control. Truman refused to consider evacuation of Korea and even defended MacArthur's decision to divide his forces for what was to be the final attack. On December 3 the president met with his closest military and foreign policy advisers to reassess the status of the war, which now seemed teetering on the edge of disaster. But little new came out of the meeting. No one seemed able to rally the American commander, who was now at a loss how to prevent collapse except to drag Chiang and his Nationalist forces on Taiwan into the battle. Marshall seemed as irresolute as the others. According to General Ridgway, "Much of the time the Secretaries of State and Defense participated in the talks, with no one apparently willing to issue a flat order to the Far East Commander to correct the state of affairs that was going from bad to disastrous."[21]

But if unfocused on how to extricate the UN forces from collapse, MacArthur was resolute in defending his reputation. He refused to take responsibility for the defeat and was soon playing the media to excuse his mistakes and blame the administration. The president and the Pentagon, he informed the editors of *U.S. News & World Report*, had imposed on him "an enormous handicap without precedent in military history." No "authoritative source," he told Arthur Krock of the *New York Times*, had suggested to him that "the command should stop at the 38th parallel or Pyongyang."[22] Angered by the misstatements, Truman now seriously considered firing the general but, fearing a public uproar, settled for the feeble order requiring that military officers and senior civilian government officials clear with appropriate officials in their departments all statements intended for the press.

Fortunately for the UN cause, on December 23, General Walker, a mediocre commander at best, died in a jeep accident, allowing the brilliant Matthew Ridgway to take over as UN combat commander. In February, Ridgway launched a counterattack that checked the enemy's advance and soon forced them to retreat. In early March UN and ROK forces retook Seoul once more. At this point, in defiance of the president's gag order of December 6, MacArthur told the head of United Press that the U.S. Eighth Army must be allowed to push north of the thirty-eighth parallel again to destroy the Communist menace. Truman reprimanded MacArthur for violating the recent directive and commanded him to report to Washington any request by Communist leaders for an armistice. He now determined to fire MacArthur but postponed the official act until he could bring Marshall, Bradley, and the Joint Chiefs aboard without dissent.

Meanwhile, whatever his superiors' wishes, the general's defiance became even more blatant. By now MacArthur had gotten wind of the administration's plan to open negotiations with the enemy for a cease-fire. The move seemed to him defeatist, and he determined to sabotage it. Following a brief trip to Korea, he issued from his Tokyo office a blustering communiqué declaring the Chinese incapable of sustaining for long their forces on the Korean peninsula, especially if the UN should expand its operations to mainland China itself. In the eyes of Lovett, Acheson, and Dean Rusk, this statement—the fifth defiance of Truman's gag order—was a deliberate attempt to undermine the administration's peace initiative by goading the enemy into a more intransigent mood. At a meeting of the three, Acheson labeled the statement "a major act of sabotage of a Government operation." The angry Lovett insisted that the general "must be removed and

removed at once." The president himself was probably the most
furious of all. MacArthur's communiqué was "the lousiest trick a
commander-in-chief can have done to him by an underling," he
told his daughter, Margaret.[23]

Worse was to follow. On March 20, in a private letter to
House Minority Leader Joseph Martin, a conservative Asia First
congressman, the general had endorsed "unleashing Chiang
Kai-shek"—that is, using Chinese Nationalist forces against the
Communists. Two weeks later, on April 5, Martin made this
statement public, setting off a firestorm. The "General's letter was
front-page news on every continent," Manchester has noted.[24]

To Truman this was the last straw. "The general," he later
wrote, "was not only in disagreement with the policy of the government but was challenging this policy in open insubordination
to his Commander in Chief."[25] MacArthur must finally go. But
the president still retained a residue of caution and turned once
more to the quartet, Marshall, Acheson, Harriman, and Bradley, for support. He did not get it; or at least not enthusiastically.
In a meeting on April 6 with the four leaders Marshall advised
caution. Rather than fire him. bring MacArthur back from Asia
for discussions. Or perhaps *he*, his Pentagon boss, should write
personally to warn the general of the serious nature of his actions. Marshall was especially concerned lest the administration
jeopardize the military appropriations bill currently pending in
Congress or hurt troop morale in Korea by offending the general
and his partisans. The others, too, for their various reasons, urged
delay. But opinion among the president's advisers soon firmed up.
The next day Marshall met with Bradley and the Joint Chiefs
and asked each to state his individual opinion of MacArthur's insubordination. All now agreed that it was unconscionable and he
must be relieved of his duties. The next morning, at still another
meeting of the president with his four close advisers, those pres-

ent concurred that the contumacious commander be dismissed. Truman sought to inform the general of his decision before it became public, but delivery of his message to Tokyo was delayed by a communication glitch. On April 11, at a late-night White House press conference triggered prematurely by a news leak, the public was officially informed that MacArthur was coming home with full honors, to be succeeded by Matthew Ridgway as overall commander in the Far East. On the thirteenth Truman gave a radio address, emphasizing his determination to prevent spread of the war and informing the public of his reasons for the relief of the general.

Despite the president's efforts, as anticipated, MacArthur's dismissal touched off a spectacular political explosion. Predictably, China Lobby Republicans furiously denounced the act. Senator Jenner raved that the country was "in the hands of a secret inner coterie which is directed by agents of the Soviet Union." He and his Ohio Senate colleague, Robert Taft, demanded that Truman be impeached. Senator McCarthy, in his coarse way, called the firing "a Communist victory won with the aid of bourbon and Benedictine."[26]

The public reaction outside the Senate's halls was equally intemperate and more worrisome politically. In Hawaii, where his plane touched down on the trip back to Washington from his Tokyo headquarters, a hundred thousand cheering citizens greeted the defrocked general. In San Francisco large approving crowds lined the streets as he drove from the airport to his hotel. In the days immediately following the recall Western Union delivered an estimated 75,000 telegrams to the White House and assorted government agencies, running 5 to 1 against the president. Some of these messages attacked Truman as an "imbecile," a "pig," a "judas," a man who deserved impeachment. The press split over the dismissal, with the *Washington Post*, the *New York Times*, and the moderate Republican *New York Herald Tribune* praising Truman, but the conservative media moguls, with McCormick and Hearst in the lead, bitterly opposed.

On April 19 MacArthur appeared at the Capitol to address a joint session of Congress. In one of the notable speeches of the mid-twentieth century, he defended his goals and strategies in Korea and repudiated the administration's. He denied any partisan or personal motives for his actions; he sought only to serve his country, he said. Aiming at Truman's negotiated-peace plans, he attacked the administration for defending the failed policy of appeasement. He, too, disliked war, he declaimed, but once a nation was at war there could be "no substitute for victory." The UN had failed to win the war in Asia, he insisted, because the American government was too politically timid and indecisive. MacArthur concluded with a bathetic review of his long public career, ending famously with the words of an old West Point barracks ballad: As he bade farewell he intoned the refrain: "Old soldiers never die; they just fade away." His last word was a whispered "Good-bye."[27]

The deafening applause that greeted MacArthur's words in the House chamber was soon reverberating across the country. In New York he received a traditional Wall Street ticker-tape parade with several million citizens lining the nineteen-mile route along Broadway. Similar enthusiasm greeted him in Chicago and in his boyhood home, Milwaukee, when he went for a visit. On May 3 the Senate Foreign Affairs and Armed Services Committees opened joint hearings on the military situation in East Asia in the Senate Office Building. MacArthur was the first witness, and his testimony would last three days. Presided over by the respected Democratic senator from Georgia, Richard Russell, the testimony went on for forty-two days and included thirteen witnesses. The sessions were closed, but edited transcripts of each day's events were released to the press.

Once again MacArthur defended his actions. He described the ongoing devastation in Korea as extraordinary. He admitted no mistakes. He denounced the concept of a "limited war," calling it "appeasement." Such a conflict would drag on indefinitely with mounting casualties and economic cost. Repeating an old theme from his days as wartime Southwest Pacific commander, he claimed that the administration, as marked by its NATO commitment, had displayed excessive concern for the wishes of America's allies in Europe and not enough for its own needs in Asia. Its preoccupation with Europe, he declared, amounted to "North Atlantic isolationism."[28] As for the talk of Soviet intervention, it was a chimera; the Russians would not go to war to defend Red China. MacArthur's attack on Europe First implied criticism of Marshall, but he was more explicit as well. The secretary's policy toward China—that is, abandoning Chiang—was, he charged, "the greatest political mistake we made in a hundred years." It was a policy the United States would "pay for . . . for a century."[29]

The administration's supporters—Secretary Acheson, Chief of Staff Bradley, members of the Joint Chiefs, Democratic senators—spent seven weeks demolishing MacArthur's arguments. Marshall's testimony immediately followed the general's and lasted for six days. It was perhaps the most effective in defense of the administration.

Marshall and MacArthur have been depicted as polar opposites, personal enemies as well as men drastically different in temperament and military ideology. But, in fact, the secretary of defense was deeply conflicted over his longtime associate. He admired his military dash and skill but deplored his vanity, his contentiousness, his political ambitions. He was not comfortable in his role as critic of "a brother army officer," he stated at the outset of his testimony. The general was "a man for whom I have tremendous respect as to his military capabilities and military performances and . . . as to his administration of Japan."[30] But, in his view, like other generals he had known, MacArthur had succumbed to the sin of "localitis." It was "completely understandable and . . . at times commendable that a theater commander should become wholly wrapped in his own aims and responsibilities, that some of the directions received by him from higher authority are not those that he would have written himself." But that the mistake was common did not validate it. Marshall sought to place the Korean conflict in the broad Cold War context that the administration espoused. It was part of a larger struggle, one against "Communist aggression and, if possible, to avoid another world war in doing so." Korea was only the latest point of conflict, though admittedly the most painful as it cost blood as well as treasure. But the general's real offense was not his narrow focus on the Far East. Nor was it even simple disobedience to military orders. "What is new and what has brought about the necessity for General MacArthur's removal," Marshall stated, "is the wholly unprecedented situation of a local theater commander publicly expressing his displeasure and his disagreements with the foreign and military policy of the United States."[31]

The hearings dragged on for almost twenty more days after Marshall's testimony, ending with the transmission of a report to the full Senate but without the usual final recommendations for action. By this time the press and the American public had lost interest in the controversy, and MacArthur had lost his popular dazzle. Clearly, it now appeared to many Americans, the administration had been within its rights to fire him and clearly, too, his policies had been dangerous. Meanwhile, on the tumultuous Asian peninsula, the enemies argued over the where and how of armistice talks, with the Americans apparently more anxious for an end to the fighting than the Communists. As they talked, bloody platoon-size clashes, raids, and counterraids between the antagonists continued with few gains for either side. In early June, Marshall flew to Korea to view the stalled battle scene for himself. Appalled by the continuing bloodshed, according to one later report, he concluded that if the enemy did not yield on negotiations it might be necessary "to give them a taste of the atom."[32]

The official armistice negotiations with the Communists finally opened in early July in Kaesong, just south of the thirty-eighth parallel. For the next two years the two sides would wrangle over terms. By the time the fighting finally ended with an armistice in late July 1953, without an official peace treaty and with the boundaries between North and South virtually unchanged, Marshall had returned to private life and could only be a distant observer of events across the Pacific.

Marshall had already become a target of the Republican right wing over his China policy. His role in the MacArthur affair, however, brought his entire career under broad attack, with the chief aggressor the emerging high priest of anti-Communism, Senator McCarthy.

On June 14, well after Marshall's congressional testimony, McCarthy rose on the Senate floor and delivered a savage diatribe against the secretary of defense. He began with a grandiose, paranoid statement that "our present situation" could only be explained as the "product of a conspiracy . . . on a scale so immense as to dwarf any previous such venture in the history of man." He then identified Marshall, along with Acheson, as prime members of the conspiracy. This conclusion he backed up by a review of some of Marshall's supposedly faulty past decisions—some valid, most imaginary—including his advocacy of a premature 1942 invasion of Europe (presumably Sledgehammer), his attempted veto of an invasion of southern Europe through Italy, his sacrifice of Allied interests to induce Soviet entry into the Far Eastern war, his "making common cause" with Stalin at Tehran, and his efforts to appease the Soviets at Yalta. His role in China and Korea received special condemnation. In collaboration with Acheson he had "created the China policy which, destroying China, robbed us of a great and friendly ally, a buffer against the Soviet imperialism with which we are now at war." As for Korea, he had fixed the boundary between the North and South where the Soviet Union, not the United States, had initially established it, and laid down the strategy that had turned the Korean conflict into "a pointless slaughter." And what was the purpose of all these dubious and conspiratorial actions? It was "to diminish the United States in world affairs, to weaken us militarily, to confuse our spirit with talk of surrender in the Far East, and impair our will to resist."[33]

McCarthy had spoken to a sparsely filled Senate chamber that shed still more listeners as he bulled his way through his hours-long rant. Yet the speech attracted wide attention if only for its outrageousness. Invited to respond, Marshall declined. "If I have to explain at this point that I am not a traitor to the United States," he replied, "I hardly think it's worth it."[34] But his partisans were not so reticent. General Wedemeyer, no champion of Marshall's China policies, came to his defense on European strategy. Senator McCarthy was "absolutely wrong" in regard to the Normandy invasion. That plan, he wrote, was honestly aimed "at winning the war on preferential terms for the West."[35] Eisenhower, rightly claiming a special friendship, gave Marshall broader support. "Now look," he told *Newsweek* reporters. "General Marshall is one of the patriots of this country. Anyone who has lived with him, has worked for him as I have, knows that he is a man of real selflessness."[36] Across the country a loud chorus of praise and defense rose to confront Marshall's intemperate critic.

Marshall may have shrugged off the Wisconsin senator's attack, but it may well have hastened his resolve to retire; that, and the partial success of his military preparedness campaign.

Though he had failed to get the UMT legislation he sought, under the goad of Korea, Congress finally passed a bill extending the 1948 draft for four more years, lengthened the military service term to two years, and approved a universal service system in principle, if not in fact.

Marshall left office on September 12, 1951, almost exactly a year after first sitting at the secretary's desk. There was a final staff meeting at the Pentagon that morning, but he had eschewed a farewell ceremony. Lovett would be taking over, and he felt confident that the department's affairs would be well managed. He thanked his staff for loyalty and praised their integrity and competence. He had, he remarked, labored for a number of policies and programs with modest success. Now he expected to sit back and observe others at work on the defense issues of the day.

In retirement, as in harness, Marshall sought to ignore McCarthy. But the grand inquisitor's malign influence continued to pursue him. In July 1952, after serving as supreme commander of NATO forces in Europe and then as president of Columbia University, Dwight Eisenhower won the Republican nomination for president. Marshall was quick to congratulate his protégé but noted ruefully that any communication from him earlier might have been "detrimental to your cause."[37] During the presidential campaign that followed, Ike was forced to confront the issue of Republican right-wing attacks on Marshall. At a press conference in Denver the reporter Murray Kempton asked him what he thought of "those people who call General Marshall a living lie?" Though previously alerted to Kempton's intentions, Ike leaped up, his face red with anger, and retorted that no one had any right to "say such a thing about General Marshall," a man who was "a perfect example of patriotism and loyal service to the United States."[38] The candidate went on to denounce Marshall's detractors in general but carefully avoided mentioning the names of the chief guilty parties. During the remainder of the 1952 presidential campaign, candidate Ike endorsed the local Republican tickets even when they included one of his patron's maligners. In Wisconsin, McCarthy's home state, Ike initially intended to insert a strong defense of Marshall into his Milwaukee campaign speech, though the senator himself, running for reelection, would be on the platform, but when his advisers warned him that it would divide the Wisconsin GOP and perhaps undermine McCarthy's bid for reelection, he deleted the paragraph. The press, however, had seen a copy of the unexpurgated speech and, to Ike's everlasting chagrin, publicized the omission as a surrender to demagogic McCarthyism. Marshall never commented publicly on Ike's weak surrender to expediency, though he told Rose Wilson, his young riding companion from his days as Pershing's Washington aide, that "Eisenhower was forced into a compromise, that's all it was."[39] In later years, in her nineties, Katherine was similarly forgiving. "Don't attack President Eisenhower about the McCarthy thing," she advised Forrest Pogue. "He did everything in the world to make it up to George and me."[40]

Once more a retiree, Marshall would divide his time, as before, between Dodona and Pinehurst. He would turn down a second Truman offer of the presidency of the Red Cross, but accepted the assignment as chairman of the American Battle Monuments Commission, a post previously held by his revered mentor General Pershing, who had died in 1948. Offers of positions in the private sector came his way, but, with the exception of a brief stint as a director of Pan American World Airways, he avoided the sort of lucrative corporate board memberships so commonly available to retired high military officers in our more avaricious times. Determined to avoid malicious gossip, he also refused to accept large publishers' advances to write his memoirs, though he eventually agreed, for the historical record, to provide Forrest

Pogue with extensive accounts of his private and public life, later transcribed and eventually posted on the Internet. If the event seemed worthy, he and Katherine also traveled abroad to attend the occasion. One of these trips was to the coronation in London in June 1953 of the young British queen, Elizabeth, daughter of his wartime friend, King George VI.

The gala celebration in Britain was steeped in fond nostalgia for Marshall. Churchill, still vigorous at seventy-nine, a participant in the religious services, hailed him warmly in Westminster Abbey as he walked past the invited guests on his way to the church's altar. Brooke and Montgomery, now both peers of the realm, also shook his hand at the ceremony. The British authorities singled out Marshall for special consideration among the foreign guests. "I received a very gracious and warm welcome on all occasions and was particularly favored in the seating at the great banquets—Buckingham Palace and Lancaster House," he wrote in a long account of the coronation he composed for former president Truman's eyes.[41] Later in the week Marshall and Katherine sat in Churchill's box at the fashionable Epsom Derby. They also visited the home of George's deceased great British friend, Sir John Dill, now owned by one of Dill's former military aides.

The Marshalls returned home and went to Pinehurst, cheered and immensely pleased by their experience. But then George came down with a cold that turned into influenza and required a stay in Walter Reed. Just before leaving for the hospital, Marshall learned that he had been chosen to receive the 1953 Nobel Peace Prize.

The award was for his authorship of the European Recovery Program, now universally called the "Marshall Plan," not for his military achievements against Hitler's tyranny. Recipients normally made a trip to Europe to receive it in person and to deliver a brief acceptance lecture. But the visit to Britain for the coronation had exhausted both Marshalls, and Katherine decided not to accompany him when he went to receive the prize in December.

Before returning to Europe, the general met briefly with reporters at the Pinehurst cottage. Disregarding the Nobel committee's citation of the ERP, he declared that his greatest contribution to world peace was in reality his success in persuading the American government in 1940 to re-arm in face of the looming totalitarian danger abroad. That struggle, not the European recovery program, had been the "hardest thing I ever did."[42] But he modestly refused to accept full credit for even this; Senator Arthur Vandenberg's help, he noted, had been vital for passage of the arms programs in Congress.

Marshall assumed that, like the awards for science and literature, the Peace Prize was conferred by the Swedish Academy in Stockholm and was surprised to learn that it was presented by the Norwegian king in Oslo. Despite his uncertain health he refused to accept the prize in absentia. But to please Katherine he took the Italian Line's new luxury liner, *Andrea Doria*, by the southern route to Europe to avoid the cold and blustery North Atlantic in winter. Arriving in Naples after eight disappointingly frigid and damp days at sea, he had not written a line of his speech. In desperation he hied off to Paris and there, at NATO headquarters, took to his bed and, with the help of Gen. Alfred Gruenther and several of his staff, managed to piece together his lecture.

Marshall flew to Norway on December 9 in a military plane to accept the award the next day at the University of Oslo auditorium. As the Norwegian presenter finished his tribute to Marshall, three men in the balcony jumped up and, while crying, "Murderer," "Murderer," tossed down leaflets accusing Marshall of ordering the pitiless atomic bomb attacks on Hiroshima and Nagasaki at the end of World War II and authoring the scheme that had "contributed to dividing the world into two hostile camps."[43] Guards quickly seized and subdued the men, reporters for a Norwegian Communist newspaper, who had gotten into the hall by flashing their press cards. As Marshall stood nonplussed at the rostrum, King Haakon VII rose from his seat in the hall, bringing the rest of the audience to their feet with loud applause. It was the first time in fifty-two years that a Nobel awards ceremony had been interrupted.

Considering the circumstances of its composition, it is no surprise that the speech delivered the following day was a platitudinous hodgepodge. In it Marshall noted that achieving peace among nations had been a goal of many generations. He related how he had first learned about the famous Pax Romana of classical times in 1918 while holed up at Pershing's American Expeditionary Force headquarters in France. This ancient experience, he said, demonstrated that the best insurance for peace had often been military preparedness—an old theme, of course, in Marshall's thinking. And yet, he conceded, large armies were not the way to achieve a peaceful world. Rather, "the most important single factor will be a spiritual regeneration to develop good will and understanding among nations." After this observation he continued with a rather naive declaration of faith in the value of teaching college and high school students about the causes of past wars so they might learn to avoid the mistakes made by their predecessors. The remainder of the address was a ramble through American ideals and international diversities, and a plea for improving the lot of the world's poor. Marshall concluded apologetically. He was aware, he said, of the inadequacy of his prescription for attaining enduring world peace. But, alluding to the award (in absentia) that very day in Stockholm of the Nobel Prize for Literature to his old friend the silver-tongued Winston Churchill, Marshall acknowledged that he "had not made clear the points that assume such preeminence and importance" in his mind. He had done his best, however, and hoped he had "sown some seeds which may bring forth some good fruit."[44] The audience applauded politely, but no one present could have been inspired by the words. Marshall himself obviously was not proud of the lecture.

Marshall returned from Europe still suffering from the effects of his recent influenza. His health would never again be good. He spent his last years predominantly in Leesburg with Katherine, where visitors, often eminent men and women, noted either his remarkable resiliency or else his unhappy decline. His mind remained clear, however. Though he confessed to being mostly concerned now with "the blackbirds eating all my marigolds" he insisted that he was "absolutely all right from the neck up."[45]

In December 1955 the *New York Times* reporter William S. White came to Pinehurst on the occasion of Marshall's imminent seventy-fifth birthday to interview the general once again. He described the Pinehurst cottage as "rather small, with a faint touch of pleasant shabbiness." Marshall himself was clearly an old man, "venerable in retirement," though the photo accompanying the article shows a handsome, healthy-looking, strong-featured gentleman, wearing a tweed jacket and tie. Present at the interview was Katherine, "a lady of subdued, relaxed gaiety."

Marshall was not on this occasion a good interview subject. He was laconic and cryptic and gave White little of interest to report beyond platitudes. He refused to acknowledge his right-wing detractors, dismissing the hostile Senator Jenner with a "Who? Jenner? Don't know him." When asked what was the "hardest job in public life," he answered: "To keep my temper." White discovered what he considered a paradox in Marshall's personality. "An aloof, aristocratic, indrawn man," he "nevertheless in his life expresses the democratic spirit as well as any person this political writer has ever known." The general's connection with his past seemed tenuous. He now saw few of his old associates. One exception was Omar Bradley, who had visited Pinehurst recently to join him on the golf links.

There was a certain air of pointless lassitude and finality hovering over the retiree's life as White reported it. When he asked Marshall what he did with his time "most of these days," he elicited: "sit quietly reading, contemplating the matters of life and watching television." As confirmation of the TV devotion, the reporter noted on the arm of the general's chair a newspaper clipping listing the evening's TV programs. Marshall acknowledged that he had not been well lately. He was still feeling the effects of a flulike virus; they limited his writing the personal letters that he felt he owed to others. As White drove off he looked back at "the tall still figure under the darkening pines" and found it "impossible to put down the melancholy thought that the truly great ones" were "falling back now into irretrievable time."[46]

In August 1958 Marshall entered Walter Reed again, this time for repair work on his teeth and to have a growth on his face removed. While in the hospital he fell and cracked a rib, delaying his discharge for several weeks. When allowed to leave he went with Katherine, earlier than usual, to the Pinehurst cottage, where he had agreed to be watched over twenty-four hours a day by an assigned Army Medical Corps sergeant. In October, Rose Page Wilson, now a married woman with three children, came for a visit. When the attentive orderly admitted her to his room she was shocked. Marshall was sitting up in bed clad in a handsome silk dressing gown, but he had aged badly. His "face was gaunt, . . . his skin stretched tightly across his jutting cheek bones and the sharp outline of his skull . . . clearly visible under his . . . hair," which "had become dead white." At that moment she realized the worst: "He's not going to get well; dear God, he's not going to get well."[47]

And he did not. In mid-January the sergeant heard gasping sounds from Marshall's room. He rushed in to discover that the general had suffered a stroke and was choking on his swallowed tongue. Marshall was rushed to nearby Fort Bragg military hospital. His life was saved, but then in mid-February he had a second, more severe stroke and in March was transferred to Walter Reed. Confined to bed and a wheelchair, Marshall could talk only in a whisper to the friends who came by to greet him and, in effect, to say good-bye. Truman visited, and Eisenhower came three times. On one of Ike's visits he was accompanied by the aged Winston Churchill, who stood at the doorway of his room with tears in his eyes while Marshall lay under the covers on his hospital bed. All through this final ordeal Katherine stayed at a guest cottage on the hospital grounds to help in any way she could. By this time he had lost his hearing and sight and could not speak. The end came on October 16. In a coma for some weeks, in the early evening he peacefully slipped away.

Marshall did not want his death to be enveloped in pomp and circumstance. George Washington had spurned a "state funeral." Marshall did, too, though he himself had organized one for Pershing in 1948. In 1956, in failing health, he had written down his funeral wishes. There should be no services in Washington's National Cathedral, nor a funeral eulogy, nor special guest lists, nor horse-drawn caissons, and no lying in state in the Capitol Rotunda. Interment should be private. Katherine amended his wishes in some details. She allowed the public to view the flag-draped coffin for a day at the cathedral. But press coverage would be restricted and the simple services conducted at the Fort Myer chapel, with interment completed privately at Arlington National Cemetery. The evening of Marshall's death President Eisenhower issued a proclamation expressing "profound grief throughout the United States" and ordering American flags flown at half staff.[48]

And so ended the life of a man whose acts, views, and decisions helped shape the course of twentieth-century world history. A man of far-ranging influence and power? Undoubtedly. He presided over the U.S. Army when it expanded from 275,000 to more than eight million men. He endorsed and vigorously promoted the strategy against the Wehrmacht that liberated Western Europe from Nazi slavery and kept it free after 1945. He skillfully managed and preserved the fragile wartime alliances and coalitions that joined disparate sovereignties and rivalrous service divisions. His own contemporaries and much later history would accord him an exalted place in the national pantheon. Few Americans, besides his own ideal, the first president, have received the dazzling encomiums Marshall did. His achievements have been summed up in Churchill's oft-repeated tag: "Organizer of Victory." Truman was even more unstinting. At his own birthday celebration in May 1948, he responded to Marshall's toast with the remark: "He won the war."[49]

Immediate praise notwithstanding, any attempt to measure Marshall's merits must acknowledge certain facts. He never commanded troops in battle. Other generals selected by him did, of course. And Marshall has been lauded for perceptive choices of commanders and ruthless weeding out of incompetents. But in fact his protégés probably varied as much in leadership quality as any random selection among the list of available officers at the time of their assingments. Marshall's "little black book"—if in fact it existed—turned up no Napoleons, Hannibals, or Alexander the Greats.

He was often admired for creating the American World War II army virtually out of nothing. And indeed the growth of the U.S. military forces between 1940 and 1945 seems almost to duplicate the cosmic inflation following the big bang. Marshall must also be commended for his effective Cassandra role during the "phony war." His dire warnings of America's unreadiness in the face of the growing international crisis undoubtedly accelerated America's preparation for war. But then he stumbled. By limiting the army's size to a spare ninety divisions he severely strained its ability to complete the job of defeating the Wehrmacht. Nor was the army he helped to create composed of highly skilled, well-trained troops, capable of taking on the veteran German enemy, though by 1944 that enemy was in the last stages of its strength. Admittedly, young American men were not ready to become soldiers. Neither the nation's peacetime values, nor its individualistic, democratic culture, were equal to the brutal demands of mid-twentieth-century military engagement. Marshall understood this and sought to improve their morale and their understanding of the stakes. But his efforts were insufficient. Nor was Marshall directly in charge of the training process. Yet however explicable the failure to turn American youths into warriors, the chief of staff cannot be acclaimed, without serious qualifiers, as the "organizer of victory."

And what should we conclude about Marshall as a military strategist, as a master planner of Allied global operations? The record is mixed. He was surely right to insist on Europe First, though it is difficult to see how, given Britain's weight in Allied councils, particularly early in the war, any other course was possible. But he also fought against dogged British opposition for a premature cross-Channel operation. The British were correct to veto his Sledgehammer plan, the part of the early cross-Channel strategy that promised to create another Dunkirk in 1942. The same goes for the contemporary aerial warfare experts who found his mid-1944 proposal for a major Allied parachute and glider drop deep within France dangerous and unworkable. On the other hand his resistance to Churchill's ambitious "underbelly" Mediterranean strategy was surely valid. The North African and

Italian operations were held to provide a valuable first "blood-ing" to green American troops and their commanders. But those dearly won campaigns failed to prevent costly mistakes in France and Germany and failed to contribute appreciably to shortening the war against Germany.

And what about the Pacific and MacArthur? Marshall's han-dling of MacArthur, the Pacific prima donna, was too deferen-tial. He excessively indulged the headstrong, histrionic general. It could be argued that so, too, did the president and almost ev-eryone else in authority. Yet however powerful and influential the Southwest Pacific commander, Marshall was his immediate boss and as such all too often failed to issue decisive orders. Further, he was mistaken to support, at least initially, Operation Downfall, the plan for invading the Japanese home islands. His estimate of probable casualties was ludicrously low; the bloodbath, both Al-lied and Japanese, would have been appalling. It is true that, when the success of the atom bomb was demonstrated, he changed his mind about invading the enemy's home islands. But his response to the dropping of the bomb itself was vacillating and equivocal almost to the very end. And then there is the question of Pacific jurisdictions. Marshall's successful advocacy of the unified com-mand principle worked well for the Atlantic theaters. Indeed it was one of his major contributions to the war—a coalition war, it should be recalled. But however impassioned his defense of the formula, faced with King's intransigence he abandoned it in the Pacific theater, with resulting costs in lives lost and time wasted.

Marshall's record on the Atlantic fronts was less ambiguous. Despite cultural differences, jealousies, rivalries, and disparities in national wealth and experience, he managed to preserve a working coalition with the British. In Europe and North Africa, World War II was a cooperative effort of the two English-speaking nations. Here Marshall excelled. His insistence on a unified command, though at times challenged by the British and at times ignored, was widely adopted and proved to be a boon. Marshall was also able to maintain good relations with Churchill and, in the end, with Britain's chief of the Imperial General Staff, Alan Brooke, with Dill serving as intermediary between the two sides.

Marshall's record as foreign policy adviser to Truman after VJ-Day displays both debits and credits. His China mission of late 1945 and early 1946 did not succeed in reconciling the Nationalists and Communists. China's problems admittedly were virtually intractable, but Marshall must take some, though by no means all, of the blame for failure to solve them. As for the Cold War, at the State Department during the crucial early months, when American policy toward postwar Russia was evolving, Marshall retained a misguided opinion of Stalin's good intentions and sought initially to restrain the most aggressive impulses of the Cold War policy hawks. He ultimately embraced their anti-Soviet ardor, but at times, as in the case of the Berlin blockade, his moderation probably served the nation well.

Marshall was only one of the many authors—a cohort that included Acheson, Kennan, Bohlen, and Clayton—of the European Recovery Program, the key American response to postwar Soviet provocation. And, indeed, the fundamental idea of preventing Communist subversion of Western Europe by restoring hope and prosperity to its people was very much in the air by 1947. All told, the program—Marshall's chief contribution to Truman-Acheson Cold War policies—was to be a shield to deflect the bitter neo-isolationist Republicans of 1946–47 and the years thereafter. Affixing his name to the ERP contributed unquestionably to that goal. And even more salient were his extensive and effective lobbying efforts in Congress and among influential citizens' groups for the ERP. But as Marshall himself insisted, the "Marshall Plan" was misnamed.

Given what is known in the second decade of the twenty-first century—whatever our sympathies for the historic perils and hopes of the world's Jewish people—it is hard to dismiss Marshall's fears that the creation of an independent Jewish state would open a Pandora's box of troubles for the United States. Assuredly there is no going back; Israel is America's staunch Middle East ally. But, as Marshall anticipated, its existence at times has complicated America's position and standing abroad, particularly in the Muslim world.

Marshall's achievements in the new Defense Department that he briefly headed were meager. But in any case they faithfully complied with the president's own wishes. It was he, even more than Omar Bradley and the other generals who testified to the congressional committee, who led to the administration's vindication. To Harry Truman, that by itself was probably a sufficient payoff for the Defense appointment.

All told, the performance of George Marshall in many of his roles was less than awe-inspiring. Yet, the far right excepted, the paeans were incessant, the applause unrelieved. The discrepancy may well have originated in Americans' yearning for a platonic ideal of a triumphant military leader above politics, deceit, and selfish ambition—in a word, a George Washington—which they located in a fallible man of sterling character but unremarkable powers. Only a very few keen observers saw beyond the conventional wisdom. In effect, the Olympian persona that Marshall himself created protected him, though imperfectly, from criticism, both in his prime and in his future historical reputation.

But whatever the reality, his life and work left a deep imprint on American life and the world during the mid-twentieth-century years of crisis and trial.

ACKNOWLEDGMENTS

This work originated as the concept of Stanley Hirshson, who tragically died before it could be significantly launched. It has been our privilege to take on the project and carry it through to completion.

We wish to thank those who contributed directly to the creation and production of our book. Alex Hoyt, once again, served as our agent, securing the contract for the work and helping to clarify its scope. Once more Hugh Van Dusen was our overall editor. His generous praise, especially at the outset, encouraged and sustained us. Immensely helpful in the production process was editor Barry Harbaugh at HarperCollins. Our copy editor, Sue Llewellyn, proved extraordinarily diligent in her reading of the manuscript. We wish also to acknowledge the generous help we received at the George C. Marshall Research Library in Lexington, Virginia, from archivist Jeffrey Kozak and director Paul B. Baron. Finally, our thanks go to Janet R. Van der Vaart of the George C. Marshall International Center for permission to use the picture of Dodona Manor.

At another level of appreciation we would like to express our thanks to many friends, particularly the following, for their encouragement during the years we spent researching and writing this book: Ralph Dannheisser, Dr. Edith Jacobs,

Dr. Howard Rock and Ellen Rock, Libby and Arnold Friedman, Norma and David Schechner, Phyllis and Jerry Reich, Betty and Jack Udelsman, Mary and Robert Nesnay, and Drs. Jennifer Roberts and Robert Lejeune.

—Debi and Irwin Unger

NOTES

CHAPTER 1: CHILDISH THINGS

1. Ed Cray, *General of the Army: George C. Marshall, Soldier and Statesman* (New York: Cooper Square Press, 2000), p. 17.
2. Ibid., p. 441.
3. Ron Chernow, *Washington: A Life* (New York: Penguin Press, 2010), pp. 122, 123.
4. Marshall Interviews, February 21, 1957, Tape 1, p. 34.
5. Andrew Roberts, *Masters and Commanders: How Four Titans Won the War in the West, 1941–1945* (New York: HarperCollins, 2009), pp. 390–91.
6. Forrest Pogue, *Organizer of Victory, 1941–1945* (New York: Viking Press, 1973), pp. 131–32.
7. Marshall Interviews, February 21, 1957, Tape 1, p. 45.
8. Ibid., February 27, 1957, Tape 1, p. 40.
9. Ibid., March 6, 1957, Tape 3, p. 99.
10. Forrest Pogue, *Education of a General, 1880–1939* (New York: Viking Press, 1963), p. 43.
11. Marshall Interviews, March 6, 1957, Tape 3, p. 98.
12. "Virginia Military Institute," http://em.wikipedia.org/wik/ virginia_military_institute, p. 7.
13. Peter Finn, *Washington Post*, August 20, 1997.
14. Marshall Interviews, March 13, 1957, Tape 4, p. 116.
15. Pogue, *Education of a General*, p. 50.
16. Marshall Interviews, March 6, 1957, Tape 3, p. 98.
17. Larry Bland and Sharon Ritenour, eds., *The Papers of George Catlett Marshall*, vol. 1 (Baltimore: Johns Hopkins University Press, 1981), pp. 18–19.

CHAPTER 2: LEARNING AND YEARNING

1. Pogue, *Education of a General*, p. 70.
2. Ibid., p. 74.
3. Marshall to General Scott Shipp, Fort Reno, March 3, 1906, in Bland and Ritenour, *The Papers of George Catlett Marshall*, vol. 1, p. 34.
4. Marshall Interviews, Tape 5, April 4, 1957, p. 156.
5. Ibid., p. 152.
6. Marshall to Colonel Bernard Lentz, October 2, 1935, in Bland and Ritenour, *The Papers of George Catlett Marshall*, vol. 1, pp. 45–46.
7. Cray, *General of the Army*, p. 37.
8. Marshall to Lesley McNair, Washington, February 23, 1939, in Bland and Ritenour, *The Papers of George Catlett Marshall*, vol. 1, p. 703.
9. Pogue, *Education of a General*, p. 106.
10. Marshall Interviews, Tape 5, April 4, 1957, p. 178.
11. Ibid., p. 172.
12. Marshall to Bruce Magruder, August 7, 1939, in Larry Bland, Sharon Ritenour Stevens, and Clarence Wunderlin, eds., *The Papers of George Catlett Marshall*, vol. 2 (Baltimore: Johns Hopkins University Press, 1986), pp. 31–32.
13. Marshall to Edward W. Nichols, October 4, 1915, in Bland and Ritenour, *The Papers of George Catlett Marshall*, vol. 1, p. 94.
14. Marshall Interviews, Tape 5, April 4, 1957, p. 178.
15. Ibid., p. 190.
16. Larry Bland and Sharon Ritenour Stevens, *The Papers of George Catlett Marshall*, vol. 5 (Baltimore: Johns Hopkins University Press, 2003), p. 221.
17. George C. Marshall, *Memoirs of My Services in the World War, 1917–1918* (Boston: Houghton Mifflin Company, 1976), p. 7.
18. Marshall Interviews, Tape 6, April 5, 1957, pp. 197–98.
19. Ibid., p. 198.
20. Pogue, *Education of a General*, p. 189.

CHAPTER 3: BETWEEN THE WARS

1. Rose Page Wilson, *General Marshall Remembered* (Englewood Cliffs, NJ: Prentice-Hall, 1968), p. 12.
2. Ibid., p. 119.

3. Bland and Ritenour, *The Papers of George Catlett Marshall*, vol. 1, pp. 203–4.
4. William Frye, *Marshall: Citizen Soldier* (Indianapolis: Bobbs-Merrill Company, 1947), p. 181.
5. Marshall Interviews, December 7, 1956, Tape 8, p. 269.
6. Ibid., April 11, 1957, Tape 7, p. 248.
7. Pogue, *Education of a General*, p. 211.
8. Bland and Ritenour, *The Papers of George Catlett Marshall*, vol. 1, pp. 234–35.
9. Ibid., p. 263.
10. Cray, *General of the Army*, p. 97.
11. Bland and Ritenour, *The Papers of George Catlett Marshall*, vol. 1, p. 281.
12. Ibid., p. 294.
13. Marshall to William H. Cocke, December 26, 1926, in ibid., p. 298.
14. Pogue, *Education of a General*, p. 246.
15. Wilson, *General Marshall Remembered*, pp. 158–59.
16. Bland and Ritenour, *The Papers of George Catlett Marshall*, vol. 1, p. 383.
17. Ibid., p. 320.
18. Pogue, *Education of a General*, p. 256.
19. Bland and Ritenour, *The Papers of George Catlett Marshall*, vol. 1, p. 320.
20. Carlo D'Este, *Eisenhower: A Soldier's Life* (New York: Henry Holt, 2002), p. 201.
21. William Odom, *After the Trenches: The Transformation of U.S. Army Doctrine, 1918–1939* (College Station: Texas A & M Press, 1999), p. 87.
22. Katherine Tupper Marshall, *Together: Annals of an Army Wife* (New York: Tupper and Love, 1946), p. 2.
23. Ibid., p. 6.
24. Ibid., p. 9.
25. Pogue, *Education of a General*, p. 272.
26. Bland and Ritenour, *The Papers of George Catlett Marshall*, vol. 1, p. 393.
27. Ibid., p. 398.
28. Pogue, *Education of a General*, p. 280.
29. Ibid., p. 282.
30. Wilson, *General Marshall Remembered*, p. 199.
31. Katherine Marshall, *Together*, p. 18.

32. Bland and Ritenour, *The Papers of George Catlett Marshall,* vol. 1, pp. 446–47.

33. Cray, *General of the Army,* p. 119.

34. Bland and Ritenour, *The Papers of George Catlett Marshall,* vol. 1, p. 482.

35. Katherine Marshall, *Together,* p. 24.

36. Ibid.

37. Frye, *Marshall: Citizen Soldier,* p. 243.

38. Bland and Ritenour, *The Papers of George Catlett Marshall,* vol. 1, pp. 533–34.

39. Robert Dallek, *Franklin D. Roosevelt and American Foreign Policy, 1932–1945* (New York: Oxford University Press, 1995), p. 152.

40. Bland and Ritenour Stevens, *The Papers of George Catlett Marshall,* vol. 3, p. 598.

41. Katherine Marshall, *Together,* p. 35.

42. Quoted in William Manchester, *The Glory and the Dream: A Narrative History of America, 1932–1972* (Boston: Little, Brown and Company, 1974), p. 189.

43. Marshall Interviews, March 6, 1957, Tape 3, pp. 108–9.

44. Ibid.

45. Frye, *Marshall: Citizen Soldier,* p. 246.

46. Cray, *General of the Army,* p. 139.

47. Katherine Marshall, *Together,* p. 43.

CHAPTER 4: PREPARING FOR WAR

1. Bland, Ritenour, and Wunderlin, *The Papers of George Catlett Marshall,* vol. 2, p. 48.

2. Dallek, *Franklin D. Roosevelt and American Foreign Policy,* p. 199.

3. Marshall Interviews, January 22, 1957, Tape 10, p. 297.

4. Bland, Ritenour, and Wunderlin, *The Papers of George Catlett Marshall,* vol. 2, p. 163.

5. Cray, *General of the Army,* p. 162.

6. Bland, Ritenour, and Wunderlin, *The Papers of George Catlett Marshall,* vol. 2, p. 263.

7. Marshall Interviews, January 22, 1957, Tape 10, p. 302.

8. Ibid., January 15, 1957, Tape 9, p. 281.

9. Ibid., Interview Notes, October 29, 1956, p. 611.

10. Winston Churchill, *Their Finest Hour*, vol. 2 of *The Second World War* (Boston: Houghton Mifflin, 1949), p. 198.

11. Mark A. Stoler, *Allies and Adversaries: The Joint Chiefs of Staffs, the Grand Alliance, and U.S. Strategy in World War II* (Chapel Hill: University of North Carolina Press, 2000), p. 13.

12. Ibid., p. 43.

13. Maurice Matloff and Edwin Snell, *Strategic Planning for Coalition Warfare, 1941–1942* (Washington, DC: Office of the Chief of Military History, Department of the Army, 1953), p. 25.

14. Louis Morton, "Germany First: The Basic Concept of Allied Strategy in World War II," in Kent Roberts Greenfield, ed., *Command Decisions* (New York: Harcourt, Brace, 1959), p. 27.

15. Matloff and Snell, p. 33.

16. Ibid., p. 26.

17. Ibid., p. 33.

18. Winston Churchill, *The Grand Alliance*, vol. 3 of *The Second World War* (Boston: Houghton Mifflin, 1950), p. 331.

19. Marshall Interviews, January 22, 1957, Tape 10, p. 319.

20. Forrest Pogue, *Ordeal and Hope, 1939–1943* (New York: Viking Press, 1966), p. 89.

21. George Marshall to Lesley McNair, Washington, September 29, 1941, George C. Marshall Papers, box 76, folder 31, George C. Marshall Research Library, Lexington, VA.

22. Bland and Ritenour Stevens, *The Papers of George Catlett Marshall*, vol. 3, p. 572.

23. Cray, *General of the Army*, p. 206.

24. Pogue, *Ordeal and Hope*, p. 152.

25. *Life*, August 18, 1941, p. 32.

26. Bland, Ritenour, and Wunderlin, *The Papers of George Catlett Marshall*, vol. 2, p. 591.

27. Marshall Interviews, January 22, 1957, Tape 10, p. 303.

28. Henry L. Stimson and McGeorge Bundy, *On Active Service in Peace and War* (New York: Harper & Brothers, 1948), p. 366.

29. Albert C. Wedemeyer, *Wedemeyer Reports!* (New York: Henry Holt, 1958), p. 17.

30. Charles E. Kirkpatrick, "Computing the Requirements for War: The
     Logic of the Victory Program of 1941," http://www.history.navy.mil/
     colloquia/cch5c.htm, p. 4.

31. Matloff and Snell, *Strategic Planning*, p. 55.

32. Russell F. Weigley, *Eisenhower's Lieutenants: The Campaign
     of France and Germany, 1944–1945* (Bloomington: Indiana
     University Press, 1981), p. 5.

33. Quoted in Cray, *General of the Army*, p. 216.

34. Dallek, *Franklin D. Roosevelt and American Foreign Policy*,
     p. 300.

35. Pogue, *Ordeal and Hope*, p. 196.

36. Ibid., p. 204.

37. Dallek, *Franklin D. Roosevelt and American Foreign Policy*,
     p. 308.

38. Quoted in Cray, *General of the Army*, p. 244.

39. John Dower, *Cultures of War* (New York: W. W. Norton, 2010),
     p. 139.

40. Pogue, *Ordeal and Hope*, p. 205.

41. Bland and Ritenour, *The Papers of George Catlett Marshall*, vol. 1,
     p. 413.

42. Pogue, *Ordeal and Hope*, p. 225.

43. Bland and Ritenour Stevens, *The Papers of George C. Marshall*,
     vol. 3, p. 7.

CHAPTER 5: RETREAT

1.   Pogue, *Ordeal and Hope*, p. 234.

2.   Bland, Ritenour, and Wunderlin, *The Papers of George Catlett
     Marshall*, vol. 2, p. 676.

3.   Marshall to MacArthur, December 11, 1941, George C.
     Marshall Papers, box 74, folder 48, George C. Marshall Research
     Library, Lexington, VA.

4.   Marshall to MacArthur, December 26, 1941, George C.
     Marshall Papers, box 74, folder 48.

5.   William Manchester, *American Caesar: Douglas MacArthur,
     1880–1964* (Boston: Little, Brown, 1978), p. 271.

6.   Roberts, *Masters and Commanders*, p. 80.

7.   Ibid., p. 70.

8. Proceedings of the American-British Joint Chiefs of Staff Conferences Held in Washington, D.C. (ARCADIA), Meeting of December 25, 1941, p. 3; World War II Inter-Allied Conference Papers. BACM Research, www.paperlessarchives.com.

9. Churchill, *The Grand Alliance*, p. 674.

10. Katherine Marshall, *Together*, p. 104.

11. Marshall Interviews, November 21, 1956, Tape 12, p. 358.

12. Churchill, *The Grand Alliance*, p. 608.

13. Pogue, *Ordeal and Hope*, p. 283.

14. Matloff and Snell, *Strategic Planning*, p. 104.

15. Richard W. Steele, *The First Offensive, 1942: Roosevelt, Marshall and the Making of American Strategy* (Bloomington: Indiana University Press, 1973), p. 66.

16. D'Este, *Eisenhower: A Soldier's Life*, p. 292.

17. Stephen E. Ambrose, *The Supreme Commander: The War Years of Dwight D. Eisenhower* (Garden City, NY: Doubleday, 1970), p. 30.

18. Stoler, *Allies and Adversaries*, p. 72.

19. Ambrose, *The Supreme Commander*, p. 33.

20. Steele, *The First Offensive*, p. 102.

21. Quoted in Mark A. Stoler, *The Politics of the Second Front: American Military Planning and Diplomacy in Coalition Warfare, 1941–1943* (Westport, CT: Greenwood Press, 1977), p. 32.

22. William Manchester and Paul Reid, *The Last Lion: Winston Spencer Churchill, Defender of the Realm, 1940–1965* (New York: Little, Brown and Company, 2012), p. 409.

23. Alex Danchev and Daniel Todman, eds., *War Diaries, 1939–1945: Field Marshal Lord Alanbrooke* (Berkeley: University of California Press, 2001), p. 246.

24. Martin Gilbert, *Road to Victory: Winston S. Churchill, 1941–1945* (Toronto: Stoddart Publishing Company, 1986), p. 86.

25. Ibid., p. 87.

26. Winston S. Churchill, *The Hinge of Fate*, vol. 4 of *The Second World War* (Boston: Houghton Mifflin, 1950), p. 309.

27. Danchev and Todman, *War Diaries*, pp. 248–49.

28. Ibid.

29. Roberts, *Masters and Commanders*, pp. 145–46.

30. Cray, *General of the Army*, p. 311.

31. Roberts, *Masters and Commanders*, p. 158.

32. Gilbert, *Road to Victory*, p. 88.

33. Steele, *The First Offensive*, pp. 180–81.

34. Pogue, *Ordeal and Hope*, p. 315.

35. Bland and Ritenour Stevens, *The Papers of George Catlett Marshall*, vol. 3, p. 164.

36. Bland, Ritenour, and Wunderlin, *The Papers of George Catlett Marshall*, vol. 2, p. 337.

37. Ibid.

38. Katherine Marshall, *Together*, p. 115.

39. Ibid., p. 118.

40. Pogue, *Ordeal and Hope*, p. 289.

41. Ibid., p. 293.

42. Quoted in Eric Larrabee, *Commander in Chief: Franklin Delano Roosevelt, His Lieutenants, and Their War* (New York: Harper & Row, 1987), p. 101.

43. Marshall Interviews, Tape 11, November 15, 1956, p. 347.

44. Foreword by Omar Bradley in Pogue, *Organizer of Victory*, p. ix.

45. Thomas Ricks, *The Generals: American Military Command from World War II to Today* (New York: Penguin Press, 2012), pp. 18, 39.

46. Stephen E. Ambrose, *The Supreme Commander: The War Years of Dwight D. Eisenhower* (Jackson: University Press of Mississippi, 1999), p. 6.

47. Marshall Interviews, February 14, 1957, Tape 15, pp. 9–10.

48. Bland, Ritenour, and Wunderlin, *The Papers of George Catlett Marshall*, vol. 2, p. 537.

49. http://en.wikipedia.org/wiki/WhyWe Fight.

50. http://www.historyarmy.mil/books/integration/JAF-02.htm.

51. John T. Whitaker, "These Are the Generals: McNair," *Saturday Evening Post*, January 30, 1943, pp. 12–14.

52. Marshall Interview Notes, September 28, 1956, p. 583.

53. Churchill, *The Hinge of Fate*, p. 298.

54. Roberts, *Masters and Commanders*, p. 176.

55. Marshall Interview Notes, October 5, 1956, p. 590.

56. Stoler, *Allies and Adversaries*, p. 78.

57. Churchill, *The Hinge of Fate*, p. 343.

58. Ibid.

59. Stoler, *Allies and Adversaries*, p. 79.

60. Bland and Ritenour Stevens, *The Papers of George Catlett Marshall*, vol. 3, p. 271.
61. Marshall to Eisenhower, July 30, 1942, George C. Marshall Papers, box 66, folder 42, George C. Marshall Research Library, Lexington, VA.
62. Stoler, *Allies and Adversaries*, p. 88.
63. Ibid., p. 85.
64. Bland, *The Papers of George Catlett Marshall*, vol. 3, p. 276.
65. Roberts, *Masters and Commanders*, p. 242.
66. Gilbert, *Road to Victory*, pp. 148–49.
67. Jean Edward Smith, *Eisenhower in War and Peace* (New York: Random House, 2012), p. 220.
68. Memorandum to the War Department classified message center, July 16, 1942, George C. Marshall Papers, box 66, folder 42, George C. Marshall Research Library, Lexington, VA.
69. Roberts, *Masters and Commanders*, p. 245.
70. Danchev and Todman, *War Diaries*, p. 282.
71. Matloff and Snell, *Strategic Planning*, p. 283.
72. Thomas Parish, *Roosevelt and Marshall: Partners in Politics and War* (New York: William Morrow and Company, 1989), p. 296.
73. Marshall Interview Notes, November 15, 1956, p. 622.
74. Churchill, *The Hinge of Fate*, pp. 425, 428.
75. Gilbert, *Road to Victory*, p. 175.
76. Churchill, *The Hinge of Fate*, p. 431.
77. Manchester and Reid, *The Last Lion*, p. 565.
78. Gilbert, *Road to Victory*, p. 178.
79. Churchill, *The Hinge of Fate*, p. 441.
80. Ibid., p. 451.

CHAPTER 6: "UNDERBELLY"

1. Eisenhower to Marshall, September 23, 1942, George C. Marshall Papers, box 66, folder 43, George C. Marshall Research Library, Lexington, VA.
2. Smith, *Eisenhower in War and Peace*, p. 239.
3. Ibid.
4. Ibid., p. 240.

5.   Bland and Ritenour Stevens, *The Papers of George Catlett Marshall*, vol. 3, p. 445.

6.   Ibid., p. 497.

7.   D'Este, *Eisenhower: A Soldier's Life*, p. 309.

8.   Joseph Patrick Hobbs, ed., *Dear General: Eisenhower's Wartime Letters to Marshall* (Baltimore: Johns Hopkins University Press, 1999), p. 23.

9.   Pogue, *Ordeal and Hope*, p. 406.

10. Steven Ossad, "Command Failures: Lessons Learned from Lloyd R. Fredendall," *Army Magazine* 53, no. 3 (March 2003), p. 50.

11. Pogue, *Ordeal and Hope*, p. 407.

12. Bland and Ritenour Stevens, *The Papers of George Catlett Marshall*, vol. 3, p. 433.

13. Rick Atkinson, *An Army at Dawn: The War in North Africa, 1942–1943* (New York: Henry Holt, 2002), p. 125.

14. Ibid., p. 144.

15. Ibid., p. 139.

16. Ibid., p. 164.

17. Matthew Cooper, *The German Army, 1933–1945: Its Political and Military Failure* (New York: Stein & Day, 1978), p. 364.

18. Bland and Ritenour Stevens, *The Papers of George Catlett Marshall*, vol. 3, p. 488.

19. John S. Eisenhower, *Allies: Pearl Harbor to D-Day* (Garden City, NY: Doubleday, 1982), pp. 230–31.

20. Atkinson, *An Army at Dawn*, p. 316.

21. Marshall Interviews, February 15, 1957, Tape 16, p. 479.

22. Ibid., p. 323.

23. http://en.wikipedia.org/wiki/lloyd_fredendall, p. 3.

24. [Eisenhower] to Fredendall, February 4, 1943, George C. Marshall Papers, box 66, folder 48, George C. Marshall Research Library, Lexington, VA.

25. Atkinson, *An Army at Dawn*, p. 322.

26. Ibid., p. 316.

27. Ibid., p. 371.

28. Harry Butcher, *My Three Years with Eisenhower: The Personal Diary of Captain Harry C. Butcher, USNR, Naval Aide to General Eisenhower, 1942 to 1945* (New York: Simon & Schuster, 1945), p. 268.

29. Atkinson, *An Army at Dawn*, p. 377.

30. Bland and Ritenour Stevens, *The Papers of George Catlett Marshall*, vol. 3, p. 525.
31. Roberts, *Masters and Commanders*, p. 543.
32. Kent Roberts Greenfield, Robert R. Palmer, and Bell I. Wiley, *The Organization of Ground Combat Troops* (Honolulu: University Press of the Pacific, 2005), p. 195.
33. Ibid., pp. 562–63.
34. Ibid., p. 65.
35. Robert Palmer, Bell I. Wiley, and William Keast, *The Procurement and Training of Ground Combat Troops* (Washington, DC: Center of Military History, United States Army, 1991), p. 3.
36. Max Hastings, *Armageddon: The Battle for Germany, 1944–1945* (New York: Vintage Books, 2005), p. 186.
37. Palmer, Wiley, and Keast, *The Procurement and Training of Ground Combat Troops*, p. 183.
38. Ibid., p. 229.
39. Larry Bland and Sharon Ritenour Stevens, *The Papers of George Catlett Marshall*, vol. 4 (Baltimore: Johns Hopkins University Press, 1996), p. 114.
40. Palmer, Wiley, and Keast, *The Procurement and Training of Ground Combat Troops*, p. 58.
41. Bland and Ritenour Stevens, *The Papers of George Catlett Marshall*, vol. 4, p. 267.
42. Pogue, *Organizer of Victory*, p. 428.
43. Ibid., p. 191.
44. Richard Overy, *Why the Allies Won* (New York: W. W. Norton and Company, 1995), pp. 272–73.
45. *New York Times,* May 11, 1943.
46. Hastings, *Armageddon*, pp. 232–33.
47. Marshall to Alexander, March 23, 1943, George C. Marshall Papers, box 66, folder 49, George C. Marshall Research Library, Lexington, VA.
48. Bland and Ritenour Stevens, *The Papers of George Catlett Marshall*, vol. 3, pp. 643–44.
49. Antony Beevor, *The Second World War* (New York: Little, Brown, 2012), p. 449.
50. Douglas Porch, *The Path to Victory: The Mediterranean Theater in World War II* (New York: Farrar, Straus & Giroux, 2004), p. 412.

51. Atkinson, *An Army at Dawn,* p. 539.
52. Stalin to Churchill, February 16, 1943, in Churchill, *The Hinge of Fate*, pp. 667–68.
53. Dallek, *Franklin D. Roosevelt and American Foreign Policy,* p. 370.
54. Roberts, *Masters and Commanders,* p. 316.
55. Cray, *General of the Army,* pp. 358–59.
56. *Casablanca Conference*, Minutes of the Joint Chiefs of Staff, January 15, 1943, p. 17. World War II Inter-Allied Conference Papers. BACM Research, www.paperlessarchives.com.
57. Ibid., January 16, 1943, p. 211.
58. Ibid., January 18, 1943, p. 392.
59. Roberts, *Masters and Commanders,* p. 330.
60. Danchev and Todman, *War Diaries,* p. 361.
61. Roberts, *Masters and Commanders,* p. 334.
62. *Casablanca Conference,* Minutes of the Combined Chiefs of Staff, January 18, 1943, p. 146. World War II Inter-Allied Conference Papers. BACM Research, www.paperlessarchives.com.
63. Ibid., January 16, 1943, p. 211.
64. Bland and Ritenour Stevens, *The Papers of George Catlett Marshall,* vol. 3, p. 557.
65. Wedemeyer, *Wedemeyer Reports!,* pp. 191–92.
66. Danchev and Todman, *War Diaries,* p. 364.
67. Maurice Matloff, *Strategic Planning for Coalition Warfare, 1943–1944* (Washington, DC: Center of Military History, United States Army, 2003), pp. 38–39.
68. Dallek, *Franklin D. Roosevelt and American Foreign Policy,* p. 374.
69. Marshall Interviews, February 11, 1957, Tape 14, p. 420.
70. Rick Atkinson, *The Day of Battle: The War in Sicily and Italy, 1943–1944* (New York: Henry Holt, 2007), p. 7.
71. Churchill, *Hinge of Fate,* p. 699.
72. Dallek, *Franklin D. Roosevelt and American Foreign Policy,* p. 393.
73. Ibid.
74. Cray, *General of the Army,* p. 386.
75. Matloff, *Strategic Planning,* p. 128.
76. Roberts, *Masters and Commanders,* p. 359.
77. Matloff, *Strategic Planning,* p. 128.

78. Ibid., p. 127.
79. *Trident Conference*, Minutes of the Combined Chiefs of Staff, May 13, 1943, pp. 328–29. World War II Inter-Allied Conference Papers. BACM Research, www.paperlessarchives.com.
80. Ibid., May 15, 1943, p. 368.
81. Ibid., May 13, 1943, p. 327.
82. Ibid., pp. 327–28.
83. Ibid., Annex A, Global Strategy of the War, Minutes of May 13, 1943, p. 334.
84. Ibid., Minutes of the Combined Chiefs of Staff, May 13, 1943, pp. 327–30.
85. Ibid., May 18, 1943, p. 392.
86. Ibid., Minutes of the Combined Chiefs of Staff, May 14, 1943, p. 345.
87. Quoted in Roberts, *Masters and Commanders*, pp. 368–69.
88. Ibid., pp. 362–63.
89. Gilbert, *Road to Victory*, p. 410.
90. Bland and Ritenour Stevens, *The Papers of George Catlett Marshall*, vol. 3, p. 708.
91. Cray, *General of the Army*, p. 398.
92. *Trident Conference*, Minutes of the Combined Chiefs of Staff, May 19, 1943, p. 407.
93. Ibid., Minutes of Meeting at Eisenhower's Villa, Algiers, May 29, 1943, p. 470.
94. Danchev and Todman, *War Diaries*, June 3, 1943, p. 417.
95. Cray, *General of the Army*, p. 401.

CHAPTER 7: PACIFIC WOES

1. Chester Wilmot, *The Struggle for Europe* (Old Saybrook, CT: Konecky & Konecky, 1952), p. 108.
2. Stephen Taaffe, *Marshall and His Generals: U.S. Army Commanders in World War II* (Lawrence: University of Kansas Press, 2011), pp. 17–18.
3. Samuel Eliot Morison, *Strategy and Compromise* (Boston: Little, Brown and Company, 1958), p. 78.
4. Marshall Interviews, November 21, 1956, Tape 12, p. 352.
5. Geoffrey Perret, *Old Soldiers Never Die: The Life of Douglas MacArthur* (Holbrook, MA: Adams Media Corporation, 1996), p. 298.

6. Ibid., p. 298.
7. Manchester, *American Caesar*, p. 285.
8. Marshall to MacArthur, August 10, 1942, George C. Marshall Papers, box 74, folder 49, George C. Marshall Research Library, Lexington, VA.
9. Taaffe, *Marshall and His Generals*, p. 23.
10. Bland and Ritenour Stevens, *The Papers of George Catlett Marshall*, vol. 3, pp. 252–53.
11. Ibid., p. 254.
12. Mark A. Stoler, *George C. Marshall, Soldier-Statesman of the American Century* (New York: Twayne Publishers, 1989), p. 117.
13. Perret, *Old Soldiers Never Die*, p. 348.
14. Marshall Interviews, November 21, 1956, Tape 15, p. 365.
15. Ibid., p. 377.
16. Manchester, *American Caesar*, p. 352.
17. Pogue, *Organizer of Victory*, p. 172.
18. Matloff, *Strategic Planning*, p. 99.
19. Pogue, *Organizer of Victory*, pp. 170–71.
20. Max Hastings, *Retribution: The Battle for Japan, 1944–45* (New York: Vintage Books, 2009), p. 97.
21. Larrabee, *Commander in Chief*, p. 333.
22. Bland and Ritenour Stevens, *The Papers of George Catlett Marshall*, vol. 4, p. 200.
23. Ibid., pp. 329–30.
24. MacArthur to War Department, June 18, 1944, George C. Marshall Papers, box 74, folder 55, George C. Marshall Research Library, Lexington, VA.
25. Marshall to MacArthur, June 24, 1944, ibid.
26. Herbert Feis, *The China Tangle: The American Effort in China from Pearl Harbor to the Marshall Mission* (New York: Atheneum, 1966), p. 140.
27. Ibid., p. 46.
28. Theodore White, ed., *The Papers of Joseph Stilwell* (New York: Sloane, 1948), p. 251.
29. Hastings, *Armageddon: The Battle for Germany, 1944–1945*, p. 283.
30. Stimson and Bundy, *On Active Service*, p. 535.

31. Marshall Interviews, "Interview Notes," October 29, 1956, p. 603.

32. Feis, *The China Tangle*, p. 60.

33. Bland and Ritenour Stevens, *The Papers of George Catlett Marshall*, vol. 4, pp. 321–22.

34. Ibid., p. 158.

35. Ibid., p. 554.

36. Danchev and Todman, *War Diaries*, pp. 441–42.

37. Bland and Ritenour Stevens, *The Papers of George Catlett Marshall*, vol. 4, p. 129.

38. Churchill, *The Hinge of Fate*, p. 702.

39. Marshall Interviews, "Interview Notes," October 29, 1956, p. 607.

40. Matloff, *Strategic Planning*, p. 350.

41. Barbara Tuchman, *Stilwell and the American Experience in China, 1911–1945* (New York: Grove Press, 1971), p. 405.

CHAPTER 8: EUROPE AT LAST

1. D'Este, *Eisenhower: A Soldier's Life*, p. 438.

2. Porch, *The Path to Victory*, p. 444.

3. Bland and Ritenour Stevens, *The Papers of George Catlett Marshall*, vol. 4, p. 92.

4. Atkinson, *The Day of Battle*, p. 183.

5. Porch, *The Path to Victory*, p. 560.

6. Atkinson, *The Day of Battle*, p. 574.

7. Ibid., p. 575.

8. Bland and Ritenour Stevens, *The Papers of George Catlett Marshall*, vol. 3, p. 516.

9. Ibid., pp. 664–65.

10. Ibid., p. 575.

11. Cray, *General of the Army*, p. 445.

12. Bland and Ritenour Stevens, *The Papers of George Catlett Marshall*, vol. 4, p. 311.

13. Andrew Rawson, ed., *Eyes Only: The Top Secret Correspondence Between Marshall and Eisenhower, 1943–45* (Stroud, UK: Spellmount, 2012), p. 67.

14. Max Hastings, *Inferno: The World at War, 1939–1945* (New York: Alfred A. Knopf, 2011), p. 248.

15. Marshall to [Archibald] MacLeish, December 25, 1944, George C. Marshall Papers, box 74, folder 45, George C. Marshall Research Library, Lexington, VA.

16. Pogue, *Organizer of Victory*, pp. 536–537.

17. Roberts, *Masters and Commanders*, p. 432.

18. Ibid., p. 433.

19. *Eureka Conference*, Minutes of Plenary Session, November 28, 1943, 4 p.m., p. 514. World War II Inter-Allied Conference Papers. BACM Research, www.paperlessarchives.com.

20. Ibid., pp. 514–15.

21. Ibid., pp. 516–20.

22. Pogue, *Organizer of Victory*, p. 300.

23. *Eureka Conference*, Minutes of November 29, 1943, 10:30 a.m., pp. 527–32.

24. Ibid., pp. 536–38.

25. Marshall Interviews, November 15, 1956, Tape 11, p. 342.

26. *Eureka Conference*, Minutes of Plenary Session, November 29, 1943, 4 p.m., p. 545.

27. Robert Sherwood, *The White House Papers of Harry L. Hopkins* (London: Eyre & Spottiswoode, 1948), vol. 1, p. xii.

28. Robert Sherwood, *Roosevelt and Hopkins: An Intimate History* (New York: Harper & Brothers, 1948), p. 803.

29. Marshall Interviews, November 1956, Tape 11, p. 330.

30. Stoler, *George C. Marshall, Soldier-Statesman*, p. 108.

31. Bland and Ritenour Stevens, *The Papers of George Catlett Marshall*, vol. 4, p. 198.

32. Sherwood, *Roosevelt and Hopkins*, p. 770.

33. Katherine Marshall, *Together*, p. 182.

34. Pogue, *Organizer of Victory*, pp. 505ff.

35. Cray, *General of the Army*. p. 442.

36. Ibid., pp. 442–43.

37. Katherine Marshall, *Together*, p. 178.

38. Cray, *General of the Army*, p. 443.

39. Bland and Ritenour Stevens, *The Papers of George Catlett Marshall*, vol. 4, p. 316.

40. Katherine Marshall, *Together*, pp. 182, 185.

41. *Time*, January 3, 1944.

42. Greenfield, Palmer, and Wiley, *The Organization of Ground Combat Troops*, p. 193.

43. McNair to Marshall, January 4, 1944, in William R. Keast, *Provision of Enlisted Replacements: Study No. 7* (Washington, DC: Historical Section—Army Ground Forces, 1946), p. 23.

44. Marshall to MacArthur, January 25, 1944, George C. Marshall Papers, box 74, folder 53, George C. Marshall Research Library, Lexington, VA.

45. Marshall to Eisenhower, May 18, 1944, George C. Marshall Papers, box 67, folder 7, ibid.

46. Eisenhower to Marshall, April 17, 1944, George C. Marshall Papers, box 67, folder 5, ibid.

47. D. M. Giangreco, "Was Dwindling US Manpower a Factor in the Atom Bombing of Hiroshima?," History News Network, July 20, 2008.

48. Churchill to Marshall to Eisenhower, April 13, 1944, in Rawson, *Eyes Only*, p. 66.

49. Matloff, *Strategic Planning*, p. 417.

50. Marshall to Eisenhower, March 20, 1944, George C. Marshall Papers, box 67, folder 4, George C. Marshall Research Library, Lexington, VA.

51. Dwight D. Eisenhower, *Crusade in Europe* (Garden City, NY: Doubleday, 1948), p. 317.

52. Mark A. Stoler, *George C. Marshall: Soldier-Statesman of the American Century* (Farmington Hills, MI: Twayne Publishers, 1989), p. 113.

53. Stanley P. Hirshson, *General Patton: A Soldier's Life* (New York: HarperCollins Publishers, 2002), p. 393.

54. Ibid., p. 460.

55. Eisenhower to Marshall, April 29, 1944, George C. Marshall Papers, box 67, folder 5, George C. Marshall Research Library, Lexington, VA.

56. Bland and Ritenour Stevens, *The Papers of George Catlett Marshall*, vol. 4, pp. 442–43.

57. Pogue, *Organizer of Victory*, pp. 380–81.

58. Eisenhower to Marshall, February 19, 1944, George C. Marshall Papers, box 67, folder 3, George C. Marshall Research Library, Lexington, VA.

59. Cray, *General of the Army*, p. 456.

60. Ibid., p. 452.

61. Rawson, *Eyes Only*, p. 115.

62. Bland and Ritenour Stevens, *The Papers of George Catlett Marshall*, vol. 4, pp. 479–80.

63. Ibid., pp. 487–88.
64. Winston Churchill, *Triumph and Tragedy*, vol. 6 of *The Second World War* (Boston: Houghton Mifflin, 1953), p. 132.
65. D'Este, *Eisenhower: A Soldier's Life*, p. 586.
66. Ambrose, *The Supreme Commander*, p. 510.
67. Cray, *General of the Army*, p. 478.
68. Gordon W. Prange, *At Dawn We Slept: The Untold Story of Pearl Harbor* (New York: Penguin Group, 1991), p. 651.
69. Ibid., p. 656.
70. Pogue, *Ordeal and Hope*, Appendix, p. 430.
71. Cray, *General of the Army*, p. 481.
72. Roberts, *Masters and Commanders*, p. 522.
73. D'Este, *Eisenhower: A Soldier's Life*, p. 596.
74. Rawson, *Eyes Only*, p. 115.
75. Ibid., pp. 138–39.
76. Montgomery to Eisenhower, September 4, 1944, in ibid., p. 138.
77. Ibid., p. 606.
78. Ibid.
79. Bland and Ritenour Stevens, *The Papers of George Catlett Marshall*, vol. 4, p. 624.
80. Marshall Interviews, February 4, 1957, Tape 13, p. 387.
81. Bernard Montgomery, *The Memoirs of Field Marshal the Viscount Montgomery of Alamein, K.G.* (London: Collins, 1958), p. 298.
82. Hastings, *Armageddon: The Battle for Germany*, p. 67.
83. Ibid., p. 81.
84. Paul Fussell, *Doing Battle: The Making of a Skeptic* (Boston: Little, Brown Company, 1996), p. 27.
85. Stephen Ambrose, *Citizen Soldiers: The U.S. Army from the Normandy Beaches to the Bulge, to the Surrender of Germany* (New York: Simon & Schuster Paperbacks, 1997), p. 285.
86. Hastings, *Armageddon: The Battle for Germany*, p. 77.
87. Ibid., p. 68.
88. Ambrose, *Citizen Soldiers*, p. 285.
89. Marshall Interviews, November 15, 1956, Tape 11, p. 323.
90. Bland and Ritenour Stevens, *The Papers of George Catlett Marshall*, vol. 4, p. 721.
91. Pogue, *Organizer of Victory*, p. 493.
92. Marshall Interview Notes, October 5, 1956, p. 591.

93. Marshall to Eisenhower, January 8, 1945, in Rawson, *Eyes Only*, p. 184.
94. Bland and Ritenour Stevens, *The Papers of George Catlett Marshall*, vol. 4, pp. 720–21.
95. Eisenhower, *Crusade in Europe*, p. 370.
96. Combined Chiefs of Staff Meeting at Malta, Tuesday, January 30, 1945, at 1200, pp. 194–96.
97. Robert Sherwood, *The White House Papers of Harry L. Hopkins* (London: Eyre & Spottiswoode, 1949), vol. 2, pp. 840–41.
98. Danchev and Todman, *War Diaries*, p. 653.
99. D'Este, *Eisenhower: A Soldier's Life*, p. 676.
100. Danchev and Todman, *War Diaries*, January 31, 1945, p. 652.
101. Eisenhower, *Crusade in Europe*, p. 372.
102. Rick Atkinson, *The Guns at Last Light: The War in Western Europe, 1944–1945* (New York: Henry Holt, 2013), p. 566.
103. Katherine Marshall, *Together*, pp. 233, 238.
104. Larry Bland, Mark Stoler, and Sharon Ritenour Stevens, eds., *The Papers of George Catlett Marshall*, vol. 6 (Baltimore: Johns Hopkins University Press, 2013), p. 401.
105. Churchill to Eisenhower, March 31, 1945, in Rawson, *Eyes Only*, p. 232.
106. Eisenhower to Montgomery, March 11, 1945, in ibid., p. 229.
107. Bland and Ritenour Stevens, *The Papers of George Catlett Marshall*, vol. 5 (Baltimore: Johns Hopkins University Press, 2003), p. 159.
108. Ibid., p. 168.
109. Pogue, *Organizer of Victory*, p. 584.
110. Bland and Ritenour Stevens, *The Papers of George Catlett Marshall*, vol. 5, p. 171.
111. Cray, *General of the Army*, p. 532.
112. Film of Marshall's talk at: http//www oscars.org/filmarchive/collections/warfilm/two-down-and-one-to-go.html.
113. Bland and Ritenour Stevens, *The Papers of George Catlett Marshall*, vol. 5, p. 172.
114. Cray, *General of the Army*, p. 655.

CHAPTER 9: JAPAN-CHINA

1. Bland and Ritenour Stevens, *The Papers of George Catlett Marshall*, vol. 4, p. 494.
2. Pogue, *Organizer of Victory*, p. 440.

3. Larrabee, *Commander in Chief*, p. 342.

4. Manchester, *American Caesar*, p. 369.

5. Perret, *Old Soldiers Never Die*, p. 407.

6. James P. Drew, "Tarnished Victory: Divided Command in the Pacific and Its Consequences in the Naval Battle for Leyte Gulf" (master's thesis, U.S. Command and General Staff College, Fort Leavenworth, KS, 2009), pp. 64–65.

7. Kent Roberts Greenfield, ed., *Okinawa: The Last Battle* (Washington, DC: Center of Military History, 2000), p. 468.

8. Hastings, *Retribution*, p. 318.

9. United States Strategic Bombing Survey, *The Effects of Strategic Bombing on Japanese Morale* (Washington, D.C.: Morale Division, June 1947), pp. 1–2.

10. "Minutes of Meeting held at the White House on Monday, 18 June 1945 at 1530," p. 1. See Bland and Ritenour Stevens, *The Papers of George Catlett Marshall*, vol. 5, p. 233.

11. D. M. Giangreco, *Hell to Pay: Operation Downfall and the Invasion of Japan, 1945–1947* (Annapolis, MD: Naval Institute Press, 2009), p. 63.

12. Marshall to MacArthur, December 26, 1944, George C. Marshall Papers, box 74, folder 56, George C. Marshall Research Library, Lexington, VA.

13. Giangreco, *Hell to Pay*, p. 50.

14. Manchester, *American Caesar*, p. 436.

15. Allis Radosh and Ronald Radosh, *A Safe Haven: Harry S. Truman and the Founding of Israel* (New York: HarperCollins, 2009), p. 201.

16. Robert H. Ferrell, ed., *Dear Bess: The Letters from Harry to Bess Truman, 1910–1959* (Columbia: University of Missouri Press, 1998), p. 30.

17. Henry L. Stimson, Memo of Conversation with General Marshall, May 29, 1945, Henry Stimson Papers, Internet version.

18. Forrest Pogue, *George C. Marshall: Statesman* (New York: Viking Penguin, 1987), p. 550 n30.

19. Bland and Ritenour Stevens, *The Papers of George Catlett Marshall*, vol. 5, p. 249.

20. From Stimson's manuscript diary for July 23, 1945. See Pogue, *Statesman*, p. 17.

21. Marshall Interviews, February 11, 1957, Tape 14, p. 27.

22. Michael D. Pearlman, "Unconditional Surrender, Demobilization, and the Atom Bomb (Combat Studies Institute, 1996), pp. 8, 15–16, http://egsc.edu/car/resources/csipearlman.asp.

23. Cray, *General of the Army*, p. 554.

24. Ibid., p. 555.

25. Katherine Marshall, *Together*, p. 273.

26. Ibid., p. 282.

27. Pogue, *Statesman*, p. 29.

28. Harry S. Truman, *Years of Trial and Hope*, vol. 2 of *Memoirs* (Garden City, NY: Doubleday and Company, 1956), p. 66.

29. Pogue, *Ordeal and Hope*, p. 431.

30. Prange, *At Dawn We Slept*, p. 687.

31. Ibid., p. 689.

32. Ibid., p. 736.

33. Ibid., p. 129.

34. *Minority Report of the Investigation of the Pearl Harbor Attack*, Senate Doc. no. 244, 79th Congress, 2d Session, pp. 305ff.

35. Truman, *Years of Trial and Hope*, p. 91.

36. Lyman Van Slyke, ed., *The China White Paper: August 1949*, vol. 2 (Stanford, CA: Stanford University Press, 1967), pp. 605–9.

37. Ibid., p. 609.

38. Dean Acheson, *Present at the Creation: My Years in the State Department* (New York: W. W. Norton, 1987), p. 139.

39. Cray, *General of the Army*, p. 563.

40. Wedemeyer, *Wedemeyer Reports!*, p. 363.

41. Pogue, *Statesman*, p. 76.

42. Cray, *General of the Army*, p. 566.

43. Pogue, *Statesman*, p. 106.

44. Ibid., p. 107.

45. Ibid., p. 106.

46. Van Slyke, *The China White Paper: August 1949*, vol. 1 (Stanford, CA: Stanford University Press, 1967), pp. 149–50.

47. Cray, *General of the Army*, p. 578.

48. Acheson, *Present at the Creation*, p. 208.

49. Truman, *Years of Trial and Hope*, p. 86.

50. Van Slyke, *The China White Paper*, vol. 1, p. 191.

51. Bland and Ritenour Stevens, *The Papers of George Catlett Marshall*, vol. 5, pp. 705–6.

52. Cray, *General of the Army*, p. 574.

53. Van Slyke, *The China White Paper*, vol. 2, pp. 686–89.

54. Pogue, *Statesman*, p. 110.

55. Truman, *Years of Trial and Hope*, p. 92.

56. Wedemeyer, *Wedemeyer Reports!*, pp. 370, 376.

57. Alan Brinkley, *The Publisher: Henry Luce and His American Century* (New York: Vintage Books, 2011), p. 337.

CHAPTER 10: AFFAIRS OF STATE

1. Bland, Stoler, and Ritenour Stevens, *The Papers of George Catlett Marshall*, vol. 6, p. 509.

2. Ibid., p. 23.

3. David McCullough, *Truman* (New York: Simon & Schuster Paperbacks, 1992), p. 535.

4. Truman, *Years of Trial and Hope*, p. 115.

5. Quoted in Pogue, *Statesman*, p. 147. See also Acheson, *Present at the Creation*, p. 213.

6. Bland, Stoler, and Ritenour Stevens, *The Papers of George Marshall*, vol. 6, p. 166.

7. John Lewis Gaddis, *George F. Kennan: An American Life* (New York: Penguin Press, 2011), p. 221.

8. Acheson, *Present at the Creation*, p. 219.

9. Harry S. Truman, Address Before a Joint Session of Congress, March 12, 1947, Avalon Project, Documents in Law, History, and Diplomacy, http.//avalon. law. yale. edu/20th_century/trudoc.asp.

10. Bland, Stoler, and Ritenour Stevens, *The Papers of George Catlett Marshall*, vol. 6, p. 97.

11. Pogue, *Statesman*, p. 189.

12. Cray, *General of the Army*, pp. 605–6.

13. James Reston, "Marshall Held Too Aloof at Conference in Moscow," *New York Times*, April 30, 1947.

14. Oral History Interview of Charles P. Kindleberger by Richard D. McKinzie, July 16, 1973, at the Truman Presidential Library, Independence, MO.

15. Bland, Stoler, and Ritenour Stevens, *The Papers of George Catlett Marshall*, vol. 6, p. 121.

16. Marshall Interviews, November 15, 1956, Tape 11, p. 324.

17. Robert D. Murphy, *Diplomat Among Warriors* (Garden City, NY: Doubleday, 1964), p. 342.

18. Acheson, *Present at the Creation*, p. 227.

19. Charles S. Kindleberger, Memorandum for the Files: "Origins of the Marshall Plan," July 29, 1948, U.S. Department of State, *Foreign Relations of the United States, 1947, The British Commonwealth; Europe*, p. 241.

20. "The Record of the Week," *Department of State Bulletin*, May 18, 1947, p. 993.

21. Acheson, *Present at the Creation*, p. 230.

22. Kindleberger, "Origins of the Marshall Plan," p. 242.

23. W. L. Clayton, Memorandum of the Under Secretary of State for Economic Affairs, May 27, 1947, *Foreign Relations of the United States,* vol. 3, p. 231.

24. Gaddis, *George F. Kennan*, pp. 266–67.

25. "Remarks by the Honorable George C. Marshall, Secretary of State, at Harvard University, June 5, 1947," *Foreign Relations of the United States, 1947, The British Commonwealth; Europe,* pp. 237–39.

26. Pogue, *Statesman*, p. 217.

27. Ibid., p. 236.

28. Avalon Project, Documents in Law, History, and Diplomacy, Yale Law School, Lillian Goldman Law Library, http:/avalon.law.yale.edu/20th_century/decade24.usp.

29. Marshall Interviews, November 19, 1956, Tape 18, p. 527.

30. *New York Times*, January 9, 1948.

31. Pogue, *Statesman*, p. 240.

32. Ibid.

33. Marshall Interviews, November 20, 1956, Tape 19, pp. 556–60.

34. Ibid., p. 556.

35. Radosh and Radosh, *A Safe Haven*, p. 24.

36. Ibid., p. 27.

37. Cray, *General of the Army*, p. 656.

38. Gaddis, *George F. Kennan*, p. 296.

39. McCullough, *Truman*, p. 595.

40. Radosh and Radosh, *A Safe Haven*, pp. 177–78.

41. Truman manuscript diary, July 24, 1947, in ibid., p. 236.

42. Truman, *Years of Trial and Hope*, pp. 164–65.

43. Radosh and Radosh, *A Safe Haven*, p. 92.

44. Ibid., p. 102.

45. Ibid., p. 118.

46. Ibid., pp. 244–45.

47. Bland, Stoler, and Ritenour Stevens, *The Papers of George Catlett Marshall*, vol. 6, pp. 209–11.

48. Ibid., p. 213.

49. Clark Clifford, *Counsel to the President* (New York: Anchor Books, 1991), pp. 4–5.

50. *Foreign Relations of the United States, 1948*, vol. 5, *The Near East, South Asia, and Africa Part 2*, pp. 972–73.

51. Radosh and Radosh, *A Safe Haven*, p. 330.

52. Ibid.

53. McCullough, *Truman*, p. 615.

54. Radosh and Radosh, *A Safe Haven*. pp. 11–12.

55. Ibid., p. 12.

56. Ibid., p. 14.

57. Ibid., p. 13.

58. Ibid.

59. Ibid., p. 15.

60. Ibid., pp. 333–35.

61. Cray, *General of the Army*, p. 661.

62. Ibid., p. 633.

63. Van Slyke, *The China White Paper*. vol. 1, pp. 251–52.

64. Wedemeyer, *Wedemeyer Reports!*, p. 476.

65. Pogue, *Statesman*, p. 299.

66. *Public Papers of the Presidents of the United States: Harry S. Truman, 1945–1953*, no. 52, "Special Message to the Congress on the Threat to the Freedom of Europe," http://Truman library.org/public papers/index.php?pid=1417&st=&st1=.

67. Pogue, *Statesman*, p. 301.

68. Cray, *General of the Army*, p. 647.

69. Bland, Stoler, and Ritenour Stevens, *The Papers of George Catlett Marshall*, vol. 6, pp. 489–90.

70. Cray, *General of the Army*, p. 649, quoting the Forrestal Diaries, p. 459.

71. Bland, Stoler, and Ritenour Stevens, *The Papers of George Catlett Marshall*, vol. 6, p. 503.

72. Pogue, *Statesman*, p. 308.
73. Ibid., p. 405.
74. Gaddis, *George F. Kennan*, pp. 333–34.
75. United States Department of State, *Foreign Relations of the United States, 1948, Western Europe*, p. 265.
76. Bland, Stoler, and Ritenour Stevens, *The Papers of George Catlett Marshall*, vol. 6, p. 509.
77. Ibid., p. 609.
78. Cray, *General of the Army*, p. 668.
79. Ibid.
80. Ibid., pp. 668–69.

CHAPTER 11: ENVOI

1. William S. White, "Mr. George C. Marshall of Leesburg, Va.," *New York Times*, August 7, 1949.
2. Bland, Stoler, and Ritenour Stevens, *The Papers of George Catlett Marshall*, vol. 6, p. 701.
3. Cray, *General of the Army*, p. 673.
4. Clay Blair, *The Forgotten War: America in Korea, 1950–1953* (New York: Times Books, 1987), p. 67.
5. *Congressional Record*, 81st Congress, 2d Session, September 15, 1950, p. 96.
6. Pogue, *Statesman*, p. 428.
7. Ibid., p. 333.
8. Cray, *General of the Army*, p. 689.
9. Ibid., p. 695.
10. *Foreign Relations of the United States, 1950*, vol. 7, p. 826.
11. D. Clayton James, "Command Crisis: MacArthur and the Korean War," in Harry R. Borowski, ed., *The Harmon Lectures in Military History, 1959–1987: A Collection of the First Thirty Harmon Lectures Given at the United States Air Force Academy*, p. 220.
12. Geoffrey Perret, *Old Soldiers Never Die: The Life of Douglas MacArthur* (New York: Adams Media, 1997), p. 561.
13. McCullough, *Truman*, p. 805.
14. Manchester, *American Caesar*, p. 629.
15. Cray, *General of the Army*, p. 696.

16. Russell Weigley, *History of the United States Army* (New York: Macmillan, 1967), p. 513.
17. Manchester, *American Caesar*, pp. 602–3.
18. Cray, *General of the Army*, p. 700.
19. McCullough, *Truman*, p. 817.
20. *Foreign Relations of the United States*, 1950, vol. 7, *Korea*, pp. 1243–44.
21. McCullough, *Truman*, p. 823.
22. Blair, *The Forgotten War*, p. 524.
23. Ibid., p. 768.
24. Manchester, *American Caesar*, p. 639.
25. Truman, *Years of Trial and Hope*, p. 447.
26. Cray, *General of the Army*, p. 712.
27. Manchester, *American Caesar*, p. 661.
28. Ibid., p. 669.
29. Ibid., p. 671.
30. Cray, *General of the Army*, p. 717.
31. James, "Command Crisis," p. 220.
32. Pogue, *Statesman*, p. 488.
33. *Congressional Record*, 82d Congress, 1st session, part 5, pp. 6556–603.
34. Cray, *General of the Army*, p. 723.
35. Wedemeyer, *Wedemeyer Reports!*, p. 154.
36. *Newsweek*, September 1, 1952.
37. Smith, *Eisenhower in War and Peace*, p. 524.
38. Ibid., pp. 526–27.
39. Wilson, *General Marshall Remembered*, p. 371.
40. Pogue, *Statesman*, p. 497.
41. Ibid., p. 502.
42. Cray, *General of the Army*, p. 730.
43. *New York Times*, December 12, 1953.
44. Ibid.
45. Cray, *General of the Army*, p. 732; William S. White, "Marshall at 75: The General Revisited," *New York Times Magazine*, December 25, 1955.
46. White, "Marshall at 75: The General Revisited."
47. Wilson, *General Marshall Remembered*, p. 387.
48. *New York Times*, October 18, 1959.
49. Bland, Stoler, and Ritenour Stevens, *The Papers of George Catlett Marshall*, vol. 6, p. 449.

BIBLIOGRAPHY

The bibliographic references in the literature for Marshall are very extensive, running to many pages. The items below represent those we found most relevant for our instruction and/or from which we borrowed quotations from primary sources.

Books

Acheson, Dean. *Present at the Creation*. New York: W. W. Norton, 1969.

Ambrose, Stephen E. *Supreme Commander: The War Years of Dwight D. Eisenhower*. Garden City, NY: Doubleday, 1970.

———. *Citizen Soldiers: The U.S. Army from the Normandy Beaches to the Bulge to the Surrender of Germany*. New York: Simon & Schuster, 1997.

Atkinson, Rick. *The Guns at Last Light: The War in Western Europe, 1944–1945*. New York: Henry Holt, 2013.

Blair, Clay. *The Forgotten War: America in Korea, 1950–1953*. New York: Times Books, 1987.

Bland, Larry, and Sharon R. Ritenour, eds. *The Papers of George Catlett Marshall*. Vol. 1. Baltimore: Johns Hopkins University Press, 1981.

Bland, Larry, Sharon Ritenour Stevens, and Clarence Wunderlin, eds. *The Papers of George Catlett Marshall*. Vol. 2. Baltimore: Johns Hopkins University Press, 1986.

Bland, Larry, and Sharon Ritenour Stevens, eds. *The Papers of George Catlett Marshall*. Vol. 3. Baltimore: Johns Hopkins University Press, 1991.

————. *The Papers of George Catlett Marshall.* Vol. 4. Baltimore: Johns Hopkins University Press, 1996.

————. *The Papers of George Catlett Marshall.* Vol. 5. Baltimore: Johns Hopkins University Press, 2003.

Bland, Larry, Mark A. Stoler, and Sharon Ritenour Stevens, eds. *The Papers of George Catlett Marshall.* Vol. 6. Baltimore: Johns Hopkins University Press, 2013.

Borowski, Harry, ed. *The Harmon Lectures in Military History, 1959–1987.* N.p.: Air Force Academy, 1987.

Brinkley, Alan. *The Publisher: Henry Luce and His American Century.* New York: Vintage Books, 2011.

Burns, James MacGregor. *Roosevelt: The Soldier of Freedom.* New York: Harcourt Brace Jovanovich, n.d.

Butcher, Harry C. *My Three Years with Eisenhower.* New York: Simon & Schuster, 1946.

Butler, J. R. M., and M. A. Gwyer. *Grand Strategy.* Vols. 3 and 4. London: Her Majesty's Stationery Office, 1964.

Byrnes, James. *Speaking Frankly.* New York: Harper & Brothers, 1947.

Chernow, Ron. *Washington: A Life.* New York: Penguin Press, 2010.

Churchill, Winston. *The Second World War.* 6 vols. Boston: Houghton Mifflin, 1948.

Clayton, W. L. *Memorandum of the Under Secretary of State for Economic Affairs.* Vol. 3. *Foreign Relations of the United States,* May 27, 1947. Washington, DC: US Goverment Printing Office, 1947.

Clifford, Clark. *Counsel to the President.* New York: Anchor Books, 1991.

Cray, Ed. *General of the Army: George C. Marshall, Soldier and Statesman.* New York: Cooper Square Press, 2000.

Dallek, Robert. *Franklin D. Roosevelt and American Foreign Policy, 1932–1945.* New York: Oxford University Press, 1995.

Danchev, Alex. *A Very Special Relationship: Field Marshal Sir John Dill and the Anglo-American Alliance, 1941–1944.* London: Pergamon, 1986.

Danchev, Alex, and Daniel Todman, eds. *War Diaries, 1939–1945: Field Marshal Lord Alanbrooke.* Berkeley: University of California Press, 2001.

D'Este, Carlo. *Eisenhower: A Soldier's Life.* New York: Henry Holt, 2002.

Dower, John. *Cultures of War.* New York: W. W. Norton, 2010.

Eisenhower, Dwight D. *Crusade in Europe.* Garden City, NY: Doubleday, 1948.

Feis, Herbert. *The China Tangle: The American Effort in China from Pearl Harbor to the Marshall Mission.* New York: Atheneum, 1966.

Ferrell, Robert, ed. *Dear Bess: The Letters from Harry to Bess Truman, 1910–1959.* Columbia: University of Missouri Press, 1998.

Frye, William. *Marshall: Citizen Soldier.* Indianapolis: Bobbs-Merrill, n.d.

Fussell, Paul. *Doing Battle: The Making of a Skeptic.* Boston: Little, Brown and Company, 1996.

Gabel, Christopher R. *The U.S. Army GHQ Maneuvers of 1941.* Washington, DC: Center of Military History, United States Army, 1992.

Gaddis, John Lewis. *George F. Kennan: An American Life.* New York: Penguin Press, 2011.

Giangreco, D. M. *Hell to Pay: Operation Downfall and the Invasion of Japan, 1945–1947.* Annapolis, MD: Naval Institute Press, 2009.

Gilbert, Martin. *Road to Victory: Winston S. Churchill, 1941–1945.* Toronto: Stoddart Publishing, 1986.

Greenfield, Kent Roberts, ed. *Okinawa: The Last Battle.* Washington, DC: Center of Military History, United States Army, 2000.

Greenfield, Kent Roberts, Robert R. Palmer, and Bell I. Wiley, eds. *The Organization of Ground Combat Troops.* Honolulu: University Press of the Pacific, 2005.

Hamby, Alonzo L. *Man of the People: Harry S Truman.* New York: Oxford University Press, 1995.

Hastings, Max. *Armageddon: The Battle for Germany, 1944–1945.* New York: Vintage Books, 2005.

———. *Retribution: The Battle for Japan, 1944–1945.* New York: Vintage Books, 2009.

———. *Winston's War: Churchill, 1940–1945.* New York: Alfred A. Knopf, 2010.

———. *Inferno: The World at War, 1939–1945.* New York: Alfred A. Knopf, 2011.

Hirshson, Stanley P. *General Patton: A Soldier's Life.* New York: Harper-Collins Publishers, 2002.

Larabee, Eric. *Commander in Chief: Franklin Delano Roosevelt, His Lieutenants, and Their War.* New York: Harper & Row, 1987.

Manchester, William. *The Glory and the Dream: A Narrative History of America, 1932–1972.* Boston: Little, Brown and Company, 1974.

———. *American Caesar: Douglas MacArthur, 1880–1964.* Boston: Little, Brown and Company, 1978.

Manchester, William, and Paul Reid. *The Last Lion: Winston Spencer Churchill, Defender of the Realm, 1940–1965.* Boston: Little, Brown and Company, 2012.

Marshall, George C. *Memoirs of My Services in the World War, 1917–1918.* Boston: Houghton Mifflin, 1976.

Matloff, Maurice, and Edwin W. Snell. *Strategic Planning for Coalition Warfare, 1941–1942.* Washington, DC: Center of Military History, United States Army, 2003.

McCullough, David. *Truman.* New York: Simon & Schuster, 1992.

Montgomery, Bernard. *The Memoirs of Field Marshal the Viscount Montgomery of Alamein, K.G.* London: Collins, 1958.

Morison, Samuel Eliot. *Strategy and Compromise.* Boston: Little, Brown, 1958.

Murphy, Robert D. *Diplomat Among Warriors.* Garden City, NY: Doubleday, 1964.

Nenninger, Timothy K. *The Leavenworth Schools and the Old Army: Education, Professionalism, and the Officer Corps of the United States Army, 1881–1918.* Westport, CT: Greenwood Press, 1978.

Odom, William. *After the Trenches: The Transformation of U.S. Army Doctrine, 1918–1939.* College Station: Texas A & M Press, 1999.

Parish, Thomas. *Roosevelt and Marshall: Partners in Politics and War.* New York: William Morrow, 1989.

Perret, Geoffrey. *Old Soldiers Never Die: The Life of Douglas MacArthur.* New York: Random House, 1996.

Pogue, Forrest C. *George C. Marshall: Education of a General, 1880–1939.* New York: Viking Press, 1963.

———. *George C. Marshall: Ordeal and Hope, 1939–1942.* New York: Viking Press, 1966.

———. *George C. Marshall: Organizer of Victory, 1943–1945.* New York: Viking Press, 1973.

———. *George C. Marshall: Statesman, 1945–1959.* New York: Viking Press, 1987.

Porch, Douglas. *The Path to Victory: The Mediterranean Theater in World War II.* New York: Farrar, Straus & Giroux, 2004.

Prange, Gordon W. *At Dawn We Slept: The Untold Story of Pearl Harbor.* New York: Penguin Group, 1991.

Radosh, Allis, and Ronald Radosh. *A Safe Haven: Harry S. Truman and the Founding of Israel.* New York: HarperCollins Publishers, 2009.

Rawson, Andrew, ed. *Eyes Only: The Top Secret Correspondence Between Marshall and Eisenhower, 1943–1945.* Stroud, Gloucestershire: Spellmount Publishers, 2012.

Ricks, Thomas. *The Generals: American Military Command from World War II to Today.* New York: Penguin Press, 2012.

Roberts, Andrew. *Masters and Commanders: How Four Titans Won the War in the West, 1941–1945.* New York: HarperCollins Publishers, 2009.

Ross, Steven T. *American War Plans, 1941–1945: The Test of Battle.* London: Frank Cass and Company, 1997.

Sherwood, Robert. *Roosevelt and Hopkins: An Intimate History.* New York: Harper Brothers, 1948.

———. *The White House Papers of Harry L. Hopkins.* London: Eyre & Spottiswoode, 1948.

Smith, Jean Edward. *Eisenhower in War and Peace.* New York: Random House, 2012.

Steele, Richard W. *The First Offensive, 1942: Roosevelt, Marshall and the Making of American Strategy.* Bloomington: Indiana University Press, 1973.

Stimson, Henry L., and McGeorge Bundy. *On Active Service in Peace and War.* New York: Harper Brothers, 1948.

Stoler, Mark A. *The Politics of the Second Front: American Military Planning and Diplomacy in Coalition Warfare, 1941–1943.* Westport, CT: Greenwood Press, 1977.

———. *George C. Marshall: Soldier-Statesman of the American Century.* Farmington Hills, MI: Twayne Publishers, 1989.

———. *Allies and Adversaries: The Joint Chiefs of Staff, the Grand Alliance and U.S. Strategy in World War II.* Chapel Hill: University of North Carolina Press, 2000.

Taaffe, Stephen. *Marshall and His Generals: U.S. Army Commanders in World War II.* Lawrence: University of Kansas Press, 2011.

Truman, Harry. *Years of Trial and Hope.* Garden City, NY: Doubleday, 1956.

Tuchman, Barbara. *Stilwell and the American Experience in China, 1911–1945.* New York: Grove Press, 1971.

Vandiver, Frank G. *Black Jack: The Life and Times of John J. Pershing.* 2 vols. College Station: Texas A & M Press, 1977.

Van Slyke, Lyman, ed. *The China White Paper: August 1949.* Vol. 1. Stanford, CA: Stanford University Press, 1967.

Wedemeyer, Albert C. *Wedemeyer Reports!* New York: Henry Holt, 1958.

Weigley, Russell. *History of the United States Army.* New York: Macmillan, 1967.

———. *Eisenhower's Lieutenants: The Campaign of France and Germany, 1944–1945.* Bloomington: Indiana State University Press, 1981.

Wilmot, Chester. *The Struggle for Europe.* Old Saybrook, CT: Konecky and Konecky, 1952.

Wilson, Rose Page. *General Marshall Remembered.* Englewood Cliffs, NJ: Prentice-Hall, 1968.

Articles

Bland, Larry L. "Fully the Equal of the Best." In *George C. Marshall and the Virginia Military Institute.* Lexington, VA: George C. Marshall Foundation, 1987.

Clayton, James D. "Command Crisis: MacArthur and the Korean War." In *The Harmon Lectures in Military History, 1959–1987,* edited by Harry R. Borowski. Air Force Academy, 1987.

Giangreco, D. M. "Was Dwindling U.S. Manpower a Factor in the Atom Bombing of Hiroshima?" *History News Network,* July 20, 2008.

Kirkpatrick, Charles E. "Computing the Requirements for War: The Logic of the Victory Program of 1941" (http://www.history.navy.mil/colloquia/cch5c.htm).

Morton, Louis. "Germany First: The Basic Concept of Allied Strategy in World War II." In *Command Decisions,* edited by Kent Roberts Greenfield. New York: Harcourt Brace and Company, 1959.

Ossad, Steven L. "Command Failures: Lessons Learned from Lloyd R. Friedendall." *Army Magazine* (March 2003).

Pearlman, Michael D. "Unconditional Surrender: Demobilization and the Atom Bomb." Combat Studies Institute, 1996.

Reston, James. "Marshall Held Too Aloof at Conference in Moscow." *New York Times,* April 30, 1947.

Whitaker, John T. "These Are the Colonels, McNair." *Saturday Evening Post,* January 30, 1943.

White, William S. "Marshall at 75: The General Revisited." *New York Times Magazine,* December 25, 1955.

———. "Mr. George C. Marshall of Leesburg, Va." *New York Times,* August 7, 1949.

Documents

Blumenson, Martin, et al. Command Decisions. Washington, DC: Center of Military History, U.S. Army, 2000.

Congressional Record. Various dates.

Keast, William R. *Provision of Enlisted Replacements: Study No. 7.* Washington, DC: Historical Section—Army Ground Forces, 1946.

Pogue, Forrest C. *George C. Marshall Interviews and Interview Notes, 1956–57.* George C. Marshall Foundation. Interviews with Forrest C. Pogue, http://marshallfoundation.org/library/pogue.html.

U.S. Department of State. *Foreign Relations of the United States.* Various dates, regions, and countries.

Archival Sources

George C. Marshall Papers. George C. Marshall Research Library, Lexington, Va.

World War II Inter-Allied Conference Papers. BACM Research, www.paperlessarchives.com.

INDEX